Library of
Davidson College

VOID

Studies in Musical Genesis and Structure

General Editor: Lewis Lockwood, Harvard University

Studies in Musical Genesis and Structure

Anna Bolena and the Artistic Maturity of Gaetano Donizetti
Philip Gossett

Beethoven's Diabelli Variations
William Kinderman

Robert Schumann and the Study of Orchestral Composition
The Genesis of the First Symphony Op. 38
Jon W. Finson

Euryanthe and Carl Maria von Weber's Dramaturgy of German Opera
Michael C. Tusa

Beethoven's 'Appassionata' Sonata
Martha Frohlich

Richard Strauss's *Elektra*
Bryan Gilliam

Wagner's *Das Rheingold*
Warren Darcy

Beethoven's Piano Sonata in E, Op. 109

NICHOLAS MARSTON

CLARENDON PRESS · OXFORD
1995

Oxford University Press, Walton Street, Oxford OX2 6DP
Oxford New York
Athens Auckland Bangkok Bombay
Calcutta Cape Town Dar es Salaam Delhi
Florence Hong Kong Istanbul Karachi
Kuala Lumpur Madras Madrid Melbourne
Mexico City Nairobi Paris Singapore
Taipei Tokyo Toronto
and associated companies in
Berlin Ibadan

Oxford is a trade mark of Oxford University Press

Published in the United States
by Oxford University Press Inc., New York

© Nicholas Marston 1995

All rights reserved. No part of this publication may be reproduced,
stored in a retrieval system, or transmitted, in any form or by any means,
without the prior permission in writing of Oxford University Press.
Within the UK, exceptions are allowed in respect of any fair dealing for the
purpose of research or private study, or criticism or review, as permitted
under the Copyright, Designs and Patents Act, 1988, or in the case of
reprographic reproduction in accordance with the terms of the licences
issued by the Copyright Licensing Agency. Enquiries concerning
reproduction outside these terms and in other countries should be
sent to the Rights Department, Oxford University Press,
at the address above

This book is sold subject to the condition that it shall not, by way
of trade or otherwise, be lent, re-sold, hired out or otherwise circulated
without the publisher's prior consent in any form of binding or cover
other than that in which it is published and without a similar condition
including this condition being imposed on the subsequent purchaser

British Library Cataloguing in Publication Data
Data available

Library of Congress Cataloging in Publication Data
Marston, Nicholas.
Beethoven's Piano Sonata in E, Op. 109 / Nicholas Marston
(Studies in musical genesis and structure)
Includes bibliographical references (p.).
1. Beethoven, Ludwig van, 1770–1827. Sonatas, Piano, no. 30,
Op. 109, E major. I. Series.
ML410.B42M25 1994 786.2' 183—dc20 94-10762
ISBN 0-19-315332-7

1 3 5 7 9 10 8 6 4 2

Typeset by Graphicraft Typesetters Ltd., Hong Kong
Printed in Great Britain
on acid-free paper by
Biddles Ltd.
Guildford & King's Lynn

Preface

RATHER like the emergence of *Fidelio* out of *Leonore*, this book is the result of a reworking of a doctoral dissertation submitted to Cambridge University in 1986. Work on the dissertation began in the summer of 1980; and even if the genesis of the book is considered to date only from 1986, it has still taken longer to write than did the Ninth Symphony or the *Missa solemnis*. Rather like Beethoven revising *Fidelio* in 1814, I have often felt that 'I could compose something new far more quickly than patch up the old with something new, as I am now doing'. But it has not merely been a question of patching up; this book differs substantially from the dissertation from which it arises, both in terms of content and structure.

It is tempting to risk a further Beethovenian analogy in relation to the number of *Skizzen* and *Urschriften* which have preceded this text, to say nothing of the geographical aspect of its genesis: like a Beethoven sketchbook, the typescript in its various stages of completion has accompanied its author to no fewer than six domestic locations and three professional ones.

Such a lengthy genesis implies a substantial debt of gratitude to those who have assisted or been caught up in all this creative activity. Jude Douglass has lived through every stage of the transition from dissertation to book; I have valued her skills as midwife to the project, and above all her unwavering insistence on a swift termination. The University of Exeter provided generous financial support which enabled me to process the music examples throughout the text; my colleagues and students at Exeter, King's College London, and Selwyn College Cambridge all indulged my constant preoccupation with this one piano sonata, and the staffs of all the libraries and archives mentioned in the text kindly allowed me frequent and lengthy access to the manuscripts in their charge. Financial support for my archival research in the early 1980s came from Cambridge University and Corpus Christi and Selwyn Colleges. A visit to the Library of Congress in 1990 was made possible thanks to a grant from the University of Exeter, and I am grateful to my hosts in Washington, Stephen and Mary Redhead. Lewis Lockwood kindly read the original dissertation and supported its appearance in this series; and Bruce Phillips of Oxford University Press deserves my

vi *Preface*

gratitude, not only for his enthusiasm for the project but also for his tolerance of the long gap between idea and realization. Reversing the positions of author and publisher, he has every right to upbraid me as Beethoven did Adolf Martin Schlesinger apropos the proof-reading of Op. 109, saying that 'I have never had a more difficult and tiresome task to cope with'.

If it is possible to trace the origins of this work to any single point, it must be to my time as an undergraduate in the Music Faculty at Cambridge, when I first became aware of the Beethoven sketchbooks and of the discipline of music analysis. It is above all to the memory of those days, and to the friends and institutions which supported and nourished me, that this book is dedicated.

N. M.

Exeter
July 1993

Contents

Editorial method in sketch transcriptions	ix
Bar numbering for Op. 109	ix
List of Examples	x
List of Tables	xv
List of Figures	xv
List of Plates	xvi
List of Abbreviations	xvii
1. Introduction	1
2. Beethoven in 1820: The Sources for the Piano Sonata, Op. 109	15
3. The Sketches for the First Movement	46
4. The Sketches for the Third-Movement Theme	81
5. The Second Movement: The First Phase	97
6. The Second Movement: The Continuity Drafts	124
7. Approaching the Variation Sketches	167
8. Plans for a Variation Set	184
9. Sketches for the Variations in the Final Version	218
10. Conclusion	252
Bibliography	261
Index	266

Editorial method in sketch transcriptions

ALL material supplied editorially is enclosed in square brackets or is written using dotted lines (barlines, ties, slurs, etc.). An exception to this rule is made for references to manuscript stave locations. Stave numbers are given in unbracketed plain type throughout each transcription; they appear above the stave for treble-clef material and below the stave for bass-clef material. In some longer drafts bar numbers are given in plain italic type and enclosed in square brackets. Words, numerals, etc. in bold type are Beethoven's.

A question mark enclosed in square brackets indicates a notation in the original which has resisted transcription; passages where the accuracy of the transcription is in doubt are identified by a horizontal square bracket broken by a question mark. Where the transcription departs radically from an unambiguous manuscript reading (for example, in replacing a sharp sign by a flat if the context demands the latter), the manuscript reading is given above the stave in the form [ms: ♯].

Local revisions are usually distinguished by size of type: the original reading, in small type, is positioned to the left of the revised one, which appears at normal size. In cases of larger-scale revision the several variants of a particular passage are presented on separate staves, with bracketed numerals ([1], [2], etc.) added to indicate the likely order in which the revisions were made.

Bar numbering for Op. 109

THE bar numbering for Op. 109 adopted throughout the text is that used in Erwin Ratz's revision of Schenker's edition of the sonata. The Schenker–Ratz edition accompanies Oswald Jonas's revision of Schenker's *Erläuterungsausgabe* of Op. 109 (see Bibliography).

List of Examples

2.1.	*a* BSk 27/75: first phrase of WoO 180 (sketch version); *b* Conversation-book entry (25 or 26 March 1820) by Joseph Czerny	17
2.2.	*a* Grasnick 20b, fol. 5ᵛ, st. 1; *b* Grasnick 20b, fol. 6ᵛ, st. 1	22
2.3.	Conversation-book entry (11–13 April 1820) for Op. 109, first movement	25
2.4.	*a* Conversation-book entries (15–25 December 1819) for the Credo of the *Missa solemnis*; *b* Wittgenstein, fols. 34ᵛ, 43ᵛ	28
2.5.	Grasnick 20b, fol. 1ᵛ: sketches for a projected sonata in E	32
2.6.	BH 108, p. 58: sketches for a 'sonata in E minor'	36
2.7.	Op. 109, second movement, bars 156–7 (Artaria 195, p. 50)	44
3.1.	*a* Grasnick 20b, fol. 3ʳ, st. 5/6–7; *b* First phrase of Ex. 3.1*a*	47
3.2.	Third phrase of Ex. 3.1*a*	48
3.3.	*a* Grasnick 20b, fol. 3ʳ, st. 9; *b* Cf. Ex. 3.3*a*	49
3.4.	Op. 109, first movement: composing-out of *x1*	50
3.5.	Grasnick 20b, fol. 3ʳ, st. 10/11	50
3.6.	Cf. Op. 109, first movement, bars 1–4	51
3.7.	The 'B-tonicizing' and 'E-tonicizing' progressions	53
3.8.	*a–c* Grasnick 20b, fol. 3ʳ, st. 12–fol. 3ᵛ, st. 1	54
3.9.	*a* Grasnick 20b, fol. 3ᵛ, st. 2; *b* Grasnick 20b, fol. 3ᵛ, st. 8/9; *c* Grasnick 20b, fol. 4ʳ, st. 9–11	55
3.10.	Cf. Op. 109, first movement, bars 60–2	58
3.11.	*a* Grasnick 20b, fol. 3ᵛ, st. 2/3–4/5; *b* Op. 109, first movement: voice-leading plan suggested by sketches	59
3.12.	Grasnick 20b, fol. 3ᵛ, st. 4–6	59
3.13.	Grasnick 20b, fol. 4ʳ, st. 4–5/6	61
3.14.	*a* Cf. Ex. 3.13, bars 8–10; *b* Cf. Op. 109, first movement, bars 12–13	62
3.15.	Grasnick 20b, fol. 4ʳ, st. 13–14	64

List of Examples xi

3.16.	Grasnick 20b, fol. 4ᵛ, st. 1, 3	65
3.17.	Grasnick 20b, fol. 4ᵛ, st. 11–16	67
3.18.	Grasnick 20b, fol. 4ᵛ, st. 16	67
3.19.	Projected voice-leading plan suggested by Ex. 3.17	68
3.20.	*a* Grasnick 20b, fol. 5ʳ, st. 1/2; *b* Projected voice-leading plan suggested by Ex. 3.20*a*	70
3.21.	*a* Grasnick 20b, fol. 5ʳ, st. 10/11–fol. 5ᵛ, st. 1; *b* Cf. Ex. 3.21*a*, bars 1–3, and Ex. 3.14	72
3.22.	*a* Grasnick 20b, fol. 5ʳ, st. 16; *b* Grasnick 20b, fol. 5ᵛ, st. 2–3; *c* Grasnick 20b, fol. 5ᵛ, st. 4–6; *d* Grasnick 20b, fol. 5ᵛ, st. 6/7; *e* Voice-leading plan for entire movement, suggested by Ex. 3.22*b* and *d*	74
3.23.	*a* BH 107, p. 39, st. 6; *b* BH 107, p. 40, st. 4–7	76
3.24.	*a* BH 107, p. 39, st. 7/8; *b* BH 107, p. 40, st. 1–2	77
3.25.	*a* BH 107, p. 41, st. 4/5–10/11; *b* BH 107, p. 43, st. 5–9 (cf. Plate 4)	78
3.26.	Op. 109, first movement: large-scale voice-leading summary	79
4.1.	Artaria 195, p. 35, st. 8	82
4.2.	Artaria 195, p. 36, st. 3/4	82
4.3.	Artaria 195, p. 36, st. 6/7–8/9	84
4.4.	*a* Artaria 195, p. 36, st. 10/11–14; *b* Cf. Ex. 4.4*a*	85
4.5.	Artaria 195, p. 36, st. 12/13–15/16	86
4.6.	Artaria 195, p. 36, st. 12/13–p. 37, st. 14/15	88
4.7.	*a* Artaria 195, p. 36, st. 15; *b* Artaria 195, p. 37, st. 16	88
4.8.	Projected arch structure for upper voice of theme	89
4.9.	Artaria 195, p. 53, st. 12–14, 16	90
4.10.	*a* Cf. Ex. 4.9, version [2]; *b* Cf. Ex. 4.9, version [3]	90
4.11.	Artaria 195, p. 53, st. 14/15	91
4.12.	Artaria 195, p. 53, st. 12/13	92
4.13.	*a* Cf. Ex. 4.7*a*; *b* Cf. Ex. 4.7*b*	93
4.14.	Cf. Op. 109, third movement, variation theme	94
5.1.	Artaria 195, p. 35, st. 10/11–14/15	100
5.2.	Op. 109, second movement, bars 1–4, left hand	101
5.3.	*a* Cf. Op. 109, second movement, bars 1–24; *b*. Cf. Ex. 5.1	101
5.4.	Artaria 195, p. 35, st. 14/15–p. 36, st. 1/2	103
5.5.	*a* Artaria 195, p. 37, st. 1/2; *b* Artaria 195, p. 37, st. 6	104

xii List of Examples

5.6.	Artaria 195, p. 37, st. 7/8–12	105
5.7.	Cf. Ex. 5.6 and Op. 109, second movement, bars 1–8	106
5.8.	*a* Cf. Ex. 5.6 and Op. 109, second movement, bars 1–16; *b* Bars 15–16	107
5.9.	Artaria 195, p. 38, st. 6–7/8	108
5.10.	Cf. Op. 109, second movement, bars 105–32	109
5.11.	*a* Artaria 195, p. 38, st. 12/13–15/16; *b* Cf. Ex. 5.11*a*, bars 1–5	110
5.12.	Artaria 195, p. 39, st. 12–14/15	111
5.13.	Op. 109, second movement: conjectural tonal structure projected by sketches	112
5.14.	Cf. Op. 109, second movement, bars 1–70	113
5.15.	*a* Artaria 195, p. 38, st. 4; *b* Op. 109, second movement, bars 162–5; *c* Artaria 195, p. 39, st. 7	114
5.16.	Op. 109, second movement, exposition transition theme (bars 25–8)	115
5.17.	Artaria 195, p. 37, st. 6	115
5.18.	Artaria 195, p. 40, st. 7–11	117
5.19.	Cf. Op. 109, second movement, bars 1–56	119
5.20.	The opposition between $\hat{3}$–$\hat{1}$–$\hat{2}$ and $\hat{3}$–$\hat{2}$–$\hat{1}$ progressions	120
5.21.	Artaria 195, p. 38, st. 9/10	120
6.1.	CD 1: Artaria 195, p. 41, st. 1/2–p. 42, st. 3/4	126
6.2.	Cf. CD 1, bars 9–25	129
6.3.	Cf. CD 1, bars 95–9, and Ex. 3.6	131
6.4.	CD 2: Artaria 195, p. 42, st. 6/7–p. 43, st. 11/12, 14	132
6.5.	Cf. CD 2, bars 1–32	136
6.6.	Artaria 195, p. 44, st. 1/2	139
6.7.	CD 3: Artaria 195, p. 44, st. 9/10–p. 45, st. 15/16	140
6.8.	Artaria 195, p. 46, st. 1/2–3/4	145
6.9.	Artaria 195, p. 44, st. 4/5–6/7	147
6.10.	*a* Artaria 195, p. 45, st. 1/2; *b* Cf. 6.10*a*	149
6.11.	Cf. CD 3, bars 76–end	150
6.12.	Artaria 195, p. 47, st. 9–14	152
6.13.	Artaria 195, p. 46, st. 10/11	154
6.14.	*a* Cf. Op. 109, second movement, bars 70–92; *b* Cf. Op. 109, second movement, bars 72–7	155
6.15.	Artaria 195, p. 49, st. 1/2–4/5	157
6.16.	Artaria 195, p. 49, st. 2–4/5	158

List of Examples xiii

6.17.	Artaria 195, p. 49, st. 2, 16	159
6.18.	Artaria 195, p. 49, st. 2, 15	159
6.19.	Artaria 195, p. 50, st. 10/11	160
6.20.	Artaria 195, p. 50, st. 10/11–13/14	161
6.21.	Cf. Op. 109, second movement	165
7.1.	*a* Artaria 195, p. 50, st. 13; p. 54, st. 1; *b* Artaria 195, p. 50, st. 13/14; p. 56, st. 1/2	172
7.2.	*a* Artaria 195, p. 57, st. 1/2; *b* Artaria 195, p. 57, st. 6/7	173
8.1.	Artaria 195, pp. 50–3: a projected set of variations	186
8.2.	*a* Artaria 195, p. 51, st. 1/2; *b* Op. 109, third movement, Variation 1, bar 8a	188
8.3.	Artaria 195, pp. 54–67: a projected set of nine variations	193
8.4.	Artaria 195, p. 68, st. 4/5–10/11 [variation 9: see Plate 5]	196
8.5.	*a* Artaria 195, p. 69, st. 1/2–3/4 (see Plate 6); *b* Artaria 195, p. 60, st. 16	199
8.6.	*a* Artaria 195, p. 55, st. 9; *b* Artaria 195, p. 56, st. 10; *c* Artaria 195, p. 61, st. 14 [variation 5]	200
8.7.	Artaria 195, p. 69, st. 3/4–9/10	201
8.8.	Artaria 195, pp. 64–9, st. 15/16: the 'overview' sketch for a variation set	203
8.9.	Artaria 195, p. 70, st. 4/5–p. 71, st. 3/4	208
8.10.	*a* Artaria 195, p. 71, st. 5–7; *b* Artaria 195, p. 71, st. 7	209
8.11.	Artaria 195, p. 73, st. 1/2	210
8.12.	Cf. Op. 109, third movement, Variation 1, bars 13–15	213
8.13.	Composing out of I–II–V^7–I/$\hat{3}$–$\hat{4}$–$\hat{3}$ in Op. 109, third movement (cf. Ex. 8.12)	214
8.14.	The relationship between theme and variation set in Op. 109, third movement	215
9.1.	Artaria 195, p. 75, st. 7–9	219
9.2.	Artaria 195, p. 59, st. 1/2–4/5	221
9.3.	Cf. Op. 109, third movement, theme and Variation 3, bars 4 and 8	222
9.4.	Artaria 195, p. 59, st. 15/16	223
9.5.	*a* Artaria 195, p. 62, st. 7/8–10/11; *b* Artaria 195, p. 64, st. 16; *c* Artaria 195, p. 78, st. 5/6; *d* Artaria 195, p. 78, st. 8/9–10/11	224
9.6.	Cf. Ex. 9.5*b*	226

9.7. *a* Cf. Ex. 9.5*c*; *b* Cf. Op. 109, third movement, Variation 5, bars 1–3 — 226
9.8. *a* Op. 109, autograph manuscript, fol. 16^r, st. 3/4: Variation 5, bars 5–8; *b* Op. 109, autograph manuscript, fol. 16^r, st. 5/6: Variation 5, bars 5–6 — 228
9.9. Cf. Op. 119 No. 11, bars 1–3 — 229
9.10. Artaria 195, p. 65, st. 1/2 — 230
9.11. *a* Cf. Ex. 9.10; *b* Cf. Op. 109, first movement, bars 58–65 — 231
9.12. Artaria 197, p. 1, st. 6–10 — 232
9.13. — 233
9.14. A 47, fol. 1^{r-v}: the *Concept* Draft for Variation [2] — 237
9.15. A 47, fols. 1^v–2^v: the *Concept* Draft for Variation [3] — 241
9.16. Cf. Op. 109, third movement, Variation 3, bars 9a–12a (17–20) — 249
9.17. Op. 109, autograph manuscript, fol. 14^r, st. 5/6–7/8 (original version only) — 250
10.1. Voice-leading connections between the movements of Op. 109 — 253
10.2. 'Abendlied unterm gestirnten Himmel', WoO 150 — 256

List of Tables

2.1.	Original concluding portion of the Wittgenstein sketchbook	20
2.2.	Proposed dating of sketches for Op. 109, first movement	25
2.3.	Contents of Artaria 195	35
2.4.	Structure of the autograph manuscript of Op. 109	42
7.1.	Variation numbering and sequence in the sketch and final versions of the Diabelli Variations	176
7.2.	Ink numbering of selected variation sketches in Artaria 195, pp. 50–69	180
8.1.	Artaria 195, pp. 50–3: a projected set of variations	185
8.2.	Artaria 195, pp. 54–67: a projected set of nine variations	192
9.1.	Sketches for the definitive set of variations in Op. 109	219

List of Figures

1.1.	Closing barlines as notated in Beethoven's autograph manuscript of Op. 109	11
9.1.	*a* The *Concept* Draft for Variation [3]: contrapuntal inversion in version [1]; *b* The *Concept* Draft for Variation [3]: contrapuntal inversion in version [2]	247

List of Plates

(Between pp. 172–73)

1. Op. 109, autograph manuscript, fol 5^v. 1st movement, bars '86–98' (*recte*: 87–99). *Wc*, Music Division, Gertrude Clarke Whittall Collection.
2. Op. 109, autograph manuscript, fol 10^v: 2nd movement, bars 166–77. *Wc*, Music Division, Gertrude Clarke Whittall Collection.
3. Op. 109, autograph manuscript, fol 19^v: 3rd movement, Variation 6 and thematic reprise, bars '35–50' (*recte*: 35–51, or 35; 1–16). *Wc*, Music Division, Gertrude Clarke Whittall Collection.
4. Puns on 'Gebauer', pocket sketches for Op. 109, first movement, and for the Credo of the *Missa solemnis*. *BNba*, BH 107, p. 43.
5. Desk sketches for Op. 109, 3rd-movement variations. *B*, Mus. ms. autogr. Beethoven Artaria 195, p. 68.
6. Desk sketches for Op. 109, 3rd-movement variations. *B*, Mus. ms. autogr. Beethoven Artaria 195, p. 69.
7. Desk sketches for Op. 109, 3rd-movement variations and theme. *B*, Mus. ms. autogr. Beethoven Artaria 195, p. 53.
8. Op. 109, *Concept* for 3rd movement, Variations [2] and [3]. *Wgm*, A 47, fol. 1^v.

List of Abbreviations

Anderson	*The Letters of Beethoven*, trans. and ed. Emily Anderson, 3 vols. (London, 1961)
B	(former) Staatsbibliothek Preussischer Kulturbesitz, Berlin
Bds	(former) Deutsche Staatsbibliothek, Berlin
BKh	*Ludwig van Beethovens Konversationshefte*, ed. Karl-Heinz Köhler *et al.*, 10 vols. (Leipzig, 1968–)
BNba	Beethoven-Archiv, Bonn
BS 2	Alan Tyson (ed.), *Beethoven Studies 2* (London, 1977)
CD	Continuity Draft for Op. 109, 2nd movement
Ea	Heinrich Schenker, *Beethoven: Die letzten Sonaten: Sonate E dur Op. 109. Kritische Einführung und Erläuterung von Heinrich Schenker*, ed. Oswald Jonas (Vienna, 1971)
JAMS	*Journal of the American Musicological Society*
JTW	Douglas Johnson, Alan Tyson, and Robert Winter, *The Beethoven Sketchbooks: History, Reconstruction, Inventory*, ed. Douglas Johnson (Berkeley, Calif., Los Angeles, and Oxford, 1985)
Kastner–Kapp	*Ludwig van Beethovens sämtliche Briefe*, ed. Emerich Kastner, rev. and enlarged Julius Kapp (Leipzig, 1923; repr. Tutzing, 1975)
Kinsky–Halm	Georg Kinsky, *Das Werk Beethovens: Thematisch-bibliographisches Verzeichnis seiner sämtlichen vollendeten Kompositionen*, completed and ed. Hans Halm (Munich and Duisburg, 1955)
PLM Draft	Paris–Landsberg–Montauban Draft
SBH	Hans Schmidt, 'Die Beethovenhandschriften des Beethovenhauses in Bonn', *Beethoven-Jahrbuch*, 7 (1971), pp. vii–xxiv, 1–443 (References in the text are to item nos.)
SG1	*Beethoven: Drei Skizzenbücher zur Missa Solemnis I: Ein Skizzenbuch aus den Jahren 1819/20 SV 81*, ed. Joseph Schmidt-Görg, 2 vols. (Bonn, 1952 (trans.), 1968 (facs.))
SG2	*Beethoven: Drei Skizzenbücher zur Missa Solemnis II: Ein Skizzenbuch zum Credo SV 82*, ed. Joseph Schmidt-Görg, 2 vols. (Bonn, 1968 (facs.), 1970 (trans.))
SG3	*Beethoven: Drei Skizzenbücher zur Missa Solemnis III: Ein Skizzenbuch zum Benedictus und zum Agnus Dei SV 83*, ed. Joseph Schmidt-Görg, 2 vols. (Bonn, 1968 (facs.), 1970 (trans.))
SG[W]	*Beethoven: Ein Skizzenbuch zu den Diabelli-Variationen und*

	zur Missa Solemnis SV 154, ed. Joseph Schmidt-Görg, 2 vols. (Bonn, 1968 (facs.), 1972 (trans.))
SV	Hans Schmidt, 'Verzeichnis der Skizzen Beethovens', *Beethoven-Jahrbuch*, 6 (1969), 7–128 (References in the text are to item nos.)
Thayer–Forbes	Alexander Wheelock Thayer, *Thayer's Life of Beethoven*, rev. and ed. Elliot Forbes, rev. edn. (Princeton, NJ, 1967)
Wc	Library of Congress, Washington, DC
Wgm	Gesellschaft der Musikfreunde, Vienna
Wn	Nationalbibliothek, Vienna

. . . le premier Allegro ici est faible, diffus, maigre dans sa diffusion. . . . Beethoven ne donnait plus sur la fin de ses jours, toute son attention à une Sonate.

La première Variation est la digne fille de cette sublime mère. . . . On peut regretter que dans les autres variations on ne retrouve plus ni l'une ni l'autre, qu'on y soit pris d'un tourbillon de notes qui aux yeux de Beethoven avaient sans doute un sens qui nous échappe.

(Wilhelm von Lenz, *Beethoven et ses trois styles,* on Op. 109)

Auch in meiner instrumental Musik habe ich iṁer das ganze vor Augen

(Beethoven to Georg Friedrich Treitschke, April 1814)

1. Introduction

This book, as its series title proclaims, is a study in musical genesis and structure. More specifically, it deals with the genesis and structure of a single musical work, Beethoven's Piano Sonata in E, Op. 109. The purpose of this introduction is to consider how these two aspects of Op. 109 have been approached and to draw attention to the limitations—some inevitable, others consciously self-imposed—by which the following chapters are constrained and shaped.

First, musical genesis. It should be obvious that no study of this kind can ever be exhaustive. A vast spectrum of experiences and impulses impinges upon the creation of an artwork: cultural, social, pyschological, emotional, and intellectual factors are all combined in a way which must ultimately be unknowable in the fullest sense, even to the artist himself. Guiding impulses of which the artist is aware will not infrequently leave no trace in the work itself, and in the absence of supporting documentation such impulses eventually become inaccessible to others. An outsider attempting to reconstruct the genesis of a musical work, then, is likely to find only very limited evidence available. There may be an amount of essentially factual information dealing, for example, with the date, place, and circumstances of composition. Then there may be statements by the composer concerning his intentions or aspirations in writing the work; such statements may be preserved in the composer's own words or as reminiscences (varying in their precision) by his contemporaries. In addition, there may be evidence in the form of the composer's working papers and sketches. All these forms of evidence demand cautious evaluation and interpretation. They do not simply speak for themselves.

In the case of Beethoven's Op. 109 there is substantial factual evidence and very little in the way of anecdote or reminiscence; but it is the compositional record, albeit necessarily partial, provided by the autograph musical sources for Op. 109 which forms the bedrock of this study. By 'autograph musical sources' are meant musical manuscripts in Beethoven's hand: the sketchleaves and sketchbooks preserving traces of the compositional process, and also the autograph manuscript of the finished work. Indeed, it is one of the

2 Introduction

self-imposed limitations of this book that the completion and submission of the autograph manuscript to the publisher Adolf Martin Schlesinger is held to mark the conclusion of the act of composing Op. 109. We shall not be much concerned with subsequent events pertaining to the preparation, publication, and correction of the first edition of the work.[1]

The historical and biographical circumstances surrounding the composition of Op. 109 are discussed in Chapter 2. As well as scrutinizing Beethoven's letters and conversation books this chapter also deals with the physical structure of the musical manuscripts, the interpretation of which then follows in Chapters 3–9. These chapters deal with each of the three movements, although not in the order in which they stand in the work. Instead, they follow the order of composition as revealed by the sketches: the first movement, the third-movement theme, the second movement, and finally the third-movement variations. This order is significant in view of the remarkable structural relationship of the third-movement theme to the first movement; and that relationship itself appears significant in view of the evidence offered in Chapter 2 that the first movement of Op. 109 was originally conceived and written as an independent composition and was only subsequently adopted as the opening movement of a sonata.

This book, then, is primarily a contribution to Beethoven sketch studies. It is concerned almost exclusively with Op. 109 and pays little attention to Beethoven's wider musical output, let alone to the cultural, social, and other factors attendant upon the composition of this one sonata. Even within this circumscribed scope, however, there are further limitations to be understood and accepted. Reference has been made above to the need to interpret evidence relating to the compositional process. In the case of Beethoven's sketches, three distinct but closely interrelated stages of interpretation are necessary. The first involves the very transcription of the sketches. The indecipherability of Beethoven's handwriting has become legendary, even if somewhat exaggerated. Scholars today are in general agreement that 'diplomatic' transcription of a Beethoven sketch, seeking as it does to reproduce the appearance of the original as faithfully as possible, is pointless. Transcriptions of this kind frequently result in musical readings which vary from the mildly eccentric to the utterly implausible. What is required is a transcription which assumes that Beethoven intended to write musical sense and

[1] The post-compositional phase is discussed in detail in W. R. Meredith, 'The Sources for Beethoven's Piano Sonata in E Major, Opus 109', Ph.D. diss. (University of North Carolina, Chapel Hill, 1985), esp. 180–236.

which interprets his actual notation in this light.² Although it is impossible to specify a general tolerance level for such interpretation, the degree of correspondence between two or more independent transcriptions of a page of sketches will often be sufficiently high to inspire confidence in the belief that they represent accurately what Beethoven apparently meant, regardless of what he actually wrote.

Such confidence notwithstanding, it remains the case that any sketch study of a Beethoven work will be based on source material which is 'interpreted' in this sense, and which is therefore already one degree removed from the original. To put it more radically, any Beethoven sketch study begins with the virtual creation of its own source material. And without prejudice to the observation made at the end of the preceding paragraph, the difference between two or more transcriptions of a single body of sketches may in some cases be so extreme as to make comparison between them meaningless: one is dealing with more or less different 'pieces' of music, despite their common derivation from a single parent source in Beethoven's hand. This point is especially relevant in the present case, for Op. 109 has been the subject of two other major sketch studies, by Allen Forte and William Meredith. These two authors' transcriptions often differ radically from each other and from those offered here; so too do their reconstructions of the probable order in which the sketches were made.³

But one does not merely transcribe Beethoven's sketches, even when allowance is made for the degree of interpretation involved: one 'realizes' them also. It is well known that the sketches often take the form of single-line drafts. Beethoven evidently notated only as much as was necessary to fix visually what he heard mentally at any point. And when transcribing sketches, particularly sketches for a work which one knows, it is well-nigh impossible to avoid reversing Beethoven's procedure and filling out the implied 'aural context' of the notes on the page. In several cases, therefore, I have not hesitated to make public here my private realizations of implied harmonies, bass lines, and so on.

This act of realization makes up the second of the three stages of sketch interpretation referred to above. The third stage consists in

[2] For a useful discussion of the notation and transcription of Beethoven's sketches, together with references to other relevant literature, see B. Cooper, *Beethoven and the Creative Process* (Oxford, 1990), 93–103.

[3] A. Forte, *The Compositional Matrix* (New York, 1961; repr. 1974); Meredith, 'Sources for Opus 109'. It would have been quite impractical, as well as inappropriate, to detail here all the many divergences between my own interpretations and those of Forte and Meredith. In the case of Forte, however, see my 'Schenker and Forte Reconsidered: Beethoven's Sketches for the Piano Sonata in E, Op. 109', *19th Century Music*, 10 (1986–7), 24–42.

interpretation or analysis, in the most common musical sense of those terms: the application to a given musical text of certain analytical or interpretative operations. That all three stages are closely interrelated is signalled by the fact that the process of what I have called sketch realization is itself partly analytical; and the same claim might be entered even for the process of transcription itself. By the same token, the results of sketch analysis cannot be separated from the material being analysed: two differing sketch transcriptions will yield differing results under the same analytical operation. Here again it is not overstressing the case greatly to say that Forte, Meredith, and I have each analysed essentially different bodies of music and that extended comparison of individual analytical conclusions is unlikely to prove fruitful.

Far from mechanically transcribing Beethoven's sketches, then, the transcriber constructs an intensely personal vision of the material for a particular work. This is obviously not to imply that there are no standards of reliability or even excellence in such matters, or that the transcriber may proceed with anything other than extreme caution. Rather, it is to stress the mutual dependence of the sketch transcriptions and analytical observations presented below. Their combination is at the heart of this book.

What of the approach to musical structure offered here? This draws heavily upon the concepts and methodology of Schenkerian analysis. Now Schenkerian analysis itself entails well-known limitations, not least in the primacy accorded to the linear properties of tonal music. Nevertheless, there are several reasons why such an approach is appropriate here. First, Beethoven's music responds particularly well to Schenkerian methods; secondly, the number of published Schenkerian analyses of complete Beethoven works remains relatively small; thirdly, the presence in Op. 109 of a set of variations offers the opportunity to explore the application of Schenkerian concepts to a genre which Schenker himself treated only marginally;[4] finally, Op. 109 features quite prominently in Schenker's own work, as the following remarks make clear.

Schenker's most extended published study of Op. 109 is his *Erläuterungsausgabe*.[5] His plan for an 'explanatory edition' of Beethoven's

---

[4] For an examination of the application of Schenkerian theory to variation movements see my 'Analysing Variations: The Finale of Beethoven's String Quartet Op. 74', *Music Analysis*, 8 (1989), 303–24. Those familiar with Schenkerian analysis will appreciate that my interpretation of the background structure of each movement of Op. 109 departs from the orthodox concept of a melodic descent from $\hat{3}$ or $\hat{5}$ to $\hat{1}$. For this reason I have avoided the conventional white-note notation of the background level in Exx. 3.26, 4.14, 6.21, 8.13–14, and 10.1.

[5] See *Ea*. Jonas's revised edn. of the four original *Erläuterungsausgaben* is problematic on at least two counts. First, it silently suppresses and rewords numerous passages in Schenker's original text; secondly, the accompanying edn. of each sonata is not Schenker's original but

last five piano sonatas, combining his own edition of each work with a substantial analytical and critical commentary, seems to have been conceived around 1910, but it was not until 1913 that the series was inaugurated with Op. 109.[6] In the foreword to this edition Schenker expressed the hope that the series would be completed in about four years. The editions of Op. 110 and 111 appeared in 1914 and 1915 respectively, but war delayed the appearance of Op. 101 until 1920. The projected final work in the series, the 'Hammerklavier' Sonata, Op. 106, was never completed: it seems to have foundered largely because of financial disagreements between Schenker and the impoverished post-war Universal Edition. Had the Op. 106 edition appeared, it would have differed from that of Op. 109 in two major respects. On an intellectual level it would have represented a much more mature stage in Schenker's musical thinking. While the Op. 109 Erläuterungsausgabe is grounded primarily in the theoretical world of the 1906 Harmonielehre and the first (1910) volume of Kontrapunkt, that of Op. 106 would have been informed by Schenker's emerging concepts of the Urlinie and structural levels in tonal music. The Op. 106 Erläuterungsausgabe would have belonged to the period of Der Tonwille and Das Meisterwerk in der Musik.

On a more practical level, the Op. 106 Erläuterungsausgabe would have differed from all the others in that Schenker would have had to abandon one of his cardinal editorial principles, namely the use of the autograph manuscript of the work as his primary source. While Beethoven's autographs for Opp. 101, 109, 110, and 111 all survive and were known to Schenker, that for Op. 106 has been missing since the early nineteenth century. Schenker believed fervently in the significance of the composer's own notation for a correct understanding of the structure of a musical work; and since it was a performer's primary task to reveal that structure, the importance of an autograph manuscript in editorial work could hardly be underestimated. Herein lies the major significance of the Op. 109 Erläuterungsausgabe, for, as Schenker was not slow to point out, it

that of Erwin Ratz's revision of Schenker's complete edn. of the Beethoven piano sonatas. This leads to seemingly incomprehensible contradictions between Erläuterung and Notentext. Further on this matter see W. Drabkin, 'The New Erläuterungsausgabe', Perspectives of New Music, 12 (1973–4), 319–30.

[6] The Erläuterungsausgabe series was published by Universal Edition in Vienna. In a letter to Theodor von Frimmel dated 13 June 1912 Schenker mentioned that he wanted to begin the series with Op. 109 because it was the most-often played of the five sonatas: see Helmut Federhofer, Heinrich Schenker: Nach Tagebüchern und Briefen in der Oswald Jonas Memorial Collection, University of California, Riverside (Hildesheim, 1985), 30. Much of the history of the Erläuterungsausgabe project can be reconstructed through the voluminous correspondence from Emil Hertzka, the director of Universal Edition, to Schenker preserved in the Ernst Oster Collection at the New York Public Library. I have drawn on this largely unpublished archive in the remarks which follow.

was the first modern edition to be based primarily on the autograph manuscript rather than on the first and other early editions, which were manifestly corrupt in many respects. So remarkable were the hitherto unexamined readings of the autograph that Schenker described his edition as 'almost an exhumation of the, so to speak, long-buried masterpiece' and boasted that Universal Edition was receiving 'the first authentic truth about Op. 109'.[7] Exaggerated as these claims may be—it will be shown below that Schenker, along with most other editors before and since, misunderstood one crucial aspect of Beethoven's notation in the autograph—there is good reason to regard the Op. 109 *Erläuterungsausgabe* as a seminal contribution to the present-day concept of the *Urtext* edition.[8]

Schenker's next published remarks on Op. 109 appeared in the essay 'The Organic Nature of Sonata Form' ('Vom organischen der Sonatenform').[9] Here Schenker was concerned to show how, in the first movement of the sonata, Beethoven employs the opening upbeat figure $g\sharp^1$–b^1 as a 'motive' in the upper voice. The figure is composed out across the development section as $g\sharp^3$–b^3 (bars 21 and 42) and then reappears in this high register at the beginning of the recapitulation (bar 48). Two further appearances, as $g\sharp^2$–b^2 in bars 95–6 and again as $g\sharp^3$–b^3 on the last quaver of bar 97, set the seal on what Schenker described as the 'world of unity and coherence' created by Beethoven's use of this two-note motive.[10] Although Schenker's essay was not published until 1926, his discovery of the role of the opening upbeat figure in creating organic coherence in the first movement of Op. 109 had been made several years earlier,

---

[7] See the original (1913) edn. of the *Erläuterungsausgabe*, 22: 'In diesem Sinne stellt die Ausgabe fast eine Ausgrabung des gleichsam längst verschütteten Meisterwerkes'; a letter to Hertzka dated 27 Nov. 1912 is quoted in Federhofer, *Heinrich Schenker*, 31: 'Die "U. E." erhält mit meiner Ausgabe die erste aut[h]entische Wahrheit über op. 109'.

[8] For Schenker's opinion of himself as 'the true founder of the discipline of autograph-study' see his *Free Composition*, trans. and ed. Ernst Oster (New York, 1979), i. 7. Correspondence relating to Schenker's search for the autograph MS of Op. 109 (today in *Wc*, but at that time in the possession of the Wittgenstein family in Vienna) is preserved in the Oswald Jonas Collection at the University of California, Riverside. The same collection also includes the MS (in Jeanette Schenker's hand) of a *kritischer Bericht* on the autograph MS. Since the Hertzka correspondence in the Oster Collection (see n. 6 above) makes clear that Schenker originally hoped to publish a facsimile edn. of the Op. 109 autograph, there can be little doubt that this critical report was intended to accompany that publication, the whole thus forming a companion publication to the *Erläuterungsausgabe*. I propose to deal more fully with this unrealized project in a separate study.

[9] *Das Meisterwerk in der Musik*, ii (Munich, Vienna, Berlin, 1926; repr. Hildesheim and New York, 1974), 43–54. A trans. by Orin Grossman was published as 'Organic Structure in Sonata Form', *Journal of Music Theory*, 12 (1968), 164–83; repr. in *Readings in Schenker Analysis and Other Approaches*, ed. Maury Yeston (New Haven, Conn. and London, 1977), 38–53.

[10] *Meisterwerk*, ii. 51: 'Den beiden Tönen des Auftaktes jagt also die Stegreif-Fantasie des Meisters in der Durchführung und in der Coda nach! . . . ihm bedeuten sie schon ein Motiv, den Schlüssel zu einer Welt von Einheit und Zusammenhang.'

in 1922. A diary entry for 22 October mentions 'marvellous discoveries made in Op. 109; in the *Urlinie*, beginning and end of the first movement and [in the] development: $g\sharp$–b!' Slightly later entries, for 11 and 12 November of the same year, mention *Urlinien* for the first and last movements of the sonata.[11]

The opening upbeat figure had in fact already caught Schenker's attention in the *Erläuterungsausgabe*. After discussing Beethoven's alterations to the left-hand semiquaver figure from bar 92 onwards in the autograph score, Schenker observed that 'if one considers the second crotchet beat in bar 97, one gets the impression of an inversion of the [opening] upbeat!' The term 'inversion [*Umkehrung*]' is not quite accurate here, for b^2–$g\sharp^2$ on the second beat of bar 97 is a straightforward retrograde of the opening upbeat. Even more immediately puzzling is the very next sentence, with which Schenker concluded his analysis of the first movement: 'the [final] cadence of the movement is an imperfect one.'[12] Even disregarding the fact that there is no actual cadence in the closing bars of the movement—the final structural V–I occurs in bars 85–6 and inaugurates a fourteen-bar tonic pedal—the reference to an 'imperfect' cadence at the close is confusing until one realizes that Schenker's notion of cadence involved melodic as well as harmonic resolution. In dealing with 'different kinds of conclusions' in his *Harmonielehre* Schenker had differentiated between the effect of a V–I harmonic progression in which the melodic line cadences on the tonic note and an identical progression in which the melodic close is on the triadic third; the former situation he described as '*a full close, a perfect cadence*', while in the latter case 'the full close here is imperfect'.[13] It is the melodic aspect of the closing bars of the first movement of Op. 109, where the upper voice remains fixed on the triadic fifth (b^2–b^3–b, bars 97–9), which explains Schenker's apparently anomalous reading in the *Erläuterungsausgabe*.[14]

---

[11] The diary entries, along with the entire text of the relevant passage in 'Vom organischen der Sonatenform', are quoted by Jonas in *Ea*, 18–19. Jonas's statement that 'Die Urlinien-Studie [von Op. 109] ist jedoch nicht erhalten' is incorrect, for Schenker's graphs of all three movements of Op. 109 are preserved in the Ernst Oster Collection. I intend to write a separate study of this unpublished analysis of the sonata, on which Schenker clearly spent considerable time and effort in 1922.

[12] *Ea*, 25: 'Betrachtet man in T. 97 das 2. Viertel, so erhält man das Bild einer Umkehrung des Auftaktes! Der Schluss des Satzes ist ein unvollkommener.'

[13] *Harmony*, ed. Oswald Jonas, trans. Elisabeth Mann Borgese (Chicago and London, 1954), 217. For a later manifestation of the same perception see *Free Composition*, 36 (§ 88) and 95.

[14] In dealing with bars 85–6 Schenker was in fact careful to observe (*Ea*, 24) that at this point 'die letzte Tonika ist erreicht. Der Harmoniengang ist zu Ende, *nicht aber noch das Melos*' (italics mine). Neither here nor in the remarks published in 'Vom organischen der Sonatenform' did he note the interesting fact that the cadence in bars 85–6 is again an 'imperfect full close' in which the melodic progression presents the opening upbeat figure in retrograde and at original pitch: b^1–$g\sharp^1$.

An appreciation of Schenker's growing interest in the role of the opening upbeat figure g♯¹–b¹ in the first movement of Op. 109 suggests the extent to which his insights on this point were a strong influence on Allen Forte's study of the movement and its related sketches. It is a vital tenet of Forte's analysis that 'to a considerable extent the melodic development of the movement resides in the composing-out of relationships which are inherent in the upper third [G♯–B, the notes of the opening upbeat figure] of the triad, where A plays a primal role.' In fact Forte hears the upper third of the tonic triad as the primary area of 'melodic development' in the second movement and the third-movement theme also (he does not analyse the variations), and concludes his study with the observation that the opening upbeat figure in the first movement is one 'of the two intervals which are to control the entire work'.[15]

The analysis of the genesis and structure of the first movement of Op. 109 developed in this book is similarly indebted to Schenker's and Forte's work on the role of the opening upbeat figure, but it draws upon other factors as well. In particular, Schenker's notion of the 'imperfect' close at the end of the movement is developed into a concept of structural 'incompleteness' or open-endedness, and this concept is seen to be applied in the way in which Beethoven composes out the opening upbeat figure throughout the course of the movement. The sketches suggest that he first intended to create a large arched linear progression from triadic third to fifth and back (G♯–A♯–B–A–G♯; or, in terms of scale degrees, $\hat{3}$–♯$\hat{4}$–$\hat{5}$–$\hat{4}$–$\hat{3}$): the fifth was to be reached by the end of the exposition, and the return to the third was to coincide with the beginning of the recapitulation. Subsequently he chose to extend this arch structure, leaving the triadic fifth 'unresolved' back to the third until the end of the movement.[16] But he finally decided to leave the structure incomplete altogether—

---

[15] *Compositional Matrix*, 19, 85. For the reading of the second movement see ex. 19, p. 48; for the third-movement theme see p. 71. A reconsideration of the structure of this theme appears in A. Forte and S. E. Gilbert, *Introduction to Schenkerian Analysis* (New York and London, 1982), 327–30. Here doubts are expressed as to whether B or G♯ is the primary melodic note (compare *Compositional Matrix*, 71: 'The fifth, B, does not constitute the main melodic note in the upper voice'), and a conventional $\hat{3}$–$\hat{2}$–$\hat{1}$ *Urlinie* is proposed: in *Compositional Matrix*, 72 the upper-voice progression a¹–g♯¹ is held to be 'superimposed' upon the final inner-voice descent g♯–f♯–e and thus to prevent 'a definitive melodic closure', while the more recent analysis holds that the *Urlinie* descent is simply 'masked' by the b¹–g♯¹ motion in the final bars.

[16] A corollary of this change is that the triadic fifth, rather than the third, acts as the primary melodic note in the recapitulation, a reading held by Schenker (*Meisterwerk*, ii. 51: 'h³ (T. 42), das zum Kopfton der Reprise werden soll (T. 48)') and Forte (*Compositional Matrix*, 23). Forte's analysis differs from mine in that he regards the motion from $\hat{3}$ to $\hat{5}$ as being completed only during the development rather than by the end of the exposition.

hence the melodic emphasis on the triadic fifth at the end of the movement.

The notion of the incompleteness of the first movement finds powerful support in a fascinating detail of Beethoven's autograph manuscript: a detail, moreover, which Schenker failed to understand. Schenker's edition of Op. 109 is conspicuous in that the first movement is given no concluding barline. The reason for this curious editorial decision emerges from the *Erläuterungsausgabe* commentary, where Schenker carefully described the several means by which Beethoven sought to link the first and second movements in the autograph. A pedalling instruction directs the pianist to depress the sustaining pedal for the final chord of the first movement and to release it only as the first chord of the second movement is struck. There is also an attacca directive at the end of the first movement, but this is deleted in pencil. At the beginning of the second movement Beethoven added a cancellation signature of three naturals in pencil before the existing E-minor key signature; also using pencil, he changed the tempo direction from 'presto' to 'prestissimo'. Now Schenker believed that Beethoven made a further pencil emendation at this stage, namely the deletion of the closing double barline at the end of the first movement. In Schenker's estimation, Beethoven probably thought that the combination of the pedalling instruction, the absence of a closing barline, and the cancellation signature amounted to a more 'energetic and reliable' way of signalling the concatenation of the two movements than the attacca directive.[17]

But Schenker misread Beethoven's autograph. The closing double barline is not deleted at the end of the first movement. The real situation is rather more complex and a good deal more interesting. What Schenker believed to be the deletion of the double barline was in fact a barline itself: the characteristic squiggle which was

[17] *Ea*, 25: these were means which Beethoven 'für energischer und verläßlicher hielt'. The details of the autograph MS discussed here can all clearly be seen in the facsimile edn., with an introd. by Oswald Jonas, published by the Robert Owen Lehman Foundation: see *Ludwig van Beethoven: Piano Sonata Opus 109* (New York, 1965), pp. 10–11. The Schenker–Ratz edn. of Op. 109 published with *Ea* conflicts with Schenker's commentary in that it correctly gives a 'double-single' barline at the end of the first movement (see below). Furthermore, Schenker's original text reads 'Ferner schrieb er hinter dem . . . Doppelstrich die Worte: "attacca il prestissimo"' whereas Jonas's revision gives 'Ursprünglich schrieb er . . .'. The unacknowledged change from 'ferner' to 'ursprünglich' spoils the connection which Schenker evidently understood between the pedalling and attacca instructions. It seems that the modification of the closing double barline originally failed to attract Schenker's attention. A handwritten text of the *Erläuterungsausgabe* commentary preserved in the Oswald Jonas Collection at the University of California, Riverside includes no reference whatever to this aspect of the autograph, while a list of proof-reading corrections relating to the text of the sonata itself reads '[Takt] 99: <u>Kein Taktstrich</u>!!! <u>trotzdem der 1. Satz zu Ende</u>'. Schenker's excitement at this late discovery is evident.

Beethoven's (and other composers') standard handwritten equivalent of the conventional double bar used to conclude a complete movement or work. What Beethoven did at the end of the first movement of Op. 109 was to replace this double barline with the more provisional form consisting of two ordinary barlines placed close together (see Plate 1). This form, here given the name 'double-single' barline, is in regular use today and usually marks a change of key or time signature (or both), or the completion of a discrete section within a work or movement. Beethoven used it very sparingly, however, so much so that his use of it in the autograph of Op. 109 takes on special significance.[18] That he substituted this form for the more conventional one clearly indicates that he imputed different meanings to the two signs. Because Schenker failed to understand this notational distinction in the Op. 109 autograph, he failed to notice that the *second* movement also ends with a double-single barline (see Plate 2: on this occasion the autograph betrays no sign of vacillation on Beethoven's part). However, he did observe more carefully the pattern of closing barlines in the third-movement variations.[19]

Fig. 1.1 provides an overview of the orthography of closing barlines in the autograph manuscript of Op. 109. One fact stands out particularly clearly: the autograph contains only one double barline, at the end of the entire sonata (see Plate 3). Provisional closes are indicated at the end of the first two movements and within the third movement (although here the double-single barlines following Variations 1 and 4 signify stronger closure than the single ones which close Variations 2, 3, 5, and 6). If the double-single barline at the end of the first movement signifies structural incompleteness, then the same sign at the end of the second movement encourages a similar reading. In distinction to Forte's reading, the analysis given in Chapters 5 and 6 below regards the lower third ($\hat{3}-\hat{2}-\hat{1}$) of the tonic triad

---

[18] For a telling example of the distinction between Beethoven's and the present-day usage of the double-single barline, compare the facsimile edn. of the autograph of *An die ferne Geliebte* (Munich, 1970) with the edition of that work in *Beethoven: Werke, XII/1: Lieder und Gesänge mit Klavierbegleitung*, ed. Helga Lühning (Munich, 1990), 151–64. The modern edition uses double-single barlines to demarcate divisions between songs and to mark changes of key and time signature. Beethoven's autograph contains no double-single barlines at all.

[19] Schenker's edn. follows Beethoven's autograph except in the case of Variation 1, where once again he misread Beethoven's double-single barline as a double barline. See *Ea*, 37–8, where Schenker promises to deal with the structural meaning of the grouping of the Op. 109 variations in his projected 'Entwurf einer neuen Formenlehre'. Schenker's misunderstanding of Beethoven's notation at the end of the first movement is all the more unfortunate in view of the continuation of the letter to Hertzka quoted in n. 7, above: '[meine Ausgabe von Op. 109] differirt, dem Autograph nach, schon in den Taktstrichen (!!!) . . .' (Federhofer, *Heinrich Schenker*, 31).

FIG. 1.1. Closing barlines as notated in Beethoven's autograph manuscript of Op. 109

1st movt	‖
2nd movt	‖
3rd movt:	
Theme	:‖
Var. 1	‖
Var. 2	|
Var. 3	|
Var. 4	‖
Var. 5	|
Var. 6	|
Them. reprise	▌

as the main area of melodic activity. Structural incompleteness here is achieved by means other than those pursued in the first movement. The sketches for the second movement suggest that Beethoven was interested in contrasting a complete *Urlinie*-like $\hat{3}$–$\hat{2}$–$\hat{1}$ descent with an incomplete form consisting of the descending step $\hat{3}$–$\hat{2}$. It is this latter form which governs the large-scale upper-voice motion in the movement and, as in the first movement, renders it melodically though not harmonically incomplete. Analysis of the second movement in these terms helps to explain one of its most interesting features, namely the unorthodox dominant preparation of the dominant rather than the tonic during the retransition to the recapitulation.

That the third-movement theme is structurally related to the first movement has already been alluded to above. The sketches suggest that in composing this theme Beethoven took up again the structural issues with which he had been concerned in the first movement. The arch structure originally intended for that movement is presented complete in the theme, and is also composed out across the six variations which follow. Thus the third movement of Op. 109, theme and variations, completes the structure left open in the first movement: in a very literal sense it is a 'recomposition' of that movement. Forte's conclusion that 'the sketches and autograph revisions suggest that [Beethoven] had in mind a plan for the entire work' applies equally well to the analysis presented here, although the route to that conclusion differs from Forte's in subtle but important ways.[20]

It should be clear from this outline summary that my analysis of Op. 109 operates within limitations which are so well known as to be almost traditional. It is largely concerned with matters of voice leading, and is therefore pitch-centred; other musical parameters—rhythm, texture, dynamics—receive scant attention. Another limitation may be felt in the emphasis placed on questions of unity, not only within individual movements but across the sonata as a whole. In reply it can only be reiterated that such limitations follow almost automatically from the adoption of a Schenkerian approach, and that no study of a musical work can possibly be exhaustive. And if, by concluding that Op. 109 is a highly unified musical structure, this study does no more than reinforce a critical commonplace, it at least tries additionally to discern something of the way in which that unity was achieved. This point brings us at last to the relationship between sketch studies and analysis: in other words, the relationship between genesis and structure. These are dangerous liaisons, apt to bring complex theoretical issues into play;[21] but in the present context they can hardly be shunned.

At a rather trivial level we may assume that genesis and structure are related to the extent that the structure of the finished work is the product of its genesis, of the unique compositional process by which it comes into existence. Being able to study the surviving evidence of that process in conjunction with the work itself, we may hope to glimpse something of the rationale behind the structure. This is a major premiss of most sketch studies and certainly of the present one, which is above all a study of Beethoven at work. It is assumed that the sketches for Op. 109 represent serious compositional activity on Beethoven's part, and that analysis of them can reveal something of what he was trying to achieve. The analysis of the final version takes its point of departure from the sketch analysis; in general it highlights structural features of the work which may be discerned in the sketches, albeit sometimes in unfamiliar guise. Some readers may wish to consider such features 'privileged', although it is not at all my claim that the purpose of music analysis is to reveal

---

[20] *Compositional Matrix*, 85.

[21] For a classic statement see D. Johnson, 'Beethoven Scholars and Beethoven's Sketches', *19th Century Music*, 2 (1978–9), 3–17; see 'Viewpoint', ibid. 270–9 for replies to Johnson by Sieghard Brandenburg and William Drabkin, together with a response by Johnson. See also P. Gossett, 'Beethoven's Sixth Symphony: Sketches for the First Movement', *JAMS* 27 (1974), 248–84. For a more recent consideration of the issue see L. Lockwood, 'The Beethoven Sketchbooks and the General State of Sketch Research', in W. Kinderman (ed.), *Beethoven's Compositional Process* (Lincoln and London, 1991), 6–13.

the composer's intentions, nor that an analysis based thereon would necessarily be more meaningful or 'correct' than one which disregarded the issue of authorial intention altogether.[22]

But in assuming that the final version somehow emerges from or partially inheres in the surviving sketches we should beware of placing excessive faith in that version as a yardstick by which to measure the sketches. To be sure, it is almost certainly impossible to avoid this pitfall altogether, because the author of a sketch study usually knows the final version of the work in question before he tackles the sketches. On the other hand, one need not go as far as Forte, who stated plainly that 'I have undertaken to interpret certain of the sketches with reference to the final version of the appropriate movement. Accordingly, I shall begin by presenting an analysis of the first movement. . . . I will then present sketches of selected passages in what I assume to be correct chronological order.'[23] Such an approach is apt to engender a wholly negative view of the sketches. By being filtered through a preconceived analytical view of the work itself, the sketches tend to become relegated to the status of failures, wrong turnings *en route* to the final version. This study of the genesis of Op. 109 tries to view the sketches in a more positive light, as the record of serious compositional decisions taken in the effort to create an as yet unwritten and (for Beethoven) unknown piano sonata. 'It is rare that a sketch, however imperfect, is admired and pondered as expression itself, with its own claims to eloquence and comprehensibility;' this book takes up the challenge thus laid down by Richard Kramer.[24]

Indeed, these observations illuminate perhaps the most fascinating role which sketch studies have to play in our thinking about musical works. Forte's approach tends towards an image of the composer as finder rather than creator: it is as if Op. 109 already exists somewhere 'out there' and the composer's job is merely to capture it on paper. Accordingly, the sketches come to seem like failed attempts to write down the 'correct answer'. But if we think (as I believe, more accurately) of the composer creating essentially *ex nihilo*, then far from appearing as 'wrong answers' which yield inexorably to the correct one in due course, the sketches come to seem like a collection of valid ideas, or potential compositions among which the

---

[22] At another level, whatever status we accord the sketches in relation to Beethoven's intentions, there can be little doubt that they may prove helpful in drawing attention to previously unnoticed or misunderstood features of a work. Therefore 'one ought to credit the sketches with the insight they afford': Drabkin, 'Viewpoint', 275.

[23] *Compositional Matrix*, 11.

[24] *JAMS* 40 (1987), 361 (review of JTW). See also Kramer, 'The Sketch Itself', in Kinderman (ed.), *Beethoven's Compositional Process*, 3–5.

composer must ultimately choose: he too confronts unavoidable limitations. The sketches, then, may deconstruct our notions of the finished work as *opus perfectum et absolutum*. They remind us that the work 'as it is' is not the work 'as it had to be'.[25] All this is not to devalue the aesthetic worth of Beethoven's final choices, nor to suggest that a performance of the sketches for a work is interchangeable with performances of the work itself. Rather, it is to suggest that there exists a continuum between genesis and structure, one which we may freely ignore or fruitfully investigate. And it is to the investigation, already long-delayed, of the genesis and structure of Op. 109 that we now turn.

[25] Further on this point, see my 'Beethoven's Sketches and the Interpretative Process', *Beethoven Forum*, 1 (1992), 225–42.

2. Beethoven in 1820: The Sources for the Piano Sonata, Op. 109

Writing of the genesis of Op. 109 in his biography of Beethoven, Thayer had this to say:

> The Sonata in E belongs unquestionably to the year 1820. The first theme of the first movement is found in the Conversation Book of April; the work was sketched in part before he began the *Benedictus* [of the *Missa solemnis*], in part while he was at work on this section, the *Credo*, the *Agnus Dei* and the Bagatelles [Op. 119 Nos. 7–11] for Starke. It was dedicated to Maximiliane Brentano, and published in November, 1821, by Schlesinger in Berlin.[1]

It is a confident, straightforward account, and one which is essentially correct. But as we attempt to probe more deeply into the writing of the sonata we shall find that the detailed course of events was considerably more complex than Thayer's account suggests. The main task of this chapter is to date all the surviving sketches for Op. 109 as accurately as possible. To do this it is necessary to take into account the other major autograph sources, namely Beethoven's letters and conversation books.[2]

I

The extant sketches for the first movement of Op. 109 are preserved in two sources: (1) a group of loose desk sketchleaves in the miscellany Grasnick 20b (*Bds*; SV 54); (2) the pocket sketchbook BH 107 (*BNba*; SV 81; SBH 665).[3] Our investigation begins with this pocket book. Like most of Beethoven's sketchbooks—and all those considered in this chapter—BH 107 does not survive in the form in which Beethoven used it. Today it consists of twenty-two leaves (forty-four pages); one leaf is missing after page 36 and page 42, and at least

---

[1] Thayer–Forbes, 762–3.
[2] Locations of letters in Anderson/Kastner–Kapp and of conversation-book entries in *BKh* are given in parentheses throughout the text. All translations from *BKh* are my own; translations from letters are Anderson's except where indicated.
[3] The *Bds* collection is briefly catalogued in Eveline Bartlitz, *Die Beethoven-Sammlung in der Musikabteilung der Deutschen Staatsbibliothek: Verzeichnis* (Berlin, 1970). For a facsimile and transcription of BH 107 see SG 1.

four more leaves must have followed after the present last page.[4] Fortunately, the leaf missing after page 42 has been identified as BSk 27/75 (*BNba*; SV 182; SBH 672). BH 107 is largely devoted to the Credo of the *Missa solemnis*, but pages 39–41 and 43 contain sketches for the first movement of Op. 109. A further sketch for the movement appears on BSk 27/75, the leaf which stood originally between the present pages 42–3. This brief sketch appears on stave 9 of the recto, beneath sketches for the *Missa*.[5] But it is to the contents of the verso of the leaf that we must turn for our first clues to the dating of the Op. 109 sketches. The verso is occupied by a draft for the canon 'Hoffmann, sei ja kein Hofmann', WoO 180, and it was probably the presence of this little composition that caused Beethoven to remove the leaf from BH 107.[6]

The 'Hoffmann/Hofmann' of Beethoven's punning text was probably the writer and critic E. T. A. Hoffmann. A series of verbal and musical entries written by Beethoven in the conversation books (*BKh* i. 318, 339, 390, 392) essentially constitute a series of sketches for the text and music of the canon. All these entries may be reliably dated between 10 and 29 March 1820. The canon is mentioned in a further entry, however, and one which probably allows us to date BSk 27/75 more precisely. The first phrase of the canon as given on BSk 27/75 is shown in Ex. 2.1*a*, while in Ex. 2.1*b* a remark and accompanying musical illustration written in a conversation book (*BKh* i. 382) by Joseph Czerny on 25 or 26 March is transcribed. The situation is easy to reconstruct: Czerny, perhaps with a copy—BSk 27/75?—of the canon in front of him, is referring to the pleasing effect made by the $a\flat^1$ in bar 5. At all events, we may be fairly certain that the version of the canon preserved on BSk 27/75 was in existence by

---

[4] Detailed reconstructions of all the sketchbooks dealt with in this chapter are given by Robert Winter in JTW. I am grateful to Winter for sharing some of his work with me prior to publication. Winter points out (JTW, 365 and 368) that a further four leaves are required to complete the first of the four sheets used to make up the sketchbook; thus there may be as many as six leaves missing at the end of the book.

[5] This Op. 109 sketch appears to have gone unnoticed in the relevant literature.

[6] That Beethoven himself was responsible for the removal of BSk 27/75 from BH 107 seems clear from an observation made by Meredith, 'Sources for Opus 109'. The draft of WoO 180 was written first in pencil and then inked over. The stub remaining from BSk 27/75 in BH 107 contains some pencil notations which continue from BSk 27/75, but no ink ones. Thus the inking-over was evidently done after the leaf was removed from the pocket book; and since Beethoven did the inking-over, he was most likely to have removed the leaf. The version of WoO 180 preserved on BSk 27/75 differs from the final one: Kinsky–Halm, 684, regards it as 'vermutlich erste Niederschrift bzw. Entwurf.' Beethoven sent the final version together with that of 'Schwenke dich, ohne Schwänke', WoO 187, to Schott on 22 Jan. 1825 (see Anderson, 1345), and it may be assumed that the removal of BSk 27/75 from BH 107 and the inking-over of the WoO 180 draft date from around this period. A sheet containing the final versions of WoO 180 and 187 was sold at Sotheby's, London on 6 Dec. 1991 (see lot 3); it is now in an American private collection.

Ex. 2.1. *a* BSk 27/75: first phrase of WoO 180 (sketch version)

b Conversation-book entry (25 or 26 March 1820) by Joseph Czerny

Das *as* nimt sich so gut aus darin

sey kein Hofman

25–6 March 1820.[7] And if we now conceptually reinsert BSk 27/75 at its original location between pages 42–3 of BH 107, we can assume a similar date for the Op. 109 sketches on the surrounding pages.

Another pun provides a second, rather less specific, chronological anchor for the sonata sketches in BH 107. Across the top four staves of page 43, immediately above the last sketches for the first movement of Op. 109, Beethoven scrawled the words 'geh'Baurer' and 'Geh'Bauer' ('go, peasant': see Plate 4). These are puns on the surname of Franz Xaver Gebauer (1784–1822), who in 1816 had become director of music at the Augustinerkirche in Vienna and in 1819 had co-founded the Spirituel-Concerte, which took place fortnightly on Fridays in the Hotel zur Mehlgrube. These concerts consisted of a symphony and a performance-rehearsal of whatever choral work was to be sung at the Augustinerkirche on the following Sunday. Standards were apparently not high; in 1821 Friedrich August Kanne, editor of the Vienna *Allgemeine musikalische Zeitung*, put this down to lack of rehearsals, noting that the original plan had been for everything to be performed at sight.[8]

Now Gebauer visited Beethoven on 16 March 1820 and wrote several entries in a conversation book (*BKh* i. 342–3). He was

---

[7] R. Winter, 'Reconstructing Riddles: The Sources for Beethoven's *Missa Solemnis*', in Lewis Lockwood and Phyllis Benjamin (eds.), *Beethoven Essays: Studies in Honor of Elliot Forbes* (Cambridge, Mass., 1984), 237, argues that the version of WoO 180 on BSk 27/75 must postdate the last relevant conversation-book entry (i. 392, dated 29 Mar.), since it is only there that the words set on the sketchleaf first appear: 'It is not very likely that the composer drafted the music before deciding upon its text.' But neither in this article nor in the list of concordances in JTW, 366 does Winter notice the entry by Czerny shown in Ex. 2.1*b*.

[8] See C. F. Pohl and J. Warrack, 'Gebauer, Franz Xaver', in S. Sadie (ed.), *The New Grove Dictionary of Music and Musicians* (London, 1980), vii. 210–11; for Kanne's remarks see Eduard Hanslick, *Geschichte des Concertwesens in Wien* (Vienna, 1869–70; repr. Farnborough, 1971), i. 186.

attempting to persuade Beethoven to put on a concert of his music in Vienna, and was offering to make all the necessary arrangements himself. In addition, he was apparently tempting Beethoven to compose something for the Spirituel-Concerte series, or at least to allow some of his existing works to be performed. Gebauer's jottings describe the musical facilities at the Augustinerkirche in glowing terms: there is a *Singschule* of thirty-two boys together with a splendid *Singmeister* called Rösner; the Court has had an attractive and large new Choir built for him at a cost of around five thousand florins; and for large works he can count on a body of 120 musicians. Beethoven seems to have taken the bait, for his Fourth and Sixth Symphonies, the Mass in C, and *Meeresstille und glückliche Fahrt* were all subsequently performed in the concert series.

It seems that Gebauer's boasts were not entirely unfounded, for on 10 April Franz Oliva wrote as follows in a conversation book (*BKh* ii. 52): 'it is said that the music at the *Augustinerkirche* has improved greatly since *Gebauer* has been in charge, and that it is now the best church music of all.' The context for this remark is likely to have been a conversation about Gebauer, whose name had been introduced in the book by Oliva just a few lines earlier. 'Because of *Gebauer*', wrote Oliva; and underneath this Beethoven wrote 'Geh'Bauer', precisely the pun that is scrawled twice on page 43 of BH 107.[9] It is risky to assume that the sketchbook and conversation-book entries are exactly contemporaneous; Beethoven could have been musing on this latest bad pun of his at least since Gebauer's visit of 16 March.[10] A date of, say, late March for the puns on page 43 of BH 107 would fit more comfortably with our relatively more reliable dating of 26 March or earlier for the draft of the canon WoO 180 on BSk 27/75, which would have directly preceded page 43 of BH 107 before being torn out. But if we assume that the sketchbook and conversation-book entries are exactly contemporaneous then we

---

[9] The pun also appears in a letter (Anderson 1066/Kastner–Kapp 1005) to the publishers Steiner and Co. Anderson dated the letter '[Vienna, 1821]', but Apr. 1820 is probably the correct date: the '*hole-and-corner musical performance*' for which Beethoven requests 'some of those *lavatory tickets*' is surely the same concert for which Oliva says he would like to obtain tickets in another part of the conversation-book entry (*BKh* ii. 52) being considered here. The *Chor* mentioned by Oliva, and by Beethoven in the letter to Steiner, is presumably *Meeresstille und glückliche Fahrt*, which was performed at two of the Spirituel-Concerte, in Apr. and May: see *BKh* ii. 392–3 (n. 144).

[10] In SG 1. 15, Schmidt-Görg does assume such a direct contemporaneity, something which has gone unchallenged by Winter both in JTW, 366 and in 'Reconstructing Riddles', 236. Neither Schmidt-Görg nor Winter mentions Gebauer's conversation-book entries of mid-Mar. 1820. The four or six leaves which originally followed p. 44 of BH 107 might of course have been used in Apr., and may have contained further sketches for the first movement of Op. 109.

must, not unreasonably, assume a short break in Beethoven's use of BH 107 between the last week of March and the second week of April 1820.

Before considering the dating of the Grasnick 20b leaves containing sketches for the first movement of Op. 109, we should look a little further back in BH 107. The two leaves (BSk 27/75 and BH 107, page 43) examined so far originally stood side by side in the sketchbook, and they both followed the beginning of sketching for Op. 109 on page 39. Can any earlier portion of the book be confidently dated? Proceeding backwards from page 39, the most useful clue is to be found on page 32, which contains the text and music of the *Scherz* 'Sanct Petrus ist ein Fels', Hess 256. The 'Saint Peter' of this musical joke was Hofrat Karl Peters, who was appointed co-guardian with Beethoven of the latter's nephew Karl when the guardianship case was eventually decided in Beethoven's favour on 8 April 1820.[11] The proposal of a co-guardian was a strategic move on Beethoven's part, and he named Peters in a letter to the Appeal Court dated 7 January 1820 (Peters's appointment was necessary, he wrote with magnificent understatement, 'since I am a little hard of hearing'!),[12] but the conversation books show that the plan was already being discussed early in the previous December. Nephew Karl asked on 8 December 1819, 'Have you already taken on Peters as co-guardian?' (*BKh* i. 120). More important, though, are these remarks written by Joseph Czerny between 9 and 15 December: 'Zmeskall and I are glad that you have turned to Peters. He'll certainly give you satisfaction, for he's an intelligent and noble man. . . . You can rely on him, when he takes something on he sees it through. He's reliable and knows the ropes' (*BKh* i. 134–5). What better impetus could there be for Beethoven's composition on a text which begins, 'Saint Peter is a rock, one can build on this'? By about mid-December 1819, then, Beethoven must have filled up to page 32 of BH 107; this is a point to which we shall return.[13]

---

[11] For details of the legal proceedings during this period see Thayer–Forbes, 746–54 and M. Solomon, *Beethoven* (London, 1977), 247–50.

[12] The letter is Anderson, iii, app. C, no. 14.

[13] In SG 1, 15 Schmidt-Görg linked the 'Petrus' *Scherz* (which he incorrectly calls 'ein Kanon') with textually related conversation-book entries (i. 187 and 245) dating from early Jan. and early Feb. 1820 respectively, and preferred to assign it to 'the first days of January 1820 at the latest'. Winter has observed (JTW, 367; 'Reconstructing Riddles', 237) that the conversation-book entries need not be tied chronologically to the *Scherz* in BH 107, but he errs more widely than Schmidt-Görg when he writes ('Reconstructing Riddles', 237) that 'at all events, there is no need to date the pocket draft [of the *Scherz*: BH 107, p. 32] much before April.' Neither Schmidt-Görg nor Winter takes account of Czerny's conversation-book entries of mid-Dec. 1819; these provide the best context for the *Scherz*.

TABLE 2.1. *Original concluding portion of the Wittgenstein sketchbook*

Wittgenstein folio	Present location
44	Wittgenstein, fol. 44
I	Grasnick 20b, fol. 2
J	Grasnick 20b, fol. 3
K	Grasnick 20b, fol. 4
L	Grasnick 20b, fol. 5
M	Grasnick 20b, fol. 6
N	Unidentified
O	Landsberg 10, pp. 95/6
P	Grasnick 20b, fol. 1
Q	Unidentified

II

Now to the desk sketches for the first movement of Op. 109. These occur on folios 3^r–5^v and 6^v of Grasnick 20b. Folios 1–6 of Grasnick 20b form a discrete group within that miscellany and are loosely stitched together with thread. Moreover, all six leaves stem from the same source, for they originally belonged at the end of the Wittgenstein sketchbook (*BNba*, BSk 1/49; SV 154; SBH 663), together with three other leaves, only one of which has so far been identified. These nine leaves followed folio 44, the present last folio of Wittgenstein, in the order shown in Table 2.1.[14]

The most useful clues to the dating of these leaves are provided by Grasnick 20b, folio 2 (leaf I) and Landsberg 10, pages 95/6 (leaf O). But these clues are useful only if we can be sure that Beethoven used the nine leaves while they were still part of the Wittgenstein sketchbook, or at least that he used them in the order in which they originally occurred there. For it is not clear when and by whom the leaves were removed; if Beethoven himself tore them from the book and used them singly, it would be unsafe to use one leaf to infer the dating of another. That Grasnick 20b, folio 3 could reliably be dated 23 February 1820, for example, would not necessarily imply that folio 4 was used immediately or some time thereafter: Beethoven could have used the leaves in any order. Inferences about chronology will carry more weight if we can be reasonably satisfied that Beethoven used these leaves while they were still part of Wittgenstein, for there is a good deal of evidence that he generally filled the pages of a sketchbook in the obvious sequence, one after another.

[14] For Winter's reconstruction of Wittgenstein see JTW, 253–9; SG[W] provides a facsimile and transcription of the surviving torso of the book. The miscellany Landsberg 10 is located in *B*.

There is good reason to believe that at least the six Grasnick 20b leaves were used before being removed from Wittgenstein. It is significant that with the exception of folio 1 they are still in the order in which they stood within the book. And the anomalous position of folio 1 can be easily explained. When tying together a bundle of papers, the knot of the thread will fall naturally on the outside of the bundle. Now the thread holding Grasnick 20b, folios 1–6 together is knotted between folios 1 and 2. To achieve a more natural position for the knot we would need only to turn folio 1 from the front to the back of the bundle: the knot would now lie outside, and the six leaves would stand in the order 2, 3, 4, 5, 6, 1—precisely their original order within Wittgenstein. This was obviously their original ordering when removed from the book and tied together; folio 1 must have been shifted from last to first position on some later occasion.[15]

There is also clear evidence that Beethoven used Grasnick 20b, folios 3–6 in the order in which they stood within Wittgenstein. In the case of folios 3 and 4 this is confirmed by sketch content: the sketches on folio 4 clearly derive from those on folio 3. As for folios 4–5 and 5–6, inkblot offsets between these two pairs of leaves furnish good evidence that Beethoven used them in their present order.[16] And such offsets would be more likely to occur between the leaves of a fairly thick sketchbook than between those of a small bundle tied loosely or not at all.

One further piece of evidence may be considered. The two very similar scale passages transcribed in Ex. 2.2*a–b* occur on stave 1 of Grasnick 20b, folios 5^v and 6^v respectively. The context of the first passage is quite straightforward: it is the continuation of a continuity draft for the first movement of Op. 109 which begins on folio 5^r and runs to stave 13 there before continuing on folio 5^v as in the example. The second passage, however, forms just as good a continuation from folio 5^r as does the first. Yet this is the only notation for Op. 109 on the whole of folio 6, and it is separated from all the preceding Op. 109 sketches by a draft of a piano piece in C minor which begins on stave 10 of folio 5^v and fills the whole of folio 6^r. The obvious explanation for this anomaly is that Beethoven, so to

---

[15] Perhaps the other three leaves missing from the end of Wittgenstein were originally bound in the bundle which now comprises only Grasnick 20b, fols. 1–6. After the removal of leaf Q (see Table 2.1), Grasnick 20b, fol. 1 would have been the last leaf in the bundle; it may have been shifted from this to its present position on top of fol. 2 to facilitate the subsequent removal of Landsberg 10, pp. 95/6, which would thereby have become the last leaf in the bundle.

[16] However, see JTW, 255 for a discussion of Paris, Ms. 77 and its curious relationship to this section of Wittgenstein.

Ex. 2.2. *a* Grasnick 20b, fol. 5ᵛ, st. 1

b Grasnick 20b, fol. 6ᵛ, st. 1

speak, turned over a new leaf: having come to the end of stave 13 on folio 5ʳ, he turned the page intending to continue his continuity draft on folio 5ᵛ. But he had mistakenly turned two leaves instead of one, and found himself writing at the top of folio 6ᵛ. Realizing his error, he abandoned the notation, turned back to folio 5ᵛ, and continued the draft as he had intended. Now a mistake such as this would be far more likely to occur when turning pages bound into a book—particularly when, as in this case, those pages occur near the end of a thick book—than when working with a small group of single leaves.

Conflating these three pieces of evidence, we may be quite confident that Beethoven used Grasnick 20b, folios 1–6 while they were still part of the Wittgenstein sketchbook. And it is not unreasonable to assume that the same is true of the other three leaves—leaf N, Landsberg 10, pages 95/6, and leaf Q in Table 2.1—which originally belonged with the six Grasnick ones. The following chronological deductions are based on this premiss; there is good reason to believe that Beethoven himself removed the leaves from Wittgenstein, but we shall assume that he did so only after using them.

III

That we can propose plausible dates for the use of Grasnick 20b, folio 2 and Landsberg 10, pages 95/6 is especially fortunate because these two leaves frame those containing the desk sketches for the first movement of Op. 109 (see Table 2.1). Grasnick 20b, folio 2 may be assigned to a period no later than mid-March 1820. The recto contains sketches for 'Abendlied unterm gestirnten Himmel', WoO 150, the autograph of which is dated 4 March 1820.[17] The sketches are not very similar to the final version of the song, so they may have been made some considerable time before this date; at any

---

[17] Kinsky–Halm, 621. The autograph is located in *Wn*.

rate, 4 March 1820 represents the latest date by which they could have been written.

The verso of Grasnick 20b, folio 2 contains sketches for a number of different works. At the bottom there are pencil sketches for the Credo of the *Missa solemnis* (sketches for this movement also occupy the top four staves of the recto), and further up there are ideas for the Ninth Symphony and for an unfinished keyboard piece. On staves 11–12 there appear the words 'Totde[n]Marsch Instrumente' and 'zule[t]zt Singstimen', followed by the opening bars of the Dead March from Handel's oratorio *Saul*. Counterpointed against the Handel quotation is a vocal bass line setting the words 'Herr Gott unser trefflicher Fürst'. A safe context for these sketches is established by fragments from newspaper reports describing the funeral of King George III of England which Beethoven copied into a conversation book around 11 March 1820 (*BKh* i. 322). Beethoven noted that the Dead March from *Saul* was played at the royal funeral, along with the cantata (*The Ways of Zion do Mourn*, 1737) which Handel composed for the funeral of Queen Caroline. Mention in the press of these solemn works by Beethoven's revered Handel seems to have prompted plans for a similar new work of his own, for he continued to write in the conversation book: 'for the *concert* [,] *variations* for full orchestra on Handel's Dead March, perhaps with voices joining in later'. Nothing is known of this projected work apart from the brief sketches on folio 2^v of Grasnick 20b. These sketches were doubtless written fairly shortly after the conversation-book entries, in the period following 11 March 1820.

Landsberg 10, pages 95/6 is taken up mainly with sketches for the Credo of the *Missa solemnis* and the song 'Gedenke mein', WoO 130. (The WoO 130 sketches begin on the lower half of page 96 and continue on Grasnick 20b, folio 1^r.[18]) What is most important for the purpose of dating is not a musical sketch but a verbal reminder penned along the top margin of page 95: 'NB: a mass or Te Deum Laudamus in the Augustiner[kirche] with these two choirs in the middle above.'[19] A context for this remark springs easily to mind. Gebauer's visit to Beethoven on 16 March 1820 and his glowing account of the musical facilities at the Augustinerkirche evidently impressed Beethoven sufficiently for him to toy with the idea of a large sacred work for Gebauer. Indeed, the plan for choral and

---

[18] The sketches for WoO 130 on Landsberg 10, p. 96 are mentioned neither in JTW, 259, nor in the inventory of Landsberg 10 given in Hans-Günter Klein, *Ludwig van Beethoven: Autographe und Abschriften: Katalog* (Berlin, 1975), 137.

[19] 'Nb: in den augustinen mit diesen 2 chören mit[t]en oben eine Messe oder tedeum laudamus.'

orchestral variations on the Dead March from *Saul* discussed above may also have been conceived with Gebauer and the Augustinerkirche in mind. Like the Handelian tribute, the projected mass or Te Deum came to nothing; but it may still have been on Beethoven's mind at the end of the month when Johann Schickh, editor of the *Wiener Zeitschrift für Kunst, Literatur, Theater und Mode,* asked in a conversation-book entry of 29 March (*BKh* i. 395): 'were you writing the mass for him? When will you write the Requiem then? Does the mass include a Te Deum?'[20]

IV

Table 2.2 provides a summary of the conclusions reached so far in this attempt to date the sketches for the first movement of Op. 109. The relevant portions of the Wittgenstein and BH 107 sketchbooks are shown in their reconstructed form, and the dates deduced above are entered at the appropriate points.[21] All dates refer to the year 1820.

The widest time frame is that for the puns on page 43 of BH 107. The most plausible date for these, assuming that the dating of BSk 27/75 is correct, is probably sometime in late March; there is no need to assume that the puns are contemporary with those in the conversation-book entry of 10 April. If this reasoning is correct, it seems that the surviving sketches for the first movement of Op. 109 belong to March 1820. It is of course possible that further sketches were written on the leaves still missing from both sketchbooks, so that sketching in BH 107, for instance, might well have extended into April. But the analysis of the sketches in Chapter 3 will show that there is no need to assume large numbers of missing sketches; by the time the sketches on page 43 of BH 107 were made, the movement must have been more or less in the form in which we know it. (Chapter 3 also confirms the fact, suggested in Table 2.2, that the sketches in Wittgenstein were made before those in BH 107.)

Further confirmation that the first movement of Op. 109 was essentially complete by late March, or at the latest by early April, is provided by another conversation-book entry (ii. 56). 'The first theme

---

[20] The eds. of *BKh* i assume that 'him' in Schickh's first question refers to Archduke Rudolph (see the reference to n. 64 [p. 419]), and thus imply that the 'mass' is the *Missa solemnis*. But Schickh may equally have been referring to Gebauer, and to the projected mass/Te Deum mentioned on Landsberg 10, p. 95.

[21] The reconstructed portion of BH 107 does not include leaves I and J from Winter's reconstruction (JTW, 368), for it is not certain that these were ever part of the sketchbook.

The Sources for Op. 109   25

TABLE 2.2. *Proposed dating of sketches for Op. 109, first movement*

Folio/page no.	Date	Remarks
Wittgenstein sketchbook		
Fol. 44		
Grasnick 20b, fol. 2	recto: before 4 March	sketches for 'Abendlied', WoO 150
	verso: after 11 March	variations on Dead March from *Saul*
Grasnick 20b, fol. 3		sketches for Op. 109
Grasnick 20b, fol. 4		sketches for Op. 109
Grasnick 20b, fol. 5		sketches for Op. 109
Grasnick 20b, fol. 6		sketches for Op. 109
Leaf N (unidentified)		
Landsberg 10, pp. 95/6	p. 95: around 16 March	projected mass/Te Deum for Augustinerkirche
Grasnick 20b, fol. 1		[piano sonata in E: see Ex. 2.5]
Leaf Q (unidentified)		
BH 107		
39/40		sketches for Op. 109
41/42		sketches for Op. 109 (p. 41)
BSk 27/75		sketch for Op. 109 (recto)
	verso: by 26 March	draft of WoO 180
43/44	16 March–10 April	puns on 'Gebauer'; sketches for Op. 109 (p. 43)
Leaf E (unidentified)		
Leaf F (unidentified)		
Leaf G (unidentified)		
Leaf H (unidentified)		

Ex. 2.3. Conversation-book entry (11–13 April 1820) for Op. 109, first movement

of the first movement is found in the Conversation Book of April', runs Thayer's account, quoted above. The entry in question (Ex. 2.3) must have been written between 11 and 13 April 1820. It is strikingly detailed, and corresponds almost exactly to the published version not only in terms of pitch but also of voicing and slurring. Such precision is uncommon in Beethoven's sketches but is easily explicable in this case. The conversation-book entry of 11–13 April is not so much a sketch as an incipit for a movement that would have been essentially complete by this time.[22]

V

At this point we should return to the pocket sketchbook BH 107 to reconsider the earlier conclusion that the 'Sanct Petrus' *Scherz* on page 32 should be dated around mid-December 1819. The grounds for this date are perfectly reasonable if taken in isolation; but if we consider the dating of page 32 in relation to that of pages 39–43, mid-December for the earlier page seems less satisfactory: can Beethoven really have filled as few as ten pocket leaves (BH 107, pages 32–42) between mid-December and late March 1819–20? In fact there are good grounds for assuming that Beethoven did very little composition in this period, and the gap suggested by dating the BH 107 leaves is supported by similar evidence from the Wittgenstein book. The route to this evidence lies within the conversation books.

In addition to their main function of facilitating communication between Beethoven and his friends and visitors, the conversation books served occasionally as a repository for Beethoven's musical ideas. The books for the period 1819–20 contain a number of jottings for the *Missa solemnis*, and it is tempting to try to correlate these with entries in the contemporary sketchbooks. Two major problems hinder such attempts. First, a degree of similarity between an entry in a conversation book and one in a sketchbook in no way guarantees that the two are contemporaneous. Secondly, even if the degree of similarity is so great as to render irresistible the idea that one entry is a direct and contemporaneous copy of the other, it will not necessarily be possible to determine which way round the copying proceeded: from conversation book to sketchbook, or vice versa? Conversation-book entries, unlike those in sketchbooks, can often be dated with considerable precision; but if Beethoven chose to copy from sketchbook to conversation book, the copying may have taken place long after the original entry in the sketchbook.[23]

---

[22] In SG 1. 15, Schmidt-Görg assumed that the conversation-book entry was a straightforward 'work in progress' sketch whose dating could automatically be transferred to the sketches in BH 107. In fact there is no basis on which to link the conversation-book and sketchbook entries beyond the fact that they are all for the same movement. The problems involved in correlating entries in these two source-types are further discussed below.

[23] Such considerations were largely ignored in SG 1, and Schmidt-Görg's conclusions were too readily adopted by Winter in JTW, 366–7 and 'Reconstructing Riddles', 235–8. Winter suggests that 'we cannot be far off in assigning the first 30 pages of [BH 107] to the period between 1819 and March 1820, with a possible break of several weeks before Beethoven then took up the Sonata Opus 109 around the beginning of April' (JTW, 367). In his reconstruction of Wittgenstein he notes the chronological implications of the sketches for WoO 150 on Grasnick 20b, fol. 2, but again postulates a break in sketching during Mar. My own conclusions below suggest that it was in precisely this month that Beethoven resumed composition in earnest.

With these problems in mind, consider Ex. 2.4a, which shows two ideas for the Credo of the *Missa solemnis* notated in a conversation book sometime between 15 and 25 December 1819 (i. 161). It happens that both ideas match sketches in the Wittgenstein sketchbook (Ex. 2.4b); in the case of the 'et vitam venturi' idea, the similarity is so close as to suggest that one is a direct copy of the other. Since the sketches occur on different pages in Wittgenstein ('et vitam venturi' is on folio 43^v, 'et sepultus est' on folio 34^v), and since both appear to be parts of larger musical units rather than self-contained entries, the most logical assumption is that in this case Beethoven copied from the sketchbook into the conversation book. The alternative—that he would have troubled to copy two ideas from a single page in a conversation book to two quite separate and apparently specially prepared locations in the sketchbook—seems highly unpersuasive.

If the copying did proceed this way round, Beethoven had evidently reached folio 43^v of Wittgenstein by the third or fourth week of December 1819 at the latest. But such a conclusion raises a problem similar to that encountered with BH 107 earlier. Setting the proposed dating of Wittgenstein, folio 43 against our earlier dating for the end of the sketchbook, the following sequence arises:

Folio 43^v: mid- to late December 1819
Folio 44:
Grasnick 20b, folio 2:   early to mid-March 1820

As with BH 107, it seems that Beethoven did very little sketching in Wittgenstein between late December 1819 and mid-March 1820. And in fact we have it on his own authority that composition was very much a low priority in the first two months of 1820. In a letter to the publisher Simrock dated 10 February 1820, Beethoven alluded to financial difficulties and admitted that, 'as has so frequently happened, I have allowed my arable field to lie fallow' (Anderson 1005/ Kastner–Kapp 953). Not that he had no good reason to neglect composition at this period, however, for it was precisely in early 1820 that the legal proceedings in the guardianship wrangle were approaching their climax. The pages of the conversation books for January and February are filled with discussions of the case; indeed, the books occasionally became 'sketchbooks' for the forty-eight-page draft memorandum to the Court of Appeal, dated 18 February 1820, with which Beethoven tried to bolster his case.[24]

---

[24] The memorandum is transcribed complete in Anderson, iii, app. C, no. 15; a facsimile and transcription was published as *Beethoven: Entwurf einer Denkschrift an das Appellationsgericht in Wien von 18 Februar 1820*, ed. Dagmar Weise (Bonn, 1953). For exx. of 'sketches' in the conversation books see *BKh* i. 191–3, and 218–20. The extraordinary effort that Beethoven must have expended on this, the longest extant non-musical document in his hand, spilled

Ex. 2.4. *a* Conversation-book entries (15–25 December 1819) for the Credo of the *Missa solemnis*

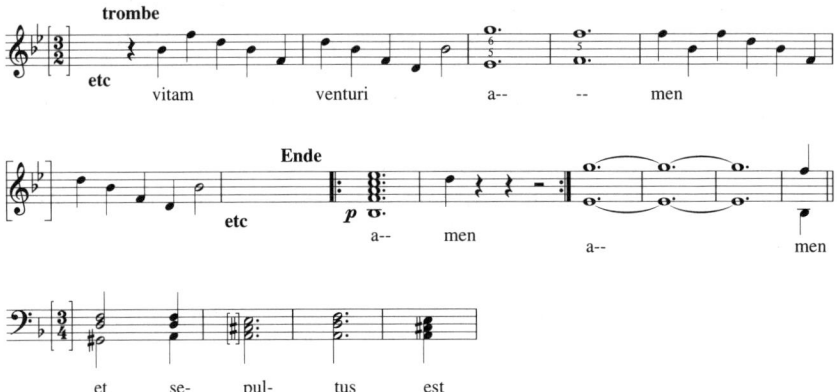

b Wittgenstein, fols. 34^v, 43^v

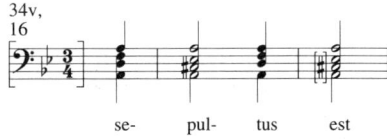

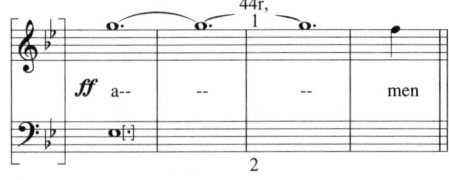

The Sources for Op. 109   29

Small wonder, then, that Beethoven found little time for musical sketching in the first two months of 1820. Perhaps the completion of the draft memorandum marked a turning point, for our dating suggests that in late February and during March he produced the 'Abendlied', WoO 150 and the first movement of Op. 109. In this connection, it may not be coincidental that the song shares the key of E major with the sonata movement; but further exploration of possible relationships between these two contemporaneous works must be reserved until Chapter 10.

VI

Thus far in this 'biography' of the first movement of Op. 109, emphasis has been almost wholly on the sketches. On the basis of the available evidence, there would seem to have been no external motivation for the composition; even if completion of the draft memorandum in February 1820 acted on Beethoven's creative faculties as a kind of catalyst, rather than simply being an obstacle whose removal allowed him once again to plough his 'arable field' without impediment, we would still be dealing with a case of internal, psychological motivation. The point is worth stressing, for if, conversely, we ignored the sketches—essentially private documents—and relied solely upon Beethoven's public statements in letters, we might be tempted to assume that the seeds of a new piano sonata were sown by the Berlin publisher Adolf Martin Schlesinger.

The first allusion in Beethoven's letters to the work which became Op. 109 comes in a letter to Schlesinger dated 30 April 1820 (Anderson 1021/Kastner–Kapp 971).[25] Towards the end of this lengthy letter Beethoven wrote: 'furthermore, I will gladly let you have new sonatas—but not at a lower price than forty ducats each. Hence a work consisting of three sonatas would cost 120 ducats.' It was an offer which eventually produced not just Op. 109 but also Opp. 110 and 111, the sonatas in A♭ major and C. Beethoven's letter was in reply to one from Schlesinger dated 11 April; the tone of his remarks suggests that Schlesinger may have asked him for new sonatas, but since Schlesinger's letter is now lost this fact cannot be verified. In any case, it is clear that even as Schlesinger put quill to paper, Beethoven was probably putting the final touches to the first

---

over even into the pages of the sketchbooks proper: see W. Meredith, 'The Origins of Beethoven's Op. 109', *Musical Times*, 126 (1985), 714.

[25] The autograph of this letter, which was not available to Anderson, was sold at Sotheby's, London, on 27 Nov. 1987, lot 234 (see also lot 235), and again at Christie's, London, on 29 June 1994, lot 102.

movement of Op. 109: the incipit transcribed in Ex. 2.3 could have been written as early as 11 April, the very day on which Schlesinger wrote to Beethoven.[26]

Once again, however, this is not the end of the matter; a much more interesting picture emerges once we penetrate a little further into the Beethoven–Schlesinger correspondence. Beethoven's letter of 30 April begins: 'I have very little time at my disposal—so I have the honour to inform you that when your letter of 11 April arrived, the Scottish themes with variations had already been given away.' The reference here is to the themes with variations which, together with the Scottish songs, Beethoven had been offering not only to Schlesinger but also to Simrock in Bonn. Simrock eventually took only the themes with variations, which he published (together with two other sets which Beethoven supplied later) as Op. 107 in 1820; Schlesinger took the songs and published them as Op. 108 in 1822.[27]

Provided that Beethoven was telling Schlesinger the truth—and in this instance there seems no good reason to assume otherwise—we must conclude that Schlesinger's letter of 11 April reached Beethoven some time after 22 April. For it was on 22 April that Beethoven dispatched the themes and variations, not directly to Simrock in Bonn but via Franz Brentano in Frankfurt. This is made clear in a letter to Simrock written on the following day, 23 April: 'I sent off the variations to Herr Brentano at Frankfurt on 22 April and am now waiting to receive from him the fee of 70 ducats for this work' (Anderson 1019/Kastner–Kapp 969).

This activity of 22 and 23 April was spurred on by Oliva, who urged Beethoven in a conversation book: 'you mustn't delay writing to *Simro[c]k* and *Brentano;—Brentano* can send you the money right away.' Just a few lines earlier Oliva had made a much more interesting suggestion: 'and maybe you could use the little new piece in a sonata for *Schlesinger*' (*BKh* ii. 87). The implications of this remark are startling. Oliva's entries must have been made before Beethoven wrote to Simrock on 22 April, and therefore presumably before Schlesinger's letter of 11 April had arrived. Given the chronology established above, the 'little new piece' to which Oliva referred can hardly have been anything other than the first movement of Op.

---

[26] The temptation to assume that Schlesinger requested sonatas in his letter can be hard to resist: e.g. in JTW, 258, Winter mentions the letter from Schlesinger 'written on 11 April and requesting sonatas'. Winter then refers in a footnote to A. Tyson, 'New Beethoven Letters and Documents', *BS* 2. 22–5. But Tyson is more cautious, observing only that 'Schlesinger *seems* also to have asked Beethoven for piano sonatas' (ibid. 24; italics mine).

[27] Beethoven's correspondence with Simrock and Schlesinger prior to the letter of 30 Apr. may be followed in Anderson 1005, 1011–13, 1015, and 1019 (Kastner-Kapp 953, 958–60, 963, and 969).

109—or, more precisely, the composition destined to become that movement: for Oliva's words strongly suggest that the work sketched at the end of Wittgenstein and BH 107 was originally intended not as part of one of Beethoven's last three piano sonatas but as an independent composition. No matter what Schlesinger suggested to Beethoven: the idea of at least one new piano sonata had already come from Oliva.

VII

Even without the evidence of Oliva's remark, we might be tempted to speculate that the first movement of Op. 109 was conceived independently of the other two. When sketching multimovement works it was Beethoven's habit to move more or less directly from one movement to the next; the first ideas for a new movement often overlap with the final sketches for the one in hand. But in the case of Op. 109 there is a conspicuous gap, filled mainly by sketching for the Credo of the *Missa solemnis*, between the first-movement sketches at the end of the Wittgenstein sketchbook and those for the second and third movements, which begin on page 35 of Artaria 195, the desk sketchbook which Beethoven used after filling Wittgenstein. It seems most likely that sketching for Op. 109 in Artaria 195 did not begin before mid-June 1820; the evidence for this dating will be examined more closely below, but first we must consider what may have been Beethoven's initial response to Oliva's suggestion that he use the 'little new piece' in a sonata for Schlesinger.

The transcriptions in Ex. 2.5 are taken from a series of sketches written on staves 4–14 of Grasnick 20b, folio 1^v. All are in E minor except for Ex. 2.5b, which is in C major. This fact and the designation '2tes Stück' accompanying Ex. 2.5e indicate that the sketches represent an overview of a projected multimovement work. Ex. 2.5a and b map out a Scherzo and Trio (only the first segment of the Scherzo is transcribed in Ex. 2.5a: in the manuscript the opening two bars return at the end of the sketch to outline the overall ABA structure). Since the position of the slow movement is specifically identified as second in the cycle, the Scherzo and Trio must have been placed third. Ex. 2.5c suggests a finale, perhaps in rondo form: the opening shown in Ex. 2.5c is followed by a new eight-bar phrase beginning in A minor and ending in C major. Following the cadence in C the sketch breaks off with the remark '3ter the[i]l in E dur durchaus', suggesting a tonic-major return of the opening

Ex. 2.5. Grasnick 20b, fol. 1ᵛ: sketches for a projected sonata in E

material.[28] Ex. 2.5*d* is clearly related to Ex. 2.5*c*; its function is more ambiguous but it probably represents the unmarked '= de' continuation from the 'Vi =' in Ex. 2.5*c*.

These sketches must have been intended for a piano sonata in E. The use of a single tonality for all movements links this projected work with Op. 109 and with Beethoven's earlier multi-movement instrumental works in E: the Piano Sonatas, Op. 14 No. 1 and Op. 90, and the second 'Razumovsky' Quartet, Op. 59 No. 2. Beyond this tonal relationship, however, links between Op. 109 and the projected sonata in E are few. The tonic–submediant relationship between Scherzo and Trio, and the recurrence of C major in the finale, are of some interest in view of the emphasis placed on the submediant in the sketches and final version of the second movement of Op. 109 (see Chapters 5 and 6). The descending chromatic bass line at the beginning of the projected slow movement might suggest the openings of the first two movements of Op. 109 (it more readily recalls the second movement of Mozart's Violin Sonata in E minor, K. 304); but such associations are hardly compelling.

More pressing is the question of how this projected sonata in E fits into events following the composition of the 'little new piece' that became the first movement of Op. 109. If, as seems most likely, Beethoven did originally conceive and write that movement as an independent composition, there may be no connection to be made with the music of Ex. 2.5. In this case, we would have to assume that despite the close physical proximity in Wittgenstein of the sonata sketches on Grasnick 20b, folio 1 and the leaves with sketches for the first movement of Op. 109 (see Table 2.2) the two projects were entirely independent of one another. On the other hand, if Grasnick 20b, folio 1 was not used until after Oliva's suggestion that Beethoven use the 'little new piece' in a sonata for Schlesinger, then the three movements outlined in Ex. 2.5 could well represent Beethoven's initial response to this idea. Whatever the relationship between these two bodies of sketches, though, it is clear that the

---

[28] Beethoven customarily used the terms 'erster Theil' and 'zweiter Theil' to indicate the exposition and development-plus-recapitulation segments of sonata form. In 'Beethoven's Understanding of "Sonata Form": The Evidence of the Sketchbooks', in Kinderman (ed.), *Beethoven's Compositional Process*, 16, William Drabkin discusses 'a late remark on the plan of the first movement of the Ninth Symphony [which] even refers to a "dritter Theil in D" (Artaria 201, p. 121), which, in the context of a movement in sonata form, can mean only the tonality at the beginning of a lengthy coda'. On the contrary, the 'third part' in this case is surely the recapitulation, opening in D major rather than the D minor of the exposition. A similar minor–major shift is clearly intended in Ex. 2.5*c*, but the overall structure of the sketch seems to preclude sonata form here.

projected sonata did not hold Beethoven's attention for long. The material of Ex. 2.5 was not developed further.[29]

VIII

In his letter to Schlesinger of 30 April 1820 Beethoven had offered to write three sonatas at forty ducats each: 'hence a work consisting of three sonatas would cost 120 ducats' (Anderson 1021/Kastner–Kapp 971). It seems that Schlesinger replied to Beethoven's letter some time during May, offering a reduced price of thirty ducats per sonata and sixty ducats for the Scottish songs, which were still available for purchase. Beethoven accepted Schlesinger's offer somewhat grudgingly in a letter of 31 May and undertook to deliver the sonatas within three months.[30] Not surprisingly, this schedule proved hopelessly unrealistic; it was to be three years rather than three months before Schlesinger finally published the last sonata, Op. 111, in 1823.

In a further letter to Schlesinger dated 28 June, Beethoven expressed his irritation that the publisher had not yet replied to the terms set out in his letter of 31 May. In the mean time, he writes, he has had the Scottish songs copied; he is under considerable pressure to sell the songs and the sonatas elsewhere, so he requests a prompt reply from Schlesinger. 'If you agree with my suggestions, . . . I shall send you the songs straight away together with one sonata which is also ready.'[31] There can be little doubt that, as far as the sonata was concerned, Beethoven was exaggerating wildly as he was wont to do when giving progress reports to publishers. The dating of the sketches for the second and third movements of Op. 109 shows that Beethoven had probably just begun work on them when he wrote to Schlesinger at the end of June.

All the known sketches for the second movement of Op. 109 and almost all those for the third survive in the sketchbook Artaria 195

---

[29] S. Brandenburg, 'Die Skizzen zur Neunten Symphonie', in H. Goldschmidt (ed.), *Zu Beethoven 2: Aufsätze und Dokumente* (Berlin, 1984), 104–5 and n. 35, deals with some of the chronological issues raised by the Grasnick 20b leaves removed from the end of Wittgenstein. Brandenburg notes the sonata sketches on fol. 1^v but claims, without further explanation, that they represent only the first two movements of the projected work.

[30] The letter of 31 May is Anderson 1024/Kastner–Kapp 977, for which only a partial and faulty French synopsis is available in the published editions. The autograph was auctioned in Paris in 1977 (Pierre Berès, Paris, 20 June 1977, lot 7), and is reportedly in a French private collection: see Marianne Helms and Martin Staehelin, 'Bewegungen von Beethoven-Quellen 1973–1979', *Beethoven-Jahrbuch*, 10 (1983), 350. I owe to Alan Tyson and Albi Rosenthal the information that the 'prix de 90 florins' mentioned in the French synopsis and published in Kastner–Kapp, Anderson, and the Berès auction catalogue reads '90 ducats' in the autograph.

[31] This letter was first published in Tyson, 'New Beethoven Letters and Documents', 22–3; a commentary, including a summary of the correspondence with Schlesinger up to this point, appears on pp. 24–5.

TABLE 2.3. *Contents of Artaria 195*

Work	Pages
Missa solemnis, Credo	1–35
Op. 109, second movement	35, 37–50, 55
Op. 109, third-movement theme	36, 37, 53
Op. 109, third-movement variations	50–73, 75, 78
Bagatelles, Op. 119 Nos. 7–11	76–80
Missa solemnis, Benedictus	80–100

(*B*; SV 11: see Plates 5–7). There are no leaves missing within the sections of the book given over to Op. 109, but further sketches for the sonata may have been written on four leaves missing between pages 80–1.[32] As the table of contents in Table 2.3 shows, a sustained period of work on the Credo of the *Missa solemnis* intervened between the composition of the first movement of the sonata in Wittgenstein and BH 107 and the beginning of work on the second movement halfway down page 35 in Artaria 195. The Credo had in fact been Beethoven's main preoccupation in Wittgenstein and BH 107 prior to the apparent break in sketching in January and February 1820; and Credo sketches re-emerge towards the end of those two books after the sketches for the first movement of Op. 109.

It is not possible to establish a precise date for the beginning of sketching for Op. 109 in Artaria 195, but a few strands of evidence give some help. Most important is the pocket sketchbook BH 108 (*BNba*; SV 82; SBH 666). This book was used after BH 107 had been filled and was probably begun in April, before Beethoven left Vienna for a short stay in Mödling.[33] At the very end of BH 108 Beethoven copied out two advertisements which had appeared in the *Wiener Intelligenzblatt* on various days early in June 1820;[34] both appeared together on 16 June, and since Beethoven's copyings were apparently superimposed on pre-existing sketches, mid-June evidently marks the date by which BH 108 had been filled. On page 58, just

---

[32] In all, ten leaves have been removed from Artaria 195: see JTW, 260–4. In his account of the contents of the book (JTW, 263) Winter erroneously attributes sketches on pp. 51–2 and 79 to the second movement of Op. 109. And in his discussion of BH 109 he suggests that 'a pocket sketchbook for the last two movements of Opus 109, used during the summer months [of 1820], has presumably been lost' (JTW, 374).

[33] The argument for this point is presented in SG 2 (though Schmidt-Görg's understanding of the original physical structure of the sketchbook was flawed) and its conclusion is essentially accepted by Winter, JTW, 369–72. While I accept the dating, I find unconvincing Winter's claim (JTW, 262; also 371) that 'the last half of [BH 108] corresponds roughly to the first 35 pages of Artaria 195' and have therefore tried to find alternative criteria by which to date the beginning of work on Op. 109 in Artaria 195.

[34] SG 2. 10; Winter, JTW, 371, gives the *Wiener Zeitung* as the source of the advertisements.

Ex. 2.6. BH 108, p. 58: sketches for a 'sonata in E minor'

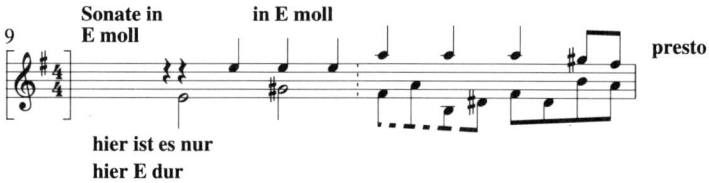

a few pages before the advertisement copyings, Beethoven made some short jottings for a 'Sonate in E moll' (Ex. 2.6). These two brief sketches use essentially the same material although one is actually in E major rather than minor, the modal change being underlined by Beethoven's remark 'hier E dur'. The major–minor contrast recalls the finale of the projected sonata on Grasnick 20b, folio 1^v (see Ex. 2.5c) but no further relationship to that earlier project seems plausible. Nor do the sketches in Ex. 2.6 appear to have anything to do with the second or third movement of Op. 109.

These sketches must have been written some little time before 16 June 1820, the approximate date for the completion of BH 108. Dated so, they correspond neatly with further pressing advice from Oliva, written in a conversation book on or just after 9 June: 'then you must have the *copying* done; then the little *sonata*' (*BKh* ii. 142). The 'copying' must be that of the Scottish songs, which Beethoven reported to be complete in his letter to Schlesinger of 28 June. The reference to a 'little sonata' is intriguing in view of Oliva's use, back in April, of the term 'little new piece' for what became the first movement of Op. 109. It is impossible to know whether Oliva was referring to a sonata which was already under way or whether he was urging Beethoven to get down to serious work on a piece of which the composer had merely given him some idea. But if Beethoven had already started work on the second movement of Op. 109 in Artaria 195 by this time, it seems odd that there are no corresponding pocket sketches in BH 108. On the whole, it seems likely that the attempted 'Sonate in E moll' on page 58 of BH 108 represents a first attempt to respond to Oliva's urgent advice and that the work on Op. 109 in Artaria 195 began somewhat later, certainly not before mid-June. Thus it is quite obvious that Op. 109 could not have been finished by 28 June, as Schlesinger would have read in Beethoven's letter of that date. Perhaps it was Beethoven's realization that, as so often, he was now very short of time in which to fulfil his commitment to Schlesinger which led him finally to abandon the idea of writing a wholly new sonata in E; if he had not already done so, he now acted upon Oliva's earlier advice and incorporated the 'little new piece' into a sonata for Schlesinger.

IX

When, indeed, was Op. 109 finished? It is difficult to be certain. The autograph is undated and therefore of no help in this respect.[35] Schindler's claim that all three sonatas for Schlesinger were written down upon Beethoven's return from Mödling to Vienna in autumn 1820 can safely be dismissed, although there may be more truth in another claim, that Beethoven, basking in the joy of having won the guardianship case, 'wrote little or no music that summer, though perhaps this only appeared to be so because the sketchbooks revealed nothing but empty pages from now on'.[36] Sketching for the second and third movements of Op. 109 must have been done during the summer months; but Beethoven may have worked in a relatively leisurely or sporadic way, so giving rise to Schindler's assertion. Certainly, another faintly chiding remark from Oliva's pen in a conversation book during the first week of August suggests that the sonata was still far from ready, and that Beethoven ought perhaps to be a little more industrious: 'you must think about the *sonata* for *Berlin*' (*BKh* ii. 195).

Two further letters to Schlesinger hold out more promise. On 20 September 1820 Beethoven explained various problems which had so far prevented him from sending the copies of the Scottish songs, and added that 'everything will go more quickly in the case of the three sonatas—The first is quite ready apart from corrections' (Anderson 1033);[37] and on 7 March 1821 he sent Schlesinger the title and dedication for 'the sonata which you must have received a long

---

[35] The autograph is located in *Wc*. A facsimile edn., with introd. by Oswald Jonas, was published by the Robert Owen Lehman Foundation as *Ludwig van Beethoven: Piano Sonata Opus 109* (New York, 1965).

[36] Anton Schindler, *Biographie von Ludwig van Beethoven*, 3rd edn. (Münster, 1860), ii. 3, and i. 272.

[37] The German text of this letter was first published in Dagmar Weise, 'Ungedruckte oder nur teilweise veröffentlichte Briefe Beethovens aus der Sammlung H. C. Bodmer—Zürich',

time ago' (Anderson 1050/Kastner–Kapp 993).[38] But even these indications are less straightforward than might be hoped. Since Beethoven had been lying through his teeth when he told Schlesinger on 28 June that the sonata was ready, can we be sure that he was being more honest on 20 September? The letter of 7 March at least provides a clear *terminus post quem non* for the completion of Op. 109; but what Beethoven meant by 'a long time ago' is unclear.

As for the Op. 109 sketches in Artaria 195, we can at least be sure that they were completed by the end of 1820, since they are followed by, and partly overlap with, sketches for numbers 7–11 of the Bagatelles, Op. 119, the autograph of which is dated 1 January 1821.[39] But the variation sketches in Artaria 195 do not come very close to the variations in the final version; that is, more sketching in other sources may have been required before the third movement was finished (the variation sketches are discussed in detail in Chapters 7–9). The only other surviving sketches for the third movement are on page 1 of Artaria 197 (*B*; SV 12). Artaria 197 follows Artaria 195 in the chronological sequence of desk sketchbooks, but it contains a number of entries which predate the main period during which Beethoven used the book.[40] Among these early entries are probably the three sketches which may be firmly linked with Op. 109. They are all on page 1: staves 3/4 and 5 contain brief pencil entries for unused variations, while on staves 6–10 there is an ink sketch for the second half of Variation 6 (see Chapter 9, Ex. 9.12). This sketch reflects a late stage of composition; it may have been contemporary with the last variation sketches in Artaria 195, or it may postdate them by a certain time.

While the sketches thus offer no conclusive evidence for Beethoven's claim on 20 September 1820 that Op. 109 was 'quite ready apart from corrections' his subsequent correspondence with Schlesinger concerning the engraving of the sonata establishes the truthfulness of the claim beyond reasonable doubt. The route to this conclusion is lengthy and somewhat obscure, and will take us from

---

Beethoven-Jahrbuch, 1 (1954), 49; Anderson's trans. of the phrase 'die erste [Sonate] ist fast bis zur *Correctur* ganz fertig' misleadingly runs 'the first [sonata] is quite ready save for correcting the copy'.

[38] For the autograph of this letter see J. A. Stargardt, Marburg, 24–5 Nov. 1981, lot 578.

[39] Kinsky–Halm, 344.

[40] See Winter's reconstruction in JTW, 265–72. On p. 269 Winter lists sketches for Op. 109 on Artaria 197, pp. 1, 28–9, and 47. Similarly, Klein's inventory (*Autographe und Abschriften*, 190–201) mentions sketches on pp. 47 and 63, though the latter attribution is considered doubtful, while what is presumably a printing error attributes the sketch on p. 1, st. 6–10 to Op. 108. Only in the case of the three sketches mentioned in the text here is the attribution to Op. 109 beyond all doubt.

1820 almost to the end of the following year. To begin, consider a further passage from the letter of 7 March 1821:

You will probably be able to read my manuscript. If you find that proofreading [*Correcturen*] is necessary, please send proofs from the songs as well as the sonata [*sowohl von den liedern als sonaten*]. But in the case of the songs you must send the manuscript as well. True, it is only a very hastily made copy of my manuscript which, however, I do not possess.[41]

Several important points arise from this. Schlesinger clearly has manuscripts of Op. 109 and of the Scottish songs. In the case of the sonata he has Beethoven's autograph manuscript, which Beethoven hopes will be sufficiently legible, while for the songs he has a copyist's score, presumably the one mentioned in Beethoven's letter of 28 June. Because Beethoven apparently does not possess his manuscript of the songs, he requires Schlesinger to return the copy to him for the purpose of checking the proofs.[42] In the case of the sonata, however, he makes no such request.

Beethoven's hopes for his handwriting were in vain. A letter of 7 June 1821 to Schlesinger (Anderson 1052/Kastner–Kapp 995) refers to a copy (*Abschrift*) of the sonata which 'seems to be almost quite correct. But the first and second proofs should have been done in Berlin from this copy and then sent to me. Thus there are now very many mistakes to *correct, including some really serious ones.*' In postscripts to this letter Beethoven apologized for the fact that his manuscript had delayed Schlesinger's work and requested that publication of the sonata be delayed 'until the corrections made in the proofs have been entered. For there really are far too many mistakes in it.' Clearly, Beethoven's autograph had been so illegible that Schlesinger had found it necessary to have a copy made in Berlin.[43] But the proofs sent to Beethoven had either been made from the autograph rather than the copy, or had been made from the copy but then checked against the autograph. Whatever the case, they were consequently riddled with errors.

On 6 July 1821 Beethoven wrote to Schlesinger: 'You are now receiving, Sir! the corrected proofs. I have never had a more difficult

---

[41] My trans., made from the German in the Stargardt catalogue (see n. 38, above). The plural *sonaten* must be a mistake on Beethoven's part.

[42] In a letter to Schlesinger dated 12 Dec. 1821 (Anderson 1063) Beethoven referred to his MS of the songs as 'practically only a sketch'.

[43] The autograph of Anderson 1052/Kastner–Kapp 995 was unavailable to Anderson. It was sold at Sotheby's, London, 12 May 1970, lot 436. The copy of Op. 109 prepared in Berlin for Schlesinger has apparently not survived. It is not to be confused with another copy, bearing corrections in Beethoven's hand, which was prepared for the library of Archduke Rudolph. This copy, or *überprüfte Abschrift*, is now in *Wgm*, VII. 17379. Q. 11967. See Meredith, 'Sources for Opus 109', 196–211; and Ch. 10, below.

and tiresome task to cope with' (Anderson 1053/Kastner–Kapp 997).[44] He went on to stress that the copy prepared for Schlesinger ('since my original manuscript was apparently not legible') should now become the primary source for the engraved edition: therefore it must be totally free of errors and must be followed in every respect. But errors remained; Beethoven sent Schlesinger a further letter and a supplementary list of mistakes, dated 13 and 14 November respectively (Anderson 1060–1), requesting that the corrections be entered in Indian ink in all engraved copies prior to distribution.[45] 'Please, please, please do follow this advice,' he pleaded, 'so that the work may appear as it should.' And he continued:

As for the other two sonatas, these will soon follow and, what is more, copied correctly. To enclose the manuscript would be too risky. For if some untoward mishap were to befall both manuscript and copy, the whole work would be lost. This is what happened the last time when on account of my ailing condition I had written down the *draft [Concept] more fully* than usual. But now that my health appears to be better, I merely jot down certain ideas as I used to do, and when I have completed the whole in my head, everything is written down, but only once.

Beethoven was writing in reply to a letter of 13 October from Schlesinger. Presumably Schlesinger had suggested that in order to avoid the problems encountered in engraving Op. 109 Beethoven should have his autograph manuscripts of the other two sonatas copied and should send the autographs and the copies to Berlin. Beethoven's statement that 'this is what happened the last time' logically refers back to the possibility that sending autograph and copy together risks losing the work entirely in the event of an accident with the post. But this cannot be what he meant; 'the last time' must refer to the events concerning Op. 109, and we know that in this case Schlesinger received Beethoven's autograph safely. (Whether he returned it to Beethoven together with the copy prepared in Berlin is unclear.) So Beethoven must have meant that he risked sending the autograph 'the last time'; and he took this risk because he already had a more than usually detailed first draft of the work himself.[46] The implication is that in the event of any 'untoward

---

[44] Anderson assumes that Beethoven is referring to the proofs of the Scottish songs, but this can hardly be the case: the letter of 12 Dec. 1821 (Anderson 1063) mentions that proof-reading of the songs is not yet finished, while Beethoven's comments on 6 July follow naturally from his remarks about the problems with the sonata on 7 June. See also Kinsky–Halm, 313, where this interpretation is supported.

[45] For the German text of Anderson 1060–1 see B. Schofield and A. D. Wilson, 'Some New Beethoven Letters', *Music & Letters*, 20 (1939), 236–8.

[46] The noun *Concept* which Beethoven used in his letter to Schlesinger is defined as 'der erste schriftliche Entwurf einer Sache, ein schriftlicher Aufsatz' in Johann Christoph Adelung,

mishap' befalling the autograph of Op. 109 *en route* to Berlin, Beethoven's draft would have preserved a version sufficiently detailed for him to be able to prepare a new score.

Fortunately, a fragment of Beethoven's draft or *Concept* for Op. 109 has survived. The manuscript (*Wgm*, A 47: see Plate 8) is a single bifolium containing detailed drafts of Variations 2 and 3 in the third movement, although neither variation is so numbered. Many features of this manuscript distinguish it from an ordinary sketchleaf: the handwriting is easy to read and the layout is clear (the apparent illegibility of the draft of Variation 3 is due to the fact that it actually consists of two superimposed drafts, each carefully written although the first is deleted); clefs, key signatures, tempo indications, dynamics, and accidentals are all notated with far more care than Beethoven habitually accorded his sketches. Finally, the drafts of both variations are very detailed, and close in content to their respective final versions. However, Beethoven decided to recast Variation 2 quite substantially (see Chapter 9), and it was probably this decision which caused him to remove the bifolium from the *Concept*.

Beethoven claimed in his letter of 13 November 1821 that poor health had been the cause of his preparing a more than usually detailed *Concept* for Op. 109. Turning back now to the letter of 20 September 1820 in which he claimed that Op. 109 was 'quite ready apart from corrections', we find that 'persistently poor health' had prevented him from completing the proofreading of the copies of the Scottish songs; and illness is also mentioned in a slightly earlier letter of 2 September (Anderson 1032/Kastner–Kapp 983) to Archduke Rudolph. Thus there is good reason to believe that Op. 109 was indeed essentially complete by late September 1820; and a similar, perhaps slightly earlier date may be assigned to the sole surviving bifolium from the *Concept* for Op. 109 occasioned by Beethoven's ill-health.

X

The only manuscript source for Op. 109 remaining to be discussed is the autograph manuscript, the source of Schlesinger's difficulties and Beethoven's consequent misery. Although it cannot honestly be described as a *Reinschrift* or fair copy of the work, it is by no means

Grammatisch-Kritisches Wörterbuch der Hochdeutschen Mundart, enlarged D. W. Soltau, rev. Franz Xaver Schönberger (Vienna, 1811), i. 1345. It was presumably on account of his *Concept* for Op. 109 that Beethoven did not specifically request the return of the autograph in his letter of 7 Mar. (Anderson 1050/Kastner–Kapp 993); in contrast, he required the copy of the Scottish songs precisely because he did not possess his own MS of them.

42 The Sources for Op. 109

TABLE 2.4. *Structure of the autograph manuscript of Op. 109*

Sheet	Folio	Watermark	Contents
I	1	2b?	Title-page
II	2	2a	*1st mvt*: 1–17
	3	1a	18–55
	4	4a	56–67
	5	3a	68–99
III	6	4b	*2nd mvt*: 1–37
	7	3b	38–73
	8	2b	74–117
	9	1b	118–49
	10	3b?	150–77
IV	11	1a	*3rd mvt*: Theme-Var. 1
	12	2a	Var. 1–2
	13	3a	Var. 2–3
	14	4a	Var. 3–4
V	15	3b	Var. 4
	16	4b	Var. 5
	17	1b	Var. 5–6
	18	2b	Var. 6
VI	19	3b?	Var. 6–reprise of theme
	20	2b?	Blank

as much of a working score as other Beethoven autographs such as that of the first movement of the Cello Sonata in A, Op. 69.[47] It contains some interesting compositional alterations, most notably in connection with Variation 3 in the third movement. These alterations are considered at the appropriate points in the succeeding chapters; of more immediate concern are the implications of the physical structure of the manuscript.

The gathering structure of the autograph manuscript of Op. 109 is shown in Table 2.4 along with a brief summary of the disposition of movements. The paper has eight staves, ruled in pairs.[48] As can be seen, the structure is fairly regular and consists mainly of gathered sheets with a separate bifolium at the very end of the manuscript.

---

[47] See L. Lockwood, 'The Autograph of the First Movement of Beethoven's Sonata for Violoncello and Pianoforte, Opus 69', *The Music Forum*, 2 (1970), 1–109; repr. in id., *Beethoven: Studies in the Creative Process* (Cambridge, Mass. and London, 1992), 17–94. The accompanying facsimile of the MS was also published separately (New York, 1970). The MS is now in *BNba*, NE 179.

[48] According to Winter in JTW, 358–9, the paper-type is the same as that found in the sketch MS *BNba*, BH 110. A drawing of the sheet watermark appears as no. 41 in JTW, 557.

It seems most likely that Beethoven wrote out each movement soon after he had finished sketching it, rather than waiting until the entire work was finished before beginning the autograph. We have seen that the first movement was composed some time ahead of the other two, and the fact that it is contained within a single gathered sheet in the autograph means that it could well have existed as an independent manuscript for some time. The interruption of the main body of sketches for the third movement in Artaria 195 by a single isolated sketch for part of the second movement on page 55 (see Table 2.3) is probably an indication that Beethoven was writing out the autograph of the movement at that time. In writing out the second movement Beethoven disrupted the regular structure of gathered sheets and completed the movement on the second leaf of a bifolium (folios 1/10), the first leaf of which forms the title-page of the autograph and encloses the first movement also. Had he been in a position to write out the third movement as soon as he had finished the second, folio 10 would surely have been the first folio of a third gathered sheet.

The use of this single bifolium as a kind of wrapper around the first two movements separates them physically from the third, and this demarcation matches a distinction to be made in the sketches. Briefly, the late sketches for the first two movements come very close to the respective final versions while those for the third movement do not (a more detailed discussion of this point is given in Chapter 7). It seems clear that the composition of the third movement ran a different course to that of the other two. The point is reinforced by the fact that the most substantial compositional changes in the autograph are connected with the third movement. In any case, the structure of the autograph suggests that the first two movements were written out ahead of the third; Beethoven may have devised the 'wrapper' formed by the bifolium 1/10 as a means of keeping them safely together.[49]

Just how close is the relationship between the late sketches and the autograph of the second movement may be illustrated by an example. Pages 47–50 of Artaria 195 contain a detailed continuity draft for the development, recapitulation, and coda of the movement (Chapter 6, CD 4); in fact this draft represents the end of sustained work on the movement in the sketchbook. Bars 156–7 gave Beethoven particular trouble; transcription reveals two complete versions of the lower voices and the beginnings of a third (Ex. 2.7). Neither version

---

[49] It is possible that the bifolium 1/10 originally formed a wrapper for the gathered sheet on which the first movement had been written out, and that Beethoven subsequently pressed its second folio into service for the end of the second movement.

44 The Sources for Op. 109

Ex. 2.7. Op. 109, second movement, bars 156–7 (Artaria 195, p. 50)

[1] nor version [2] corresponds to the final version; but this was not always the case. When he came to write out bars 156–7 in the autograph (folio 10ʳ) Beethoven unhesitatingly wrote out version [2] from the draft. What is more, he did not revise these bars immediately. Bar 158 must already have been in place at the beginning of the next system when he did so, for after deleting the existing version of bars 156–7 he was forced to squeeze the new, final one into the small space remaining at the right-hand side of the staves, which even had to be extended into the margin.

The exact correspondence between these bars in Artaria 195 and the autograph manuscript of the second movement strongly suggests that Beethoven was actually copying from the sketchbook: for a short time, the sketchbook version [2] was actually the final version of this passage. Thus the relationship between the sketches and the autograph of Op. 109 is an intimate one. On a broad level, the gathering structure of the autograph reflects the pace of composition; at a more detailed level such as that just discussed the distinction between sketch and autograph becomes severely blurred, if not wholly erased.

XI

Thayer was right: 'the Sonata in E belongs unquestionably to the year 1820'. But in proving this simple statement correct we have encountered many questions of which Thayer was probably never aware. Nor has it been possible to answer all of those questions satisfactorily. To take one example, the precise relationship between the E-minor sketches on Grasnick 20b, folio 1^v (Ex. 2.5) and the 'little new piece' destined to become the first movement of Op. 109 remains unclear. Nor is it possible to establish with any certainty just what was the pattern of work on Op. 109 during the summer of 1820, or exactly when Beethoven completed the writing of the autograph. It is especially fortunate that scrutiny of the sources can reveal as much as has been discussed here; to insist on explanations and reasons at every stage would be unrealistic.

'Yet if one insists on discovering reasons, then there are surely far more noble motives to which one can ascribe a dedication of that kind': writing to Franz Brentano on 20 December 1821, Beethoven apologized for not asking permission before dedicating Op. 109 to Brentano's daughter Maximiliane and asked that Brentano should 'regard this work as a token of my lasting devotion to you and your whole family' (Anderson 1064). Thus was the link between Op. 109 and the Brentano name sealed for posterity. The much more palpable link between Op. 109 and Oliva, however, has had to be rescued here from the spare and reticent evidence of the conversation books. No dedication or honour marks Oliva's involvement in the genesis of the sonata; but we should not underestimate the significance of what was presumably a purely chance remark to Beethoven. The 'little new piece' is the subject of the next chapter; the consequences of its incorporation into 'a sonata for Schlesinger' unfold in Chapters 4–9.

3. The Sketches for the First Movement

Formal Synopsis

Exposition (1–15):
First group (1–8)
Second group, first statement (9–11)
 varied repeat (12–14)
Codetta (15)

Development (15–48):
First part (15–21)
Second part (21–42)
Retransition (42–8)

Recapitulation (48–65):
First group (48–57)
Second group, first statement (58–60)
 varied repeat (61–4)
Codetta (65)

Coda (65–99)

The Desk Sketches: Grasnick 20b, folios 3^r–5^v, 6^v

Grasnick 20b, folio 3^r is not given over entirely to Op. 109. On staves 1–2 there is a sketch for the Credo of the *Missa solemnis*, and on staves 3/4 an incipit for a piano composition in F minor which was not pursued further. On staves 5/6 Beethoven shifted from F minor to E major and wrote the sketch shown in Ex. 3.1a. If this was indeed his very first sketch for Op. 109, it is clear that little effort on paper was required before he reached a satisfactory opening for the work.[1] The analysis in Ex. 3.1b shows how the first phrase of the sketch grows from the initial upper-voice interval b^1–$g\sharp^1$ (x:

---

[1] This remark applies far more readily to pitch and rhythm than to metre, about which Beethoven remained undecided for some time. His indecision may be reflected in the almost total lack of authentic barlines in Ex. 3.1a. Beethoven vacillated between 2/4 and 4/4 metre for some time, and it is not always clear which metre is intended in a particular sketch. Viewed in their entirety, the sketches suggest a gradual transition from 4/4 to 2/4 as the basic metre of the movement, and it is on this basis that editorial barlines and time signatures have been supplied where necessary. The assumed metre of a sketch obviously needs to be taken into account when phrase-lengths are under discussion.

Ex. 3.1. *a* Grasnick 20b, fol. 3ʳ, st. 5/6–7

b First phrase of Ex. 3.1*a*

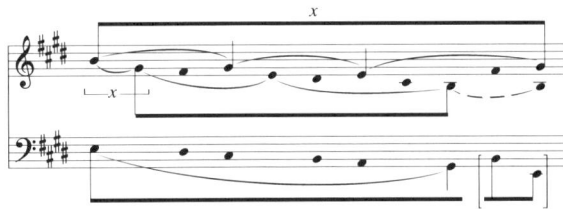

see the bracketed notes). This interval is composed out in the upper voice by means of a triadic descent from b^1 to e^1 followed by a stepwise return to $g\sharp^1$. The middle-voice descent through the sixth $g\sharp^1$–b composes out an inverted retrograde of *x*.

In the remainder of the sketch Beethoven tired of writing the persistent semiquaver-dotted quaver rhythm and adopted a shorthand notation using only a single crotchet for each beat. The phrase just discussed is followed by a second which leads to a tonicization of the dominant. Like the first phrase, this one closely matches the course of the final version; but there is one significant difference. In the sketch the resolution of $a\sharp^2$ to b^2 takes place directly to secure the establishment of B major, while in the final version (bars 8–9) $a\sharp^2$ falls to a^2 simultaneously with the switch from 2/4 to 3/4 time and the beginning of the second group. The b^2 expected in bar 9 is delayed until the end of the exposition.[2] The third phrase in Ex. 3.1*a*

---

[2] William Kinderman discusses the sketch transcribed as Ex. 3.1*a* in connection with the 'parenthetical enclosure' of the second group within the first: see 'Thematic Contrast and Parenthetical Enclosure in the Piano Sonatas, Opp. 109 and 111', in H. Goldschmidt (ed.), *Zu Beethoven 3: Aufsätze und Dokumente* (Berlin, 1988), 43–59.

Ex. 3.2. Third phrase of Ex. 3.1a

begins with a return to the original register as b^1 is reintroduced through its upper neighbour $c\sharp^2$. Thereafter a further composing-out of x, this time as a linear progression through the third b^1–a^1–$g\sharp^1$, implies a cadence in E major (Ex. 3.2).

A fourth phrase, similar to the third, breaks off after only five beats. On the next stave (stave 8) Beethoven abandoned musical notation in favour of words. First he wrote the phrase 'fällt ein cis moll u.[nd] schließt darin'; then he added the words 'in eine[r] Fantasie' above the original phrase and used a curved line to insert them between 'u.[nd]' and 'schließt'. This verbal instruction captures the essential features of what was to become the second group in the final version: the way in which it breaks in unexpectedly on the first group and substitutes an improvisatory, fantasia-like style of keyboard writing for the previously established figuration. Most interesting, however, is the tonal implication of the original sentence: 'fällt ein cis moll u.[nd] schließt darin'. Assuming that Ex. 3.1a was intended for a sonata-form movement, this remark can only mean that Beethoven now planned to close the exposition not in the dominant, B major, but in the submediant, C♯ minor.[3] This tonal scheme is unprecedented in his music: where the submediant is used elsewhere for the second group of a sonata-form exposition it is invariably in the major rather than the minor mode. But the instruction attached to Ex. 3.1a is merely the first sign of the special position which C♯ minor held in Beethoven's thoughts during the composition of the first movement of Op. 109, as the following pages will show.

Admittedly, C♯ minor is a good deal less prominent in the final version than in the sketches; for example, the exposition closes in the dominant with only a passing reference to the submediant at the

---

[3] A sketch on fol. 3^r, st. 12, although perhaps written at a different time to Ex. 3.1a and its accompanying remark, may nevertheless be significant in this context. It consists simply of a four-bar phrase in 2/4 time based on the opening of Ex. 3.1a and modulating directly from E major to C♯ minor.

Ex. 3.3. *a* Grasnick 20b, fol. 3ʳ, st. 9

b Cf. Ex. 3.3*a*

beginning of the second group. And Beethoven soon had second thoughts about the tonal plan outlined in connection with Ex. 3.1*a*. An alternative continuation for that sketch, marked 'oder' and intended to follow the tonicization of B at the end of the second phrase, is shown in Ex. 3.3*a*.[4] This apparently new material turns out to be an expansion of the third phrase of Ex. 3.1*a*. The initial b^2 is now transferred down through two octaves to b; b^2 and b^1 each give rise to descending third-progressions; and the final g♯ again implies tonic harmony. The various composed-out statements of *x* in this expanded phrase are highlighted by brackets in the analysis shown in Ex. 3.3*b*.

If Ex. 3.3*a* is read in its proper context as a continuation for the first two phrases of Ex. 3.1*a*, an even larger composing-out of *x* can be traced from the initial b^1 (Ex. 3.1*a*) to the closing g♯ (Ex. 3.3*a*). The implied harmonic underpinning of this composite sketch is a broad I–V–I progression, the tonicization of V coinciding with the melodic arrival on b^2. There are significant connections here with the first movement of Op. 109, which likewise composes out a I–V–I progression on the largest level. As in Ex. 3.1*a*/3.3*a*, the upper voice of the entire movement is bounded by the two notes of its initial interval: $g\sharp^1$–b^1 (*x1*) is inverted to become $g\sharp^1$–b (Ex. 3.4).[5] Even the low-register ending of the final version is anticipated by

---

[4] In the MS the initial b^2 of Ex. 3.3*a* is roughly aligned beneath the b^2 which concludes the second phrase of Ex. 3.1*a*.

[5] In view of the special relationship between the first movement and the third-movement theme it may be significant that the opening right-hand chord of the theme presents $g\sharp^1$–b: a synoptic reference, as it were, to the melodic structure of the movement from which the theme takes its origin (see Ch. 4, below).

Ex. 3.4. Op. 109, first movement: composing-out of *x1*

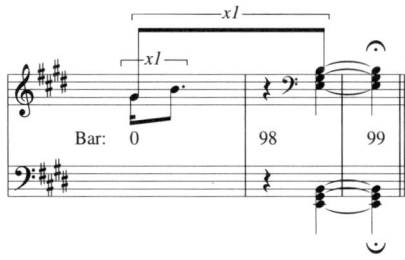

Ex. 3.5. Grasnick 20b, fol. 3^r, st. 10/11

the closing g♯ of Ex. 3.3a. Furthermore, we have seen that the tonicization of the dominant and the corresponding melodic arrival on b² are present in the final version, although displaced from their expected position in bar 9 to the end of the exposition in bar 15.

While recognizing the extent to which these first sketches already hint at important features of the final version, we must also try to take them on their own terms. It seems clear that Beethoven was especially interested in exploring the large-scale unifying potential of the initial upper-voice interval *x*. Coupled with this is his tendency to use G♯, the triadic third, as a melodic signifier of the tonic note and key. Later sketches support the view that the composition of this movement turned largely on an exploration of the alternative harmonic identities which could be assigned to G♯; even Beethoven's repeated attempts to emphasize the submediant, C♯ minor, may ultimately be seen as an aspect of his preoccupation with G♯.

That preoccupation can be sensed in the next sketch (Ex. 3.5), which is a revision of the first two phrases of Ex. 3.1a. The most significant change is the reversal of the initial upper-voice interval:

Ex. 3.6. Cf. Op. 109, first movement, bars 1–4

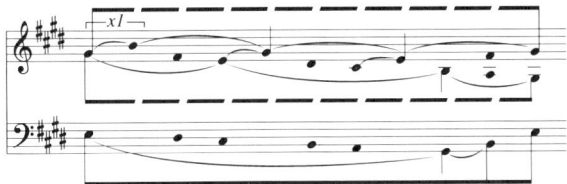

b^1–$g\sharp^1$ (x) becomes $g\sharp^1$–b^1 ($x1$), and the direction of the intervals on the following beats is reversed accordingly. One consequence of this change was that the triadic third gained in prominence over the fifth: while x controls the first phrase of Ex. 3.1a, the revised phrase in Ex. 3.5 proceeds from and returns to $g\sharp^1$. Moreover, while the ascent e^1–$f\sharp^1$–$g\sharp^1$ in bars 2–3 of Ex. 3.1a is rhythmically subordinate to the repeated b, even these priorities are reversed in Ex. 3.5: the ascent to $g\sharp^1$ is articulated on the beat and the repeated b is relegated to the second semiquaver. The substitution of $g\sharp^1$ for b^1 at the opening of the movement is further emphasized by a metrical shift, for Ex. 3.5, unlike Ex. 3.1a, begins unequivocally on the downbeat of bar 1. However, this change necessarily weakened the placement of $g\sharp^1$ at the end of the phrase: whereas in Ex. 3.1a it occurs within a downbeat, in Ex. 3.5 it enters on the last beat of bar 2.

The substitution of $x1$ for the original x at the beginning of the movement proved an important compositional decision. Looking ahead to the final version, which uses 2/4 metre and an upbeat opening, we can see that Beethoven took further steps to reinforce G♯ throughout the first phrase. In both sketches considered so far, the middle voice consists of a stepwise descent from $g\sharp^1$ to b—an inversion of $x1$. But in the final version the descent continues down to g♯ and the completion of the octave-progression $g\sharp^1$–g♯ coincides with the return to $g\sharp^1$ in the upper voice (Ex. 3.6).

Why was Beethoven so concerned with the articulation of G♯ at the beginning of the movement, and why did he reject b^1–$g\sharp^1$ (x) in favour of $g\sharp^1$–b^1 ($x1$) as the initial upper-voice interval? Such questions arise from the preceding discussion and need to be answered at this stage in order to clarify the direction of much that is to follow. It is naturally impossible to give an exhaustive explanation of Beethoven's preoccupation with G♯: beyond a certain point we must simply accept it as a given element in the compositional process. And if we believe that Beethoven wanted this movement to be 'about' G♯ in some sense, we should not be surprised to find him emphasizing that pitch at the outset. The substitution of x_1 for x assists this emphasis by making G♯ the first note heard.

But the substitution has a larger aim. The idea that G♯ (more specifically, $g\sharp^1$) acts as a melodic signifier of the tonic note and key has been put forward above. Building on this idea, we might similarly understand the interval $g\sharp^1$–b^1 as a signifier of the two tonal areas, tonic and dominant, underlying Exx. 3.1a and 3.5, and the exposition in the final version. The original interval x could of course be interpreted in the same terms; but b^1–$g\sharp^1$ would imply the succession B major–E major (V–I) which, in this movement, can only occur once the dominant has been established.

This last point implies that the initial upper-voice interval signifies not only tonal areas but also motion between them. And Beethoven had found a means of representing such motion by composing out the interval as a third-progression. This is seen most clearly in Exx. 3.2 and 3.3b and their associated sketches: the implied tonal progression from dominant back to tonic is coordinated with the upper-voice descent B–A–G♯. But another linear expression of the initial interval is present in Exx. 3.1a and 3.5, although it is stated less directly. In both sketches $g\sharp^2$ is introduced in the upper voice prior to the tonicization of the dominant at the end of the second phrase. This $g\sharp^2$ represents an octave transfer of $g\sharp^1$ from the first phrase; it connects by step to $a\sharp^2$, which then resolves to b^2 to complete the cadence in the dominant.[6] Essentially the same is true of the final version, where $g\sharp^2$ is reached in bar 7 and connects with $a\sharp^2$ in the following bar. (The resolution to b^2 is delayed until bar 15, as discussed above.)

Thus the initial upper-voice interval $g\sharp^1$–b^1 (x_1) has voice-leading as well as tonal implications; it defines the large-scale melodic course of the upper voice up to and including the tonicization of the dominant. In summary, we may say that these first sketches show Beethoven exploring the organizational possibilities inherent in his chosen opening interval. Its two constituent notes signify the tonic and dominant tonalities respectively; and motion from tonic to dominant or from dominant back to tonic can be expressed linearly by the addition of the appropriate passing note, A♯ or A. We shall refer to these two opposed and balancing third-progressions as the 'B-tonicizing' and 'E-tonicizing' progressions (Ex. 3.7); they will figure prominently in the remainder of this chapter.

---

[6] More precisely, $g\sharp^2$ leads to $f\sharp^2$ which then gives rise to $a\sharp^2$ by means of *Übergreifung* or 'reaching over': see Schenker, *Free Composition*, i. 47–9 and fig. 41. This does not invalidate the linear succession $g\sharp^2$–$a\sharp^2$–b^2.

Ex. 3.7. The 'B-tonicizing' and 'E-tonicizing' progressions

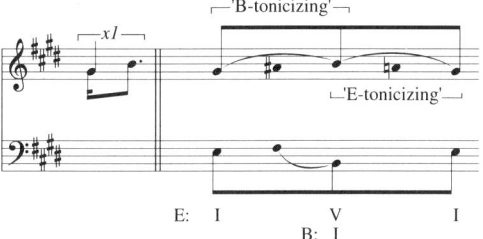

Implicit in the foregoing is the assumption that even at this early compositional stage Beethoven was concerned with the large-scale structure of the movement, with 'the whole'. This impression is strengthened by the next sketch, which shows not only an elaboration of the second group in the exposition but also a projected ending for the movement. The three parts of this sketch (Ex. 3.8) are not musically continuous, but their physical characteristics suggest that they represent a single compositional act. Ex. 3.8a maps out the exposition and is clearly indebted to the two sketches already discussed. The metrical inconsistency in the first three bars is amusingly suggestive of Beethoven's concern for the articulation of $g\sharp^1$. In Ex. 3.5 he had adopted a downbeat opening so that the initial $g\sharp^1$ received strong metrical support. But that decision shifted $g\sharp^1$ to a weak beat at the end of the first phrase, whereas in Ex. 3.1a it had occurred on a downbeat at that point. Here in Ex. 3.8a Beethoven tried to get the best of both worlds: the downbeat opening ensures strong metrical support for the initial $g\sharp^1$, and the foreshortening of the second bar by one crotchet beat results in a downbeat articulation for the closing $g\sharp^1$ also! Moreover, this is the downbeat of a 2/4 rather than a 4/4 bar, so that the opening of the second phrase heralds the metrical scheme which Beethoven eventually adopted.

The second phrase takes the same direction as in earlier sketches: $g\sharp^1$ is transferred up to $g\sharp^2$, which connects with $a\sharp^2$ two beats later. But this $a\sharp^2$ does not resolve directly to b^2: it falls instead to a^2 on the first beat of a 3/4 bar (Beethoven expressly indicates the new time signature). The deceptive resolution and ensuing material clearly foreshadow the eventual second group, but it is the differences rather than the similarities between sketch and final version which are most interesting here. For example, the sequential pattern of descending fifths (a^2–$d\sharp^2$, $g\sharp^2$–$c\sharp^2$, $f\sharp^2$–b^1) in the first two bars suggests that in spite of the notated 3/4 Beethoven was still thinking basically in terms of duple metre: the presence of a barline only after the sixth

Ex. 3.8a–c Grasnick 20b, fol. 3r, st. 12–fol. 3v, st. 1.

crotchet (b^1) points to an underlying hemiola scheme, with three 2/4 bars combining to create a larger triple (3/2) metre. A more important difference concerns the melodic motion in the sketch. The descending line which begins with the unexpected fall from $a\sharp^2$ to a^2 continues only as far as e^2, following which a change in direction leads back to $g\sharp^2$, emphasized by the accompanying pause mark. If the transcription in Ex. 3.8a is basically correct, it seems that this $g\sharp^2$ was to connect with $a\sharp^2$ at the end of the phrase, implying a second attempt to reach b^2 and the dominant key by means of the 'B-tonicizing' progression, harmonized locally as ii–V–I in B major. In the final version the 'B-tonicizing' progression is even more remote from the musical surface; as Oswald Jonas has explained, '[Beethoven] integrates the entire second theme into a descending seventh-progression, which is derived from the inversion of the second, $a\sharp^2$–b^2, which is expected'.[7]

---

[7] O. Jonas, *Introduction to the Theory of Heinrich Schenker*, trans. and ed. John Rothgeb (New York and London, 1982), 142, ex. 210.

Ex. 3.9. *a* Grasnick 20b, fol. 3ᵛ, st. 2   *b* Grasnick 20b, fol. 3ᵛ, st. 8/9

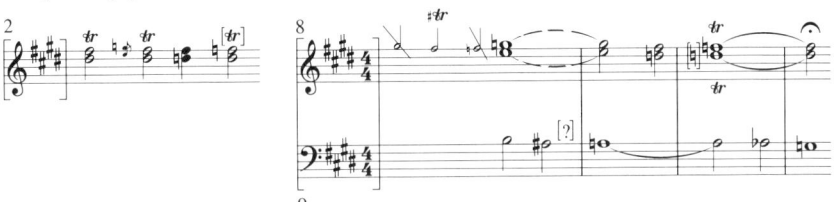

c Grasnick 20b, fol. 4ʳ, st. 9–11

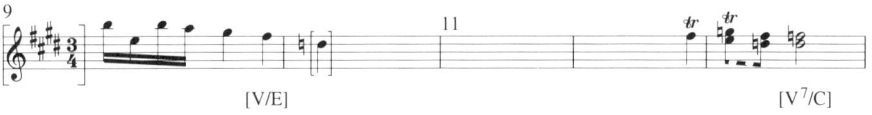

The projected ending for the movement (Ex. 3.8*c*) appears complete with concluding double barline. The material already bears considerable similarity to the beginning (bars 65–74) of the coda in the final version. But contrary to that version, the high right-hand register is maintained to the very end and there is a strong linear ascent to the concluding e^4 (Ex. 3.8*b* may represent an earlier attempt to fix this ascent). The ending of the final version is considerably less definitive.

The few sketches considered so far occupy a total of only twelve staves, from folio 3ʳ, stave 5 to folio 3ᵛ, stave 1. Yet the first movement of Op. 109 seems already to have taken definite shape; the exposition is more or less fixed in Ex. 3.8*a*, and Ex. 3.8*c* from the same sketch brings much of the coda into focus. It is tempting to assume that Beethoven himself had a firm grasp on the movement by this time (as will become clear, the first sketches for the second movement convey a quite different impression in this respect). But any such assumption is shattered by the next sketch, on folio 3ᵛ, stave 2 (Ex. 3.9*a*). Judging from its position relative to the surrounding sketches, it may have been written only after one (Ex. 3.9*b*) which occurs several staves further down folio 3ᵛ; but such is the close relationship between them that these two sketches need to be discussed together.

What is most disconcerting about Ex. 3.9*a* and *b* is the apparently 'abstract' nature of the sketching: the melodic and rhythmic features of the final version, so evident in previous sketches, are entirely absent here, and Ex. 3.9*b* in particular looks more like something from a *Harmonielehre* than anything to do with a late Beethoven piano sonata. But the relationship of both sketches to the first movement of Op. 109 is clarified by a later continuity draft, on folio 4^r. The draft extends as far as the second group in the recapitulation and breaks off with material (Ex. 3.9c) which is clearly derived from Ex. 3.9a and b. Drawing on our knowledge of the recapitulation in the final version we may begin, cautiously, to interpret the material shared by the three passages transcribed in Ex. 3.9. They attempt to fix the astonishing shift to C major with which the varied repeat of the second group in the recapitulation begins (bars 61–2). They are the only extant sketches for this part of the movement, and reveal little development in Beethoven's formulation of it; rather, they need to be read in conjunction with one another in order to clarify a single stage of thought. The 'abstract' appearance already alluded to is important in this respect. Alone of all the sketches for the first movement, these three show little or no attempt to fix surface melodic and rhythmic detail. But this very facelessness focuses attention on their harmonic implications; it was in the harmonic domain that Beethoven's main problems lay.

Ex. 3.9b is the easiest to deal with, for it includes a bass line which helps to clarify harmonic and voice-leading functions. The bass descends chromatically from b, supporting g^2/e^2, to g, supporting f^2/d^2—a chord which in this context may be interpreted as a dominant seventh of C.[8] The pair f^2/d^2 is also the goal of Ex. 3.9a and c, though these begin with $f\sharp^2/d\sharp^2$ and $f\sharp^2$ respectively—notes which probably represent the dominant chord of E, if we assume that some form of the bass descent shown in Ex. 3.9b was intended for these two sketches also.

We may suppose that the three sketches in Ex. 3.9 are directed towards achieving a smooth connection between the dominant of E and that of C. How do they compare with the final version in this respect? There the dominant of C appears to result immediately from the chromatic alteration of the diminished seventh at the end of bar 60; a strong sense of connection between the two chords is engendered partly through our recollection of the corresponding passage in the exposition, where the diminished seventh reached on the last quaver of bar 11 is repeated, albeit in a different position, at

[8] This is of course not the only possible interpretation of $f^2/d^2/g$. The chord might also resolve as an augmented sixth on the flattened submediant of B; but since these sketches evidently relate to the second-group area in the recapitulation it is unlikely that such a dominant-key orientation would have been intended. It is worth noting the close voice-leading correspondence between Ex. 3.9b and bars 45–9 in the *second* movement of Op. 109, a passage in which f^2/G is first approached and resolved as V^7/C although it is subsequently reinterpreted (bars 55–6) as $VI^{\flat 6}/b$.

the beginning of bar 12.[9] What is less apparent—or less audible—is that the diminished seventh at the end of bar 60 is itself a chromatic alteration of a previous chord, the dominant of E reached at the end of the first group (bar 57): f♯^{2} and d♯^{2} in this chord are replaced by e♯^{2} and d^2 at the beginning of bar 58 and e♯^{2} is renotated as f^2 at the end of bar 60. Thus the progression from the dominant of E to that of C implied by the sketches in Ex. 3.9 also underlies this remarkable passage in the final version, although it is considerably obscured there by the complex surface activity.

A closer look at Beethoven's use of register helps to focus attention on some of the more important distinctions between Ex. 3.9 and the corresponding part of the final version. When the second group breaks in at bar 58 the low bass register used prior to that point is abruptly quitted: the right hand is unaffected, but the supporting bass leaps up to the middle-register third b–g♯ (compare Ex. 3.9b). On the last quaver of bar 60 the bass plunges back down to introduce the decisive chromatic shift G♯–G which transforms the diminished-seventh harmony into a dominant seventh. It is largely by means of this careful manipulation of bass register that the connection between bars 57 and 60–1 is forged.

In the bass of Ex. 3.9b Beethoven had envisaged a smooth stepwise connection between the dominant of E and that of C; and g^2 had already appeared in the upper voice before being reached in the bass. In the final version, on the other hand, G figures nowhere in the upper voice; and the stepwise bass descent is replaced by the low-register progression B–G♯–G. The middle-register events separating B from G♯ throw a good deal of emphasis on to the shift G♯–G. Furthermore, the return from C to E major is achieved very economically in the second half of bar 62 by the exact reversal of this shift: G returns to the G♯ last heard at the end of bar 60, and brings with it a return to tonic harmony. Once we perceive the special attention given to the semitone shifts G♯–G and G–G♯ in the final version, a reinterpretation of the varied repeat of the recapitulation second group seems possible. The tonicization of C major in bars 61–2 may be understood as subordinate to the larger progression G♯–G–G♯: in other words, C prolongs its dominant, G. Ex. 3.10 illustrates the point.

This somewhat laborious charting of events leads us back, then, to the crucial pitch G♯. In the recapitulation of the second group Beethoven momentarily 'negates' G♯ by replacing it with G. While

---

[9] In *Harmony*, 305–6, Schenker cited this repetition in bars 11–12 as an example of the way in which 'Beethoven, especially during his last period, loved to anticipate the whole subsequent scale-step'.

Ex. 3.10. Cf. Op. 109, first movement, bars 60–2

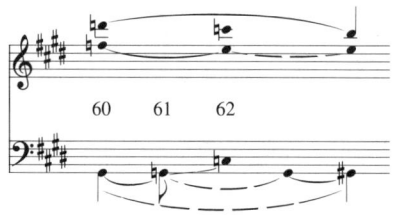

this point will be taken up again later, we may close this discussion by noting that none of the three sketches in Ex. 3.9 actually shows the V–I cadence in C major which appears in the final version: evidently it was the arrival on the dominant of C—in other words, the establishment of G in place of G♯—which was uppermost in Beethoven's mind.

Sandwiched between Ex. 3.9a and b on Grasnick 20b, folio 3ᵛ, are two other sketches whose relationship to Op. 109 is immediately clear. The first (Ex. 3.11a) is an idea for the retransition. It outlines an arrival on the submediant—a further appearance, this, of the key which loomed so large in Beethoven's plans for the movement—followed by a flourish on the dominant seventh (clearly implied, although no triadic root is present) which leads into the recapitulation.

The (displaced) resolution of the seventh, a^2, to $g\sharp^3$ at the beginning of the recapitulation is quite clear in Ex. 3.11a. The observation would be superfluous were it not for the importance in so many of these sketches of linear progressions between G♯ and B. The large-scale voice-leading plan illustrated in Ex. 3.11b shows a broad arch structure resulting from the composing-out of $x1$, the initial upper-voice interval $g\sharp^1$–b^1, and should be compared with Ex. 3.7. Just as the 'B-tonicizing' progression was to span the exposition, so the 'E-tonicizing' progression was to span the development: as the retransition sketch shows, the return from B through A to G♯ would be completed in the upper voice at the beginning of the recapitulation, simultaneously with the re-establishment of the tonic key.

The second of the two remaining sketches on folio 3ᵛ is shown in Ex. 3.12. It is another sketch for the exposition second group and should be compared with its predecessor in Ex. 3.8a. Despite the initial absence of barlines, the implied harmony and metre are better correlated here than in the earlier sketch: there is no lingering sense of duple time. One consequence of this metric-harmonic realignment was a stronger articulation of the descent from a^2 to $g\sharp^2$. In Ex. 3.8a, $g\sharp^2$ falls on the (weak) third beat of the first 3/4 bar; in Ex. 3.12

Ex. 3.11. *a* Grasnick 20b, fol. 3ᵛ, st. 2/3–4/5

b Op. 109, first movement: voice-leading plan suggested by sketches

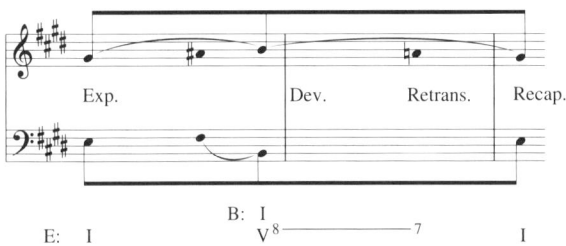

Ex. 3.12. Grasnick 20b, fol. 3ᵛ, st. 4–6

it falls on the downbeat of the second bar in the group and accordingly receives more stress. Like its counterpart in the final version, this $g\sharp^2$ is set in the context of submediant harmony. The strong articulation of a^2–$g\sharp^2$ at this point in the movement seems significant, for it replaces the resolution $a\sharp^2$–b^2 expected at the end of the first group (not a part of Ex. 3.12, but inferable here on the basis of previous sketches). As Exx. 3.7 and 3.11*b* make clear, the tonal implications of the semitone steps A♯–B and A–G♯ are diametrically opposed, leading towards the dominant and tonic respectively. The *submediant* harmonization of a^2–$g\sharp^2$ at the beginning of the second group thus makes its substitution for the expected $a\sharp^2$–b^2 doubly deceptive.

Comparison of Exx. 3.12 and 3.8a reveals further developments of the second-group material. Whereas in the earlier sketch the linear descent from a^2 had reached only as far as e^2, in Ex. 3.12 it extends down to $c\sharp^2$ (although $g\sharp^2$ is substituted for e^2 on the second quaver of bar 3). And the apparent attempt at the end of Ex. 3.8a to re-introduce the 'B-tonicizing' progression in the second group is replaced in Ex. 3.12 by the first attempt to fix the varied repeat, a passage which serves precisely to delay further the completion of the 'B-tonicizing' progression in the final version. The most notable feature of the varied repeat as it appears in Ex. 3.12 is the absence of the unexpected D$\sharp$-major harmony found in bars 12–13 of the final version. In fact this harmony appears nowhere in the sketches for the second group, although an apparently insignificant element in the next sketch to be discussed may be regarded as its most immediate progenitor.

This next sketch is the continuity draft, extending as far as the second group in the recapitulation, from which Ex. 3.9c was extracted. It builds on the previous draft (Ex. 3.8) by incorporating some of the material developed in the intervening sketches. Ex. 3.13 gives a transcription of the draft up to the beginning of the recapitulation. The only significant development in the first group is the decision to begin on an upbeat rather than a downbeat, although the 4/4 metre of Ex. 3.8a is retained. It is clear from the layout in the manuscript that Beethoven did not at first sketch all the varied repeat of the second group; the diagonal line following the bass-clef A sufficed to indicate what had already been notated in more detail in Ex. 3.12, and Beethoven proceeded directly to the beginning of the development. At some later point he returned to the varied repeat and added the material identified as version [2] in the transcription.

As far as the first statement of the second-group material is concerned, we need only observe that, in contrast to Ex. 3.12, e^2 had now been incorporated into the linear descent from a^2. It is the varied repeat which requires attention. As already explained, Beethoven did not at first notate the repeat in full because he had already done so in an earlier sketch (Ex. 3.12). Thus it is not surprising to discover that the material added in version [2] introduces a new element, one not present in that earlier sketch. Comparing Exx. 3.12 and 3.13, we can see that the new element is a registrally displaced passing note, g^1, inserted between $g\sharp^2$ and $f\sharp^2$ in the descent from a^2. Ex. 3.14a shows a reduction of the relevant passage from the sketch, with the passing note now located in its 'obligatory' register; Ex.

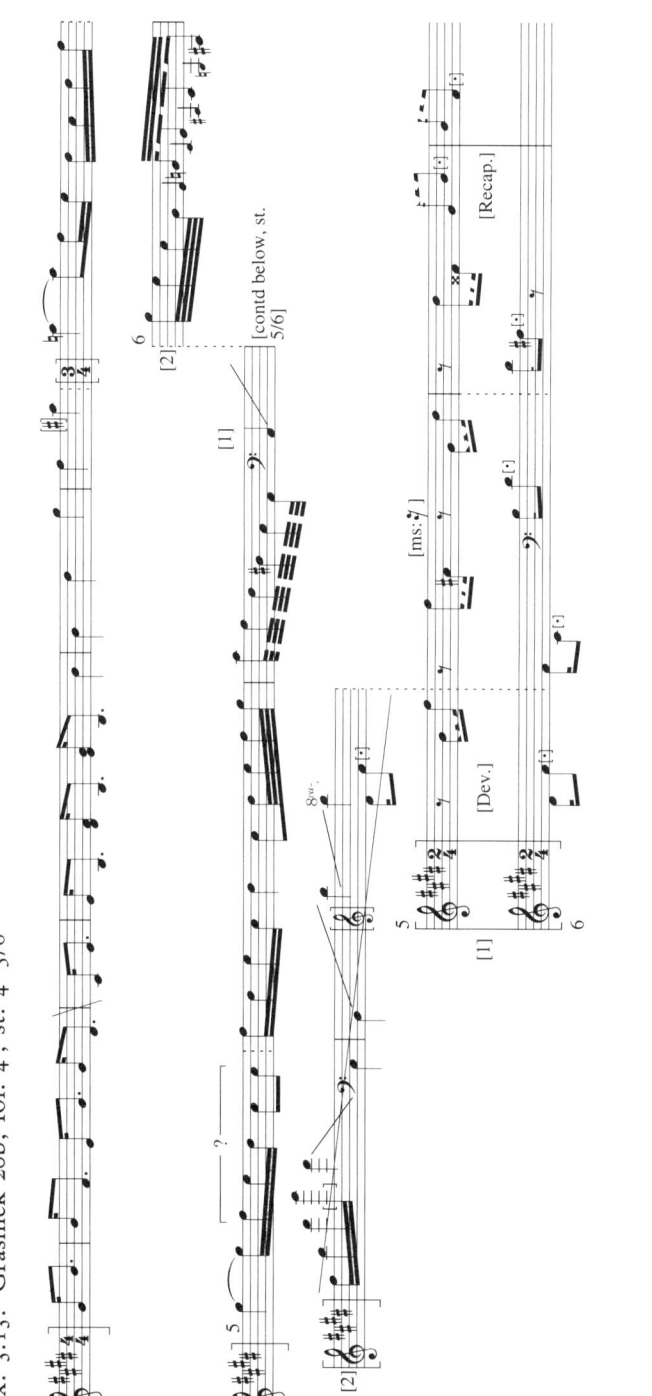

Ex. 3.13. Grasnick 20b, fol. 4ʳ, st. 4–5/6

Ex. 3.14. *a* Cf. Ex. 3.13, bars 8–10

b Cf. Op. 109, first movement, bars 12–13

3.14*b* gives a similar reduction of the corresponding passage from the final version.

The final version, with its emphatic D♯-major harmony in bar 13, is a good deal more striking than the sketch: indeed, such is the force of D♯ major here that it is g♯^{3} which seems to be a passing note, linking a^3 and f𝄪^{3}. Yet the origin of the striking harmony supporting f𝄪^{3} between g♯^{3} and f♯^{3} in the upper voice may lie in the addition of the chromatic passing note g^1—enharmonically, f𝄪^{1}—in Ex. 3.13. Nor is this all that can be said about that g^1. It is interesting that the continuity draft in which it appears breaks off not at any significant formal juncture but part way through the varied repeat of the second group in the recapitulation. (The final bars of the draft are transcribed in Ex. 3.9*c*.) Our earlier analysis of this part of the movement, and of the three sketches for it, suggested that Beethoven was principally concerned with the introduction of G as a negation of G♯. Now he may have broken off the continuity draft at this point because he had not yet finalized the material which was to follow. On the other hand, it may have been the planned introduction of G in the recapitulation second group which gave him the idea of introducing the same note, again in a close linear relationship to G♯, in the corresponding part of the exposition.[10] Thus he broke off the draft at the point shown in Ex. 3.9*c*, returned to the exposition and inserted the version [2] material shown in Ex. 3.13. Any connection between f𝄪^{3} supported by D♯-major harmony in bar 13 and G supporting V^7/C in bar 61 of the final version seems remote. But the sketches speak in favour of such a connection and suggest that, for Beethoven at least, the introduction of F𝄪/G in the exposition was a belated response to the appearance of G already planned for the recapitulation.

Whatever its relationship to the final version, the passing g^1 in Ex. 3.13 has other resonances within the continuity draft of which it forms part. The draft is the first to contain any hint of the development.

---

[10] The relationship of G to G♯ is a contrapuntal one in both cases. In the exposition, both in the final version and in Ex. 3.13, G/F𝄪 functions as a passing note between G♯ and F♯; in the recapitulation G functions as a chromatic lower neighbour to G♯: see Ex. 3.10.

That part of the movement is represented simply by the first four beats of the exposition, transposed to the dominant and with the right- and left-hand parts exchanged (see Ex. 3.13). The transposition dictates that the fifth beat (corresponding to bar 2, beat 2 in the final version) should bring in the subdominant of B major. This triad is of course also the tonic of E major, and in the draft it serves to initiate a very premature recapitulation. It is unclear whether Beethoven had allowed for the literal 'quotation' of the opening of the movement which would inevitably occur if the first group were transposed to the dominant; certainly, in the final version (bars 15–16) he transposed only the first two beats before continuing differently. In any case, what is more important for our purposes is that the transposition in the continuity draft is not wholly precise. For it to be so, the harmony on the fourth beat (that is, the beat immediately preceding the recapitulation in Ex. 3.13) should be D♯ minor. But Beethoven substituted D♯ major, which functions locally as the dominant of G♯ minor. While we might observe merely that this harmony foreshadows the eventual tonicization of G♯ in the final version (bars 21–8), the substitution of f𝄪^{1} for an expected f♯^{1} again points to the g^1 which was later inserted in the exposition second group: despite the enharmonic notation, the pitch identity (f𝄪^{1}/g^1) is exact.

To summarize: the continuity draft on Grasnick 20b, folio 4^r from which Exx. 3.9c and 3.13 are transcribed suggests a compositional relationship between (1) the introduction of G (within V^7/C) in the recapitulation second group; (2) the introduction of f𝄪^{1} (within V/g♯) in the development; and (3) the subsequent insertion of g^1 as a chromatic passing note between G♯ and F♯ in the exposition second group. In the final version the chromatic passing note became elaborated as F𝄪 (within a D♯-major harmony), a notational and harmonic change which obscures its possible relationship to G in bars 61–2 of the recapitulation while clarifying its relationship to F𝄪 and the tonicization of G♯ minor in bars 21–8 of the development.[11]

Beneath this continuity draft there is another sketch for the retransition; it is transcribed in Ex. 3.15. Compared to Ex. 3.11a, the previous sketch for the retransition, one important difference stands out. In Ex. 3.11a the arrival on the dominant seventh of E is projected as an event of some significance: Beethoven envisaged a rhetorical flourish, presumably wide-ranging scales in the right hand

---

[11] In *Compositional Matrix*, 21–2 Forte regards the D♯-major harmony in bar 13 of the final version as a dominant preparation for the appearance of G♯ minor in the development. Schenker, on the other hand, argued that D♯ major in bar 13 does not at all imply G♯ minor: see *Ea*, 9–10.

Ex. 3.15. Grasnick 20b, fol. 4^r, st. 13–14

above a dominant pedal in the left. But in Ex. 3.15 the dominant is considerably underplayed, particularly in relation to the preceding emphasis on the submediant. The weakening of the dominant seventh of E in favour of the submediant during the retransition was to continue in later sketches. In the present instance it should be noted that the upper voice still carries the resolution of the seventh, a^2, to g$\sharp^2$ at the beginning of the recapitulation; thus at this stage Beethoven still intended to complete the arch structure illustrated in Ex. 3.11b.

Folio 4^v is mostly taken up with a detailed continuity draft for the exposition and development; the right-hand part of bars 1–8 is shown in Ex. 3.16.[12] Beethoven's revisions here reveal some surprising decisions. The pattern of ascending thirds and descending fourths familiar from earlier sketches was notated first, only to be replaced by a pattern in which sixths and fourths alternate (version [2]). Beethoven soon became dissatisfied with this new pattern, for it extends no further than the upbeat to bar 2. He then reinstated the original scheme (version [3]) and added crotchet stems to the first note of each pair in order to emphasize the sequence g$\sharp^1$–b^1–e^1–g$\sharp^1$ . . . Although not rigorously retained in succeeding sketches, these stems were incorporated into the final version.

The new pattern tried out in version [2] invites explanation, despite having been relatively short-lived. A considerable amount of space has been devoted above to Beethoven's interest in the initial upper-voice interval g$\sharp^1$–b^1 as a source of large-scale voice-leading progressions. How, then, are we to explain his abandonment of that

[12] Beethoven evidently still thought of the movement in 4/4 rather than 2/4 at this stage. It seems that the first barline to be written in Ex. 3.16 was the deleted one in the middle of the present bar 2. Thus the sketch originally began with a complete 4/4 bar, without an upbeat. Having decided to opt again for an upbeat, Beethoven added a barline after the first beat, deleted the existing barline and reinstated it one beat later. He then proceeded in 4/4 for another two bars. The only barline left unaccounted for in Ex. 3.16 is thus the second one, which produces an initial 2/4 metre. This barline was the result of a later revision, however, for it cuts through part of the musical notation in the MS. In the next continuity draft in Grasnick 20b (see Ex. 3.20a) 4/4 metre is again used explicitly.

Ex. 3.16. Grasnick 20b, fol. 4ᵛ, st. 1, 3

interval in favour of the rising sixth g♯¹–e²? The explanation may yet depend on considerations of large-scale structure. Up to this point in the Grasnick 20b sketches there is only one indication of how Beethoven intended to end the movement: and as Ex. 3.8c shows, he chose e⁴ as the final upper-voice note. The next indication of the ending of the movement, in a continuity draft beginning on folio 5ʳ, shows e³ as the final upper-voice note. By substituting g♯¹–e² for g♯¹–b¹ as the initial upper-voice interval, Beethoven appears to have forfeited the foreground statement of the intervallic space to be composed out in the upper voice prior to the recapitulation (see Ex. 3.11b); but in its place he now defined, again at the immediate foreground level, the larger space through which the upper voice would move during the entire movement. In this respect the initial interval g♯¹–e² in Ex. 3.16 represents a halfway stage between earlier sketches and the final version, in which g♯¹–b¹ not only defines large-scale linear progressions but combines the initial and final upper-voice pitches of the movement also.

Only one other important change in the conception of the exposition is reflected in the continuity draft on folio 4ᵛ. Up to this point Beethoven had always cast the first group as a pair of equal-length phrases. The underlying equality is perceptible even when the last bar of the second phrase is elided with the first bar of the second group. In the final version, however, the phrase structure of the first group is 4 + 5 bars (again, the understood fifth bar of the second phrase is elided with the first bar of the second group). The reason for the extension is unclear, but it seems first to have been charted in a pencil revision to the second phrase in Ex. 3.16 (version [4]). Later sketches, including the first of the pocket sketches, show the two-bar extension found in the corresponding part (bars 52–8) of the recapitulation.[13]

The version of the development in this draft is a good deal more extensive than the few bars tried out previously (see Ex. 3.13). As Ex. 3.17 shows, at least four stages of work on this section can be distinguished. Stage [1] bears comparison with Beethoven's previous attempt. The dominant-key transposition of the first group is abandoned after two beats, and the ensuing pairs e^1–$g\sharp^1$ and $g\sharp^1$–$d\sharp^1$ suggest a deflection towards the submediant (compare the final version, bars 16–17). But then the first-group material reappears at its original pitch-level ($g\sharp^1$–b^1, b^1–$f\sharp^1$ . . .) for several beats before turning towards F♯ minor. This was evidently unsatisfactory, for in stage [2] Beethoven deleted this material and substituted an abrupt turn to G♯ minor which motivates a sequence of ascending thirds ($g\sharp$–b–$d\sharp^1$–$f\sharp^1$) similar to that in bars 26–33 of the final version. The ascending sequence was retained in stage [3] and linked to an expansion of the preceding material. Stage [4], which includes further modifications, was initially superimposed on stage [3]: Beethoven used upward stems to distinguish notes belonging to the later stage until he could continue it on a separate stave (after stave 14 stage [3] joins up with stage [2] on stave 15; stage [4] continues separately from stave 14 to stave 16).

The result of all this revision was a passage of music which eventually served as the basis of bars 15–33 in the final version. But while the remainder of the development in the final version functions essentially as dominant preparation for the recapitulation, the continuity draft on folio 4^v takes a very different direction. The dominant seventh of E does indeed appear at the end of stages [2/3] and [4]; but it is preceded by a climactic arrival on the dominant of C♯ minor with a sustained G♯ in the upper voice. The harmonic setting of G♯ suggested by the figured-bass numerals in stage [2/3] is made clearer in a subsidiary sketch accompanying the draft (Ex. 3.18).

Comparison with Ex. 3.15, the previous sketch for the retransition,

---

[13] It may have been his decision to extend the second phrase of the first group in this way which led Beethoven ultimately to cast the movement in 2/4 rather than 4/4. Seen against the originally prevailing 4/4 metre of Ex. 3.16 (cf. n. 12, above), the phrase-extension (which is identical to that in the final version) involves adding an extra *half*-bar; this metrical problem is avoided if 2/4 metre is adopted.

Ex. 3.17. Grasnick 20b, fol. 4ᵛ, st. 11–16

Ex. 3.18. Grasnick 20b, fol. 4ᵛ, st. 16

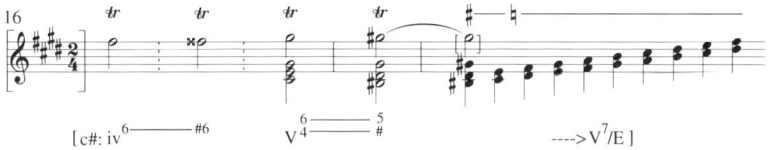

is instructive. Ex. 3.15 revealed an emphasis on the submediant at the expense of the dominant seventh of E. What is so striking in the present instance is the idea of replacing the submediant triad by its own dominant, G♯: the change serves as a powerful means of undermining the (E-major) tonic force of the pitch G♯ at precisely the point where we would expect that force to be strongly asserted.

Ex. 3.19. Projected voice-leading plan suggested by Ex. 3.17

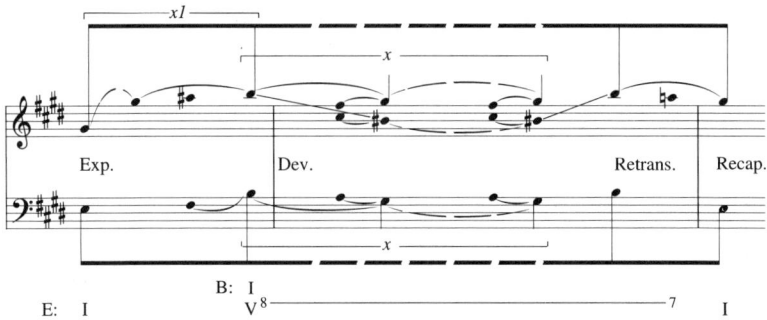

And now we may begin to see that the emphasis laid on the submediant in earlier sketches may have been prompted more by the fact that its dominant is G♯ rather than by Beethoven's desire to explore a direct relationship between E major and C♯ minor.

Closer scrutiny of the various stages of work in Ex. 3.17 offers yet further insight into Beethoven's exploration of G♯ and the submediant. The climactic arrival on G♯ noted above was first tested in stage [2]. In stage [3] Beethoven went on to introduce material which was eventually taken over into the left hand of bars 17–27 in the final version. That material includes the important arrival on the dominant of C♯ minor in bar 21, an arrival which marks the end of a distinct subsection within the development. As discussed in Chapter 1, Schenker noted the importance of this moment and the 'motivic' connection $g\sharp^3-b^3$ between bars 21 and 42 which he believed resulted from Beethoven's composing-out of the initial upbeat interval. What the sketch material suggests is that this intermediate harmonic goal (V/C♯ minor) in bar 21 of the final version was conceived at a time when the main climax of the development was set to occur on the identical harmony, and with G♯ in the upper voice. With this in mind, Ex. 3.19 tries to suggest how Beethoven may have understood the tonal structure of the exposition and development at this stage in the composition of the movement. The arch structure shown earlier in Ex. 3.11b remains unaffected; but within the prolonged dominant of E there now occurs a prolonged dominant of C♯ minor, so that during the development the interval B–G♯ is composed out in both outer voices. While Schenker's reading of the final version is not applicable to the development as sketched in Ex. 3.17, Beethoven's aim—to compose out the initial upper-voice interval $g\sharp^1-b^1$—seems to have been essentially the same in each case.

One final illustration of Beethoven's continuing fascination with

G♯ in this continuity draft remains to be considered. In Ex. 3.17, the arpeggiated dominant seventh of E at the end of stage [2/3] concludes with the notes f♯², f𝕩², each marked with a trill. (Ex. 3.18 shows f𝕩² in an implicitly different harmonic setting.) No doubt f𝕩² was intended as a passing note leading to g♯² at the start of the recapitulation, in which context g♯² would naturally be heard as the triadic third in E major. But the implied progression f𝕩²–g♯² seems also to recall two earlier events. In the first place it suggests the tonicization of G♯ minor earlier in the development. But a more remote connection is even more significant. In the continuity draft from which Ex. 3.17 is taken, the varied repeat of the second group in the exposition includes the chromatic passing note G which had first been introduced in the preceding draft on folio 4ʳ (see Ex. 3.13 and the related text; the actual pitch succession in the present draft, on folio 4ᵛ, is g♯³–g³–f♯³). Thus the progression f♯²–f𝕩²–[g♯²] leading into the recapitulation would recall and reverse the descending line in the exposition: while G leads away from G♯ to F♯, F𝕩 leads up from F♯ to re-establish G♯. In view of Beethoven's apparent interest in G/F𝕩 and its relationship to G♯ in earlier sketches, the presence, however fleeting, of f𝕩² here should not go unremarked.[14]

Ex. 3.19 shows that Beethoven's plans for the development section had so far left the large-scale 'E-tonicizing' progression intact. The next (and final) continuity draft was to change all that. This draft, which begins at the top of folio 5ʳ, starts with the end of the development and continues through the recapitulation to the close of the movement. The opening is shown in Ex. 3.20a.

The re-establishment of the tonic at the beginning of the recapitulation is now deprived of any dominant (that is, V/E) preparation; instead, the development ends with a sustained dominant of C♯ minor and the recapitulation begins after a brief pause. Although such a procedure is by no means unprecedented in the classical period,[15] its use here is undoubtedly less a matter of stylistic choice than the logical outcome of the increasing emphasis given to the submediant and its dominant, G♯, in Beethoven's plans for the

---

[14] Although F𝕩 does not link F♯ and G♯ at the beginning of the recapitulation in the final version, an analogous chromatic link is to be found between the end of the recapitulation and the beginning of the coda. In bar 65, following the ascending E-major arpeggio spanning more than four octaves, the unharmonized pair b²–b♯² is heard in longer note values and within a ritardando. Although both notes are heard in the context of the tonic-key arpeggio, the leading-note function of b♯² recalls earlier tonicizations of the submediant, in the second group of the exposition and in the development. This time no such tonicization takes place: c♯³ at the beginning of the coda occurs within subdominant harmony. Yet the *suggestion* of a tonicized submediant remains, albeit more visually than aurally.

[15] See e.g. the first movement of Haydn's String Quartet in E♭, Op. 64 No. 6, bars 95–8.

Ex. 3.20. *a* Grasnick 20b, fol. 5ʳ, st. 1/2

b Projected voice-leading plan suggested by Ex. 3.20*a*

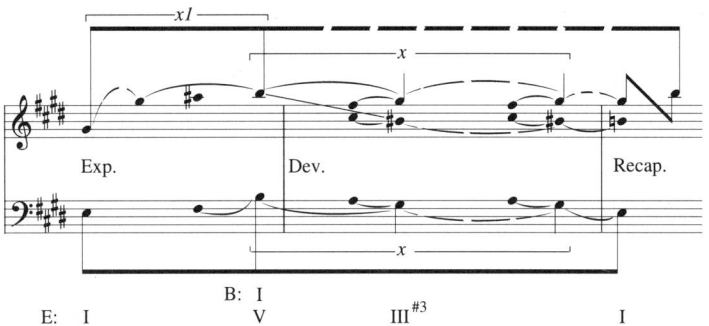

development and retransition. And the voice-leading consequences of this revised retransition may be read in Ex. 3.20*b*: the suppression of the dominant of E necessarily prevents the completion of the 'E-tonicizing' progression. Although G♯ returns in the upper voice at the beginning of the recapitulation, the B which has been in force since the beginning of the development remains melodically active also.[16]

Although it was clearly conceived as a sketch for the first movement, Ex. 3.20*a* bears upon the genesis of the second movement of Op. 109 in two respects. First, it is obvious that the sketches for the first movement betray a keen concern for the submediant, a concern probably engendered by Beethoven's more general interest in G♯, which happens to be the dominant of the submediant in E major. The sketches for the second movement, in E minor, likewise reveal a concern for the submediant degree; and this concern again led

---

[16] B, the melodic goal of the 'B-tonicizing' progression, is of course also a member of the tonic triad of the movement. My argument is that Beethoven's plan demanded that B, reached from G♯ via the 'B-tonicizing' progression spanning the exposition, be 'resolved' back to G♯ via the 'E-tonicizing' progression; that progression was necessary to counterbalance the events of the exposition and to re-establish G♯ as the principal melodic pitch (in Schenkerian terms, the *Kopfton*), since B could otherwise function in this capacity in the recapitulation precisely by virtue of its membership of the E-major triad.

Beethoven to a radical reconsideration of the form of the whole movement at one stage. Secondly, and more importantly, the retransition (bars 97–104) in the second movement bears a close relationship to the idea tried out for the first movement in Ex. 3.20a. In the second-movement retransition there is no dominant preparation of E minor; instead, bars 97–104 prepare the dominant of the dominant, B minor, so that the recapitulation seems initially to begin on the subdominant in that key. While it is disappointing that no sketches for this part of the second movement exist, it may not be entirely fortuitous; since he had tried out and eventually rejected a similar plan for the first movement, Beethoven may have been able to rely largely on these earlier sketches when composing the second movement.

The remainder of the continuity draft for the recapitulation need not detain us long. Beethoven seems to have suffered a temporary lapse of concentration when writing out the second phrase of the first group, for in its earliest form it followed the exposition model exactly, preparing B instead of E major as the key of the second group. This lapse may have occurred because Beethoven was literally copying from an earlier draft: taken as a whole, this recapitulation certainly seems closely modelled on the immediately preceding exposition draft (folio 4^v; cf. Exx. 3.16–17). Similarly, Beethoven's immediate correction of the offending phrase appears to borrow directly from the corresponding one in his previous attempt at the recapitulation, in the draft on folio 4^r; two further stages of revision were necessary on folio 5^r to establish the six-bar second phrase which appears in the recapitulation first group (bars 52–8) in the final version.

Things went more smoothly once the tonal orientation of this second phrase had been settled. The treatment of the varied repeat in the second group (Ex. 3.21a) is surprising on two counts. First, there is no sign of the introduction of G as the dominant of C major, as in earlier sketches (Ex. 3.9) and in the final version. Instead, a chromatic passing note, c^3, is introduced between $c\sharp^3$ and b^2 in the descending line from d^3. This passing note corresponds to the g^1 first introduced in the exposition (see again Ex. 3.13). The second surprise, one related to the inserted c^3, is the substitution of an F$\sharp$-major arpeggio for the expected F$\sharp$-minor one in the second bar of the varied repeat. Ex. 3.21b gives an interpretation of the voice leading implied in this passage and shows that the major-mode arpeggio derives from the interpolation of another chromatic passing note, this time in the bass. Whereas the upper-voice pair d^3–$c\sharp^3$ would properly be supported in tenths by B–A in the bass (compare

Ex. 3.21. *a* Grasnick 20b, fol. 5^r, st. 10/11–fol. 5^v, st. 1

b Cf. Ex. 3.21*a*, bars 1–3, and Ex. 3.14

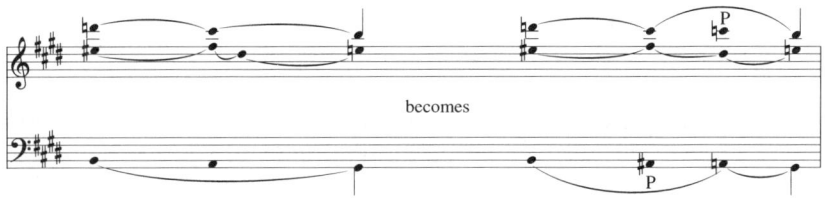

the final version, bars 58–9), A♯ is introduced as the support for c♯^{3} so that A remains free to support the interpolated passing c^3. The resultant F♯-major harmony has a similarly bright and startling effect to that of the D♯ major in the corresponding bar (bar 13) of the exposition in the final version.

As well as omitting the appearance of C major in the second group, the recapitulation draft beginning on folio 5^r does not include a coda, plans for which had been adumbrated considerably earlier (see Ex. 3.8*c*). Instead, the movement ends with wide-ranging scales leading up to e^3 as the final pitch: the scales grow out of the cadence which closes the varied repeat of the second group. But ideas for a coda do emerge in subsequent revisions to the draft and in a series of sketches filling the rest of folio 5^{r-v}. Most of these ideas use the material presented in Ex. 3.8c and themselves form the basis of the first section (bars 65–74) of the coda in the final version. None of the sketches shows the passage of chords in bars 75–85 of the final version; this must have been formulated later, for the only surviving sketches appear in the pocket sketchbook BH 107.

Of the coda sketches on Grasnick 20b, folio 5^{r-v}, four which indicate a new approach to the ending of the movement are particularly interesting (Ex. 3.22a–d). Ex. 3.22a and d are written in pencil; Ex. 3.22b and c are written in ink. It is likely that the ink sketches were written first, but this chronology cannot be firmly established.[17] What is clear at a glance is that Beethoven's plan to end the movement on a high note (literally, e^3: see Exx. 3.8c and 3.21a) had now been abandoned. Particularly noticeable is the consistent final rhythmic gesture, further articulated by means of dynamic emphasis in Ex. 3.22a and c. But it is the return of the 'E-tonicizing' progression in Ex. 3.22b and d which catches the eye and ear most strongly. The complete progression, b–a–g♯, appears at the end of Ex. 3.22d—the low register is reminiscent of the ending of Ex. 3.3a, and also foreshadows the final version—while in Ex. 3.22b a^2–$g\sharp^2$ forms the final melodic cadence, implying V^7–I in E major.[18] There can be no doubt that the reappearance of the 'E-tonicizing' progression here is directly related to its suppression in the retransition to the recapitulation. The tension between G♯ and B resulting from that suppression was now to be resolved only at the very end of the movement, and the span of the broad arch structure illustrated in Ex. 3.11b was to be correspondingly extended.

Ex. 3.22e summarizes this latest large-scale structural plan. But the decisive closure and neat symmetry suggested here are in fact already challenged by Ex. 3.22a and c. In a sense, these two sketches each contain not one but two endings. First there is an arrival on $g\sharp^1$ or $g\sharp^2$, stressed by the forte dynamic and preceding crescendo (in Ex. 3.22c $g\sharp^2$ is even introduced from a^2). But this arrival is immediately undercut by the ensuing afterbeats, both piano. In Ex. 3.22c these beats articulate nothing other than the reverse of the initial upper-voice interval: b^2–$g\sharp^2$. This reinforces the situation at the beginning of the recapitulation, where b^2 is not 'resolved' through

---

[17] The sketch transcribed in Ex. 3.22c (the opening bars are omitted) is the only one of the four which Beethoven supplied with a closing double barline. Might this indicate that it was the first to be written, the other three being conceived later in its wake?

[18] The literal absence of b^2 here is not critical to the 'E-tonicizing' function: it is the semitonal progressions A♯–B (implying V–I/B) and A–G♯ (implying V^7–I/E) which most fundamentally distinguish the 'B-' and 'E-tonicizing' progressions in terms of which the sketches and final version are analysed in this chapter.

74 Sketches for First Movement

Ex. 3.22. *a* Grasnick 20b, fol. 5^r, st. 16

b Grasnick 20b, fol. 5^v, st. 2–3

c Grasnick 20b, fol. 5^v, st. 4–6

d Grasnick 20b, fol. 5^v, st. 6/7

e Voice-leading plan for entire movement, suggested by Ex. 3.22*b* and *d*

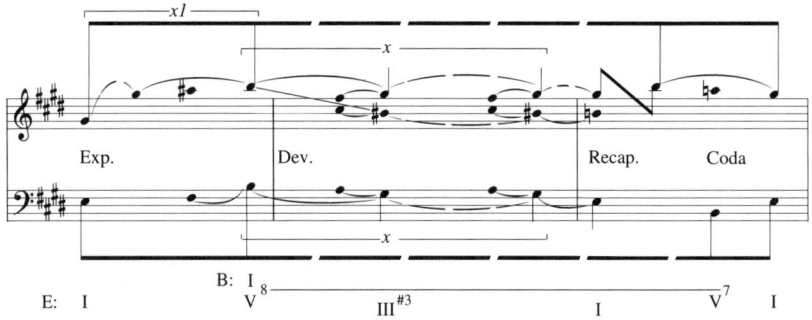

a^2 to $g\sharp^2$ (see Ex. 3.20): the movement ends with the tension between the triadic third and fifth left unresolved. The other sketch, Ex. 3.22a, may be thought to go further, since $g\sharp^1$, introduced from below rather than above, is followed by the pair b^1–e^1. This outlining of the tonic triad could be seen as a step *en route* to the closed-position triads at the end of the final version. To see that ending emerge in greater detail we must put aside the desk sketchleaves in Grasnick 20b and open the pocket sketchbook.

The Pocket Sketches: BH 107, pages 39–41, 43; BSk 27/75, folio 1ʳ

Anyone coming to the pocket sketches for the first movement of Op. 109 after making a thorough study of those on the Grasnick 20b leaves is bound to be struck by their different characteristics. There are no continuity drafts among the pocket sketches; only strictly delimited passages of the movement are presented. Viewed in their entirety, the Grasnick sketches give a fairly clear picture of the growth of the whole movement, of the grafting of new details and refinements on to an existing framework; by comparison, the pocket sketches provide only glimpses of particular details caught at a single evolutionary stage. To turn from the desk to the pocket sources is to substitute still photography for a movie film. But this is not to devalue the pocket sketches: on the contrary, their limited scope is itself significant in relation to what we know already from the Grasnick 20b leaves.

This last point becomes clearer when we consider that of the total of fourteen pocket sketches, eight deal with only two parts of the movement: there are four sketches for the end of the development and the retransition, and four for the very end of the movement. Moreover, most of the lengthier pocket sketches are included among these eight. Beethoven's concentration on these two areas is easy to understand: the Grasnick sketches show that his decision to suppress the 'E-tonicizing' progression at the retransition profoundly affected his approach to the ending. Although they show that further revisions had taken place, the pocket sketches reinforce the theory that changes made in one of these two areas of the movement inevitably entailed corresponding changes in the other.

The sketches for the end of the development and retransition show that Beethoven had abandoned the idea of a climax on the dominant of C♯ minor with no subsequent dominant preparation of E. Indeed, there is no trace of the submediant now; the dominant of E is the solitary goal, and the upper voice drives towards b^2 or beyond to b^3 (Ex. 3.23a–b). But although the dominant of E is reinstated, it is

Ex. 3.23. *a* BH 107, p. 39, st. 6

b BH 107, p. 40, st. 4–7

significant that the sketches show no sign of a parallel reinstatement of the 'E-tonicizing' progression in the upper voice.

Correspondingly, the 'E-tonicizing' progression now disappears at the end of the movement also. The strongest trace of it is to be found in Ex. 3.24*a*, a sketch which is clearly derived from those transcribed above in Ex. 3.22. Here in BH 107 the upper voice does at least drive towards the progression a^1–$g\sharp^1$; but the bass B♮ gives a submediant inflection to the harmony and strongly undermines any tonic implications expected of $g\sharp^1$. (The first two bars of Ex. 3.24*a* were later taken over into bars 75–8 of the final version.) Ex. 3.24*b* is more typical of the sketches for the ending. Here the final note is indeed the triadic third, g♯; but it is overshadowed by the preceding thrice-repeated b^2, whose registral prominence further stresses the disconnection—the absence of a linking A, as in the 'E-tonicizing' progression—between the two pitches. As well as revealing Beethoven's growing tendency to stress B at the expense of G♯ at the close of the movement, Ex. 3.24*b* suggests the extent to which the ending was more generally modelled on the new shape adopted for the development and retransition. Just as in Ex. 3.23*b* (to take one example) there is an upward sweep from the middle register to b^2 and beyond, so in Ex. 3.24*b* the melodic line arpeggiates up from b to b^2 before returning to g♯ for the close.

Ex. 3.24. *a* BH 107, p. 39, st. 7/8

b BH 107, p. 40, st. 1–2

The last two pocket sketches (Ex. 3.25*a*–*b*) make the connection with the development and retransition even more obvious in that they eschew the low-register conclusion. The final ascent from b reaches up instead to b^2 or b^3—the precise melodic goals of the retransition sketches—and stays there. Ex. 3.25*a* is one of two sketches which show something of the passage of block chords in bars 75–85 of the final version; it also shows that Beethoven considered omitting the material which follows that passage there (bars 86–97), although something close to it had already appeared in Ex. 3.24*b*. Most telling in Ex. 3.25*a*, though, is the way in which it ends with G♯ and B, the two notes of *x1*, the initial upbeat interval, fused into a vertical unit with B significantly doubled in the right hand.

Conclusion

The sketches studied in this chapter reveal much about the genesis of the first movement of Op. 109. There is, moreover, a comforting logic to the sequence of events: early, relatively vague ideas gradually yield to more concrete formulations, and the final version seems to grow before our eyes as one continuity draft succeeds another and new details are incorporated into the existing framework. If any series of sketches were to convince us that musical composition, for Beethoven, consisted in an unerring and inexorable progression from chaos to order, it might be this one. And yet composition rarely proceeds in such a fashion; we must distinguish the order which we impose on the sketches—themselves only a partial record of the creative process—from any order imposed by the composer. Yet notwithstanding such caveats, these sketches for the first movement of Op. 109 lend powerful support to the idea that in this case

78 *Sketches for First Movement*

Ex. 3.25. *a* BH 107, p. 41, st. 4/5–10/11

b BH 107, p. 43, st. 5–9 (cf. Plate 4)

Ex. 3.26. Op. 109, first movement: large-scale voice-leading summary

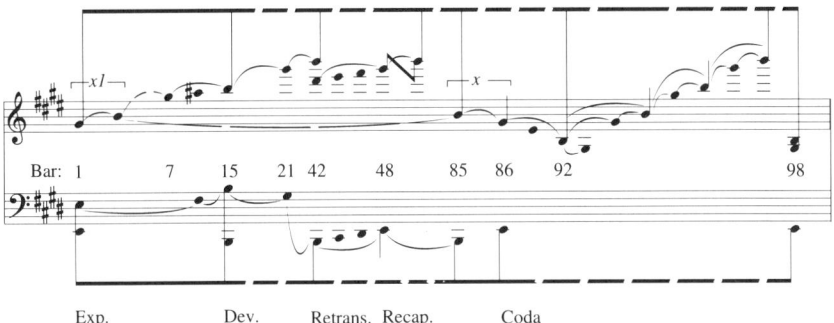

Beethoven was working against the background of a controlling plan.

That plan centred upon the derivation of large-scale voice-leading progressions in the upper voice from the initial upper-voice interval. The two notes of the interval, G♯ and B, were to signify the tonic and dominant keys respectively. The tonicization of B underpinning the exposition would be correlated with the 'B-tonicizing' progression G♯–A♯–B in the upper voice. The development and retransition would support the 'E-tonicizing' progression B–A–G♯, so that the V^7–I cadence introducing the recapitulation and the return of the tonic key would simultaneously confirm the melodic 'resolution' of B back to G♯. Beethoven subsequently chose to leave the 'E-tonicizing' progression incomplete until the end of the movement, thereby creating a tension between B and G♯ during the recapitulation; and the final pocket sketches show him suppressing the 'E-tonicizing' progression even at the close. The melodic primacy of G♯ is assured only in the first group of the exposition.

The same is true of the final version, a voice-leading summary of which is given in Ex. 3.26 (compare Exx. 3.19, 3.20b, and 3.22e which provide similar, partially conjectural summaries based on the sketches). The 'B-tonicizing' progression spans the exposition, but the 'E-tonicizing' progression is avoided at the retransition: b^3 is hammered out thirteen times between bars 42–8, and although a^3 is present as an inner voice Beethoven carefully avoids any direct connection between it and the melodic $g♯^3$ at the start of the recapitulation. The emphasis given to b^3 during the retransition carries through into the first two beats of the recapitulation. This, coupled with the fact that $g♯^3$ is introduced by an ascent from $d♯^3$ as opposed to a descent from b^3, creates the impression that b^3 is the primary upper-voice pitch while $g\sharp^3$ is part of an inner voice; unlike the beginning of the exposition, the primacy of $g\sharp^3$ over b^3 is now not clearly established. Ex. 3.26 suggests that the lack of melodic closure at the point of recapitulation also affects the bass: the return of the tonic in bar 48 is interpreted as part of a larger dominant prolongation which extends to the final structural cadence in bars 85–6 (compare Ex. 3.22e).

That B has effectively replaced G♯ in the upper voice is made clear early in the coda when the initial upper-voice interval is reversed (b^2–$g\sharp^2$ in bar 67, b^1–$g\sharp^1$ in bar 69) to take the form it assumed in the very first sketches for the movement.[19] This same reversal occurs together with the final structural cadence in bars 85–6. And the point is reinforced in the last phrase, which begins in bar 92. The two notes of the initial interval, each one introduced from an upper appoggiatura, are stated in a rising sequence in alternate bars. Significantly, the sequence begins with B (specifically, b) rather than G♯; and since the first bar of each two-bar group is relatively strong (the strong–weak grouping of two-bar units begins in bar 86), B receives greater metrical stress than G♯. In addition, the reverse form of the initial interval (that is, x rather than $x1$) reappears attached to b, b^1, and b^2 in bars 92, 94, and 96. The rising sequence demands that $g\sharp^3$ appear in bar 97, but in fact b^2 is repeated from bar 96. Only on the last quaver beat of bar 97 does the expected $g\sharp^3$ arrive, together with b^3: a fleeting reminiscence, in this highest register, of the opening event of the movement. Finally, the closing triads return to the registral point of origin in bar 92: the notes of the initial interval are fused into a vertical unit with b above g♯. This *unvollkommener Schluß* (Schenker's term, discussed in Chapter 1) confirms that the symmetrical structure contemplated in the sketches has been left incomplete. And the double-single barline which Beethoven substituted for the original double one at the end of the first movement in the autograph (again, see Chapter 1) constitutes a particularly vivid sign of his sense of this structural incompleteness. His decision to leave the movement unfinished, so to speak, had far-reaching consequences for the next part of the sonata which he composed: not the second movement, but the third-movement theme. The sketches for this are the subject of Chapter 4.

[19] The reversal also appears at a significant point near the beginning of the recapitulation. In the exposition, the inner-voice descent $g\sharp^1$–g♯ in bars 1–4 ends with a restatement of the initial upper-voice interval at the lower octave (g♯–b). At the corresponding point in the recapitulation, Beethoven rewrote the inner voice so that the main descent reaches only as far as b^2: a^2–$g\sharp^2$ in bars 51–2 merely prolongs b^2. As a result, the *reversed* initial interval b^2–$g\sharp^2$ appears on the downbeat of bar 52. The subtle rewriting of this first phrase in the first group of the recapitulation neatly conveys the changed relationship between G♯ and B.

4. The Sketches for the Third-Movement Theme

In Chapter 2 it was argued that the composition of the first movement of Op. 109, originally as an independent work, probably marked Beethoven's return to serious composition after a period of relative inactivity caused by the mounting struggle for guardianship of his nephew Karl. Having thus renewed his compositional drive, he worked hard at the Credo of the *Missa solemnis*. This new burst of activity overflowed from the Wittgenstein sketchbook into Artaria 195, the first thirty-four pages of which are entirely taken up with Credo sketches. But work on the Mass peters out halfway down page 35, and the sketch transcribed in Ex. 4.1 appears on stave 8. This could hardly be called a 'sketch' for Op. 109 in any strict sense; yet the implicit key and explicit time signature call to mind the second movement of the sonata. Ex. 4.1 is perhaps best regarded as a kind of route marker indicating a change of direction, a turning aside from sacred music on the grandest scale to the more intimate world of the piano: the semiquaver figuration seems appropriate to that instrument.

The remainder of page 35 and staves 1/2 of page 36 were taken up with two other sketches which definitely belong to the genesis of the second movement (they are discussed in Chapter 5). But this seems to have been as much work on that movement as Beethoven was prepared to commit to Artaria 195 for the time being. The next sketch on page 36 (Ex. 4.2) was clearly intended for something else. The melodic profile of this short entry links it closely with the variation theme, while the suggestion of a two-part form employing inversion of the outer voices ('2ter the[i]l rechte Hand den Bass linke H.[and] den Gesang') conjures up both the binary structure of the theme and the display of invertible counterpoint in Variation 3; moreover, we shall see that in the final version of the theme itself there is indeed a subtle contrapuntal relationship involving not only the upper voice and bass but some inner voices also. If the physical position of Ex. 4.2 corresponds to its chronological one (and there is little reason to doubt this), then Beethoven may already have worked on the theme elsewhere, either on other sketchleaves or at the piano. However, the sequence of six sketches for the theme

Ex. 4.1. Artaria 195, p. 35, st. 8

Ex. 4.2. Artaria 195, p. 36, st. 3/4

et[c] 2ter the[i]l rechte Hand den Bass linke H.[and] den Gesang

which fills the rest of page 36 and the bottom three staves of page 37 suggests that any such work had not been extensive.

Before analysing these sketches—and since there are only six of them they may all be transcribed and studied—a little more should be said about their physical characteristics. With one small exception, they are written entirely in pencil. The exception occurs in the second of the six (Ex. 4.4a); the main body of this sketch is written in pencil, but at some point Beethoven revised the last four bars in ink. When did he do so? Although ink sketching begins on page 38, and ink remains the primary medium until page 71, there is good reason to link this four-bar revision with two much later sketches for the theme, on page 53 (see Plate 7). By the time he had reached this page, Beethoven had finished sketching the second movement and had begun working on the third-movement variations, sketches for which begin on page 50.[1] Both of the sketches for the theme on page 53 are written in ink. The second one, on staves 12–16, is extremely detailed, heavily revised, and very similar to the final version. It was undoubtedly the last of the surviving theme sketches to be written and may be regarded as a preliminary autograph version. Now the ink revision to the sketch on page 36 is closely related to a layer of revisions in this detailed sketch on page 53. And the other theme sketch on

[1] A last, isolated, sketch for the second movement appears in pencil on p. 55, a page otherwise taken up with part of a variation sketch. The pencil sketch clearly belongs outside the main phase of composition for the second movement, and may have been occasioned by problems which Beethoven encountered in writing out that movement in the autograph MS.

page 53 is really no more than a copy, with slight modifications, of the bass line of a further sketch on page 36 (see Ex. 4.5). It seems clear, then, that before making his final assault on the theme in Artaria 195 Beethoven looked back at his earlier sketches on pages 36–7 and transferred the bass line of one of them to page 53, where he was then working; it was probably at this time also that he made the anomalous ink revision to the second of those earlier sketches.

Finally, it is noticeable that the variation sketches on pages 50–3— that is, those preceding the final, detailed sketch for the theme— imply certain details which do not appear in the theme sketches on pages 36–7. For instance, the parallelism between bars 1–2 and 5–6 of the final version is not apparent in the sketches on pages 36–7 but is clearly implied in a variation sketch on pages 50–1. This suggests either that Beethoven made other sketches for the theme which no longer survive or that certain refinements did not require recourse to pen and paper.[2] Whatever the explanation for this anomaly, let us now turn to a more detailed examination of the surviving sketches for the variation theme in Op. 109.

The first sketch from page 36 is transcribed in Ex. 4.3. In its original form, prior to the 'Vi = de' revision, it consisted of a single four-bar phrase. Although the first two bars already come very close to the final version—the descending thirds $g\sharp^1$–e^1 and $d\sharp^1$–b in the upper voice remain unchanged throughout the sketching—bars 3 and 4 are considerably different. Despite the sharply rising contour of the foreground, the underlying direction of the phrase is downward rather than upward. This downward motion, shown on the analytical stave placed above the transcription in Ex. 4.3, is quite different to the ascending line from $g\sharp^1$ to b^1 found in bars 3–4 of the final version. Beethoven's later revision and extension of Ex. 4.3 remained committed to descending motion in the upper voice. No reductive analysis is required to show the stepwise descent $g\sharp^1$–$c\sharp^1$ spanning the first half ($f\sharp^1$ is implied by the bass $F\sharp$ in the second bar of the '= de' extension) or the descent from a^1 (functioning as upper neighbour to $g\sharp^1$) to e^1 in the second half. The upper voice of this completed theme composes out an easily perceptible $\hat{3}$–$\hat{2}$–$\hat{1}$ ($g\sharp^1$–$f\sharp^1$–$e\sharp^1$) *Urlinie*.

---

[2] A further possibility which might be considered has been aired by Christopher Reynolds in connection with the variation finale of the Violin Sonata in A, Op. 30 No. 1: 'The genesis of the theme was not a question of arduous work that had to be completed before commencing the variations. Instead, the refinements of the theme are products of the variations ostensibly generated by them. What has been thought to be a derivative relationship now should be viewed as reciprocal.' See 'Ends and Means in the Second Finale to Beethoven's Op. 30, No. 1', in L. Lockwood and P. Benjamin (eds.), *Beethoven Essays: Studies in Honor of Elliot Forbes* (Cambridge, Mass., 1984), 142. In the case of Op. 109 there appears to be no evidence to support the claims which Reynolds makes for Op. 30 No. 1.

84 Sketches for Third-Movement Theme

Ex. 4.3. Artaria 195, p. 36, st. 6/7–8/9

The revised version of Ex. 4.3 results in a binary-form theme (4 + 4 bars with repeats: presumably Beethoven intended the first half to be repeated as well as the second) which already shares several features with the final version. There is the parallelism between bars 1 and 3; the pervasive use of the sarabande-like ♩ ♩. ♪ rhythm; and the melodic sequence in the second half. Also prophetic is the arrival on a^1 above an implied supertonic triad at the beginning of the second half. This event was to reappear at the beginning of the last phrase (bars 13–16) in the final version, following the G♯-minor cadence in the preceding bar. (The sketch even foreshadows the melodic succession $g\sharp^1$–a^1, although the harmonic implications are different and the metrical placement of a^1 in relation to $g\sharp^1$ is much weaker: compare the final version, bars 12–13.) But none of these similarities should blind us to the differences between the revised Ex. 4.3 and the final version; the most glaring disparity between the two is the central cadence on the submediant, as opposed to the dominant, in the sketch.

The next sketch (Ex. 4.4a) records further developments. Although it presents only the second half of the theme, it implies certain changes

Ex. 4.4 *a* Artaria 195, p. 36, st. 10/11–14

b Cf. Ex. 4.4*a*

in the first half. Most obvious is the replacement of the submediant by the dominant at the central cadence.[3] And the fact that this second half is now eight rather than four bars in length suggests a corresponding expansion of the first half of the theme. The use of a sequence around the circle of fifths in bars 2–6 may be regarded as an outgrowth of the sequence in the second half of the revised Ex. 4.3. Other connections with that earlier sketch include the rhythmic augmentation, in the last two bars of Ex. 4.4*a*, of the stepwise descent $g\sharp^1$–$f\sharp^1$–e^1 in the last bar of Ex. 4.3, and the fact that in Ex. 4.4*a* a middleground descent, in this case from B to E, controls both outer voices (see Ex. 4.4*b*).

---

[3] The letter 'h' at the beginning of Ex. 4.4*a* stands for B [major] and seems to underline the altered central cadence already expressed in the sketch itself.

86 *Sketches for Third-Movement Theme*

Ex. 4.5. Artaria 195, p. 36, st. 12/13–15/16

The changes to the first half of the theme implied by Ex. 4.4*a* are made explicit in Ex. 4.5, which directly follows that previous sketch in Artaria 195. The length of the first half has indeed been doubled from four to eight bars, and the harmonic goal both of the first four-bar phrase and of the entire sketch is no longer the submediant but the dominant, B major. But Ex. 4.5 testifies to a much more radical change in Beethoven's conception of the theme. Whereas in earlier sketches the underlying direction in the upper voice had been downward, now it is ascending motion which controls the linear flow in both outer voices. The change is especially noticeable in the bass, which climbs relentlessly through two and a half octaves from E to b^1, but it also effects a major reshaping of the upper voice. An ascending third-progression, $g\sharp^1-a\sharp^1-b^1$, now spans the first four bars and is repeated an octave higher in bars 6–8 as the melodic line continues to rise. The revisions in bars 7–8 emphasize Beethoven's concern for this third-progression. At first a^2 intervened between $g\sharp^2$ and $a\sharp^2$; it was removed, making the approach to $a\sharp^2$ more direct. And bar 8 was totally rewritten in order to retain $a\sharp^2$ in the upper voice for two further beats before its upward resolution to b^2. (The original upper voice in this bar, $b^2-g^2-f\sharp^2$, was modified and transferred to the inner voice as $g^2-e^2-d\sharp^2$.)

The similarity between Ex. 4.5 and the final version of bars 1–8 will be obvious. The main difference between the two concerns the register of bars 5–8. In the sketch these bars effect an upward register transfer, from $g\sharp^1-b^1$ to $g\sharp^2-b^2$. The final version takes the opposite direction: the upper voice descends to $g\sharp$ on the downbeat of bar 7, and a stepwise ascent through a♯ to b then follows. This downward shift may have been determined by Beethoven's decision to repeat bars 1–2 in bars 5–6 (as we shall see, this repeat was at first more literal than it was to become in the final version); the repetition of bar 2 necessarily took the upper voice down to b, forcing Beethoven to forgo the continued ascent which characterizes the second half of Ex. 4.5.

One similarity between Ex. 4.5 and the final version is perhaps not so obvious: the use of submediant harmony in bar 7 in association with a melodic G♯. In Ex. 4.5 the two events coincide: the submediant falls on the downbeat of bar 7 as the bass reaches its highest point, c♯^{2} (!), while above it the upper voice has g♯^{2}, tied over from the previous bar. In the final version the submediant harmony and appearance of G♯ are not coordinated, for g♯ occurs on the downbeat of bar 7 as part of a tonic chord while the following e^1 is harmonized as the third of the submediant triad. Several factors combine to stress this moment. The bass, which has been rising by step since bar 5, changes direction and falls a third from e to c♯; and unlike all previous notes in the bass voice, the c♯ (and the following c) is doubled at the lower octave. Simultaneously with the falling third in the bass, the upper voice leaps upward through a sixth—a large interval in the context of this theme—from g♯ to e^1. And although e^1 is expected, on the basis of its previous appearances on the second beat of bars 1, 3, and 5, the submediant harmony is surprising: e^1 has previously been heard only as part of a tonic triad.

It is precisely the weight, the emphasis given to this submediant in bar 7 of Ex. 4.5 and of the final version which is so important. We have seen that by the time he wrote Ex. 4.5 Beethoven had abandoned the idea of a central cadence in the submediant. Yet he seems to have wanted to stress this harmony in some other way. Further evidence for this claim is provided by an alternative to bars 5–8 written at the bottom of page 37 and cued into Ex. 4.5 by means of an 'oder 6ô' connective. Ex. 4.6 shows the composite new eight-bar first half. The second four-bar phrase is now controlled by submediant harmony as far as the second beat of bar 7. It is interesting to note the gradual stepwise ascent from g♯^{1} (bar 1) to e^2 (bar 6): the emphatic leap g♯–e^1 in bar 7 of the final version may owe something to this progression.

Only two of the six sketches on pages 36–7 remain to be discussed, and since they are very similar in content they may be presented together (Ex. 4.7a–b). They were probably the last of the six to be written, so it seems appropriate that they both deal with the end of the theme. The identity between the revised first bar (d♯^{1}–e^1–f♯^{1}) of

88 Sketches for Third-Movement Theme

Ex. 4.6. Artaria 195, p. 36, st. 12/13–p. 37, st. 14/15

Ex. 4.7. *a* Artaria 195, p. 36, st. 15   *b* Artaria 195, p. 37, st. 16

Ex. 4.7a and bar 6 of Ex. 4.4a in its original, pencil version suggests that Ex. 4.7a may have been conceived specifically as a revised ending for that sketch.

The most significant development recorded in these two sketches is the replacement of the melodic close on the tonic note, as in Exx. 4.3 and 4.4a, by one on the triadic third, g♯^{1}, preceded by a^1. Given that Beethoven was by now planning for the upper voice to unfold the ascending third G♯–A♯–B during the first half of the theme, the purpose of this new ending seems to have been to reverse that ascent over the course of the second half, giving a broad symmetrical arch structure to the upper voice as a whole (Ex. 4.8).[4]

Finally we come to the last sketch of all, the detailed one on staves 12–16 of page 53 in Artaria 195 (see Plate 7). It does indeed bear the hallmarks of a preliminary autograph version: the entire theme is sketched, including all inner and outer voices (but no phrasing); it is provided with the performance direction 'con molto sentimento ed espressivo', which became 'Andante molto cantabile ed espressivo' in the final version; in short, it is a fully performable composition.

---

[4] The linear ascent from g♯^{1} to b^1 is already implied in Ex. 4.4a, which shows the second half of the theme beginning on the dominant and with b^1 in the upper voice. But as Ex. 4.4b shows, the second half of the theme as conceived here is structured around an upper-voice descent to the tonic rather than to the triadic third.

Ex. 4.8. Projected arch structure for upper voice of theme

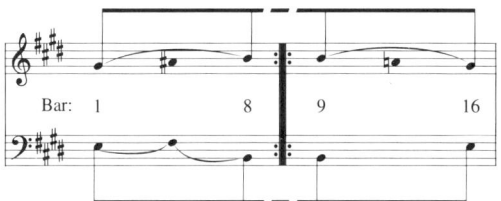

But despite the evolutionary 'gap' between it and the earlier sketches on pages 36–7, and despite its close similarity to the final version, in some ways it still represents work very much in progress. It bears several layers of revisions and corrections (the complexity of which makes it impractical to reproduce a full transcription), and some of the changes made may be more easily related to the earlier sketches than to the final version.

In general the upper voice corresponds almost exactly to that in the final version. There is only one difference in the first half: bar 5 was originally identical to bars 1 and 3, with g♯¹–e¹–f♯¹ allied to the sarabande rhythm. Only subsequently did Beethoven substitute b¹ for g♯¹ on the downbeat and insert g♯¹ before f♯¹, splitting the original quaver here into a pair of semiquavers. The substitution of b¹ for g♯¹ might be explained as a means of consolidating the linear ascent g♯¹–a♯¹–b¹ in bars 1–4; but although this revision to bar 5 was evidently made at quite a late stage (it is in pencil rather than the prevailing ink, which suggests that it dates from a later revisionary pass through the sketches), the retention of b¹ at the beginning of bar 5 already occurs in Ex. 4.5, the first sketch to record the ascending linear motion in the first half of the theme.

Ex. 4.9 shows the upper voice of bars 9–12 as given in this sketch. Beethoven's revisions repay close study. In all three versions the phrase leads to a cadence in G♯ minor. In versions [1] and [2] this cadence brings the descending third b¹–a♯¹–g♯¹ in the upper voice; but the function of this progression is not quite the same in each case. In version [1] the upper voice in bars 9–11 is identical to that in the final version; it articulates a clear middleground descent through the third b¹–a¹–g♯¹, thereby reversing the ascent through that same third which underlies the first half of the theme and prefiguring the larger descent from b¹ to g♯¹ which spans the entire second half. The cadential progression in bar 12 thus restates or summarizes this descending third-progression, although a♯¹ has to be substituted for a¹ in deference to the tonicization of G♯. In version [2] Beethoven

90   Sketches for Third-Movement Theme

Ex. 4.9. Artaria 195, p. 53, st. 12–14, 16

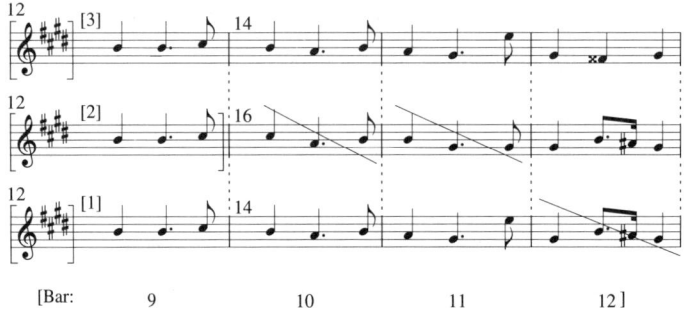

Ex. 4.10. *a* Cf. Ex. 4.9, version [2]   *b* Cf. Ex. 4.9, version [3]

tried replacing the appoggiaturas b^1 and a^1 at the beginning of bars 10 and 11 with a repetition of the preceding note ($c\sharp^2$ and b^1 respectively). But the effect of this was to keep b^1 active by means of its upper neighbour $c\sharp^2$ and thus to weaken the linear descent to $g\sharp^1$. As Ex. 4.10*a* shows, it is only with the foreground cadential progression in bar 12 that the descent from b^1 to $g\sharp^1$ is completed in this case. In version [3], therefore, Beethoven reinstated version [1] of bars 9–11; but he also transferred the foreground third-progression from the upper voice in bar 12 to the tenor, where it appears in equal crotchets, and substituted the simpler neighbour-note figure $g\sharp^1$–f_x^1–$g\sharp^1$ in the upper voice. Of the three versions it is this last, corresponding to the final version, which most directly expresses the middleground descent b^1–a^1–$g\sharp^1$ over the course of bars 9–12 (Ex. 4.10*b*).

The biggest surprise in the sketch on page 53 is reserved for the closing bars. Ex. 4.11 shows what appears to have been Beethoven's first idea for bars 15–16. While there is admittedly some doubt as to the exact motion in bar 15, there is none whatsoever about the last bar. The stepwise descent ($f\sharp^2$–e^2) to the final tonic note marks a return to the world of Exx. 4.3 and 4.4*a*, in which the upper voice of the theme composes out a $\hat{3}$–$\hat{2}$–$\hat{1}$ ($g\sharp^1$–$f\sharp^1$–e^1) *Urlinie*. And a concrete link with those earlier sketches is provided by the ink revision to Ex. 4.4*a* which, it has been argued, was probably added to that

Ex. 4.11. Artaria 195, p. 53, st. 14/15

sketch on page 36 at the time when Beethoven was working on page 53. In the ink revision to Ex. 4.4a the upper voice again closes on the tonic note, despite the fact that it must have been made *after* the two sketches shown in Ex. 4.7, both of which show the upper-voice close on g♯^{1} rather than e^1.

To be sure, the a^1–g♯^{1} close recorded in Ex. 4.7 is reinstated in revisions to the sketch on page 53. Yet to regard Ex. 4.11 as a passing whim, or even as a serious compositional 'U'-turn, might be to respond too naïvely to this new/old ending. The sudden leap up to the e^2 register here at the very end of the theme is curious: with the single exception of the fleeting e^2 in bar 11 (as in the final version) this register is not touched upon anywhere else. In view of this, the f♯^{2}–e^2 close in Ex. 4.11 is best regarded as a covering progression, one deriving from the doubling of the inner-voice pair f♯^{1}–e^1 (in fact the octave doubling is explicit in Ex. 4.11). Accordingly, the true upper-voice descent in the final bar remains a^1–g♯^{1}. Ex. 4.11 is an attempt to have one's structural cake and eat it, to preserve the elegant arch structure shown in Ex. 4.8 while at the same time creating a firmer sense of closure by means of a $\hat{3}$–$\hat{2}$–$\hat{1}$ *Urlinie*.

Before leaving this final, detailed theme sketch on page 53 a word is in order about Beethoven's treatment of the lower voices. The sketches on pages 36–7 deal mainly with the shaping of the upper voice, but sufficient indication of the melodically inclined bass is also given (see particularly Ex. 4.5). Yet in the sketch on page 53 Beethoven first tried out a much more static, homophonic accompaniment involving an inner-voice dominant pedal whose low register gives it considerable aural prominence (Ex. 4.12). This pedal was sustained until the first beat of bar 7 and then reintroduced one octave higher in bars 9–11. Although Beethoven eventually reinstated the moving bass in the first half, he retained the pedal in bars 9–11 of the final version, where it appears in the tenor voice.

92 Sketches for Third-Movement Theme

Ex. 4.12. Artaria 195, p. 53, st. 12/13

Conclusion

If the foregoing pages have at times induced a sense of *déjà lu*, this has been both intentional and inevitable. The single most important fact about the genesis of the variation theme in Op. 109 is that it appears to have run an almost identical course to that of the first movement of the sonata. Returning to the piano sonatas for Schlesinger after lengthy sketching for the Credo of the *Missa solemnis*, Beethoven took up again the compositional issues with which he had been concerned in the 'little new piece' later to become the first movement of Op. 109.

The parallels are remarkably specific. Consider three of Beethoven's early plans for the first movement: the idea of deriving large-scale voice-leading progressions from the initial upper-voice interval; the intended close on the tonic note (e^3) at the end of the movement; and the plan to close the exposition in the submediant. All three reappear in the first sketches for the theme. It seems that the theme was always to begin on $g\sharp^1$, the pitch Beethoven had chosen for the beginning of the first movement; and the initial upper-voice interval in the theme, $g\sharp^1-e^1$, was to be composed out as a $\hat{3}-\hat{2}-\hat{1}$ *Urlinie* (see Exx. 4.3 and 4.4*a*), a plan which inevitably entailed a close on the tonic note. Lastly, Ex. 4.3 shows that Beethoven at first envisaged a cadence in the submediant at the midpoint of the theme—a location comparable in structural status to the close of the exposition in a sonata-form movement. Going beyond this last point, recall that after he had decided to make the dominant the goal of the central cadence in the theme, Beethoven tried to emphasize the submediant elsewhere. Likewise, his decision to close the exposition of the first movement in the dominant instead of the submediant by no means inhibited him from experimenting with the submediant at other points, such as the end of the development and retransition.

The decision to close the first half of the theme in the dominant presumably led to the idea of composing out the third-progression G♯–A♯–B in the upper voice during bars 1–8. This marks another

Ex. 4.13. *a* Cf. Ex. 4.7*a*   *b* Cf. Ex. 4.7*b*

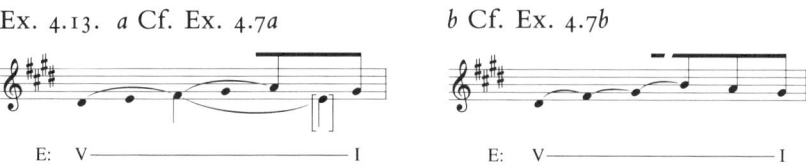

point of close contact with the sketches for the first movement, in which the 'B-tonicizing' progression G♯–A♯–B, derived from the initial upper-voice interval g♯¹–b¹, is composed out during the exposition. And renewed consideration of Ex. 4.5, the first sketch to show this ascending third-progression during the first half of the theme, powerfully reinforces the sense of a 'return' to the first movement which so many of these sketches convey. It was pointed out above that bars 5–8 of Ex. 4.5 differ markedly in register from the corresponding bars in the final version of the theme; and it was suggested that the low register reached in the final version is a consequence of the parallelism between bars 1–2 and 5–6, a parallelism not yet present in Ex. 4.5. But if we now think of Ex. 4.5 in relation not to the final version of the theme but to the first movement, it becomes clear that its deployment of register—the transfer of the initial g♯¹ to g♯² followed by the ascent a♯²–b²—directly matches what happens in the exposition of that earlier movement: g♯¹ is transferred up to g♯² in bar 7, a♯² follows in bar 8, and the b² expected in bar 9 is delayed until the close in bar 15.

The adoption of the 'B-tonicizing' progression in the first half of the theme led to the corresponding adoption of the 'E-tonicizing' progression B–A–G♯ in the second half; this much, at least, is suggested by the two sketches transcribed in Ex. 4.7, which show Beethoven's attempts to recast the final bars as a descent through a¹ to g♯¹ rather than through f♯¹ to e¹, as in Exx. 4.3 and 4.4*a*. (Ex. 4.7*a–b* must have been written after Ex. 4.5, in which the 'B-tonicizing' bars 1–8 make their first appearance.) Closer analysis of the endings sketched in Ex. 4.7 underlines how carefully Beethoven now sought to avoid any suggestion of a final descent to e¹. Ex. 4.13*a* shows that f♯¹ in Ex. 4.7*a* strongly implies resolution to e¹ in the last bar; Ex. 4.13*b*, on the other hand, shows that Ex. 4.7*b* avoids any such implication. In the final version of the theme the upper voice avoids descending below g♯¹ during the whole of the second half (the sole, insignificant exception is f𝄪¹, lower neighbour to g♯¹ in bar 12); if there are any implications of a descent through f♯¹ to e¹ in the final bar here, they are so weak as to be negligible.

The symmetrical arch structure created in the upper voice of the theme by the balancing 'B-tonicizing' and 'E-tonicizing' progressions

Ex. 4.14. Cf. Op. 109, third movement, variation theme

is simultaneously the most important example of Beethoven's reworking of ideas originally conceived for the first movement and the one which most obviously breaks the pattern. Beethoven had indeed envisaged such a symmetrical structure for the first movement: the 'E-tonicizing' progression was to be completed at the beginning of the recapitulation, but that completion was later delayed until the end of the movement (see Exx. 3.11, 3.20*b*, and 3.22*e*). But Beethoven eventually suppressed it altogether, leaving the first movement structurally incomplete (Ex. 3.26). In the third-movement theme, the 'E-tonicizing' progression is not suppressed; on the contrary, it is expressed with the utmost clarity and simplicity, as the analysis of the final version given in Ex. 4.14 shows.[5]

In bars 1–8 the 'B-tonicizing' progression appears twice, first within bars 1–4 as $g\sharp^1$–$a\sharp^1$–b^1 and then within bars 1–8 as $g\sharp^1$–$g\sharp^1$–$a\sharp$–b.[6] The subtle imitation between the upper voice and bass is particularly

---

[5] The ambiguous ending for the theme shown in Ex. 4.11 should not be forgotten, however; this attempt to combine a complete 'E-tonicizing' progression with an *Urlinie*-like descent to e^2 ($\hat{1}$) is reminiscent of the 'double' endings for the first movement transcribed in Exx. 3.22*a* and *c*.

[6] The detail of the progression from $g\sharp^1$ to $a\sharp^1$ in bars 1–4 is another element which recalls the first movement: $g\sharp^1$ falls to $f\sharp^1$, which then gives rise to $a\sharp^1$. Compare the progression $g\sharp^2$–$a\sharp^2$ in bars 7–8 of the first movement, where *Übergreifung* produces $a\sharp^2$ from the preceding $f\sharp^2$.

noteworthy: the foreground progression g♯–a♯–b in bars 3–4 imitates the middleground ascent in the upper voice, and the upper-voice descent b–a–g♯ in bars 6–7 is prepared by the same descent an octave lower in the bass of bars 4–5. Both these descending third-progressions B–A–G♯ are preparatory in the further sense that they prepare the 'E-tonicizing' progression which governs the second half of the theme. Again, the progression appears twice in the upper voice, in bars 9–12 and 9–16. Again, there is an element of imitation, in that the foreground tenor progression b–a♯–g♯ in bar 12, in addition to reversing the bass in bars 3–4, imitates the middleground upper-voice descent b^1–a^1–$g♯^1$. And just as ascending and descending progressions between b and g♯ appeared in the upper voice in bars 6–8, so in bars 14–16 the foreground is saturated with progressions through the third b^1–$g♯^1$. The balanced construction of the two halves of this theme is extraordinary.[7]

Extraordinary too is the relationship between the theme and the first movement. Taken by themselves, the sketches analysed in Chapter 3 already give strong support to the theory that the first movement of Op. 109 is structurally incomplete; but the evidence of the sketches for the third-movement theme confirms that theory in almost every detail.[8] After his work on the *Missa solemnis*, Beethoven's first act in fulfilling his obligations towards Schlesinger seems to have been to recompose the 'little new piece' which by now he surely intended to incorporate into a new sonata. It was a recomposition in at least two senses: not only does the course of compositional events leading to the variation theme run closely parallel to that which produced the first movement, but the theme is also a recomposition in that it reworks the basic material of the first movement and achieves precisely the structural closure which Beethoven had suppressed there.

At this point we are in a position to reconsider an issue left open in Chapter 2: the question of whether Beethoven himself removed from the Wittgenstein sketchbook the leaves bearing sketches for

---

[7] For a similar and more detailed analysis of the theme see Forte and Gilbert, *Introduction to Schenkerian Analysis*, 327–30, where an orthodox *Urlinie* descent to î (e^1) is offered. My reading of a 3̂–♯4̂–5̂–4̂–3̂ structural line in the upper voice is of course much indebted to my analysis of the first movement.

[8] The close relationship between the first movement and the variation theme suggests at least one further possible way of reading the latter, a reading which goes some way towards clarifying a slightly disturbing element. Compared to the second half of the theme, in which the 'E-tonicizing' progression unfolds in a single register, the first half, with its use of two registers, might seem a little diffuse. But the falling sixth $g♯^1$–b played out during this first half unites the initial and final pitches of the first movement. In this sense bars 1–8 of the theme recall the incomplete first movement while bars 9–16 present its completion: the structural 'problem' and its 'resolution' are juxtaposed.

the first movement of Op. 109. The decision to rework that material in the sketches for the third-movement theme on pages 36–7 of Artaria 195 would certainly have provided a strong impulse for him to do so, if only in order to avoid having two sketchbooks in use at once. And having concluded this compositional 'unfinished business' (to borrow Edward Cone's apt phrase) he was now in a position to proceed to the second movement.[9]

---

[9] The reference is to E. T. Cone, 'Schubert's Unfinished Business', *19th Century Music*, 7 (1983–4), 222–32; repr. in id., *Music: A View from Delft*, ed. R. P. Morgan (Chicago and London, 1989), 201–16.

5. The Second Movement: The First Phase

Formal Synopsis

Exposition (1–65):
First group, first part (1–8)
  second part (9–24)
Transition (25–32)
Second group, first part (33–42)
  second part (42–56)
Closing group (57–65)
Development (66–104):
Main part (66–96)
Retransition (97–104)

Recapitulation (105–67):
First group, first part (105–12; 112–19)
Transition (120–31)
Second group, first part (132–43)
  second part (143–57)
Closing group (158–67)
Coda (168–77)

Artaria 195, pages 35–40

Whereas the sketches for the first movement and for the third-movement theme have each been discussed in a single chapter, those for the second movement and the third-movement variations require two chapters each (the variation sketches also require a substantial introduction: see Chapter 7). In the case of the second movement the division into two chapters stems not only from the fact that there are a larger number of sketches to be dealt with but also from important differences in sketch-type. A brief overview of the sketches will help to make this clear.

At the beginning of Chapter 4 reference was made to the first two sketches which may safely be related to the second movement of Op. 109: they occupy the bottom half of page 35 and the top two staves of page 36 in Artaria 195. After writing them Beethoven switched his attention away from this movement and concentrated instead on the third-movement theme. The return to sketching in E minor came at the top of page 37 with one of those apparently inconsequential contrapuntal doodlings which litter the sketchbooks; this one proved of considerable consequence, however, for it contained the kernel of the first part of the first group (bars 1–8) in the second movement; we shall examine the gradual emergence of these bars below. After filling staves 7–13 of page 37 with an embryonic draft of the exposition in which the first-group material is already close to its final form, Beethoven turned to page 38 and worked almost uninterruptedly on the second movement until the bottom of page 50.

The first layer of sketches on page 37 was written in pencil, but Beethoven made a number of later additions and revisions in ink. The exposition draft on staves 7–13 was partly written over in ink; in two places Beethoven added connectives ('Vi = 100; 30') whose counterparts appear in sketches on page 39, a fact which helps to suggest the point at which the ink additions to page 37 were made. Other ink sketches evidently added later to page 37 are also connected with material on pages 38–9; so it seems that the main change from pencil to ink occurred more or less simultaneously with the turn to page 38. Beethoven continued to work in ink until the sketching was finished, resorting to pencil only for a few revisions to pages 49 and 50 and for the very last sketch, on page 55. The close relationship between these final sketchbook entries for the movement and the version in the autograph score was discussed above in Chapter 2.

Ignoring the break represented by the third-movement theme sketches on pages 36–7, we can regard the second-movement sketches on pages 35–40 of Artaria 195 as belonging to an initial phase of work. This phase is characterized chiefly by short sketches for various parts of the movement. In some cases the relationship between sketch and final version is direct and obvious; in others it is more oblique. An exposition draft on page 37 has already been referred to; in fact this and a series of sketches on the lower half of page 39 provide virtually all the material for the exposition in the final version.

This last point is of course easily made with hindsight. Beethoven's own reaction to the material on pages 35–40 was either to modify it considerably or to discard it totally. The next phase of work began with an abrupt change in musical detail and in the method of sketching: pages 41–5 contain three continuity drafts, the first and third of which outline movements whose form is quite different to that of

Second Movement: First Phase 99

the final version. A few shorter sketches relating partly to these drafts intervene on pages 46–7 before a fourth and final continuity draft begins on the lower half of page 47 and continues to the bottom of page 50, where sketches for the variations take over.

From our perspective, therefore, the surviving sketches for the second movement divide fairly neatly into a phase of activity in which Beethoven concentrated on short sketches for specific parts of the movement or (as we shall see) for specific compositional ideas, and a subsequent phase in which he worked at integrating those ideas in the context of an entire movement or formal section. This chapter deals with the first phase; the continuity drafts will be discussed in Chapter 6. It goes without saying that the division argued here is to some extent pragmatic and arbitrary; if evidence survived of work carried out in parallel with the sketching in Artaria 195 it might well obscure the suggested distinction between shorter sketches and continuity drafts. Moreover, it will become clear during the course of Chapter 6 that, despite appearances, the switch from short sketches to continuity drafts did not involve any real discontinuity of purpose: although the drafts seem to present substantially new conceptions of the movement, Beethoven's underlying compositional concerns remained remarkably consistent.

This consistency notwithstanding, it would still be unwieldy to deal with all the second-movement sketches in a single chapter. There is a remarkable diversity of material here; and in many of the shorter sketches Beethoven seems to have been less concerned with working out foreground musical detail than with establishing compositional ideas *in abstracto*. Whereas the very first and most of the succeeding sketches for the first movement relate to the final version in a fairly obvious way, the same is not true of the second-movement sketches. For this reason it seems more useful to discuss the sketches on pages 35–40 not strictly in the order in which they are presumed to have been written but in terms of the compositional ideas which they illustrate. This approach is by no means ideal; but it offers perhaps the best way of defining what, in Beethoven's mind, the second movement of Op. 109 seems to have been 'about'.

The first sketch is transcribed in Ex. 5.1. The prevailing metre here, as in many later sketches, is 12/8 rather than the eventual 6/8, although individual 6/8 bars do occur. Beethoven's indecision over the most appropriate metre recalls his vacillation between 2/4 and 4/4 in the sketches for the first movement. In order to facilitate comparisons with the final version, however, editorial barlines have been added in Ex. 5.1 to create a consistent 6/8 metre; and in the following discussion all references are to 6/8 bars.

Ex. 5.1. Artaria 195, p. 35, st. 10/11–14/15

Although the sketch is superficially quite different from the final version, several similarities stand out. Most important is the placement of the triadic third, g^2, on the first downbeat—although the upbeat beginning of this and the succeeding phrases is quite foreign to the final version. This last point aside, the phrase structure of Ex. 5.1 is close to that of the final version: a complementary pair of four-bar phrases (the implied harmony in Ex. 5.1 is I–V; in the final version bars 1–8 are supported by I–V–I) is followed by a third such phrase, which is repeated almost exactly. The rhythmic figure allied to the interval of a descending third is common to this phrase and to bars 9–10 and their repetitions in the final version.

Beethoven's revisions to the first phrase of Ex. 5.1 wrought a

Ex. 5.2. Op. 109, second movement, bars 1–4, left hand

Ex. 5.3. *a* Cf. Op. 109, second movement, bars 1–24

b Cf. Ex. 5.1

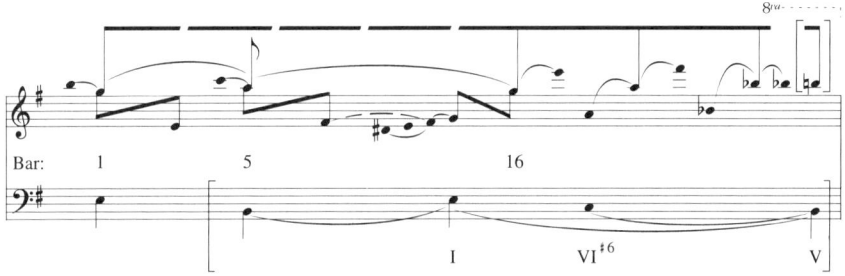

subtle change in the melodic rhythm of the upper voice. In the first version each beat in bars 1 and 2 is marked by a change of pitch. In the revision this change occurs only on each downbeat, with the result that the descending arpeggio from g^2 to e^1 is articulated by a rhythm of two dotted minims followed by two dotted crotchets and a final dotted minim. And as Ex. 5.2 shows, this is the rhythm which is hammered out, in the bass rather than the upper voice, in bars 1–4 and 5–8 of the final version.

A further relationship between Ex. 5.1 and the final version emerges if we consider aspects of voice leading. To take the final version first: the initial upper-voice g^1 connects with a^1 on the downbeat of bar 9, at the beginning of the second part of the first group (Ex. 5.3*a*). In Ex. 5.1 the initial downbeat g^2 connects similarly with a^2 (implicitly supported by a bass B) at the beginning of the second four-bar phrase; the intervening arpeggiation from the e^2 to the e^1

register matches the corresponding ascent throughout bars 1–8 of the final version (Ex. 5.3b).

The upward registral transfer during bars 1–8 of the final version forces a^1 (bar 9) into an inner voice. This a^1 is prolonged during the following bars and resolves back to an inner-voice g^1 at the cadence which closes the first group in bar 24 (Ex. 5.3a: the voice-leading structure of bars 1–8 and 1–24 is examined more closely in Exx. 5.7 and 5.8). Four bars from the end of Ex. 5.1 a^2 likewise resolves to g^2 (see Ex. 5.3b). This resolution within the rising E-minor arpeggio is short-lived, for the following two arpeggios bring back a^2 followed by $b\flat^2$, which is then transferred up an octave to $b\flat^3$ before the sketch breaks off. This final note is intriguing: did Beethoven actually hear it as $a\sharp^3$, part of an augmented-sixth chord on the submediant which would demand upward resolution to b^3? Or did he hear $b\flat^3$, in which case a downward resolution to a^3 would presumably follow? Both readings are possible; indeed, it will become clear that precisely this harmonic ambiguity plays a major role in the final version. Ex. 5.3b opts for the upward resolution in its analysis (necessarily somewhat conjectural) of the upper-voice motion throughout Ex. 5.1. At the largest level there is a linear ascent through the third g^2–b^2; that interval is first defined (as b^2–g^2) by the initial upbeat–downbeat succession at the beginning of the sketch. (The a^2 reached in bar 5 finds temporary resolution in a lower octave in the third and fourth phrases, which are governed by the linear descents a^1–e^1 and a^1–g^1, before the larger ascent resumes in the original register.)

At this point one might conclude that with Ex. 5.1 Beethoven had formulated almost everything except the actual foreground detail of the first group in the final version. One of the most glaring differences between Ex. 5.1 and the final version is the absence of the stark descending octaves in the left hand of bars 1–8: the two repeated tonic triads at the beginning of the sketch suggest that Beethoven was thinking rather in terms of static pedal harmonies. But the next sketch to be considered marks a decisive change in his conception of the bass. Ex. 5.4 clearly projects a linear progression through the tonic octave, although in an ascending rather than a descending direction.[1] Other foreground features of the final version also appear more clearly here: the succession of dotted minim and dotted crotchet pulses is made more explicit (compare Ex. 5.2), and the upper voice accompanies the bass in parallel tenths.

The rising progression through the tonic octave in Ex. 5.4 is

---

[1] The rising bass of Ex. 5.4 bears comparison with that of the third-movement theme, the sketches for which appear directly after Ex. 5.4 in Artaria 195.

Ex. 5.4. Artaria 195, p. 35, st. 14/15–p. 36, st. 1/2

immediately repeated a third lower on the submediant, C. The parallel treatment of the tonic and submediant in this sketch is noteworthy in that C major plays an important part in the final version of the movement, particularly in the recapitulation transition (bars 120 ff.) where it is not only juxtaposed abruptly with the preceding tonic harmony but also replaces the appearance of that harmony in the corresponding passage (bars 25 ff.) in the exposition.

We come now to the contrapuntal doodling at the top of page 37 which was referred to at the beginning of this chapter. The first two bars are transcribed in Ex. 5.5a; Ex. 5.5b shows a sketch which Beethoven wrote immediately beneath.

The source of the first half of Ex. 5.5b is obvious: Beethoven fashioned a four-bar antecedent from Ex. 5.5a and added a four-bar consequent. But what is most remarkable about this transformation of Ex. 5.5a is the way in which, more or less at a stroke, it brings bars 1–8 of the second movement of Op. 109 sharply into focus. The neighbour-note motion b^1–c^2–b^1 in bars 1–2 might seem to recall the initial upbeat figure from Ex. 5.1; but the rhythm in bars 1, 3, and 5 and the 4–♯3 suspension in bar 4 were taken over directly into the corresponding bars of the final version, as was the $\hat{4}$–$\hat{1}$ (a^1–e^1) motion controlling the consequent phrase, though it was transferred from the upper voice to the bass.

It is difficult not to believe that the formation of this eight-bar period marked a decisive compositional step, for immediately beneath Ex. 5.5b Beethoven wrote out the embryonic draft of the exposition mentioned earlier; the draft is transcribed in Ex. 5.6. Bars

104 Second Movement: First Phase

Ex. 5.5. *a* Artaria 195, p. 37, st. 1/2

b Artaria 195, p. 37, st. 6

1–16 of the movement now appear essentially in their final form.[2] The remark 'erster theil in H moll' reveals that Beethoven had already chosen the dominant minor as the key of the second group; and in the original, pencil layer of the draft this choice is made plain in the third and final eight-bar period, which consists basically of arpeggiated B-minor harmony. (The final b^2 was presumably intended to mark the end of the exposition.) When he returned to revise the draft in ink, Beethoven replaced this period with the repeat of bars 9–16 which stands as bars 17–24 in the final version.[3]

The ink revisions to the upper voice of bars 1–16 may appear slight, but they are none the less revealing. In their original form, bars 11–12 were very similar to bars 3–4; evidently too similar for Beethoven's liking, for he recast bars 11–12 decisively, replacing the implied imperfect cadence with a weak (feminine) perfect one; the

[2] Moreover, Beethoven opted initially for a 6/8 metre, as in Ex. 5.5*b*. The notated '12/8' and corresponding deletion of barlines at the beginning of Ex. 5.6 date from the stage of ink revisions.

[3] The repetition of bars 9–16 in the revisions to Ex. 5.6 was left incomplete because Beethoven ran out of space; he had to extend staves 10/11 well into the right-hand margin in order to accommodate as much of the repeat as he notated. The connective '30' with which the repetition breaks off refers to p. 39, st. 8/9, where Beethoven began working out the transition and second group. 'Vi = 100' following the revisions to bars 1–8 leads to p. 39, st. 1/2, where a rapid modulation from E to B minor is sketched; it seems that at this stage Beethoven was considering an even more terse and compressed exposition than the one in the final version.

Ex. 5.7. Cf. Ex. 5.6 and Op. 109, second movement, bars 1–8

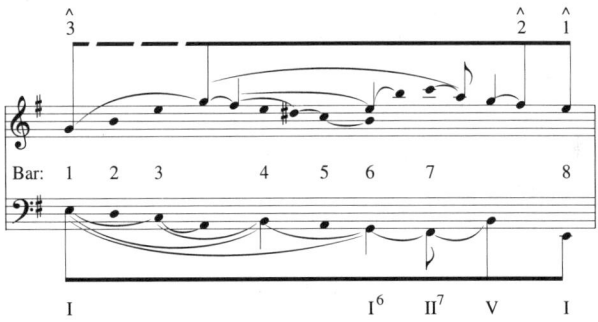

4–♯3 suspension was shifted from bar 12 to bar 4 in the process. The revision of the cadence in bars 15–16 (a revision again involving the substitution of a feminine for a previously masculine phrase-ending) may also have been intended to make it rhythmically and melodically more distinct from that in bars 7–8. But these changes were prompted by more than a desire for varied cadences; Beethoven was also responding to the linear structure of bars 1–8. We may consider that structure more closely, bearing in mind that for our purposes bars 1–8 in Ex. 5.6 are essentially identical to the corresponding bars in the final version.

Ex. 5.7 shows that the upper voice in bars 1–8 is controlled by a $\hat{3}$–$\hat{2}$–$\hat{1}$ descent. The triadic third is transferred up an octave from g^1 to g^2 before leading to $f\sharp^2$, which is prolonged by the foreground descent to $d\sharp^2$ in bar 4. There is an intermediate descent to e^1 in bar 6 as the descending arpeggiation of the tonic triad in the bass reaches G; and before the definitive $\hat{2}$–$\hat{1}$ is completed in bars 7–8, a^2 enters as an upper neighbour to g^2. Returning to the ink revisions in bars 9–16 of Ex. 5.6, it emerges that the syncopated $f\sharp^2$ introduced in bars 11 and 15 creates a stepwise connection with e^2 in bar 8 and leads first to g^2 (bar 12) and then back down to e^2 (bar 16). Ex. 5.8a illustrates this middleground voice leading and shows how the space between g^2 and e^2 composed out in bars 1–8 continues to be explored in bars 9–16 (and bars 17–24 in the final version). A further refinement made after the ink revisions in Ex. 5.6 and incorporated into the final version underlines Beethoven's sensitivity to these linear connections between e^2 and g^2. As Ex. 5.8b shows, the succession e^2–$d\sharp^2$–e^2 in bar 16 of Ex. 5.6 was replaced in the final version by $d\sharp^2$–$f\sharp^2$–e^2. The reintroduction of $f\sharp^2$ immediately prior to e^2 helps further to consolidate the middleground descent g^2–$f\sharp^2$–e^2.

This is a good point at which to pause and take stock of the

Ex. 5.8. *a* Cf. Ex. 5.6 and Op. 109, second movement, bars 1–16

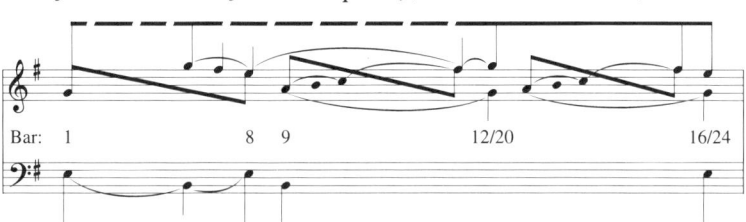

b Bars 15–16

sketches—a mere five of them—discussed so far. One of the most striking developments to note is the almost wholesale rejection of the movement begun in Ex. 5.1: the static pedal harmonies of that sketch were replaced by the strongly directed bass of Ex. 5.6; upbeat-based phrases gave way to downbeat-based ones; and upper-voice motion between the triadic third and fifth ceded to motion between the triadic third and the tonic. The composition of the second movement of Op. 109 was now well under way; as we know, Beethoven was about to turn to page 38 of Artaria 195 and begin the long series of ink sketches which would continue almost unbroken to the bottom of page 50. What were the compositional ideas which would shape the course of that work, and how would Beethoven develop them?

First there was the idea of using the submediant prominently in the movement. We have already seen the juxtaposition of E minor and C major in Ex. 5.4 and noted that it brings to mind the choice of those two keys in the exposition and recapitulation transitions respectively. But in earlier sketches (for example, the beginnings of Exx. 5.1 and 5.5*b*) the submediant also plays a melodic role as upper neighbour to the dominant; and it is this neighbouring role which is suggested, at a more large-scale level, in a sketch for the development section on page 38 (Ex. 5.9).

The sketch is tantalizingly incomplete: what, for example, was to link the A-minor version of the first-group main theme and the extended F-major harmony? Even more teasing is the failure to show

Ex. 5.9. Artaria 195, p. 38, st. 6–7/8

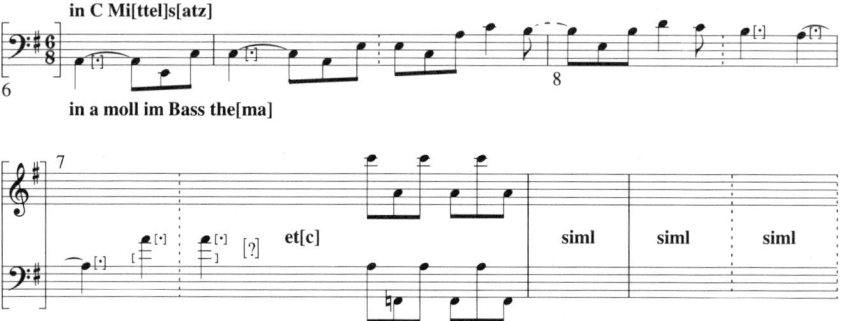

how the recapitulation would have been prepared: the preparation of the dominant rather than the tonic key in the retransition of the final version is one of the most extraordinary features of the movement, yet no sketches for the passage have survived.[4] What is immediately clear, though, is the intended tonicization of C major within the development, referred to here as the 'Mi[ttel]s[atz]'.[5] That this was to occur near the beginning of the development section is confirmed by a sketch at the bottom of page 38 (see Ex. 5.11a). The end of the exposition is represented in this sketch by a descending B-minor arpeggio; this is followed by a rising stepwise progression through F (as opposed to F♯) to G, marked with a pause sign: evidently a dominant preparation for C. This strategy sets up C major as the first local tonic following the establishment of B minor in the exposition, and the upper-neighbour relationship C–B is thus composed

---

[4] For two discussions of this retransition see Forte, *Compositional Matrix*, 51–2, and E. T. Cone, 'Analysis Today', in P. H. Lang (ed.), *Problems of Modern Music: The Princeton Seminar in Advanced Musical Studies* (New York, 1960), 37, repr. in Cone, *Music: A View from Delft*, 42–3. My own explanation appears in the Conclusion to Ch. 6. In Ch. 3, above (pp. 70–1) it was suggested that Beethoven may have been able to rely on his abortive sketches for the retransition in the first movement when working on the parallel passage in the second.

[5] Beethoven's use of *Mittelsatz* to denote the development section appears rather idiosyncratic; it was a term more commonly used to denote the 'second subject' in sonata-form movements, or an inner movement of a multi-movement work. Both these usages appear e.g. in E. T. A. Hoffmann's review of the Piano Trio in E♭, Op. 70 No. 2: see S. Kunze (ed.), *Ludwig van Beethoven: Die Werke im Spiegel seiner Zeit* (Laaber, 1987), 136, 138. The earliest printed appearance of the term in connection with a development section seems to be H. Birnbach, 'Über die verschiedene Form grösserer Instrumentaltonstücke aller Art und deren Bearbeitung', *Berliner allgemeine musikalische Zeitung*, 4 (1827), 285–7. See also F. Ritzel, *Die Entwicklung der 'Sonatenform' im musiktheoretischen Schrifttum des 18. und 19. Jahrhunderts* (Wiesbaden, 1974), 216, and Drabkin, 'Beethoven's Understanding of "Sonata Form"', 18. Another Beethoven sketch in which *Mittelsatz* appears to denote a sonata-form development is transcribed in R. Winter, *Compositional Origins of Beethoven's Opus 131* (Ann Arbor, Mich., 1982), 166.

Ex. 5.10. Cf. Op. 109, second movement, bars 105–32

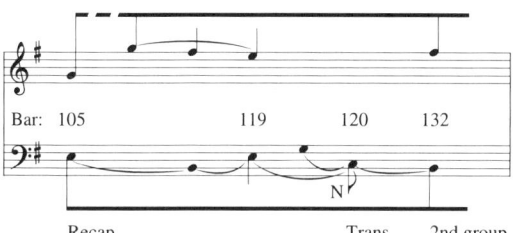

out harmonically. Essentially the same move occurs in the final version, where the sustained B-minor pedal on which the development opens shifts up to C in bar 79. And the procedure is reversed in the recapitulation, where the abrupt lurch to C at the beginning of the transition (bar 120) may be understood as the composing-out of an upper neighbour to the dominant, on which the second group begins in bar 132 (Ex. 5.10).

A further significant appearance of submediant harmony, in bars 49–54 of the final version, also relates to the interval C–B but is best explained in relation to another semitonal pair, G–F♯ (see below). Before entering upon that explanation, which involves a detailed examination of large-scale voice leading in the movement, we may examine a second compositional idea which Beethoven developed further in the sketches. This was the idea of the stepwise descending bass in bars 1–8 of Ex. 5.6 and the final version.[6] Several sketches reveal attempts to replicate this prominent foreground feature at deeper levels.

Consider Ex. 5.11a, the sketch referred to above in which the tonicization of C is approached through a stepwise ascent from B to G. The progression around the circle of fifths in the first five bars represents the first attempt in the sketches at connecting E minor and B minor, the two tonal centres of the exposition. Although the harmonic sequence may initially seem pedestrian, a moment's thought—and Beethoven's careful notation—uncovers the rationale of the plan. Embedded within the sequence is a stepwise descent through the B octave, divided into two descending fourths (or tetrachords): b^1–$f\sharp^1$ in the middle voice (note the separate rhythmic articulation) and e^1–b in the bass (Ex. 5.11b). The relationship of this

[6] The first version of the descending bass in Ex. 5.6 presents the octave e–E without the intervention of A in bar 3 or of B in bar 7. The subsequent inclusion of B was no doubt dictated by the desire for a strong cadential dominant; the elaboration of c–B as c–A–B in bars 3–4 may have been adopted in order to avoid implied parallel fifths (g^2/c–f♯^{2}/B) in the outer voices.

Ex. 5.11. *a* Artaria 195, p. 38, st. 12/13–15/16

b Cf. Ex. 5.11*a*, bars 1–5

idea to the descending bass in bars 1–8 of the movement is obvious. And Beethoven clearly thought enough of the idea to make plans for its transposed reappearance in the recapitulation, for a sketch added in ink to page 37, staves 13/14 in Artaria 195 shows the beginning of the circle-of-fifths progression which would yield an embedded descent through the E rather than the B octave.

Page 39 of Artaria 195 is largely given over to sketches for the exposition transition and second group: sketches, like Ex. 5.11*a*, which involve working out the tonicization of B minor. In a series of entries on the lower half of the page Beethoven actually reached what was to form the basis of the final version of this part of the movement. But he then took up again the idea illustrated in Ex.

Second Movement: First Phase

Ex. 5.12. Artaria 195, p. 39, st. 12–14/15

5.11a: E and B minor are linked by a progression around the circle of fifths, although with C now substituted for the C♯ of the earlier sketch. Ex. 5.12 shows that the stepwise progression through the fourth E–B was to be articulated by a bold three-note motive and was to be stated twice, with the motive first in the top voice and then in the bass. But the end of this example reveals a surprising new twist. The progression around the circle of fifths extends beyond B, through E to A; although the three-note motive is abandoned, its shape is still implicit in the movement of the bass. The

Ex. 5.13. Op. 109, second movement: conjectural tonal structure projected by sketches

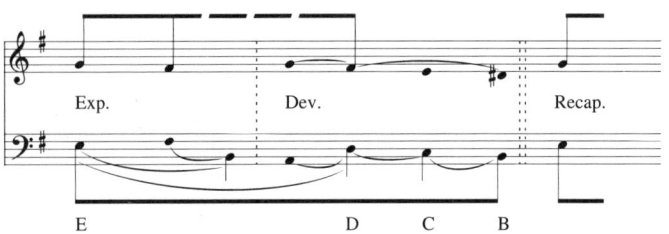

purpose of this extension seems to be the preparation of A as the dominant of D, although the sketch breaks off before any cadence in D is actually realized. At the top of the very next page of Artaria 195 (page 40, staves 1–2) there is a sketch showing a melodic idea in D minor; it is tempting to suppose that this was connected with the plan adumbrated in Ex. 5.12, but there is no direct musical continuity between the two sketches to support this point. (It is even possible that the sketch on page 40 is unrelated to Op. 109 altogether.)

Despite the inconclusive ending of Ex. 5.12 it is probably safe to assume that Beethoven was considering a move to D. And since B minor already seems to have been so firmly fixed as the key of the second group, it might be best to interpret Ex. 5.12 as a plan for a tight fusion of exposition and development. That is, there would be no exposition repeat, and little formal articulation of the close of this section; exposition and development would instead be bonded by the force of the circle-of-fifths progression pushing beyond B minor to A in preparation for D. The two sections are similarly fused in the final version, where the closing cadence of the exposition is elided with the beginning of the development so that the music continues in an unbroken sweep.[7]

Ex. 5.13 is an attempt to interpret the move to D projected in Ex. 5.12 in the light of other evidence gathered from the sketches so far. Admittedly, the example necessarily makes two major assumptions: first, that Beethoven still intended to introduce C major prominently in the development, and secondly, that the retransition would have involved a conventional dominant preparation of the tonic.

---

[7] On the other hand, might Beethoven have considered a D-major close for the exposition in Ex. 5.12? Precedents for such an unusual tonal scheme include the slow movement of the 'Ghost' Trio, Op. 70 No. 1 (D minor–C major, a scheme later employed in the second movement of the Ninth Symphony) and the third movement of the 'Razumovsky' Quartet in E minor, Op. 59 No. 2, in which the first section (bars 1–8) modulates from E minor to D major. (The last movement of this quartet, like the second movement of Op. 109, places great emphasis on the submediant.)

Ex. 5.14. Cf. Op. 109, second movement, bars 1–70

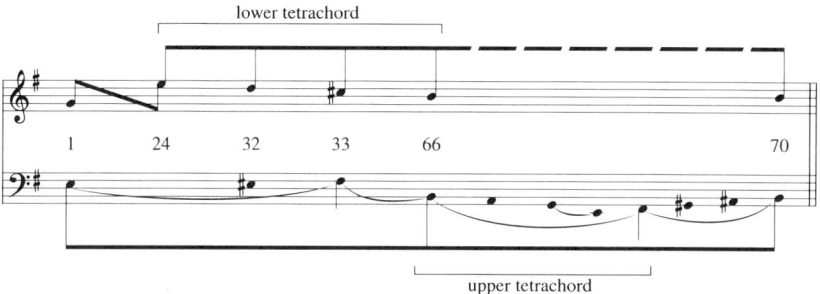

Now none of the sketches made prior to Ex. 5.12 gives any clue to Beethoven's plans for the retransition; but the few later ideas which are recorded all involve dominant preparation of E minor rather than the preparation of B minor found in the final version. It is at least reasonable, then, to assume that the conventional dominant preparation was foreseen when Ex. 5.12 was written.

The relationship of Ex. 5.13 to the descending bass in bars 1–8 of the movement will again be obvious. If the above interpretations are sound, then the sketches imply the composing-out of the descending fourth E–B at two middleground levels: during the exposition, as part of the tonicization of B minor (Ex. 5.11), and in the combined exposition and development, leading up to the recapitulation. However conjectural it may be, the reading in Ex. 5.13 can at least claim the merit of plausibility, for the proposed integration of detail and structure, of foreground and middleground, is typically Beethovenian. Chapter 6 will show that Beethoven continued in his attempts to use the descending bass of bars 1–8 in such ways; but as a temporary conclusion here, we may note that the experiments of Exx. 5.11a and 5.12 were not without effect on the final version. Ex. 5.14 shows that the lower tetrachord of the B octave (e^2–b^1) is composed out during the second half of the exposition; when b^1 arrives at the cadence in bar 66, the development opens with the complementary upper tetrachord (B–F♯) in the bass.

The third and most far-reaching compositional idea documented in the sketches on pages 35–7 of Artaria 195 is that of linear motion between the triadic third and tonic. The discussion of Ex. 5.6 showed that Beethoven's revisions to bars 9–16 served to extend the motion between $\hat{3}$ and $\hat{1}$ (g^2 and e^2) which governs bars 1–8. Ex. 5.15a, which comes from stave 4 of page 38, further testifies to Beethoven's concern with this particular melodic space. This sketch is one of a number

Ex. 5.15. *a* Artaria 195, p. 38, st. 4

b Op. 109, second movement, bars 162-5

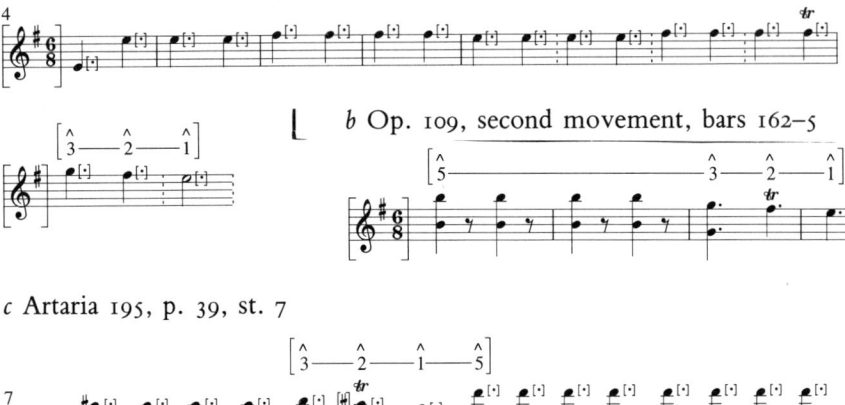

c Artaria 195, p. 39, st. 7

at the top of page 38 whose relationship to the movement is rather obscure; but its emphatic dotted-crotchet rhythm and the closural melodic shape suggest a connection with the recapitulation closing theme in the final version (Ex. 5.15*b*). What is chiefly missing in the sketch is the emphasis on the dominant note ($\hat{5}$) found in the final version; but that feature appears in Ex. 5.15*c*, written on page 39 and visible in Artaria 195 at the same time as Ex. 5.15*a*, since pages 38–9 form a single opening. Ex. 5.15*c* assumes a background tonic of B rather than E minor and thus relates rather to the exposition than to the recapitulation closing theme. Allowing for the transposition, its first two bars are identical to the last four of Ex. 5.15*a*; the repeated dominant note which makes up the second half of Ex. 5.15*c* was to become the first element in the final version, preceding the $\hat{3}$–$\hat{1}$ motion.

The very position of Ex. 5.15*c* on page 39 of Artaria 195 is thought-provoking in the context of the present discussion. In addition to occurring almost immediately opposite Ex. 5.15*a* it stands directly above the first appearance in the sketches of the exposition transition theme. This theme (Ex. 5.16), which appears more or less in its final form here on page 39, is melodically similar to the closing theme in that it too combines a $\hat{3}$–$\hat{1}$ descent with a repeated dominant note, one embellished in this instance by a double neighbour-note figure. Comparison of Exx. 5.15*b* and 5.16 helps to highlight the shared melodic elements; the fact that the first sketches for both themes

Ex. 5.16. Op. 109, second movement, exposition transition theme (bars 25–8)

Ex. 5.17. Artaria 195, p. 37, st. 6

occur so close to one another tempts one to suppose that the melodic similarities were the product of conscious shaping rather than a matter of coincidence.[8]

But if the sketches support the idea that the melodic motion $\hat{3}$–$\hat{2}$–$\hat{1}$ was important to Beethoven, they also show that he soon began to consider ways of reordering those three scale degrees. Consider Ex. 5.17, a pencil fragment on page 37 which follows directly after Ex. 5.5*b* above. The repeated three-note motive G–E–F♯ ($\hat{3}$–$\hat{1}$–$\hat{2}$) is a reordering of G–F♯–E ($\hat{3}$–$\hat{2}$–$\hat{1}$). The reordering changes the harmonic implications of the motive: whereas in the various sketches considered so far, $\hat{3}$–$\hat{1}$–$\hat{2}$ motion implies an *Urlinie*-like I–V–I harmonization (and this is of course how it is treated in the first group in the final version), the $\hat{3}$–$\hat{1}$–$\hat{2}$ motive in Ex. 5.17 implies IV–V in B minor. This motive inevitably conjures up the retransition in the final version, a passage for which, as already mentioned, no sketches survive. It is unlikely that Ex. 5.17 was itself intended for that part of the movement; in fact Ex. 5.17 may even form the continuation of Ex. 5.5*b*, although certain physical evidence in the sketchbook— an unnatural gap between the end of Ex. 5.5*b* and the beginning of Ex. 5.17, and the slightly different shade of pencil in which Ex. 5.17 is written—suggest that it was appended to the earlier sketch at some stage rather than having formed an original part of it. In any case, if we read Exx. 5.5*b* and 5.17 as one continuous musical idea, then this composite sketch shows a closed area in the tonic key followed by a dominant preparation for the dominant. In other words,

---

[8] It is also interesting to compare the third and fourth bars of the transition theme shown in Ex. 5.16 with the first two bars of Ex. 5.5*b*, above: the upper-neighbour figure B–C–B, another important element in the sketches, is common to both.

the G–E–F♯ motive in Ex. 5.17 would appear to be connected with the exposition transition rather than with the retransition to the recapitulation.

The association of the G–E–F♯ motive with the exposition transition and second-group area is reinforced by Ex. 5.18. This is a conflation of two originally separate sketches on page 40 of Artaria 195. The first, labelled A, covers staves 7/8–9/10; the second is written on staves 10/11. At some point Beethoven decided to expand sketch A by inserting the last four bars of this second sketch. He cued in the expansion, labelled B in Ex. 5.18, by means of the numbers '10' and '100'. Ex. 5.18 was clearly meant for the end of the exposition (which Beethoven apparently intended to repeat at this stage), and it shows the G–E–F♯ motive in various guises. It appears in bars 4–5 of version A1, with e^1 perhaps altered to $e\sharp^1$. The first two bars of version A2 give the motive in the e^2 register, and the chromatic alteration of e^1 is no longer in doubt in the inserted B segment, which shows G–E–F♯ prolonged in two senses: first in the literal sense that it is presented in longer note values (the string of dotted minims calls up the retransition in the final version even more strongly than does Ex. 5.17); and secondly in that the intervals g^1–e^1 and e^1–$f\sharp^1$ are prolonged by passing notes, $f\sharp^1$ and $e\sharp^1$ (the expected final $f\sharp^1$ of the motive is supplied an octave lower by the first note of the closing theme). Version B2 includes material which bears further on the treatment and significance of the G–E–F♯ motive. The motive appears in the upper voice (again, the final $f\sharp^1$ must be understood as supplied by the ensuing closing theme) and is accompanied in the bass by its inversion, E–G[–F♯]. The chromatic passing note $e\sharp^1$ is harmonized as part of an augmented-sixth chord which is poised to resolve on to the dominant of B minor at the beginning of the closing theme.

Whither so much detailed analysis? We have apparently established no more than that our interpretation of Ex. 5.17 was probably right, and that the G–E–F♯ motive, far from being connected with the retransition, definitely appears in association with the exposition second group in Ex. 5.18, where it enters emphatically before the beginning of the closing theme. But to begin to sense the real significance of the various elements combined in Ex. 5.18 we must take a harder look at what happens in the exposition of the final version.

To recapitulate: we have seen that the main middleground motion in the upper voice in both parts of the first group is between $\hat{3}$ (g^2) and $\hat{1}$ (e^2). But this motion takes place in a higher register than that in which the movement begins. What happens to the *initial* $\hat{3}$, g^1

Ex. 5.18. Artaria 195, p. 40, st. 7–11

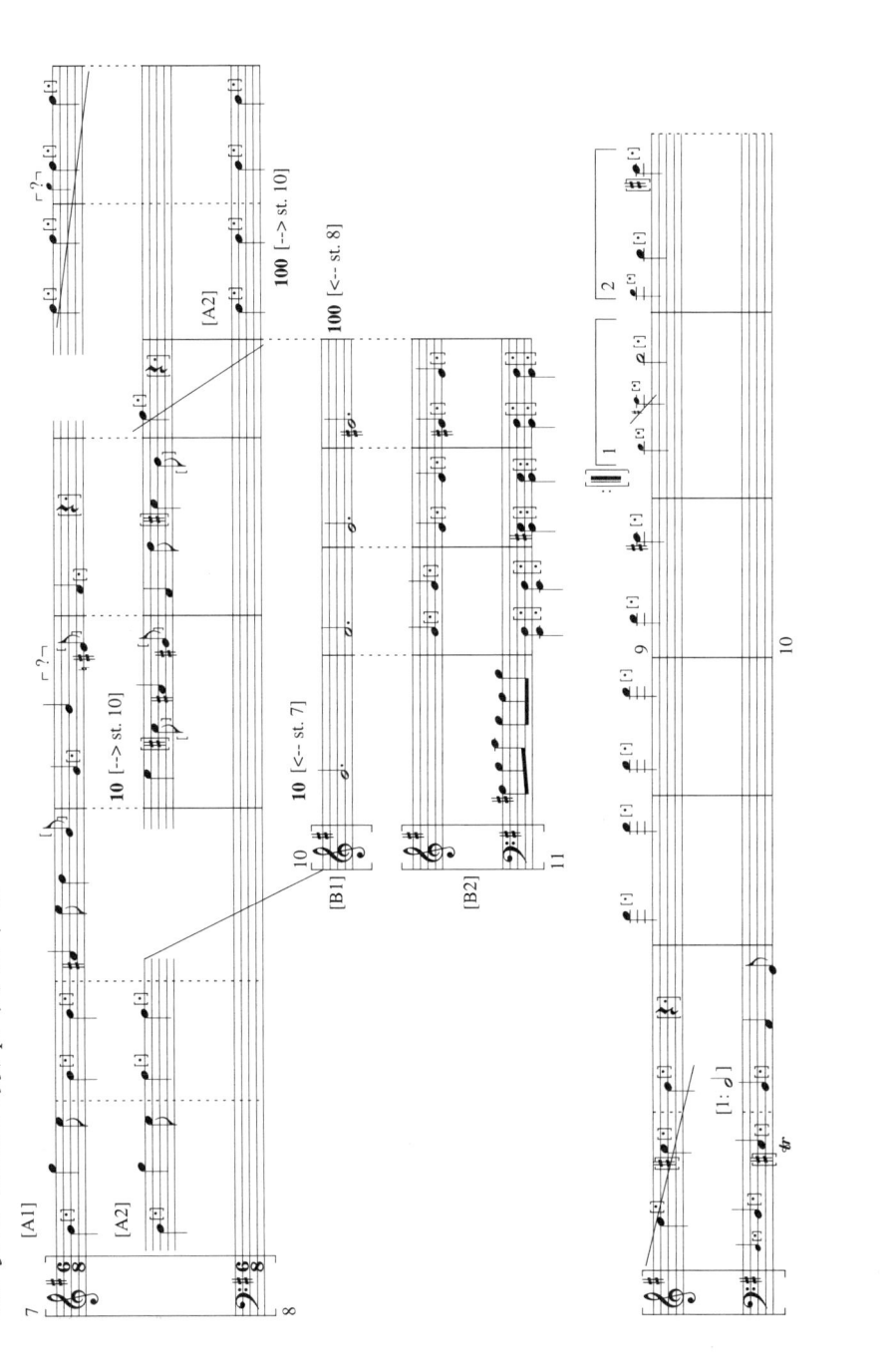

rather than g^2? Within the first group, it moves out to a^1 in bar 9 and returns definitively to g^1 only with the resolution of the dominant pedal on the second beat of bar 24, where the first group ends (see Ex. 5.3a). But by this stage g^1 has become an inner voice beneath e^2, which marks the end of the $\hat{3}$–$\hat{2}$–$\hat{1}$ activity worked out in the revisions to bars 9–16 of Ex. 5.6, the principal sketch for the exposition first group. To locate the point at which the initial g^1 is properly regained in the upper voice and carried forward, we must look ahead to bars 55–6, where g^1 moves not to a^1 but to $f\sharp^1$. A textural detail—the return of left-hand octave doubling—underscores the connection between bars 55–6 and 1–8.

Bars 55–6 are crucial. They break decisively a progression around the circle of fifths begun in bar 43, after the eight-bar dominant pedal in B minor has been resolved (bars 33–42). The bass, which disguises the underlying root progression in fifths by means of a linear chromatic descent, reaches G in bar 49; and G functions in its immediate context as a dominant seventh of C. In bar 50 the outer voices exchange notes: f^2 is transferred to the bass and G moves to the upper voice. During the next four bars the bass F twice falls to E, giving the effect of a V_2^4–I^6 progression in C, the next point around the circle of fifths from G. In bar 55, then, the scene is set for a third such resolution; but this time the bass F resolves upward to F$\sharp$, the dominant of B minor, and pulls the upper-voice g^1 down to $f\sharp^1$ with it. Bars 55–6 restore a firm sense of the prevailing dominant-minor tonality and expose the sequential passage begun in bar 43 as a harmonic digression.

The passage between bars 49–56 turns entirely on the aural ambiguity of the augmented-sixth sonority: an augmented-sixth chord in one key sounds like, and may be treated as, a dominant seventh in another. Thus the apparent dominant seventh of C set up at bar 49 is in reality an augmented sixth on G, the submediant degree in B minor. Beethoven exploits the double resolution potential of the chord by treating it twice as V^7/C before revealing its true identity; F in bar 55 should more properly be notated as E$\sharp$.

To sum up, Ex. 5.19 shows how bars 55–6 relate to the preceding part of the exposition. The most basic progression is shown in Ex. 5.19a: g^1 over E in bar 1 leads to $f\sharp^1$ over F$\sharp$ in bar 56. In Ex. 5.19b the augmented-sixth/dominant-seventh sonority on G is introduced; this produces a chromatic voice exchange, with g^1 transferred to the bass and the bass E proceeding to an upper-voice $e\sharp^1$. In Ex. 5.19c $e\sharp^1$ is notated as f^1 and is re-exchanged with the bass G so that the upper voice again proceeds directly from g^1 to $f\sharp^1$. The last elaboration is shown in Ex. 5.19d: the bass F transferred from the upper voice falls

Ex. 5.19. Cf. Op. 109, second movement, bars 1–56

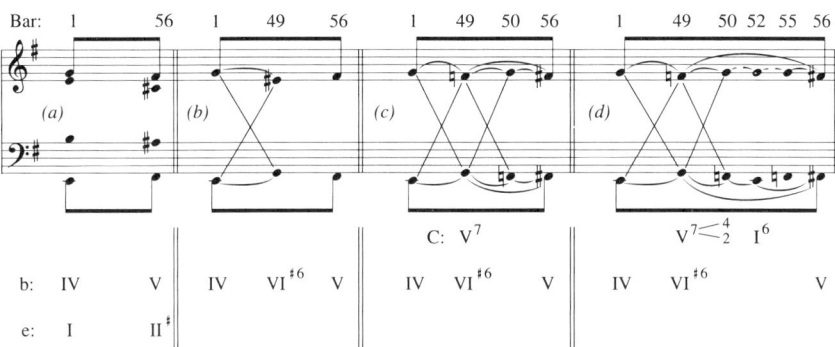

to E, producing the apparent C-major triads in bars 52 and 54 before resolving to F♯.

The relationship of the B segment in Ex. 5.18 to the final version now emerges somewhat more clearly. The events worked out in that segment—the combination of the G–E–F♯ motive with its own inversion, and the introduction of the chromatic passing note e♯^{1}, harmonized as part of an augmented-sixth chord—all correspond to elements of the middleground progressions analysed in Ex. 5.19. In Ex. 5.18 those events are located at a single point in the exposition (it is in fact the crucial point, corresponding to bars 55–6 in the final version), while in the final version they unfold over a much longer span. And now we can appreciate the full import of the G–E–F♯ motive and its relationship to the G–F♯–E motions played out in various sketches and in the final version. While on an immediate level G–E–F♯ appears to be a simple reordering of the linear descent G–F♯–E, it is used in the sketches and the final version in such a way as to truncate that descent and to prevent its completion. Ex. 5.20a, whose relationship to the various stages of Ex. 5.19 is obvious, shows that g^1–e^1–f♯^{1}, when combined with its inversion in this harmonic context, elaborates the partial linear descent g^1–f♯^{1}. The outer voices converge on the dominant of B minor, and completion of the $\hat{3}$–$\hat{2}$–$\hat{1}$ descent in E minor cannot take place until the bass moves to B (Ex. 5.20b). So the relationship between these two three-note melodic figures ($\hat{3}$–$\hat{2}$–$\hat{1}$ and $\hat{3}$–$\hat{1}$–$\hat{2}$) proves to be fundamentally antithetical; and the particular melodic formula used in Ex. 5.18—g^1–f♯^{1}–e^1–e♯^{1}[–f♯^{1}]—further sharpens the antithesis by using a complete $\hat{3}$–$\hat{2}$–$\hat{1}$ motion to elaborate the larger, incomplete $\hat{3}$–$\hat{1}$–$\hat{2}$ progression.

Although the crucial position of bars 55–6 within the final version of the exposition may be appreciated at this stage, an assessment of

Ex. 5.20. The opposition between $\hat{3}$–$\hat{1}$–$\hat{2}$ and $\hat{3}$–$\hat{2}$–$\hat{1}$ progressions

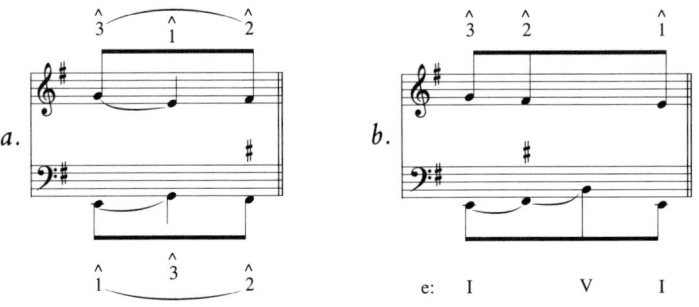

Ex. 5.21. Artaria 195, p. 38, st. 9/10

their role in the structure of the complete movement must await the conclusion of Chapter 6. Meanwhile Ex. 5.21 presents another sketch which bears on the voice-leading issues just raised in connection with those bars. The sketch does not at first relate obviously to any passage in the final version. The alternation between d^2 and g^2 in the upper voice together with the bass motion g–f might hint at the beginning of the passage spanning bars 49–56, but there is no actual C-major harmony in the sketch; on the contrary, the G-major triads turn out to represent the neapolitan degree in F♯ minor. Yet this is precisely the crux of the matter: the truncated $\hat{3}$–$\hat{2}$–$\hat{1}$ descent in E minor, realized now as the neapolitan relationship G–F♯, lies at the heart of this sketch despite being approached in a way quite different to that chosen in the final version and illustrated in Ex. 5.19.

If an analysis of the important voice-leading function of g^1–$f\sharp^1$ in the final version helps to shed light on the 'idea' behind this sketch, the neapolitan relationship in Ex. 5.21 opens the way to a further level of interpretation of the final version: the neapolitan relationship between C, the key fleetingly touched upon in bars 49–54, and B minor, the true goal of those and the succeeding bars. It is better termed a 'latent' relationship, for C does not function as a conventional 'neapolitan sixth'; the Janus-faced dominant-seventh/augmented-sixth chord on G mediates between the two keys and prevents a true ♭II⁶–

V–I cadence in B minor. Nevertheless, the close association of these neapolitan-related keys gives Beethoven another opportunity to explore the melodic step C–B and adds a further layer of meaning to this passage in the final version. C–B is again brought to the fore in the parallel passage (bars 152–7) in the recapitulation, where G–F♯ from the exposition (see Ex. 5.19) is transposed down a fifth to C–B.[9]

Mention of this recapitulation passage brings us full circle in our exploration of compositional ideas in these early sketches for the second movement; we return to the unresolved $b\flat^3$ at the end of Ex. 5.1. The two resolutions suggested above—$a\sharp^3$–b^3 or $b\flat^3$–a^3—depend precisely on whether the note is heard as part of a dominant seventh in F or an augmented-sixth chord on the submediant in E minor; but at this distance it is precisely Beethoven's failure to indicate either resolution which impresses most strongly. The harmonic ambiguity raised at the end of this early, seemingly inconsequential sketch, is of the essence; while it relates by transposition to bars 55–6 of the exposition, it relates directly to the parallel passage in the recapitulation, bars 156–7.

Conclusion

We have now considered most of the sketches for the second movement of Op. 109 on pages 35–40 of Artaria 195. The numerous short entries on these six pages offer a wealth of material, the relationship of which to the final version is not always immediately obvious. It needs to be stressed that the often startling discontinuities between adjacent entries have been largely filtered out above because of the restricted focus adopted. Rather than examining all the sketches in their presumed chronological sequence, a process of selection based on sketch content has enabled us to isolate three compositional ideas which appear to have guided Beethoven's imagination: the idea of the submediant as a prominent melodic and harmonic scale degree; the use at middleground levels of the descending bass first heard in bars 1–8; and the use in the upper voice of the related progressions $\hat{3}$–$\hat{2}$–$\hat{1}$ and $\hat{3}$–$\hat{1}$–$\hat{2}$, one connoting a cadential progression in the tonic, E minor, the other preparing the dominant of the dominant, B minor.

It is appropriate now to introduce a fourth idea, one which embraces the other three: the idea that these sketches, like those for the third-movement theme, seem to be largely motivated by the

---

[9] Sketches for this recapitulation passage appear in Artaria 195, p. 38, st. 1/2, and p. 40, st. 5–6.

concerns which dogged Beethoven while composing the first movement. The submediant is conspicuous in the sketches for both movements, although it is employed differently (the upper-neighbour relationship of C to the dominant of E minor has little or no parallel in the first-movement sketches, for instance); and we should remember that whereas Beethoven eventually played down the importance of C♯ minor in the first movement, he gave C major considerable prominence in the second. As for the bass descent in bars 1–8, this relates to the first movement in a more direct way. It is not so much that Beethoven's use of the descent at middleground levels has a direct parallel in the sketches for the first movement, but rather that the descent itself recalls the similar descending bass in the first phrase (bars 1–4) of that movement.[10]

The apparent re-engagement with the concerns which had already shaped the first movement and the third-movement theme is at its most compelling when we consider Beethoven's treatment of the $\hat{3}$–$\hat{2}$–$\hat{1}$ and $\hat{3}$–$\hat{1}$–$\hat{2}$ progressions. These are clearly analogues of the 'E-tonicizing' and 'B-tonicizing' progressions discussed in Chapter 3; indeed, were it not for the terminological confusion which might result we could apply the same labels here, for $\hat{3}$–$\hat{2}$–$\hat{1}$ is the paradigmatic *Urlinie* progression, a linear unfolding of a segment of the tonic triad, while the reordering $\hat{3}$–$\hat{1}$–$\hat{2}$ served Beethoven as a preparation for the dominant of the dominant. The two first-movement tonicizing progressions are of course also reorderings (or rather, reversals with appropriate chromatic alteration) of one another: $\hat{3}$–$\sharp\hat{4}$–$\hat{5}$ (G♯–A♯–B) becomes $\hat{5}$–$\hat{4}$–$\hat{3}$ (B–A–G♯; cf. Ex. 3.7).

The matter of these linear progressions may be pursued a little further. Although the second movement is characterized by linear motion (complete and incomplete) between $\hat{3}$ and $\hat{1}$, the first sketch for the movement in Artaria 195 (see Ex. 5.1) shares the space $\hat{3}$–$\hat{5}$ with the first movement. Now Ex. 5.1 was followed shortly by the sketches for the third-movement theme on page 36; and we have seen that in those sketches Beethoven first emphasized linear motion between $\hat{3}$ and $\hat{1}$ before basing the theme around the $\hat{3}$–$\sharp\hat{4}$–$\hat{5}$–$\hat{4}$–$\hat{3}$

---

[10] In *Compositional Matrix*, 85, Forte illustrates the relationship between the opening bass lines of the first and second movements and of the third-movement theme. The sketches are powerless to prove or disprove the real or consciously intended 'existence' of any such relationship; but they can alert us to the disparity between the simple movement-to-movement relationship heard in the work and the more complex circumstances of its genesis. The ascending bass in the variation theme was evidently formulated before the descending bass in the second movement (see Ex. 4.6). And yet Ex. 5.4, ostensibly a sketch for the second movement, begins with a minor-mode version of the bass in that theme! Ex. 5.4, moreover, predates not only the sketches for the third-movement theme but also Ex. 5.6, in which the descending bass in bars 1–8 of the second movement first appears.

progression originally intended for the first movement. It is only after those theme sketches that we find Ex. 5.6, the sketch for the first group of the second movement in which motion between $\hat{3}$ and $\hat{1}$, as opposed to $\hat{3}$ and $\hat{5}$, is now the guiding factor. The shifting focus on the two halves of the tonic triad in these early sketches for the second and third movements seems to represent a search for balance, and a response to the choices already made in the first movement.

Such faith in Beethoven's manipulation of these linear progressions may seem over-zealous. But it receives strong support from an aspect of Ex. 5.18 which was passed over when that sketch was introduced above, namely the intended exposition repeat.[11] Taking the first-time bar, the repeated f♯³ in the closing theme leads to d³–c♯³–b²—$\hat{3}$–$\hat{2}$–$\hat{1}$ in B minor. Taking the second-time bar, $\hat{3}$–$\hat{2}$–$\hat{1}$ is reordered as $\hat{3}$–($\hat{2}$)–$\hat{1}$–$\hat{2}$: d³–(c♯³)–b²–c[♯]³. The explicit juxtaposition of the two progressions cannot be misconstrued: the one is to be *heard* as a reordering of the other.[12]

---

[11] The exposition repeat was evidently an afterthought, for the material in the second-time bar in Ex. 5.18 was originally allotted to the first-time one.

[12] Compare the first- and second-time bars in the exposition of the first movement of the 'Hammerklavier' Sonata, Op. 106: when the repeat is taken we hear G–A–B as a deliberate alteration of the previously played G–A–B♭.

6. The Second Movement: The Continuity Drafts

As explained in Chapter 5, Beethoven's sketching in Artaria 195 for the second movement of Op. 109 falls fairly naturally into two phases of activity: the first phase is marked by the shorter sketches on pages 35–40 of the sketchbook, the second by the four continuity drafts which occupy almost all of pages 41–50. This second phase might be further broken down into two subphases, one covering pages 41–5, which contain three continuity drafts along with a small number of closely related sketches, the other represented by the fourth draft, a detailed version of the development and recapitulation which begins on the lower half of page 47 and continues to the bottom of page 50. This draft marks the end of continuous work on the movement in Artaria 195. Page 46 and the top half of page 47 are filled by a few shorter sketches which relate to the third and fourth drafts. Finally, on staves 1–2 of page 47 there is a sketch in E minor and 2/4 time which is unrelated to the sonata; it seems not to have been written with the quill used for the surrounding material and may therefore date from a different period.

In this chapter the three drafts on pages 41–5 will be transcribed in full. They merit such extended presentation precisely because the conceptions of the total movement (or complete formal sections) which they document are strikingly different from Beethoven's eventual choices. The fourth draft, on the other hand, is generally much closer to the final version and is therefore not transcribed complete. The discussion of it below will focus on three areas: Beethoven's conception of the development section, his problems with the recapitulation transition, and his work on the coda.

CD 1

Pages 40–1 of Artaria 195 form a single opening, and are therefore both visible simultaneously. As the eye travels from one to the other, contrasts leap almost literally from the page. Page 40 presents

Second Movement: Continuity Drafts

a haphazard collection of fragmentary sketches, some deleted, some probably unrelated to Op. 109; there are several changes in handwriting and almost half the page is unused. Page 41, on the other hand, is filled from top to bottom; the staves are paired, the pairing emphasized by braces (little different in appearance from Beethoven's ordinary barlines) at the left-hand edge; the handwriting is totally consistent; there are few deletions. Nothing on pages 35–40 gives any warning of the extensive draft of nearly 130 bars which begins here.

Not only is the extent of the draft unprepared; one is also taken aback by its content, much of which is quite new. To put this novelty in better perspective, recall that in the course of writing the shorter sketches on the preceding pages Beethoven had already arrived more or less at the final form of the exposition first group on page 37 (Ex. 5.6), and had captured on page 39 almost all the essentials of what became the transition and second group; only the closing theme was lacking, and even that made its appearance on page 40 (Ex.5.18).

The notated metre in CD 1 fluctuates between 6/8 and 12/8, as in earlier sketches; thus editorial barlines have again been added in the transcription (Ex. 6.1) to create a consistent 6/8, and the bar numbering below refers exclusively to bars of 6/8. The barring begins at bar 9, however, for the first bar of the draft clearly corresponds to that bar in the final version. The transcription shows that Beethoven did in fact begin the draft at bar 1, then broke off after bar 2 and started again at bar 9: this is a good indication that he was satisfied with the form of bars 1–8 already worked out (see Ex. 5.6) and saw no need to write them out again. Indeed, bars 1–8 may be regarded as a fixed element against which ideas for other parts of the movement are tested.

The structure of the second part of the first group in CD 1 differs from that in Ex. 5.6, which formed the basis of the final version. Instead of a repeated eight-bar period made up of two four-bar phrases, Beethoven tried a single sixteen-bar period built from two eight-bar phrases (CD 1, bars 9–16 and 17–25; the final cadence is delayed and elided with the beginning of the next phrase). The difference in phrase structure—essentially a doubling of the earlier proportions—is less significant than the new conception of the melodic line, particularly with respect to register. Ex. 5.8 showed that Beethoven was at pains to establish strong linear motion between e^2 and g^2 in this part of the movement. But in CD 1 the e^2 register is never reached: the upper voice remains in the initial register, and the entire passage is bounded by the resolution of the

Ex. 6.1. CD 1: Artaria 195, p. 41, st. 1/2–p. 42, st. 3/4

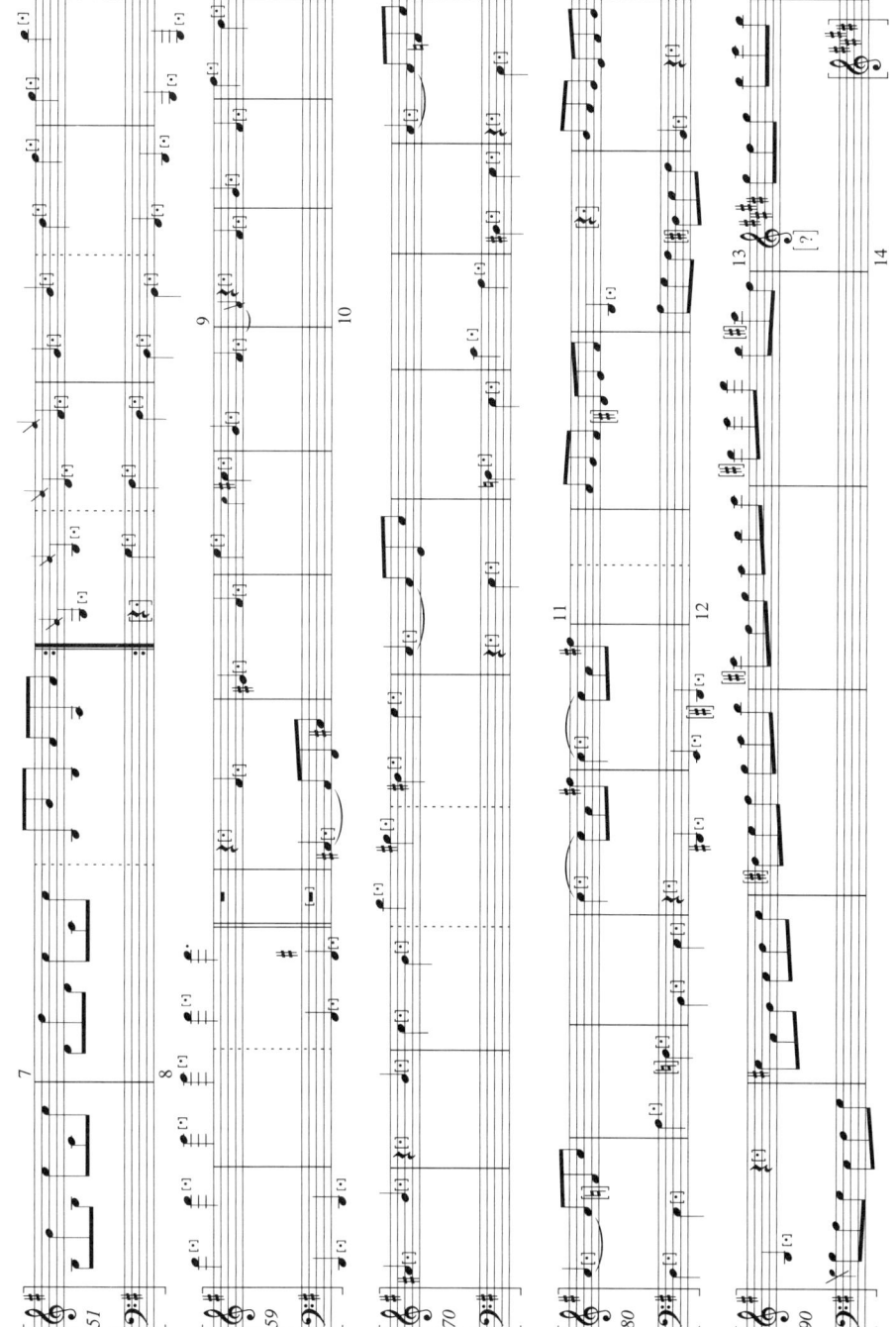

Ex. 6.1. contd.

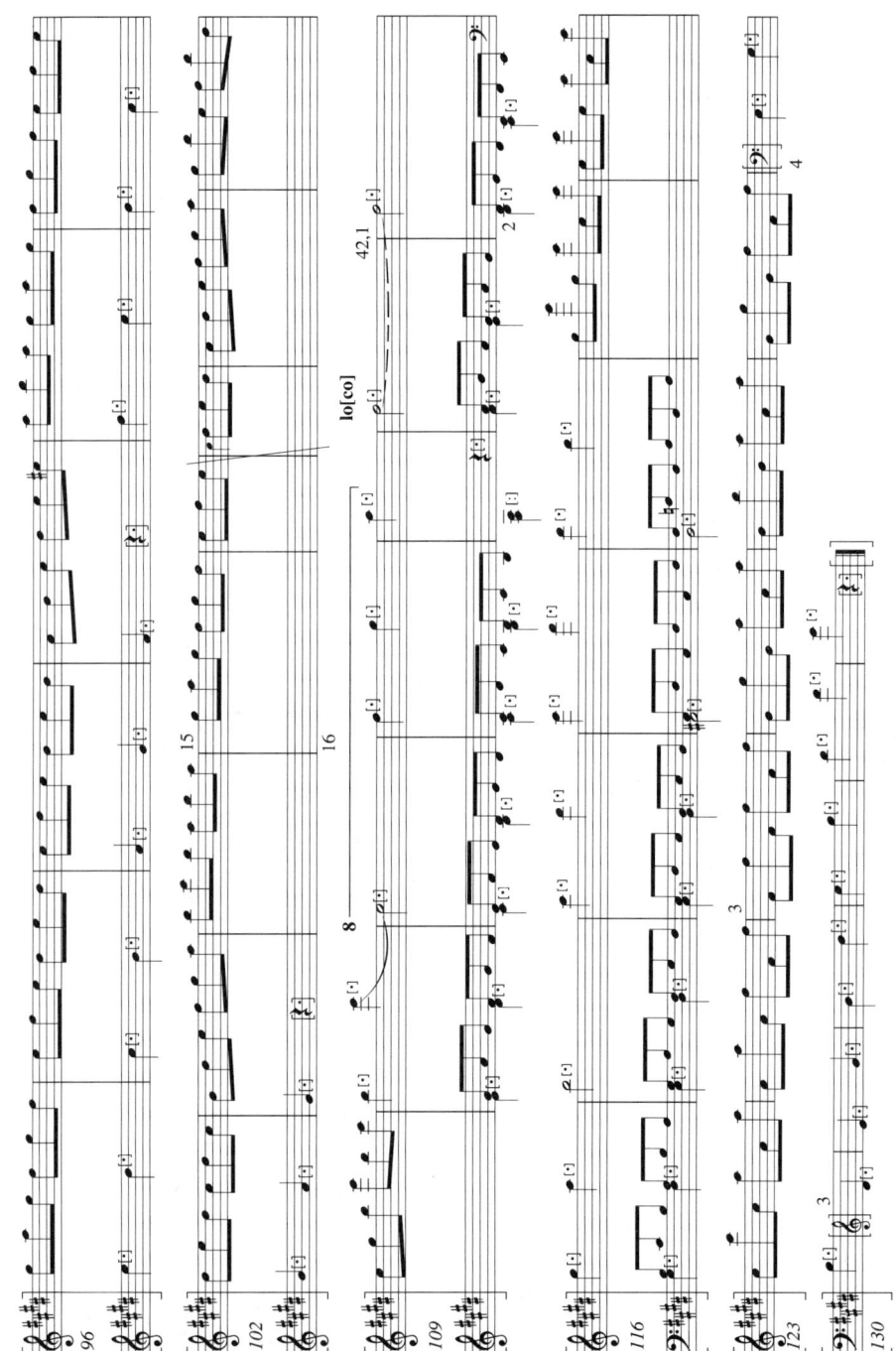

Ex. 6.2. Cf. CD 1, bars 9–25

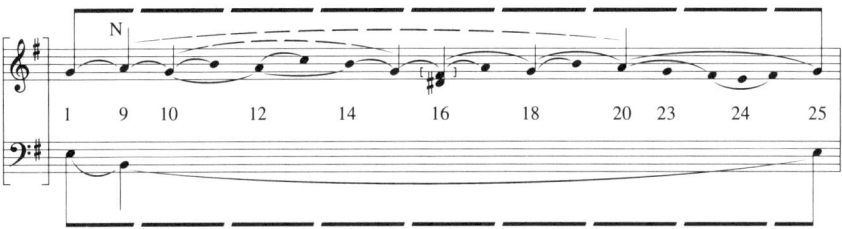

initial a^1 in bar 9 to g^1 in bar 25. This may be understood as a return to the initial sonority of the movement, g^1/E (Ex. 6.2).[1]

The arrival of g^1 in bar 25 heralds the start of a six-bar transition (bars 25–30). This springs the first major surprise in the draft, for the transition prepares not B minor, the second-group key fixed firmly in earlier sketches, but G major. During the transition the upper voice ascends by step to a^2 before falling to g^2 at the beginning of the second group: Beethoven again insists on the resolution A–G.

The second group comprises three parts. The descending theme in the first part (bars 31–45) could be heard as a derivative of the ascending line in the transition, but its true origin is surely the descending bass in bars 1–8, out of sight in this draft but hardly out of Beethoven's mind. However, the most interesting feature of this tripartite second group is its end. A closing theme (bars 54–61) built from G-major arpeggios in contrary motion carries the upper voice back up to g^3, on which note the second group began. But just before the double bar g^3 falls to a repeated $f\sharp^3$; the addition of the bass F♯, together with the A♯ implied by the figured-bass notation, leaves no doubt that the tonality has turned abruptly here to the dominant of B minor.

Fully to grasp this ending we must consider the exposition as a whole, including the unwritten but intended bars 1–8. While this exposition draft seems superficially to be quite different to anything projected in earlier sketches, the differences are in fact born of an adherence to previously established ideas. The upper voice prolongs a large-scale $\hat{3}$–$\hat{2}$ (G–F♯) progression above the bass motion E–F♯: Beethoven maintains the triadic third as *Kopfton* until the very end, when g^3 falls to $f\sharp^3$ as the dominant of B minor. Although the tonal scheme, with the relative major standing as the key of the second group, might be seen as something of a bow to tradition, there is a

---

[1] The higher register used in bars 9–24 of the final version forces the resolution a^1–g^1 into an inner voice: see Ex. 5.3.

more specific and rigorous explanation for the appearance of G major here. The harmonic underpinning of this exposition (E minor–G major–F♯ as dominant of B minor) represents a composing-out of the bass counter-motive to G–E–F♯, the upper-voice $\hat{3}$–$\hat{1}$–$\hat{2}$ progression which prevents the completion of a $\hat{3}$–$\hat{2}$–$\hat{1}$ descent in E minor (see Ex. 5.20). Thus despite its seemingly novel surface, there is no fundamental discontinuity between the exposition in CD 1 and the ideas worked out on pages 35–40 of Artaria 195.

The development, which is less well worked out than the exposition and recapitulation, does however seem to represent an almost complete break with earlier plans. Most importantly, there is no sign here of C major, the key which had formerly been chosen as the first tonal goal of the development; the tonicization of B minor prepared at the end of the exposition is confirmed in bars 63–70 instead. And A minor and F major, which had been indicated as significant keys in the development sketch on page 38 (Ex. 5.9), receive only a passing glance. There is an apparent break after bar 84, and the notation resumes in bar 87 with what is presumably the beginning of the retransition. Moving above an implied dominant pedal, the upper voice presents a middleground linear ascent from a^1 (bar 87) to the left-hand e^2 in bar 96, but this is somewhat obscured by the faster ascending motion and upward registral transfers in the foreground.

The middleground ascent recalls the exposition transition. Nor is the reminiscence accidental, for what follows the retransition here is precisely what followed the transition earlier: the second group, now slightly altered and stated in the tonic major. The alterations consist mainly in the more extended treatment afforded to the first part. The initial statement of the descending theme (bars 96–103), now in the left hand beneath an accompaniment moving in parallel thirds, clearly proclaims its kinship with bars 1–8 of the movement. It is this clear revelation, in the tonic key, of the thematic relationship between the first and second groups which allows Beethoven to omit the first group entirely from this recapitulation.

But bars 1–8 of the second movement are themselves kin to the first phrase of the first movement, in that they are underpinned by a descending progression of parallel tenths above the bass. The tonic-major recapitulation of the second group in CD 1, allied to the parallel-third motion in bars 96–103, seems calculated to underline the movement-to-movement connection also, and it is perhaps in this connection that bar 95 is to be explained. This bar stands isolated within an otherwise regular series of strongly defined four-bar groups (bars 87–90, 91–4; 96–9, 100–3) and functions like an inserted upbeat

Ex. 6.3. Cf. CD 1, bars 95–9, and Ex. 3.6

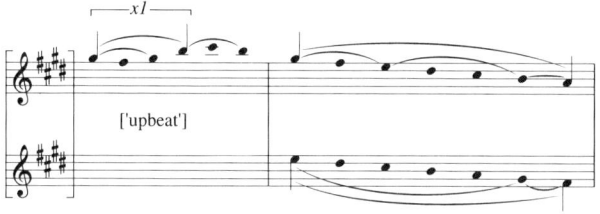

to the beginning of the second group. Is it coincidental that the main notes, g♯² and b², mimic the opening upbeat interval in the first movement? Ex. 6.3 should be compared to Ex. 3.6.

As well as setting up these retrospective links with the first movement, the E-major recapitulation in CD 1 shades into the beginning of the third-movement theme, which was of course substantially composed by this time. When the closing theme reappears (bars 129–35), the rising thirds E–G♯ and B–D♯ prepare the bass which will support the falling thirds g♯¹–e¹ and d♯¹–b at the beginning of the third movement.

CD 2

CD 2 (Ex. 6.4) covers the exposition only. With the exception of the first group, it shares no material with CD 1 but rather represents a return to the ideas sketched on pages 37 and 39 of Artaria 195. This in turn means that the transition and second-group material corresponds closely to what we know as the final version. The 'return' to earlier sketches was in some cases a very specific one: as we shall see, one section of CD 2 is an almost literal copy of one of the sketches from page 39.

Unlike CD 1, CD 2 contains all of bars 1–8, and these correspond almost exactly to their final form. Together with the fact that the opening of the draft is written with considerable care (there is even an elaborate scrolled brace at the left-hand edge of the first system), this suggests that Beethoven was intending to write what would amount virtually to a fair copy of the complete movement. The urge to attempt this at such an early stage is characteristic of Beethoven, as is also the early failure and abandonment of the attempt.[2] It is

---

[2] On this point see also R. Kramer, '"Das Organische der Fuge": On the Autograph of Beethoven's String Quartet in F major, Opus 59 No. 1', in C. Wolff (ed.), *The String Quartets of Haydn, Mozart, and Beethoven: Studies of the Autograph Manuscripts* (Cambridge, Mass., 1980), 224.

Ex. 6.4. CD 2: Artaria 195, p. 42, st. 6/7–p. 43, st. 11/12, 14

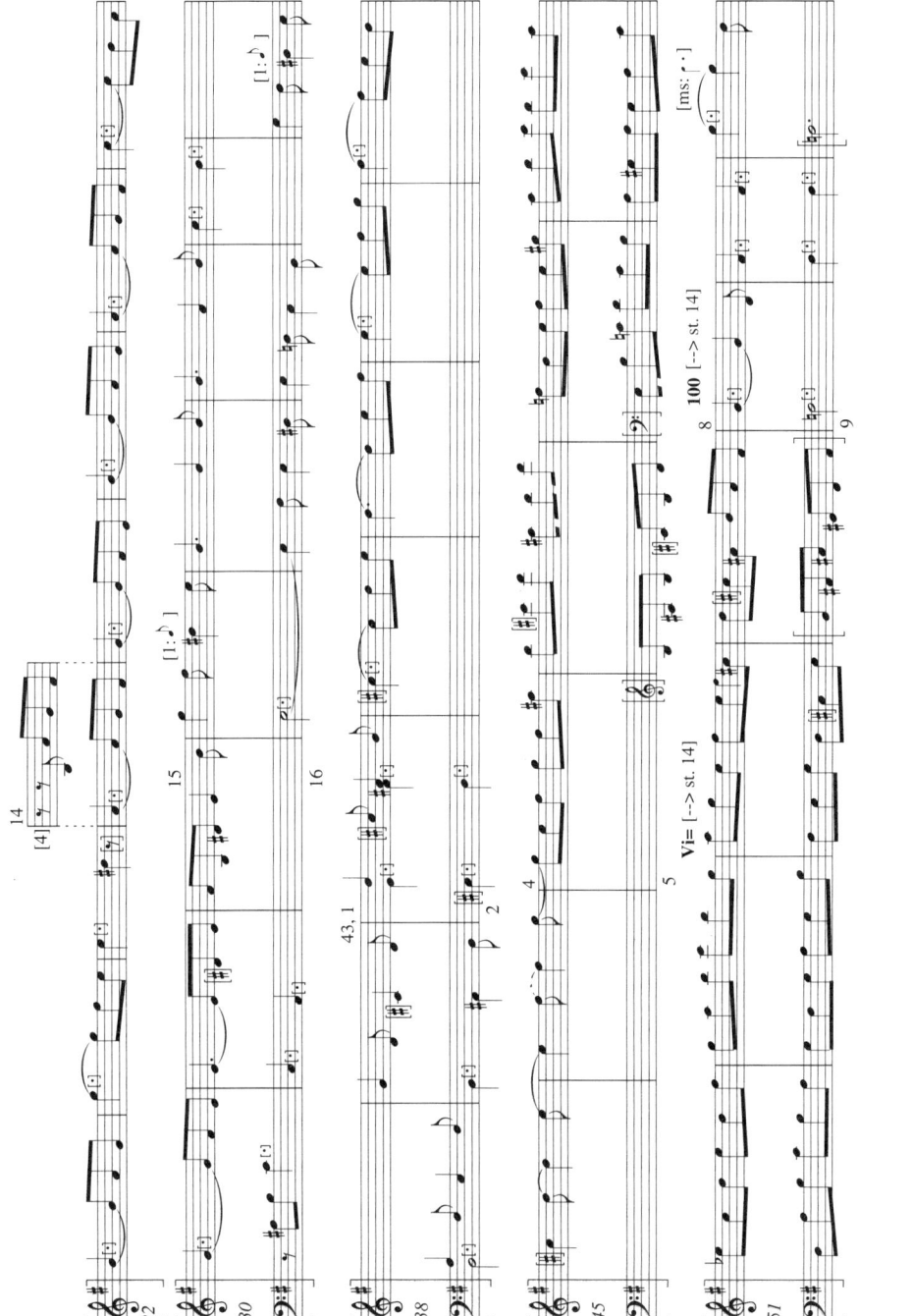

Ex. 6.4. contd.

clear from CD 2 that bars 1–8 were the only part of the movement in which Beethoven had complete confidence, for problems set in immediately thereafter.

The treatment of the second part of the first group is interesting, and shows clearly Beethoven's reliance on earlier sketches. Version [1] marks a return to the seminal sketch transcribed in Ex. 5.6, in which bars 9–16 were initially cast as an antecedent–consequent pair with a 4–♯3 suspension in the fourth bar of the antecedent (bar 12). The same formula is adopted in CD 2 (even the leap up to g^2 is preserved) but is abandoned two bars into the consequent phrase. Version [2], on the other hand, borrows directly from CD 1: Beethoven began copying out the eight-bar antecedent phrase with which that draft begins. But this was evidently not satisfactory either, for version [2] breaks off after only five bars.

What eventually satisfied Beethoven, at least temporarily, was a near-exact repeat of bars 1–8 (Ex. 6.4, version [3]). Apart from the tie between bars 9 and 10, this repeat contains a single, startling alteration: b^1 is substituted for e^2 at the final cadence (bars 15–16). The note is clearly written, and it is not easy to imagine Beethoven absent-mindedly substituting b^1 for e^2 at such a point. We must assume, then, that the change was intentional. If so, what was its purpose? The main consequence of the missing e^2 is a lack of melodic closure: the $\hat{3}$–$\hat{2}$–$\hat{1}$ (g^2–$f\sharp^2$–e^2) progression spanning bars 1–8 (see Ex. 5.7) is left incomplete because $f\sharp^2$ does not fall to e^2 at the cadence.

This incomplete progression is reinforced in the second part of the first group (bars 17–32), to which Beethoven again now turned his attention. The formulation he adopted is a conflation of the previously abandoned versions [1] and [2]: the sixteen-bar (8 + 8) structure of version [2] (and CD 1) is retained, but the melodic detail of the antecedent—specifically, the ascent to g^2 and the 4–♯3 suspension in bars 23–4—is derived from version [1] and Ex. 5.6. There is an underlying $\hat{3}$–$\hat{2}$ descent in the antecedent phrase, in that g^2 (bar 23) falls to an implied $f\sharp^2$ (bar 24: $f\sharp^2$ is replaced by the foreground motion to $d\sharp^2$). By comparison, the consequent phrase (bars 25–32) avoids the e^2 register but closes with a complete $\hat{3}$–$\hat{2}$–$\hat{1}$ progression in the lower octave.

Ex. 6.5 summarizes the upper-voice motion in the first group of CD 2 and illustrates the importance of the $\hat{3}$–$\hat{2}$–$\hat{1}$ progression. The progression is twice stated complete, the higher-register statement in bars 1–8 being nested within the lower-register one covering the entire group (bars 1–32). As we have seen, the progression in the higher register is left incomplete after bars 1–8. Beethoven's

Ex. 6.5. Cf. CD 2, bars 1–32

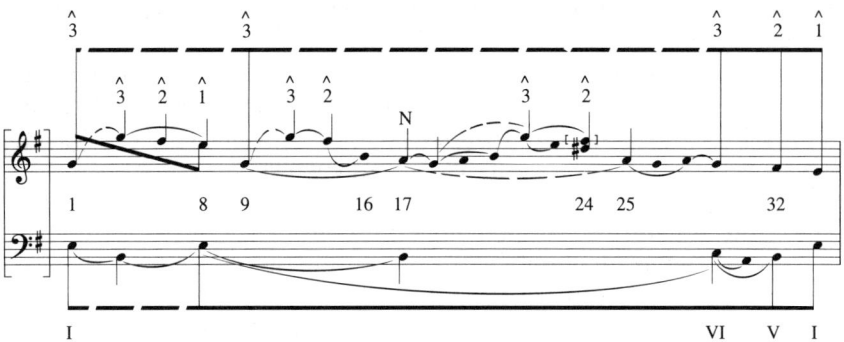

treatment of the upper voice in CD 2 is thus quite different to that in Ex. 5.6 where, as in the final version, complete statements of the $\hat{3}$–$\hat{2}$–$\hat{1}$ progression are confined to the higher register in both parts of the first group. Meanwhile the initial g^1 is elaborated within an expanded upper-neighbour progression g^1–a^1–g^1 which becomes an inner voice during bars 9–24 (Ex. 5.3a). CD 1, on the other hand, takes a middle course: the higher register is avoided altogether after bars 1–8, which are not written out in full, and both parts of the first group are unified by the expanded upper-neighbour progression g^1–a^1–g^1, now firmly set in the upper voice (Ex. 6.2).

The organization of the transition in CD 2 (bars 33–40) corresponds closely to that in the recapitulation of the final version (bars 120–31): a harmonized statement of the transition theme is followed by a pseudo-contrapuntal counterstatement, with four overlapping entries creating a gradual rise in pitch.[3] And the transition is followed by the first part of the second group (bars 41–6). This is considerably shorter than its counterpart in the final version which, like the rest of the second group, had been essentially fixed in sketches on page 39. The two versions also differ in that the single phrase in CD 2 ends with a V–I cadence (a pedal F♯ is implied in the bass of bars 41–7) which proves to be the first step in a sequential progression around the circle of fifths. By contrast, the corresponding cadence in the final version is not simultaneously part of such a progression: after the cadential motion f♯–b in bars 41–2 the bass

[3] In the recapitulation of the final version the polyphonic 'entries' follow one another at an interval of two bars rather than one, as in CD 2. In his first sketch for the exposition transition (Artaria 195, p. 39, st. 8/9) Beethoven had initially opted for a harmonized statement of the theme which was to be repeated; the replacement of the repeat by an initial statement in octaves, as in the final version, was a later addition.

moves up a step from B to c♯, and it is from this note (functioning as V/f♯) that the circle-of-fifths progression begins.

It is the treatment of the second part of the second group in CD 2 which most clearly shows the influence of earlier sketches. The circle-of-fifths progression just mentioned begins with a passing tonicization of B minor, thereby establishing the local tonic for the first time. The sequential repetitions in bars 49–50 and 51–2 similarly touch on A and G, but the sequence is discontinued thereafter. The tenth b^2/g in bar 52 leads to $a^2/f♯$ in bar 53, and the remainder of that bar is built from a stepwise descent in parallel tenths between the upper voice and bass. The upper-voice descent continues in bar 54, reaching $a♯^1$ on the fifth quaver. Beethoven omitted the bass in this bar, but he presumably intended it to continue in parallel tenths with the upper voice, reaching F♯ as the upper voice arrived on its $a♯^1$.[4]

In essence, then, bars 53–4 consist of a prolonged F♯ supporting the chromatic progression A–A♯ in the upper voice. And in a wider context, the bass f♯ in bar 53 marks the end of a descending fourth-progression b–a–g–f♯ which begins in bars 47–8. The progression is not new: in an earlier sketch on page 38 (Ex. 5.11a) Beethoven had tried to integrate linear descents through the complementary tetrachords of the B octave (that is, B–F♯ and E–B) with the modulation from tonic to dominant minor which was to underpin the exposition; here in CD 2 he was using the upper tetrachord within the second group itself.

The influence of the sketch from page 38 did not stop here. The rest of CD 2 is very close in content to the remainder of the exposition (bars 51–65) in the final version; but underneath the draft, on stave 14 of page 43, Beethoven wrote an extension to the phrase (bars 47–54) we have just been considering and cued it into the draft by means of 'Vi = de' and '1oo' connectives.[5] This extension turns out to be a close adaptation of another earlier sketch, the one on page 39 in which the progression from E to B minor is articulated by means of a descending fourth-progression E–D–C–B (Ex. 5.12). The version in CD 2 preserves not only the three-note motive from

---

[4] The missing bass in bar 54 has been supplied editorially in Ex. 6.4.

[5] A literal interpretation of the 'Vi = de' connection results in the omission of bars 53–4, which upsets the larger phrase structure: bars 47–54 form an eight-bar group, and the '= de' extension consists of two more such groups (the first two bars of the extension may be disregarded since they effectively duplicate the next two; Beethoven abandoned the quaver figuration in favour of the three-note motive and simply failed to delete his first thoughts). The omission of bars 53–4 would also result in an awkward harmonic progression from bar 52 to the first bar of the extension. In all probability, then, the 'Vi =' referent is misplaced and should follow bar 54.

the earlier sketch but also the double statement of the fourth-progression, first in the upper voice and then in the bass. The result of this extension to CD 2 is clear: both tetrachords of the B octave are now presented, B–F♯ in bars 47–54 and E–B in the added material. This linear statement of the composed-out B octave contrasts with the superimposition of the two tetrachords in Ex. 5.11a and was surely designed to complement the bass descent through the E octave in bars 1–8 of the movement. Whereas the first part of the second group in CD 1 presented a simple foreground derivative of that descending bass, Beethoven's plan in CD 2 involved a rather more subtle middleground reference.

Finally, we should consider more closely the material which was originally to follow bars 53–4 of CD 2, prior to the insertion of the extension. The eight-bar phrase in bars 55–62 begins and ends with a statement of the progression which eventually appeared in bars 55–6 of the final version; the crucial role of that progression within the exposition was examined at length in Chapter 5. The change in upper-voice register between the first and second statements here in CD 2 seems important in view of Beethoven's treatment of melodic closure within the first group. Ex. 6.5 shows that closure is achieved in the e^1 register by means of a complete $\hat{3}$–$\hat{2}$–$\hat{1}$ progression, and that after bars 1–8 this progression is consistently truncated in the e^2 register. In bars 55–6 of CD 2 Beethoven now reverses the situation in the lower register—g^1–$f\sharp^1$ cannot proceed satisfactorily to e^1 in these harmonic circumstances—while again reinforcing the lack of closure in the higher register by means of g^2–$f\sharp^2$ in bars 61–2.

Much of the force of bars 55–6 in the final version comes, of course, from Beethoven's manipulation of the double resolution potential of F: F–E creates a momentary tonicization of C in bars 51–2 and 53–4, and the upward resolution of F to F♯ in bars 55–6 is unexpected. In CD 2 this double resolution is again pressed into service, but in a less effective way. The downward resolution in the upper voice (f^2–e^2, bars 58–9) is sandwiched between the two upward ones on either side.[6] What this version does perhaps achieve is a slightly more emphatic tonicization of C: the editorially supplied bass in bars 57–60 suggests that the shift of f from the bass to the upper voice would allow a root-position C-major triad to support e^2.

The final phrase in CD 2 (bars 63–73) needs little comment, except to point out that there is no indication here of a repeated exposition (compare Ex. 5.18). On the other hand, the firm cadence in

---

[6] The final version of bars 51–6 had already emerged in sketches on p. 39 of Artaria 195, but it was to be some time before Beethoven was convinced that this relatively early formulation was the most suitable.

Ex. 6.6. Artaria 195, p. 44, st. 1/2

bars 71–3, involving a $\hat{3}$–$\hat{2}$–$\hat{1}$ descent in B minor not found in the final version, suggests that Beethoven did not envisage an elision with the beginning of the development; a return to the opening of the draft could therefore follow on quite naturally from this point. Plans for the beginning of the development appear in a sketch (Ex. 6.6) at the top of the next page (page 44) in Artaria 195. The handwriting of this sketch is very similar to that of CD 2; so similar, in fact, that it may have been written as a continuation of the draft, for it too follows naturally from the cadence in bars 71–3.

The clear and direct motion towards C major illustrated in Ex. 6.6 seems to be yet another indication that Beethoven had now decisively rejected the plans outlined in CD 1 in favour of his earlier ideas for the movement. This notion, however, is shattered by the next sketch on page 44; but that is better considered in relation to CD 3.

CD 3

Two features of the physical layout of this draft deserve mention before we consider its musical substance. First, the draft continues from page 44, staves 15/16 to page 45, staves 3/4. A separate sketch for the coda, labelled 'Ende', occupies page 45, staves 1/2; it must have been written before Beethoven began CD 3—or at the latest, before he had filled page 44—for if staves 1/2 had been empty when he turned to page 45 he would surely have used them for the continuation. Secondly, it will be noticed that the bar numbering in the transcription (Ex. 6.7) does not include the blank bar following bar 60. The musical continuity between bars 60–1 is perfectly assured, and we need not suspect a break here. At precisely this point in the sketchbook, in fact, there is a large smudge extending from stave 7 to stave 8, on which the right-hand part of CD 3 is written. Beethoven must have marked off the blank bar, perhaps along with several

Ex. 6.7. CD 3: Artaria 195, p. 44, st. 9/10–p. 45, st. 15/16

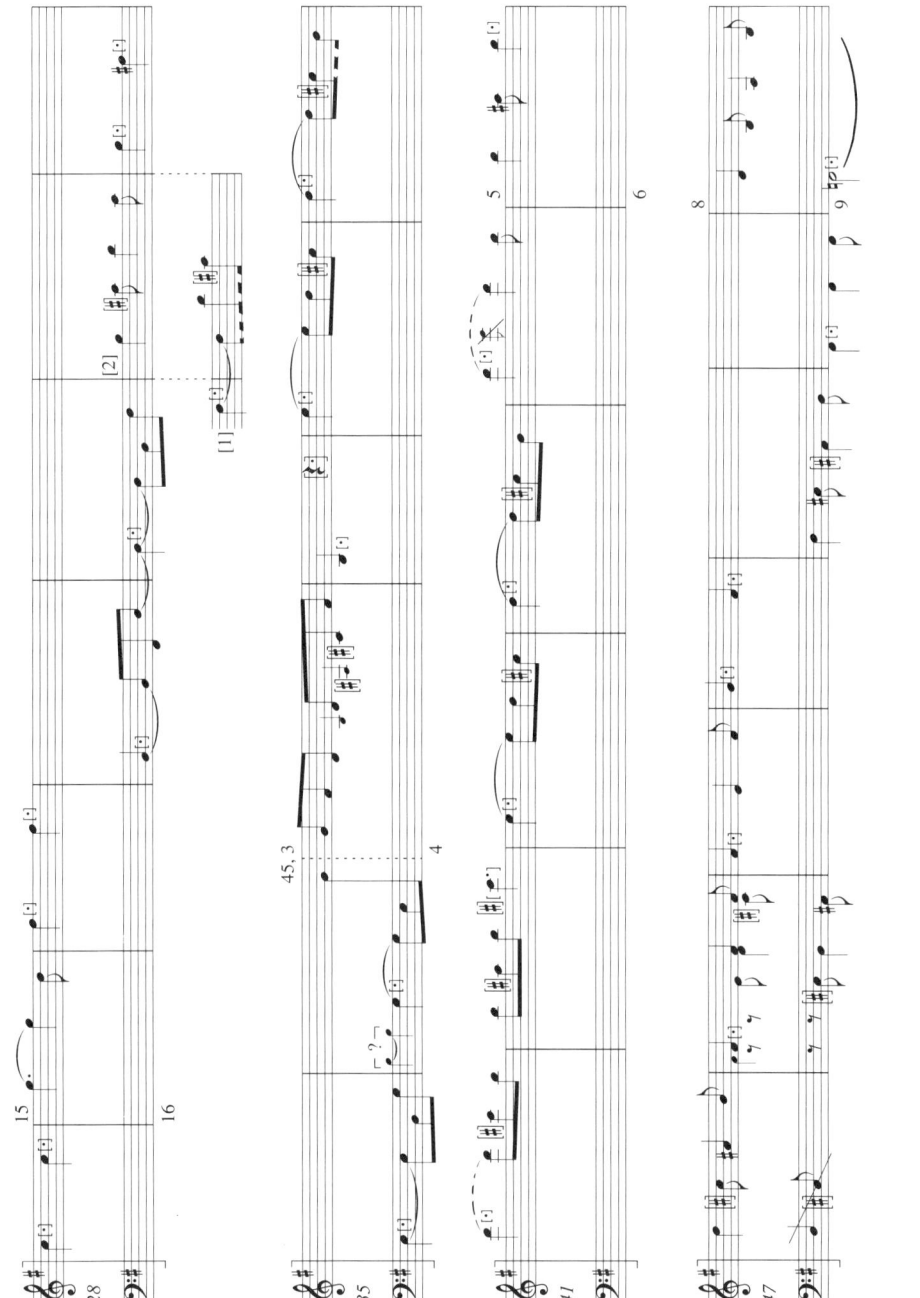

Ex. 6.7. contd.

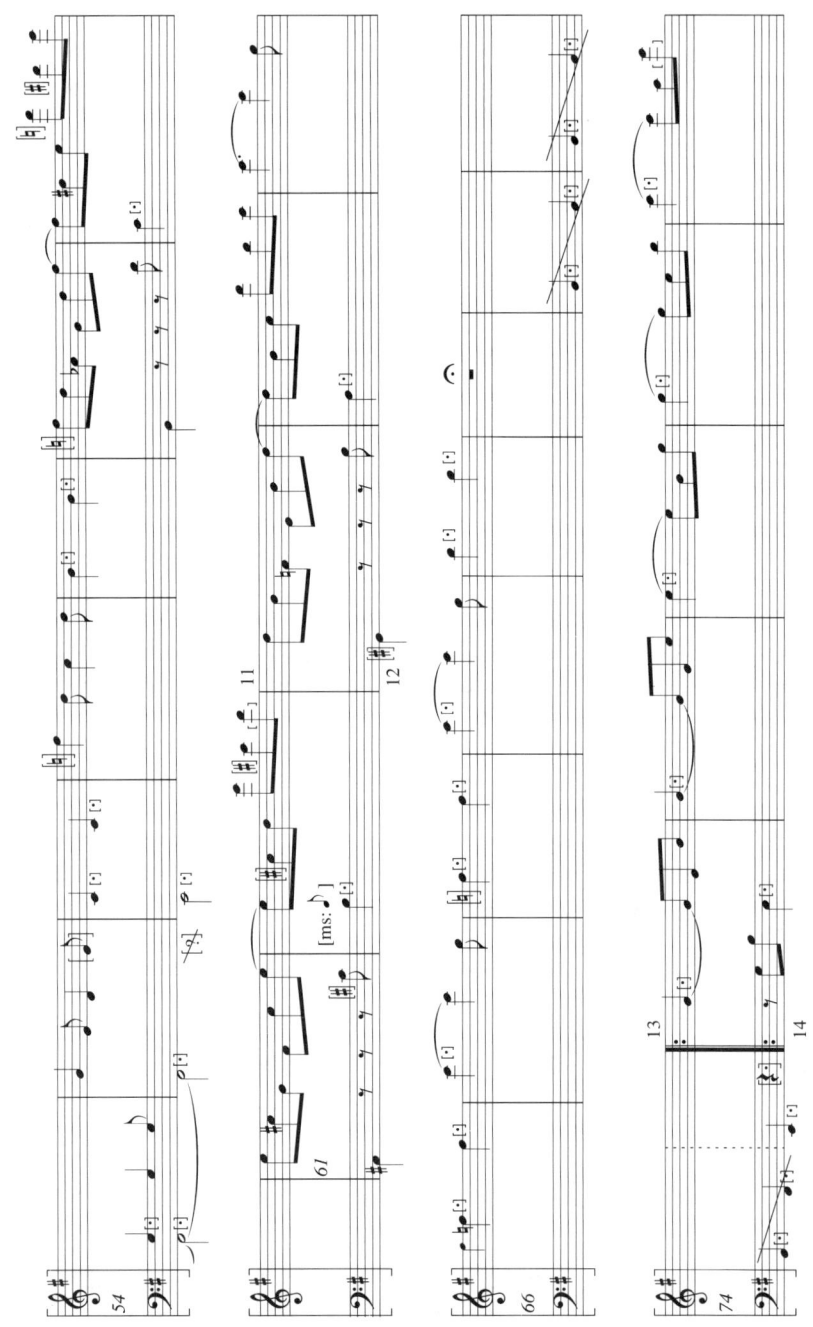

others, before realizing that the smudge would prevent him from filling it.

CD 3 testifies to another radical recasting of the form of the second movement of Op. 109. The draft clearly does not begin at the beginning; indeed, the material of bars 1–24 is almost without precedent in previous sketches. But things become clearer from bar 25 onward, for all of the remaining material is familiar from earlier sketches. In particular, the content and sequence of events in bars 31–75 runs closely parallel to that in CD 2; the major difference is that CD 2, the exposition draft, begins in E minor and closes in B minor while bars 31–75 of CD 3 move in the opposite direction, from B minor to E minor. Bearing this in mind, and noting also that bars 25–30 and 65–70 of CD 3 are identical apart from the transposition, it begins to seem that this draft projects a baroque-style binary-form movement with the harmonic scheme I–v : v–I. The second part begins in bar 31 and is presented complete; the first part, however, is only partially represented.

What is missing from the first part? By examining both the draft itself and two closely related sketches we can obtain a plausible answer to this question. There is good reason to assume that the movement would have begun with some version of the first-group material familiar from earlier sketches and from the final version: first, because this material represents such a secure part of Beethoven's conception of the movement that it is difficult to imagine him abandoning it, even in this context; and secondly, because the formal model adopted in CD 3 presupposes that both parts will begin and end with the same basic material. In other words, we may to some extent infer the material missing in the first part from the complete second part, and may assume that the movement would have begun with an E-minor version of bars 31–46.

CD 3 continues (bars 47–58) with the transition, which begins in B minor (compare the corresponding passage, bars 33–40, in CD 2). The likely assumption that this material, suitably transposed, would also have appeared in the first part of the movement is bolstered by Ex. 6.8, a sketch which follows immediately after CD 3 at the top of page 46. The close correspondence between this sketch and bars 47–60 of CD 3 speaks for itself.

Both in Ex. 6.8 and in CD 3 the transition leads directly into the progression around the circle of fifths which, to speak in terms of the final version, belongs to the second part of the second group: the first part is omitted in these sketches (again, compare the corresponding passage in CD 2, where at bar 41 the transition leads into the familiar phrase built over a dominant pedal in B minor). But a

Ex. 6.8. Artaria 195, p. 46, st. 1/2–3/4

variant of that omitted material turns up in the last six bars of a sketch which immediately precedes the beginning of CD 3 on page 44 (Ex. 6.9).

Ex. 6.9 testifies to another radical rethinking of familiar material. In place of the expected bass resolution c♯–d in bars 5–6, Beethoven breaks the sequential progression around the circle of fifths and reaches instead towards F major through the reinterpretation of the augmented-sixth chord in bar 7 (the parallel with events in bars 150–7 of the final version will be obvious). F major is not sustained but is replaced by the six-bar section referred to above. This introduces the second-group material omitted from Ex. 6.8 and CD 3, but in a new harmonic context: now it is the dominant of C major, rather than of E or B minor, which is the pedal harmony. (The incongruous diminished-seventh chord with which Ex. 6.9 breaks off further muddies the uncharted waters into which Beethoven had drifted here.)

While the V^7/C pedal at the end of Ex. 6.9 may not be consonant with our expectations, derived from earlier sketches and the final version, it is nevertheless entirely consonant with the first two bars of CD 3, which are built on the same harmony. Moreover, if we compare the first two bars of Ex. 6.9 with the last two of Ex. 6.8 we see that these also are basically identical. From a purely musical point of view, then—there is no physical continuity between the two sketches—Ex. 6.8 runs into Ex. 6.9, and Ex. 6.9 runs into CD 3. These overlaps are probably not fortuitous. In other words, Exx. 6.8 and 6.9 combine to supply much of the material missing from the first part of the movement outlined in CD 3; we may prefix them to the draft conceptually, and may similarly prefix Ex. 6.8 with a suitably transposed version of the first-group material in the second part (bars 31–46) of CD 3 in order to provide a plausible reconstruction of the missing opening portion of this projected binary-form movement.

We may pause to savour for a moment the stage in the genesis of the second movement represented by CD 3, for in writing this draft Beethoven reached a point at the furthest remove from his eventual formulation. Robert Winter has remarked that 'Beethoven seems to have been best able to make responsible aesthetic choices after a compositional or expressive problem had been defined in terms of extremes';[7] the rejection of sonata form in CD 3 represents one such extreme, while the rejection in CD 1 of the tonal-thematic scheme

---

[7] R. Winter, 'The Sketches for the "Ode to Joy"', in id. and B. Carr (eds.), *Beethoven, Performers, and Critics* (Detroit, 1980), 194.

Ex. 6.9. Artaria 195, p. 44, st. 4/5–6/7

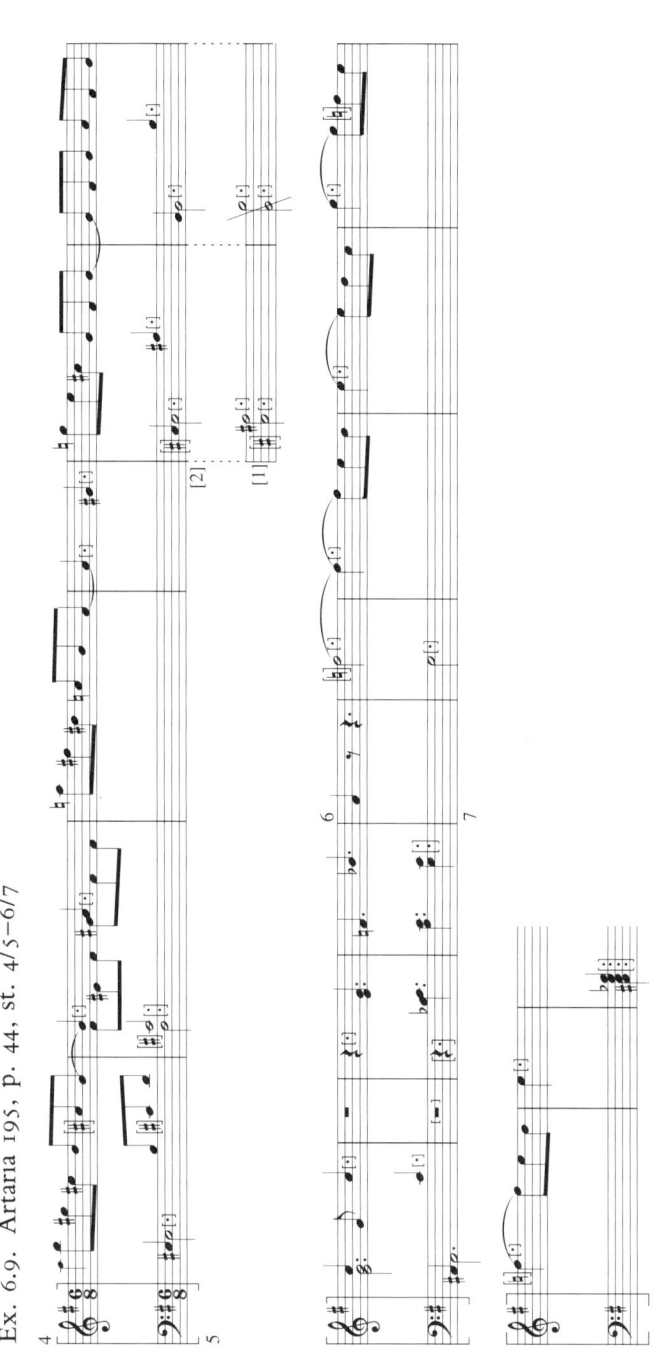

worked out in earlier sketches (and eventually adopted in the final version) might be said to represent another.

But just as the radical features of CD 1 were shown to result largely from the reinterpretation of familiar ideas, so too does the severe rupture between CD 3 and preceding sketches begin, on reflection, to seem more apparent than real. One explanation for the rejection of sonata form in CD 3 hangs on Beethoven's continuing exploration of the submediant. A Schenkerian reading of bars 1–30 of CD 3 would identify a prolongation of the $VI^{\sharp 6}$–V/b progression governing bars 49–56 of the final version: the antecedents of this passage were discussed at length in Chapter 5. The most notable feature of the prolonged version in CD 3 is the increased emphasis afforded to C major. The long-range resolution of the chord in bar 1 is to the (implied) dominant of B minor in bar 30; but in its immediate context it resolves as a dominant seventh and ushers in nine bars of root-position C major.

As a precedent for this expansion of the submediant we may recall bars 55–62 of CD 2, where the appearance of f^2–e^2 in the upper voice rather than the bass allows for the possibility of root-position as opposed to first-inversion C-major harmony. And fully to appreciate the reappraisal of the movement undertaken in CD 3 we should recall that in the first phase of sketching, described in Chapter 5, the most significant appearance of C major was apparently earmarked for the development section. Now the binary-form movement projected in CD 3 obviously has no separate development section; but what it does include, if the above reconstruction of the incomplete first part is correct, is a section of music which emphasizes the submediant and which has no correlate in the second part. This independent section may be understood as a substitute development which has become absorbed into the first part of the movement. If, in Beethoven's mind, the basic purpose of the development was to explore and emphasize the submediant, then that section is merely relocated, rather than omitted, in CD 3.[8]

Only the coda of CD 3 remains to be discussed, but we should first examine the independent coda sketch at the top of page 45. Although this sketch must have been written before the coda in CD 3, the two are closely related. Ex. 6.10a provides a transcription; the

---

[8] The appearance of developmental material in binary-form movements of the kind on which CD 3 is evidently modelled is by no means uncommon; what *is* unusual here is the appearance of such material in the first rather than the second section. See M. Tilmouth, 'Binary Form', in Sadie (ed.), *New Grove Dictionary of Music and Musicians*, ii. 708, where Scarlatti's Sonata in C, K. 460, is cited as an example of a movement in which 'a great deal of development in the first section makes it almost twice the length of the second'.

Ex. 6.10. *a* Artaria 195, p. 45, st. 1/2

b Cf. Ex. 6.10*a*

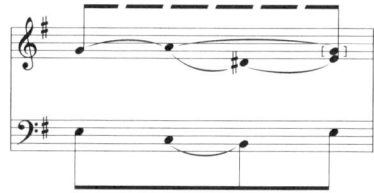

sketch begins with a straightforward reference to the beginning of the movement, and proceeds almost entirely within that initial register. Ex. 6.10*b* illustrates the voice-leading implications of the final bars: the sustained a^1 is left unresolved at the cadence, as the upper voice leaps down to bring in $d\sharp^1$–e^1. Were the a^1 to be explicitly resolved, then the final upper-voice pitch would have to be g^1, creating a return to the initial sonority of the movement and, more locally, of this coda.

The idea of a reference to the opening of the movement is taken up in the coda to CD 3 (bars 76–end). Compared to Ex. 6.10*a*, this version is registrally more wide-ranging, and it closes in the e^2 register associated with the second part of the first group in the final version. But the most significant moment comes in bar 84, where the tonic major replaces the minor: the last nine bars are effectively an expanded *tierce de picardie* above a tonic pedal. Ex. 6.11 highlights two aspects of the linear motion in these bars. The stepwise descent from

Ex. 6.11. Cf. CD 3, bars 76–end

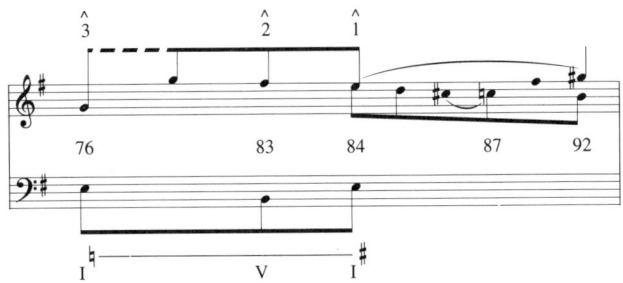

e^2 to b^1 serves as a further reminder of the descending bass in bars 1–8 of the movement, while the rising line from e^2 to $g\sharp^2$ opens out the space between the tonic and triadic (major) third, effectively replacing the initial sonority of the movement with its major-mode equivalent. It is significant that in these two versions of the coda Beethoven arranges for the triadic third to remain active at the final cadence, even if, as shown in Ex. 6.10b, it is only implicitly so.

The turn to the tonic major in the coda of CD 3 recalls the E-major recapitulation in CD 1. That recapitulation, it was shown, engenders connections with the first and third movements of the sonata; and much the same is true of this coda. While the disposition of the final chord in CD 3, with $g\sharp^2$ at the top, prepares the first chord of the ensuing variation theme, its surprising metrical placement, on the second rather than the first beat of the final bar, recalls the ending of the first movement, where the unbroken motion of bars 86–97 is abruptly terminated by the silent downbeat which precedes the arrival of the final chord.

After completing CD 3 (and presumably also Ex. 6.8, the related sketch for the transition in the first part) Beethoven made a few shorter sketches before his last major sketching effort, represented by CD 4. The most telling of these sketches is one on page 47, staves 6–7, which shows segments of the first part of the exposition second group as it appears in the final version. The sketch is mainly significant in that it marks the 'rehabilitation' of sonata form: the emphasis given to the dominant of B minor in this part of the movement is essential to the polarization of tonic and dominant, E and B minor. That polarization, crucial to a sonata-form exposition, is less important in the kind of binary-form movement projected in CD 3, from which—as we have seen—the first part of the second group had been meticulously omitted.

CD 4

CD 4 begins on page 47, stave 9 in Artaria 195 and continues down to page 50, staves 13/14. As explained above, this draft for the development, recapitulation, and coda will not be transcribed in full here. Instead, discussion will concentrate on (1) the development, (2) the transition in the recapitulation, and (3) the coda. These areas have been chosen for different reasons: the development is poorly represented in the sketches for the movement, and the version preserved in CD 4 is the only detailed and continuous one prior to the final version; the recapitulation transition provides a good opportunity to examine in detail Beethoven's handling of a particularly difficult passage; and the composition of the coda raises issues relevant to the large-scale structure of the movement—issues which will be further explored in the Conclusion below.

1. The Development Ex. 6.12 shows the development as it appears in CD 4. The first two bars (compare bars 55–6 in the final version) mark the end of the exposition, and the development proper begins with bar 3. What is perhaps most immediately obvious about this section is its length, particularly in comparison with the final version. A second feature is Beethoven's reliance on the ideas recorded earlier on page 38 of the sketchbook (Ex. 5.9). The development in Ex. 6.12 comprises three distinct sections, all based on eight-bar groupings. The first section (bars 3–18: the deletion of much of this section will be discussed below) begins with a chromatic ascent from b^1 to g^2. An ascending octave leap brings in g^3, from which note a partly chromatic descent leads towards c^3, implied at the beginning of bar 19: $g^3-f\sharp^3-f^2-e^2/e^3-d^3[-c^3]$. These events correspond precisely to Beethoven's earlier plans: C was to be the first harmonic goal of the development, and its dominant (G) was to be approached by a rising stepwise progression from B (cf. Ex. 5.11a).

The second section (bars 19–26) should therefore be understood as beginning in C major. The purpose of this eight-bar phrase is to lead from C to A minor, the key in which the third (and longest) section begins. The choice of A minor as the next harmonic goal after C is again no surprise: both keys had been projected in Ex. 5.9, and Beethoven's accompanying remarks there ('in C Mi[ttel]s[atz]'; 'in a moll im Bass the[ma]') make the tonal succession quite clear. The cadence in bars 26–7, like that in bars 18–19, elides the ending of this section with the beginning of the next.

It was from the third section (bars 27–58) that the development in the final version was eventually to spring. Both in its surface detail

Ex. 6.12. Artaria 195, p. 47, st. 9–14

and its larger organization, this section once again draws directly upon the descending bass in bars 1–8 of the movement. That bass is immediately obvious as the source of the octave-descents beginning on A, G, F♯, and E (bars 27, 35, 43, and 49). Each descent is presented canonically, the lower voice acting as *dux* and the upper as *comes*. The middleground tetrachord A–E defined by the key notes of the four octaves is of course also derived from the descending bass in bars 1–8.

It seems that the F♯ octave-descent in bars 43–50 proved the most influential segment of this third section. Whereas the A and G octaves are unfolded complete in both voices, only the upper (and, in this case, augmented) tetrachord, $f\sharp^2-c^2$, of the F♯ octave appears in the *comes* entry in bars 45–8. Nor is the F♯ octave treated consistently as *dux*: it is split into its two constituent tetrachords and the lower one ($b^2-f\sharp^2$, bars 47–50) is placed above *comes*. This registral dislocation of the two tetrachords in *dux* creates the impression of a new contrapuntal voice appearing above *comes*: the two-part texture is supplanted by an implied three-part one.

It is likely that the special treatment of the F♯ octave was bound up with the prevailing eight-bar phrase structure. Each octave-descent requires eight bars; and since *comes* follows *dux* at an interval of two bars, a two-bar extension would have been required at the end of the development to accommodate the completion of the E octave in *comes*. But by splitting the *dux* statement of the F♯ octave in the manner just described, Beethoven was able to bring in the E octave in bar 49, two bars earlier than would otherwise have been the case. This obviated the need for the two-bar extension (the third section of this development comprises four eight-bar phrases) although it necessarily entailed two 'dead' bars (57–8) in *dux*; Beethoven used these for an 'Eroica'-like false start to the recapitulation.

Another aspect of the treatment of the F♯ octave deserves mention. In the A and G octaves Beethoven carefully differentiated the approaches to the dominant and the tonic: the melodic formula $\hat{6}-\hat{4}-\hat{5}$ prefaces the dominant, while the $\hat{2}-\hat{5}-\hat{1}$ motion allows the insertion of the dominant directly before the closing tonic (both formulae are of course adopted from the descending bass in bars 1–8 of the movement). When he came to the F♯ octave Beethoven again did things differently. The F♯ tonic in bar 50 is approached through the 'dominant' formula, with the result that this lower tetrachord of the F♯ octave becomes indistinguishable from the upper tetrachord of a B octave: $b^2-a^2-g^2-e^2-f\sharp^2$ ($\hat{8}-\hat{7}-\hat{6}-\hat{4}-\hat{5}$). This ambiguity was to be pursued in the final version.

Another stage *en route* to the final version of the development is

154 Second Movement: Continuity Drafts

Ex. 6.13. Artaria 195, p. 46, st. 10/11

recorded in Ex. 6.13. This sketch, entered on page 46, appears to be a replacement for almost all Ex. 6.12, which occurs on the facing page 47 in the sketchbook. Beethoven's rejection of Ex. 6.12 is indicated by the deletion of bars 1–12 and the addition of a 'Vi = de' connective linking it with Ex. 6.13. Neither the extent of the deletion nor the position of the 'Vi =' should be taken literally, however. The clue to understanding how Exx. 6.12 and 6.13 fit together is provided by the last two bars of the latter, which duplicate bars 55–6 of Ex. 6.12. Ex. 6.13, then, is a replacement for bars 1–56 of CD 4; the duplication of bars 55–6 marks the point at which the substitute passage feeds into the continuity draft.

Beethoven had clearly decided upon a considerable reduction in the length and scope of the development section, for Ex. 6.13 is a mere fourteen bars long and draws exclusively upon the third section of Ex. 6.12. Only two octave-descents, through B and E, are now used; and their treatment springs largely from that afforded the F♯ octave in Ex. 6.12. In *dux* the lower tetrachord of the B octave is placed above *comes* (bars 5–8). In *comes*, however, this tetrachordal split is not observed: the B octave is presented complete in bars 3–10, with the result that bars 9–10 duplicate bars 7–8. The E octave is also split, with the lower tetrachord of *dux* entering above *comes* in the penultimate bar; but this time the canonic pattern is altered, for *comes* begins in bar 11 with the lower rather than the upper tetrachord. In effect, *dux* appears to be imitating *comes* in the presentation of the A–E tetrachord during the last four bars.

Indeed, the chief result of the registral separation of the two tetrachords making up each octave-descent is that the tetrachord, rather than the octave, becomes the governing interval. This effect

Ex. 6.14. *a* Cf. Op. 109, second movement, bars 70–92

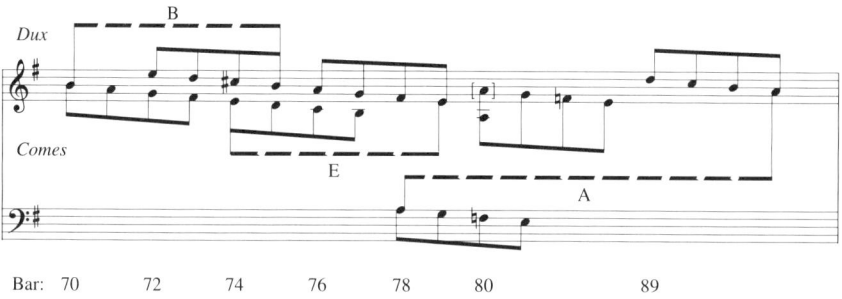

b Cf. Op. 109, second movement, bars 72–7

is heightened in the final version, where each octave-descent is divided between *dux* and *comes*, the former taking the upper tetrachord and the latter 'imitating', at the fourth above, with the lower tetrachord. It is the fourth, not the octave as in Ex. 6.12, which is the guiding interval here (Ex. 6.14).

Ex. 6.14*a* shows that the B, E, and A octaves are unfolded in the final version, although the entrance of the lower tetrachord of the A octave is delayed by the contrasting material in bars 83–8.[9] Ex. 6.14*b* shows how Beethoven responded to the ambiguity which had surfaced in his treatment of the F♯ octave in Ex. 6.12. He rejected the $\hat{2}$–$\hat{5}$–$\hat{1}$ approach to the tonic in the lower half of the tetrachord altogether and substituted $\hat{2}$–$\sharp\hat{7}$–$\hat{1}$. Through the flattening of $\hat{2}$ and $\hat{7}$ this lower tetrachord could be converted into the upper tetrachord of the octave a fifth below the original: thus the lower tetrachord of the B octave in bars 72–5 (e^2–d^2–$c\sharp^2$–$a\sharp^1$–b^1, $\hat{4}$–$\hat{3}$–$\hat{2}$–$\sharp\hat{7}$–$\hat{1}$) reappears transformed as the upper tetrachord of the E octave in bars 74–7 (e^1–d^1–c^1–a–b, $\hat{8}$–$\flat\hat{7}$–$\hat{6}$–$\hat{4}$–$\hat{5}$), and so on.

One last observation: although Beethoven had lost his cherished harmonic goals, C major and A minor, somewhere between Exx. 6.12

---

[9] The principle of imitation at the fourth gives way temporarily to the former one of imitation at the octave in bars 80–3, when *comes* answers *dux* with the upper rather than the lower tetrachord of the A octave.

and 6.13, he restored them in the final version. The B pedal gives way to C in bar 79, just as the E octave is being completed, and C-major harmony is maintained for the next six bars. C is succeeded by A minor, a key defined by its own octave-descent (Ex. 6.14). Thus the final version mediates between Exx. 6.12 and 6.13, combining the material concision of the latter with the broader harmonic scheme of the former.

2. The Recapitulation Transition Before beginning to examine the problem of the recapitulation transition in CD 4, a brief summary of the recapitulation up to that point may be helpful. The first part of the first group (bars 1–8 in the exposition) is stated twice: first in its original form and then with the right- and left-hand parts inverted (compare the final version, bars 105–19).[10] Whereas in the final version Beethoven omitted the second part of the first group (bars 9–16 and 17–24 in the exposition) from the recapitulation, he not only included it in full in CD 4 but again inverted the parts in the repeat of the basic eight-bar phrase (the inversion is implied in CD 4 by the fact that the upper voice is transferred to the left hand; the right-hand stave is blank). In this repeat he also substituted f^2 for $f\sharp^2$ in the bars corresponding to 19 and 23 in the exposition, so as to prepare the arrival of C major at the beginning of the transition. The final bar of the repeat had to be slightly altered to accommodate the abrupt turn to C.

The model for the transition in CD 4 was the corresponding part of CD 3 (Ex. 6.7, bars 47–58): an initial, harmonized statement of the four-bar theme followed by a series of two-bar units using the first half of the theme to create a pseudo-polyphonic texture. It was a model which was retained in the final version. In CD 4 there was no problem with the harmonized statement, nor with the ultimate goal of the transition, namely the reappearance, on the dominant of E minor, of the first part of the second group (compare bar 132 of the final version: the continuation into the second group is omitted from the transcription in Ex. 6.15). Beethoven's difficulties centred rather upon the series of two-bar units. His first attempt is shown in Ex. 6.15; the bottom stave summarizes the voice leading and shows that c is regained in the bass by means of a chromatic descent from g.

This version was evidently unsatisfactory, perhaps because it required five rather than four two-bar units to reach its goal. At all

---

[10] As Ex. 6.4 shows, Beethoven chose to repeat bars 1–8 in the exposition when he wrote CD 2. Was he already planning to repeat those bars in the recapitulation also?

Ex. 6.15. Artaria 195, p. 49, st. 1/2–4/5

events, the next attempt involved only four units. Beethoven replaced the descending chromatic bass with a diatonic progression through the third G–F♯–E (he did not actually notate the bass in the final bar, but the upper voice clearly implies tonic harmony). Ex. 6.16 shows this new version and again includes a summary of the voice leading.

The 'Vi =' sign in the fifth bar connects with a '= de' attached to a supplementary sketch on stave 16 of the same page. This was to be Beethoven's third attempt at organizing the passage, one in which he reinstated his earlier idea of a descending chromatic bass. This version (Ex. 6.17 shows it in the context of CD 4) is distinguished from Ex. 6.16 by the appearance of a new pitch, F, in the chromatic line. (At some later stage Beethoven pencilled in F♯–F on the main draft and supplied the F with an upper part indicating F-major harmony.)

A comparison with the final version shows that the arrangement in Ex. 6.17 eventually proved more satisfactory than the previous two; but any advance perceived in the shaping of the descending bass must have been offset by the return to a series of five rather

Ex. 6.16. Artaria 195, p. 49, st. 2–4/5

than four two-bar units. So Beethoven deleted the third (F♯–F) and fifth (C–B¹) units of Ex. 6.17 in pencil and wrote his fourth and final attempt, again in pencil, on stave 15. This version, when incorporated into the main draft, produces a bass which corresponds to that in bars 124–31 of the final version (Ex. 6.18).[11]

The deletion of the F♯–F and C–B¹ units in Ex. 6.17 shows clearly that Beethoven had now pinpointed the trouble-spots in this passage. In all previous attempts he had separated the goal of the descending bass in the transition from the beginning of the second-group dominant pedal: in Exx. 6.15 and 6.17 there is a cadence on the dominant before the second group begins, while in Ex. 6.16 the cadence is on the tonic. By deleting the two-bar unit C–B¹, then, Beethoven signalled that this part of the passage needed revision. Simply to remove the arrival on B¹ from the series of two-bar units in Ex. 6.17 and to elide it with the beginning of the second group, however,

---

[11] A pencilled 'Vi =' in the bar in CD 4 corresponding to bar 129 of the final version may have been intended to cue in the pencilled revision on stave 15, although that revision is supplied with no corresponding '= de' referent. Moreover, Beethoven would surely have intended the revision to fit into the draft at the point corresponding to bar 126 (Ex. 6.18 reflects this assumption). Given the confused appearance of this part of CD 4, however, with so many versions of this problematic passage superimposed on one another, it is hardly surprising that he should have misplaced the 'Vi =' referent.

Ex. 6.17. Artaria 195, p. 49, st. 2, 16

Ex. 6.18. Artaria 195, p. 49, st. 2, 15

would result in the creation of an odd half-unit; another bar had to be deleted in order to restore a series of four complete units. Thus the deletion of the F♯–F unit in Ex. 6.17 reflects the location of the second bar to be omitted. Beethoven removed the F♯, which was already present in the second bar of the second two-bar unit, G–F♯ (the removal of B^1 from the fifth unit similarly avoided duplication of the bass note on which the second group was to begin). This removal shifted F, a sensitive pitch both in the sketches and the final version of the movement, to the first (strong) rather than the second (weak) bar of a two-bar unit, thereby giving it greater prominence; in the final version F is thrown even further into relief by the registral break between bars 127–8.

3. The Coda The remaining part of CD 4 to be discussed is the coda. Beethoven's first idea here was eventually to be his last: he ended the draft by writing out a bass line corresponding to bars 170–7 of the final version, the only difference being that the last three notes—F♯, B, and E—are each spaced one bar apart, giving the effect of a composed ritardando. This coda follows directly from the end of the closing theme, as if bar 170 in the final version followed directly after bar 165 with the intervening four bars omitted. But

Ex. 6.19. Artaria 195, p. 50, st. 10/11

before he had sketched any upper voices above this bass Beethoven deleted it in favour of something else (Ex. 6.19).

The material corresponding to bars 166–9 of the final version now makes its first appearance. Most significant here is Beethoven's treatment of the cadence in bars 168–9. At first the upper-voice f♯^{1} resolved just as one would expect—to e^1; but Beethoven replaced e^1 by b, causing an unexpected downward leap in the upper voice which also creates consecutive fifths by contrary motion with the bass.[12] The reasons for this melodic substitution will be discussed in the Conclusion, below; meanwhile it should be recalled that Beethoven had already done something similar on a previous occasion: in the repeat of bars 1–8 at the beginning of CD 2 he had substituted b^1 for the e^2 expected in the last bar (see Ex. 6.4, bars 15–16).

The nine-bar drive to the final cadence in Beethoven's first attempt was condensed into five bars following the newly inserted material in Ex. 6.19. The upper voice transcribed here shows only one of several versions present in the manuscript; this voice clearly gave Beethoven trouble, and it is not possible to separate some versions from one another with any certainty. What is certain is that Beethoven had now rejected the idea of a direct reference to the upper voice of bars 1–8, as in the coda of CD 3 (see Exx. 6.7 and 6.10a). On the other hand, the stepwise bass descent from e to E is clearly a final reference to the opening of the movement. And one particular feature of the coda from CD 3 which is retained in Ex.

---

[12] Schenker delightedly pointed out this solecism in *Ea*, 34: 'Quinten-"Antiparallele" bei den äußersten Stimmen!'

Ex. 6.20. Artaria 195, p. 50, st. 10/11–13/14

6.19 is the displacement of the final tonic (presumably now minor- rather than major-mode) from the first to the second beat of the bar; Beethoven was evidently still content with this allusion to the final chord of the first movement.

The five-bar close in Ex. 6.19 was eventually replaced by the eight-bar one which became the final version. Again, the sketchbook presents a bewildering array of upper voices which can be disentangled only with considerable difficulty and a certain amount of judicious speculation. It is clear that at one stage Beethoven wrote out an upper voice corresponding exactly to that in the final version, although the inner voices are not completed. But before writing that version he entered a fragmentary right-hand part which reveals an interesting attention to linear motion (Ex. 6.20). The upper voice closes on the tonic note, as it does in all versions of the coda found in CD 4: this much, at least, is certain. But the inner voice descending from e^2 closes on g^1, thereby reasserting the initial upper-voice pitch of the movement and effectively restating the opening sonority: g^1 above E, triadic third and tonic. The triadic fifth is omitted.

Conclusion

With this long survey of the sketches for the second movement of Op. 109 at last complete, the task of this Conclusion is to summarize the results of Chapters 5 and 6 and to examine the relationship to the final version of the compositional issues raised by the sketches.

The division of the second-movement sketches into two separate groups was prompted by the obvious change in sketch-type between pages 40 and 41 of Artaria 195. This change made it appropriate to speak of two phases of activity, one marked by the writing of relatively short, fragmentary sketches (some of which relate directly to the surface of the movement as we know it while others do not), the other characterized by a series of lengthy continuity drafts in which Beethoven attempted to chart the course either of a large formal section, such as an exposition, or of an entire movement.

The change in sketch-type appears to coincide with a radical change in Beethoven's conception of the movement. By the time he turned to page 41 in Artaria 195 he had, albeit unknowingly, sketched all the eventual material of the exposition, and had also fixed other basic features such as the appearance of C major in the development and recapitulation. But in CD 1 he rejected virtually all of that material and drafted a movement with a second group in the relative major which is recapitulated in the tonic major. CD 2 presents a version of the exposition which corresponds much more closely to the earlier sketches and to the final version, while Beethoven's continuing fascination with the submediant led in CD 3 to another radical reformulation: a binary-form movement the first part of which, tonally speaking, is an amalgamation of previous exposition and development material.

But the discontinuity between the two phases of sketching is more apparent than real. The novel features of CD 1—the tonal scheme in the exposition, the recapitulation of the second group in the tonic major—can all be understood in relation to compositional ideas which were elaborated in the first phase of sketching. Three such ideas were proposed in Chapter 5: the importance of the submediant; the use, at foreground and middleground levels, of the stepwise descending bass in bars 1–8; and a concern for large-scale linear motion between $\hat{3}$ and $\hat{1}$ in the upper voice, together with the avoidance of such motion by the reordering of $\hat{3}$–$\hat{2}$–$\hat{1}$ to yield the unclosed progression $\hat{3}$–$\hat{1}$–$\hat{2}$.

In the Conclusion to Chapter 5 it was suggested that these three ideas may be understood as aspects of a fourth, inclusive one: the idea of reworking the compositional premises of the first movement of the sonata. This leads to the establishment of various links between the two movements. For instance, the stepwise descending bass at the outset of the second movement engenders an audible foreground connection with the similar opening of the first movement. Beethoven's many attempts to use this descending bass at middleground levels in the second movement seem on the whole not to have survived the sketch stage—although the divided descent through the B octave which unites the second half of the exposition

Second Movement: Continuity Drafts 163

and the beginning of the development in the final version has been noted (Ex. 5.14). The submediant plays a prominent and sometimes disruptive role in the sketches for the first and second movements: in the latter case its effect on the form of the movement is most acute in CD 3. (As in the case of the first movement, however, the role of the submediant in the second-movement sketches was attenuated in the final version.) Then there are the allusions to the tonality and final chord of the first movement (and to the opening of the third-movement theme) built into the end of CDs 1, 3, and 4: these too bespeak Beethoven's continuing desire to create audible links between the individual movements of Op. 109.

But it is the suggestion of an underlying conformity between the long-range linear aspects of the first and second movements which requires the most careful scrutiny. The functional parallel between the 'E-tonicizing' and 'B-tonicizing' progressions in the first movement and the G–F♯–E ($\hat{3}$–$\hat{2}$–$\hat{1}$) and G–E–F♯ ($\hat{3}$–$\hat{1}$–$\hat{2}$) progressions which emerge in the second-movement sketches may be clear enough; but does the parallel extend to the final version? Can the second movement, like the first, be said to be 'incomplete' in some sense? There are strong reasons for believing so.

Beethoven's treatment of the related progressions G–F♯–E and G–E–F♯ in the exposition of the second movement has already been examined in Chapter 5. To recapitulate: in bars 1–8 the triadic third is established in two registers, g^1 and g^2. Throughout the first group, strong closure is provided in the higher register as g^2 descends repeatedly through $f\sharp^2$ to e^2 (bars 7–8, 15–16, 23–4). The initial g^1, however, is succeeded by its upper neighbour, a^1, at the beginning of bar 9; and the resolution back to g^1 in bars 15–16 and 23–4 is relegated to an inner voice. Beethoven's concern with voice-leading obligations in these two distinct registers is documented both in the shorter sketches (Exx. 5.7 and 5.8) and in the continuity drafts which include the exposition (Exx. 6.2 and 6.5). The lower register remains undeveloped until bars 55–6, the crucial moment in the exposition when the chord set up as a dominant seventh in C is revealed as an augmented-sixth chord which must resolve to the dominant of B minor. The sudden plunge through two octaves from g^3 to g^1 dramatizes the return to the initial upper-voice pitch, which now falls to $f\sharp^1$ to meet the arrival of F♯ in the bass. Of course, the prevailing harmonic context prevents E from following F♯ in any register to complete a $\hat{3}$–$\hat{2}$–$\hat{1}$ descent in the tonic. At the largest level, then, the upper voice in the exposition composes out the incomplete descent g^1–$f\sharp^1$ ($\hat{3}$–$\hat{2}$) counterpointed by E–F♯ in the bass.

One obvious location for the completion of the descent is at the beginning of the recapitulation, where the expected V–I resolution could easily support f♯^{1}–e^1 in the upper voice. But it is precisely here that Beethoven plays the masterstroke: G–E–F♯ and its mirror, E–G–F♯, control the outer voices in bars 93–104 and prepare not E minor but B minor. The development proper could be said to end with the sustained dominant of B minor in bar 96 which brings back f♯^{1} in the upper voice; thus the $\hat{3}$–$\hat{2}$ progression composed out in the exposition is nested within a larger statement spanning the exposition and development. In the retransition (bars 97–104) Beethoven concentrates on the higher register opened up at the beginning of the movement, this time emphasizing the lack of a complete $\hat{3}$–$\hat{2}$–$\hat{1}$ descent.[13]

The return to g^1 at the beginning of the recapitulation sets the scene for another attempt at completion of the descent in the lower register. The opportunity comes at the beginning of the coda where the appearance in bar 168 of f♯^{1}, harmonized now as a dominant seventh in E minor, seems certain to lead at last to an upper-voice e^1 over root-position tonic harmony. Ex. 6.19 shows that Beethoven at first allowed this to happen but subsequently rejected e^1 in favour of the surprising leap down to b. And whereas he had previously entertained the idea of a coda which opened like the beginning of the movement, he now made it the business of bars 170–7 to re-establish just the opening sonority—essentially, the space between $\hat{3}$ and $\hat{1}$—in the two principal registers. The g^1 in bar 173 is approached by step from b^1; the pair g^2/e^2 is introduced above it and dominates the rest of the coda. As the top voice reaches e^3 in bar 175, c^3 introduces a descending line which leads back to g^2 over e^2 via a neighbouring a^2. The completion of the neighbour-note motion a^2–g^2 is prolonged by the insertion of f♯^{2}, and the resulting progression a^2–f♯^{2}–g^2 ($\hat{4}$–$\hat{2}$–$\hat{3}$) in the last two bars echoes G–E–F♯ ($\hat{3}$–$\hat{1}$–$\hat{2}$), the principal agent of melodic incompletion in the movement.

The graph in Ex. 6.21 provides a summary of the foregoing analysis and interprets the large-scale voice-leading structure of the movement as an unorthodox example of a Schenkerian interrupted structure. The upper voice descends conventionally from $\hat{3}$ to $\hat{2}$ prior to the recapitulation, but this motion is accompanied by I–II♯ in the bass

---

[13] It might be argued that a conventional dominant preparation in bars 93–104 would not have undermined an upper-voice F♯–G progression at the point of recapitulation. But a V–I cadence introducing the recapitulation would strongly imply the melodic descent F♯–E even if this were not explicitly stated in the upper voice. By treating F♯ as V/B minor, Beethoven was able to keep such implications at bay. In bars 93–104 F♯ functions as a passing note between E and G in both outer voices. Because of the contrary motion between upper voice and bass, the bass progression F♯–E in bars 104–5 forces the upper-voice f♯^{1} up to g^1: there can be no suggestion of consecutive octaves F♯–E.

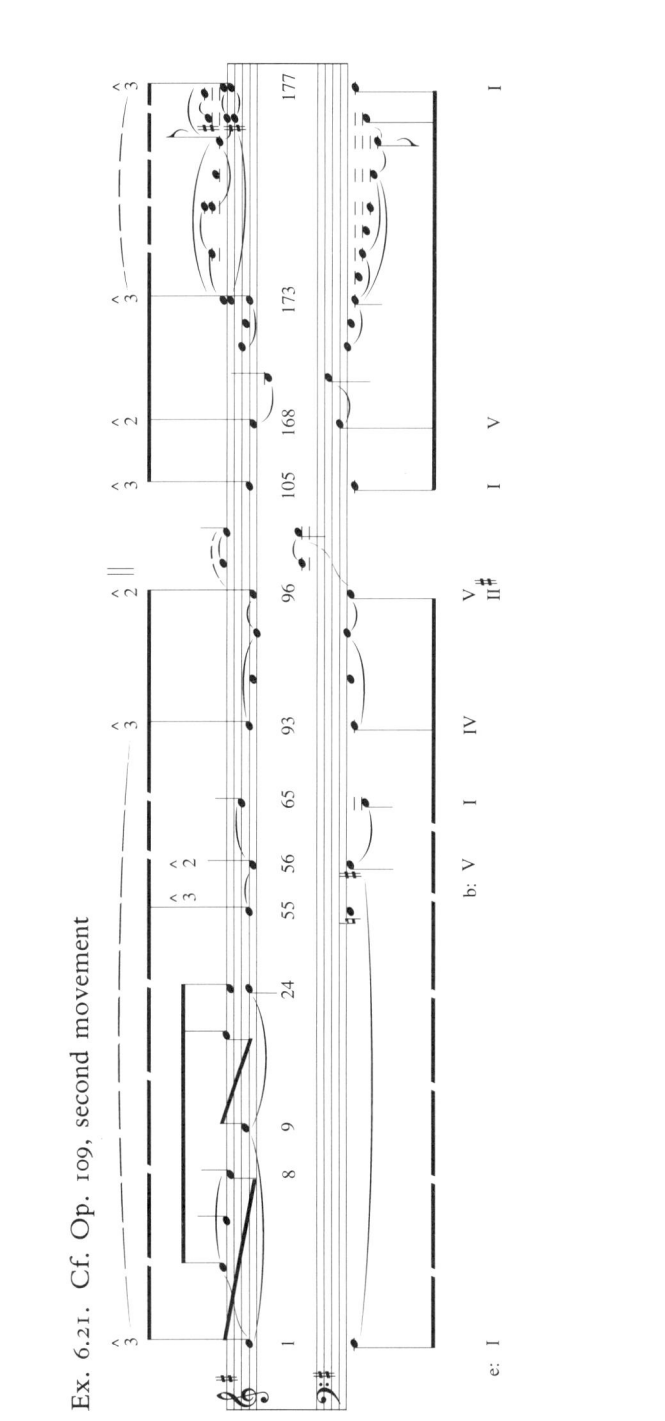

Ex. 6.21. Cf. Op. 109, second movement

rather than by the usual I–V progression. In the second half of the structure it is the bass which behaves conventionally (I–V–I) while the upper voice departs from the norm: the expected $\hat{3}$–$\hat{2}$–$\hat{1}$ is replaced by the $\hat{3}$–$\hat{2}$–$\hat{3}$ motion.

The parallels between this analysis and that of the first movement given in Chapter 3 are too striking either to ignore or to dismiss as coincidental. The second movement of Op. 109 may indeed be regarded as incomplete in much the same sense as the first. The two linear progressions involved in each case are reorderings of a three-note figure derived from the initial sonority of the movement. That opening sonority is recalled in the closing one, which thus serves as a reminder of the tonal space within which satisfactory melodic closure has been suppressed. Moreover, both in the first movement and in the second the retransition to the recapitulation plays a vital role in the avoidance of closure. The first-movement sketches show that Beethoven suppressed the 'E-tonicizing' progression at the retransition, initially in order to delay its appearance until the end of the movement before he decided to suppress it altogether; the importance of the retransition in the second movement has just been discussed. It was suggested in Chapter 3 that the second-movement retransition may have been closely modelled on rejected sketches for the corresponding part of the first movement. That remodelling, if it did indeed occur, may account partly for the lack of sketches for the second-movement retransition itself.

But to describe the second movement as another 'recomposition' of the first would threaten to overload that term, which has already been used to characterize the close relationship between the third-movement theme and the first movement. In searching to categorize the genesis of the second movement in relation to that of the first, a more appropriate term might be 'variation'; a term, moreover, which would by now have been uppermost in Beethoven's mind as, without bothering to turn the page on CD 4, he began sketching the third-movement variations in the bottom right-hand corner of Artaria 195, page 50.

7. Approaching the Variation Sketches

The sketches for the first two movements of Op. 109 reinforce a commonly held perception of Beethoven's compositional process as one during which initially inchoate or vague musical ideas become transformed into something approximating the work in its definitive public form. That the sketches document only a part—perhaps a very small part—of the total process of composition should no longer need any emphasis; even Nottebohm, whose writings on the sketches probably did more than any others to propagate the view being discussed here, was insistent that the sketches 'reveal to us not the entire creative process, but only single isolated incidents from it. What we term the organic development of a work of art is far removed from the sketches.'[1] More recently, Lewis Lockwood has warned against 'uncritical acceptance' of 'the view of [Beethoven's] creative work as being normally a process of assiduous labor by which once commonplace musical thoughts were transformed by gradual stages into artistic substance'. Lockwood's argument is essentially that, rather than speaking *in abstracto* of Beethoven's 'compositional process', we should think in terms of a multiplicity of such processes: 'Enough is known of the chronology of Beethoven's works to suggest not a single mode of compositional procedure but a broad spectrum of structural problems to which a variety of approaches must have been necessary.'[2]

Pace Nottebohm, Beethoven's sketches often do seem to convey at least something of 'the organic development of a work of art', although this may be so because we, who come to the sketches not only post-Nottebohm but also post-Schenker, tend to confuse a perceived organic coherence in the work itself with the organic process of its coming into being. The sketches for the first two movements of Op. 109 conform closely to the 'standard view', however illusory that view may be. For example, it is not difficult to sense

---

[1] Nottebohm, *Zweite Beethoveniana: Nachgelassene Aufsätze und Mittheilungen*, ed. E. Mandyczewski (Leipzig, 1887), ix. The trans. is taken from Johnson, 'Beethoven Scholars and Beethoven's Sketches', 5.
[2] 'Beethoven's Sketches for *Sehnsucht* (WoO 146)', in A. Tyson (ed.), *Beethoven Studies*, i (New York, 1973; London, 1974), 97, 98; repr. in Lockwood, *Beethoven: Studies in the Creative Process*, 95, 96.

168 *Approaching the Variation Sketches*

a logical progression towards the final version in the sketches for the first group in the first movement. But to turn from the sketches for the first two movements to those for the third-movement variations is to enter a different world: literally, a different compositional world, for Beethoven did not compose variations in the same way as sonata forms. The issues to be addressed were different in many respects, and they dictated a different method of sketching.

Apart from the difference in sketching methods, a more obvious difference is likely to strike someone reading through all the sketches for the sonata. To illustrate this, albeit crudely, let us imagine that all known copies and recordings of Op. 109 have been destroyed, leaving the sketches as the only evidence for the work. It is not unreasonable to suggest that a musicologist armed with a reliable guide to the correct chronological sequence of the sketches would be able to reconstruct the first two movements quite successfully; the suggestion hinges on the fact that the eventual form of these movements is already quite fully established in the later sketches. But this does not hold for the third-movement variation sketches. Of a total of nearly sixty ideas, only eight can be related unequivocally to variations in the final version. Variations 3 and 6 are represented by one fragmentary idea each, and there are four attempts, again fragmentary, for what became Variation 5. The other two sketches, which belong to a late stage of composition, are comparatively complete: one presents the melodic line of Variation 1 while the other focuses on the right-hand figuration in bars 9a–16a (17–24) of Variation 6. Except for the drafts of Variations 2 and 3 preserved on the A 47 bifolium in Vienna, these eight sketches are the only ones which allow us to examine the genesis of specific details in individual variations. And leaving aside the fact that no comparable sketching for the other variations survives, our intrepid musicologist would not even be able to tell that the material in these sketches for Variations 1, 3, 5, and 6 was destined for inclusion in the final version. No clear picture of the third movement of Op. 109 emerges from the sketches: neither the detail of individual variations nor their sequence in the total form is potentially reconstructible.

The factors which would prevent a successful reconstruction of the movement itself also hinder attempts to reconstruct its genesis. In addition to the fact that so little of the surviving sketch material relates directly to the published variations, it is clear that a large amount of material is missing: as explained in Chapter 2, the A 47 bifolium is apparently the sole survivor from a former extensive draft (*Concept*) of the sonata, and it is likely that a pocket book containing sketches for the second and third movements has also been lost. But before we surrender entirely to these problems, we should ask to what extent the Op. 109 sketches are typical of Beethoven's variation sketches; for if the qualitative difference between the variation sketches and those for the first two movements is to be explained in terms of differing compositional methods and aims, the variation sketches might yet prove informative. This chapter begins with a general consideration of Beethoven's variation sketches and proceeds to compare the Op. 109 sketches with those for the other two great piano variation sets from this period: the second movement of the Sonata in C, Op. 111, and the Diabelli Variations, Op. 120, the composition of which straddled both Op. 109 and 111. Finally, a close study of the physical characteristics of the Op. 109 sketches will help to distil a sense of purpose from what might otherwise seem a mass of intractable material, and will in its turn suggest ways in which an analysis might be formulated.

Several studies of the sketches for individual variation sets have been published in recent years, but the most useful general introduction to Beethoven's sketching methods for such works remains a short article by Sieghard Brandenburg.[3] Brandenburg distinguishes three basic types of sketching activity:

1. 'Initial' sketches or 'initial' ideas (*erste Entwürfe, erste Einfälle*). These occur at the beginning and during the course of virtually all Beethoven's sketching for variation sets. They are single-voice fragments, usually no more than a few bars long, and make use of standard variation techniques; there is nothing particularly original about them. They were probably written down quickly and were rarely worked upon or revised to any extent; they give the impression of having been produced with little or no effort. Even if they were subsequently rejected, Beethoven often left them undeleted; he would have been confident of not confusing them with sketches which were directly relevant to the composition in hand, and may have wished to preserve them as a kind of *aide-mémoire* or spur to further ideas.

2. 'Elaboratory' sketches (*Ausarbeitungsskizzen*). If the function of the 'initial' sketches was merely to record a particular variation-type, that of the 'elaboratory' ones was to shape an individual variation in

---

[3] 'Beethovens "Erste Entwürfe" zu Variationenzyklen', in C. Dahlhaus *et al.* (eds.), *Bericht über den Internationalen Musikwissenschaftlichen Kongress Bonn 1970* (Kassel, 1971), 108–11. Studies of individual works include C. Reynolds, 'Beethoven's Sketches for the Variations in E♭ Op. 35', in A. Tyson (ed.), *Beethoven Studies*, iii (Cambridge, 1982), 47–84; Reynolds, 'Ends and Means in the Second Finale to Beethoven's Op. 30, No. 1', in Lockwood and Benjamin (eds.), *Beethoven Essays*, 127–45; W. Kinderman, *Beethoven's Diabelli Variations* (Oxford, 1987). My review of Kinderman's book pursues sketch-related issues: see *19th Century Music*, 12 (1988–9), 80–9.

considerable detail. In some cases the material elaborated and revised is taken from a prior 'initial' sketch. Notable characteristics of 'elaboratory' sketches are the presence of more than one voice, and of dynamic or instrumental indications; the sketches are often copied, extended, and revised several times over until the final version of the composition begins to emerge clearly. The presence of various layers of revision, sometimes distinguished by a change of writing implement, can present difficulties of transcription. Unwanted sketches of this type are often heavily deleted, since their continued presence might become confusing during later stages of work.

3. 'Overview' sketches (*Übersichtsentwürfe*). These occur particularly in connection with works from Beethoven's middle and late periods, and involve the combination of a number of already planned variations to form a larger formal unit. Like 'elaboratory' sketches, they are subject to revision, usually in their opening bars. Normally only a single voice (not necessarily the most characteristic one for each variation) is present throughout, and the closing bars are more hurriedly notated than the opening. 'Overview' sketches may be written out repeatedly, often with only slight modifications being made between one version and the next.

Brandenburg accounts for the emergence and special characteristics of 'overview' sketches in terms of Beethoven's stylistic development as a composer of variations. In early sets, he claims, the sequence of variations found in the 'initial' sketches corresponds more or less to that in the final version. But in later works (among which Brandenburg includes even Op. 35) the 'initial' sketches no longer determine the larger structure of the set to the same extent: that function is assumed by the 'overview' sketches. The 'initial' sketches simply fix particular variation types, and they may now occur at any stage in the compositional process; they come to represent a reservoir of variation possibilities whose suitability for inclusion in the set is tested at the 'overview' stage before the selected variations are elaborated in detail. The 'overview' sketches thus act as a filter for inappropriate material. And Brandenburg suggests that the originality of Beethoven's early variation sets lies in the individuality of the separate variations, whereas in the later works it derives more from the cyclic conception of the whole.

It is not easy to apply Brandenburg's criteria to the Op. 109 variation sketches. There is one obvious 'overview' sketch in Artaria 195, written on staves 15/16 of pages 64–9 and also staves 1/2 of that last page; it contains incipits for six variations and a coda. However, none of the incipits corresponds closely to any of the other sketches in this sketchbook or in Artaria 197. Thus, this overview appears not to have played the characteristic filtering role described by Brandenburg; in his terms, it consists rather of a combination of several 'initial' ideas. However, the presence of a number at the head of certain sketches in Artaria 195 does attest to a filtering process of some kind; these numbered sketches will be dealt with in more detail below.

The total number of ideas for variations recorded in Artaria 195 and 197 was estimated above as about sixty.[4] If we now exclude from this number the early sketch on page 36 of Artaria 195 (Ex. 4.2) which belongs outside the main period of sketching for the variations; the six incipits in the 'overview' sketch on pages 64–9; and two sketches which represent internal fragments of variations rather than their openings, we are left with some fifty sketches. Of these, no fewer than thirty-eight may readily be classified as 'initial' sketches: they cover no more than half the length of the theme (twenty-five cover less than half), and are generally unrevised, undeleted, and so on. The remaining twelve sketches cover the full extent of the theme, but only three of them correspond at all well to Brandenburg's 'elaboratory' type, exhibiting more than one voice throughout and (in two cases only) clear signs of critical reflection and revision.[5] Two of the three may be reworkings of earlier 'initial' sketches (see Ex. 7.1); on the other hand, any relationships between these 'initial' and 'elaboratory' sketches may be purely fortuitous—a possibility which will be discussed at greater length below. The other nine sketches are less fully notated; although they cover the full extent of the theme, many bars are left blank or are only partially notated.[6]

Above all, it is the lack of any clear interrelationships which emerges most strongly from a close examination of the variation sketches for Op. 109. The twenty or more consecutive pages of variation sketching in Artaria 195 largely fail to communicate any real sense of commitment on Beethoven's part: here and there an idea is

---

[4] This and other numbers are necessarily approximate since it is not always clear whether a given notation should be counted as a sketch in its own right or as a revision of another sketch. As in so many matters, the interpretation of the sources and their interrelationships plays a decisive role here.

[5] These three sketches begin at the following locations in Artaria 195: p. 54, st. 1/2, p. 56, st. 1/2, and p. 67, st. 1/2. On page 75, st. 7–10 the melodic line of Variation 1 is sketched complete (although not quite in its final form); but precisely because of its close relationship to a variation in the final version, and because of its evidently late position in the compositional process, this sketch does not really belong in the same category as the three 'elaboratory' ones being discussed here.

[6] The presence of blank bars, which are also common to the 'initial' sketches, underlines the extent to which Beethoven's sketching methods were dictated by the musical form with which he was working. Since the length of each variation was essentially determined by that of the theme, Beethoven could begin by marking out the requisite number of bars before proceeding to enter any musical material.

172 *Approaching the Variation Sketches*

Ex. 7.1. *a* Artaria 195, p. 50, st. 13; p. 54, st. 1

b Artaria 195, p. 50, st. 13/14; p. 56, st. 1/2

subjected to a measure of critical scrutiny (the four attempts, at three different points in the sketchbook, to forge the opening of what became Variation 5 are a case in point), but in general one gets the impression that Beethoven was simply churning out ideas unreflectively, with little thought for their ultimate viability. The single 'overview' sketch reinforces this point in that it too consists of yet more new ideas rather than a sifting of old ones. In short, it seems that, with the exception of the late sketch for the melodic line of Variation 1 on page 75, the variation sketches in Artaria 195 correspond most closely to Brandenburg's type 1: they are 'initial' sketches which formed a reservoir of variation possibilities. That Beethoven subjected them to a modicum of critical assessment is shown by the addition of numbers to certain sketches, but the formulation of the movement as we know it seems to have taken place almost entirely outside Artaria 195 and 197. The A 47 bifolium, with its drafts of Variations 2 and 3, undoubtedly represents a part of that formulation.

Before going on to consider the sketches for Op. 111 and the

1. Op. 109, autograph manuscript, fol. 5ᵛ: 1st movement, bars '86–98' (*recte*: 87–99). *Wc*, Music Division, Gertrude Clarke Whittall Collection (reproduced with permission of the Library of Congress).

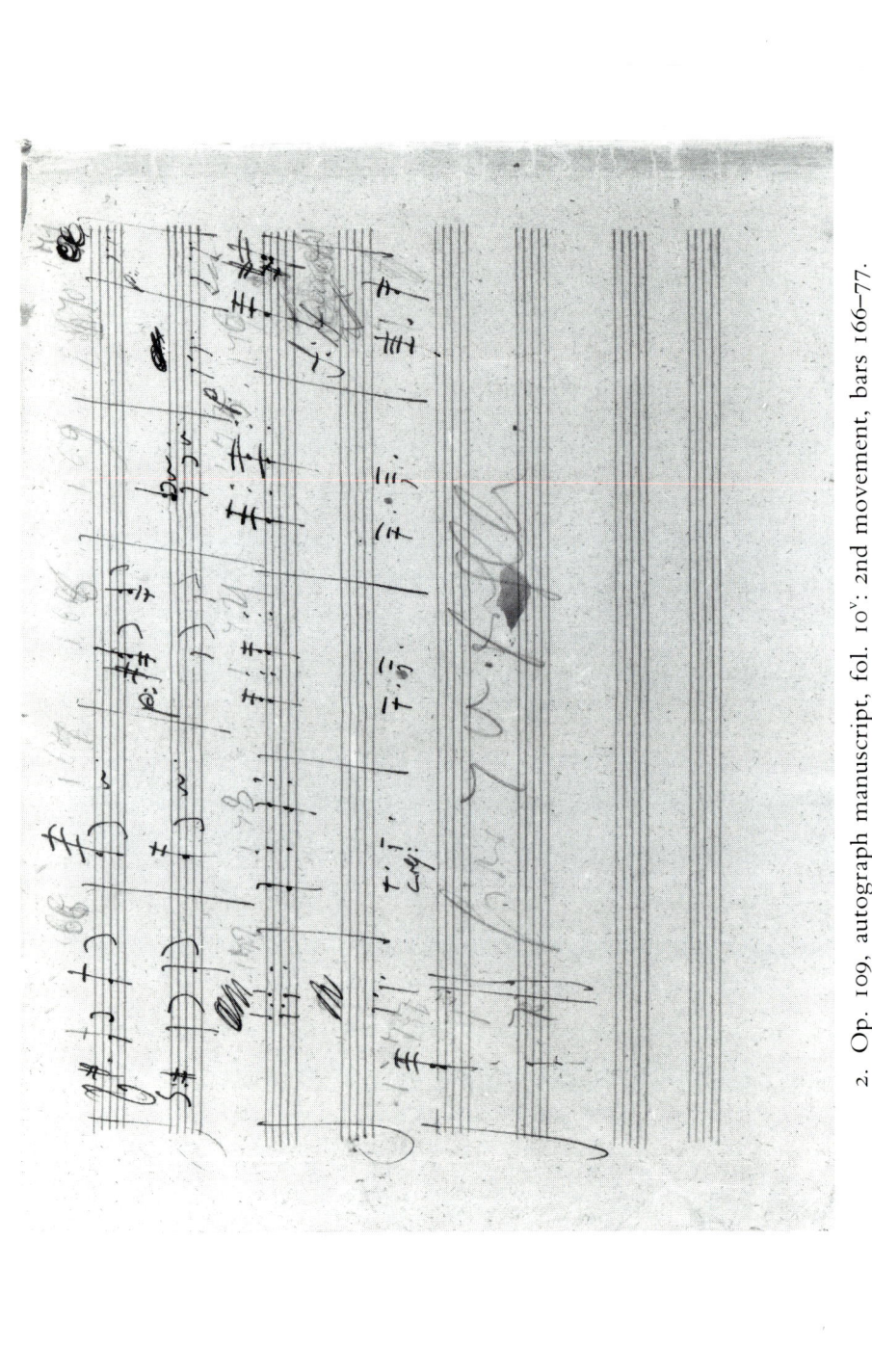

2. Op. 109, autograph manuscript, fol. 10ᵛ: 2nd movement, bars 166–77. W c, Music Division, Gertrude Clarke Whittall Collection (reproduced with permission of the Library of Congress)

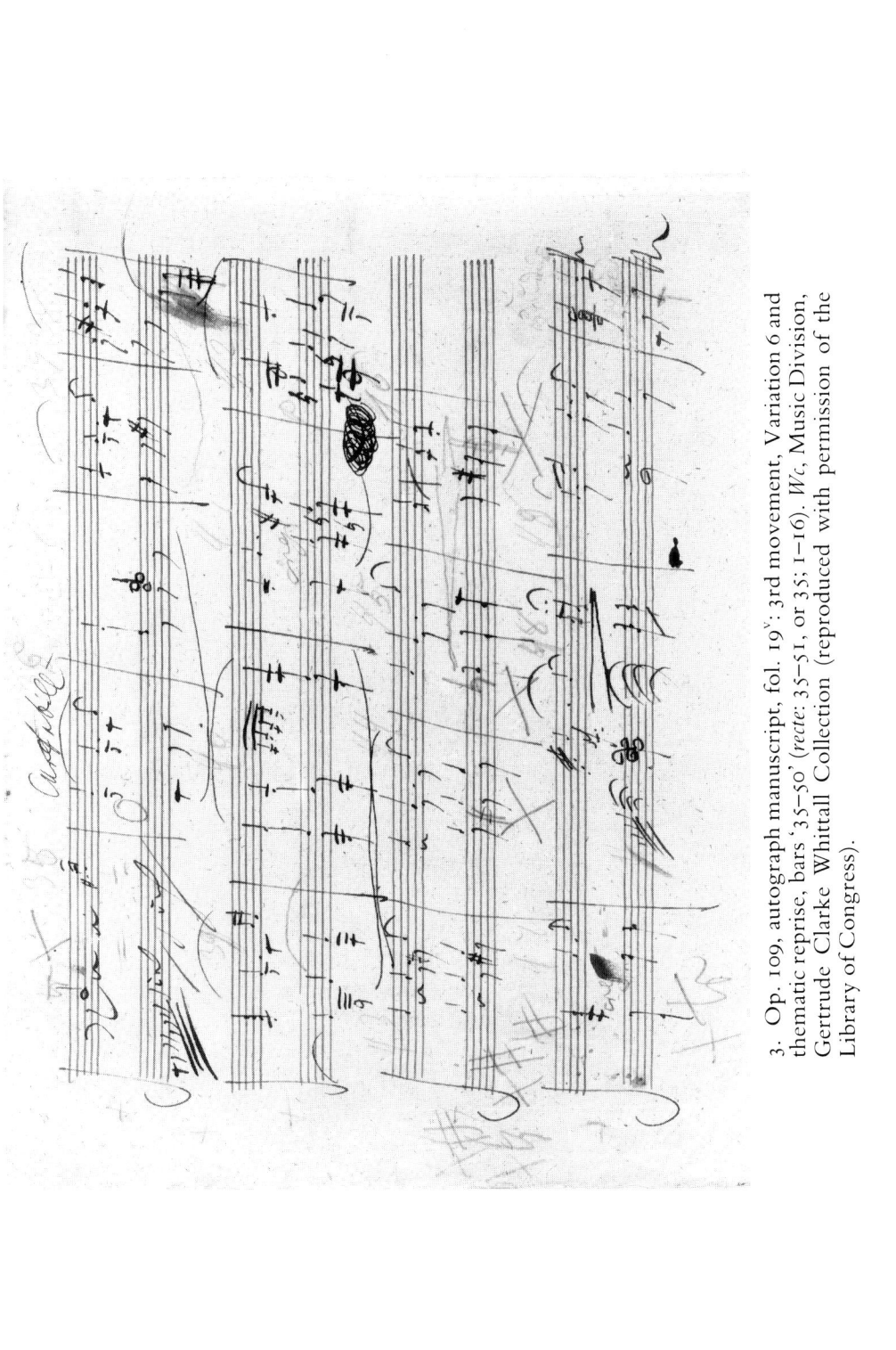

3. Op. 109, autograph manuscript, fol. 19ᵛ: 3rd movement, Variation 6 and thematic reprise, bars '35–50' (*recte*: 35–51, or 35; 1–16). *Wc*, Music Division, Gertrude Clarke Whittall Collection (reproduced with permission of the Library of Congress).

4. Puns on 'Gebauer', pocket sketches for Op. 109, first movement, and for the Credo of the *Missa solemnis*. BNba, BH 107, p. 43 (reproduced with permission of the Beethoven-Haus, Bonn).

5. Desk sketches for Op. 109, 3rd-movement variations. B, Mus. ms. autogr. Beethoven Artaria 195, p. 68 (reproduced with permission of the Staatsbibliothek zu Berlin – Preußischer Kulturbesitz, Musikabteilung).

6. Desk sketches for Op. 109, 3rd-movement variations. *B*, Mus. ms. autogr. Beethoven Artaria 195, p. 69 (reproduced with permission of the Staatsbibliothek zu Berlin – Preußischer Kulturbesitz, Musikabteilung).

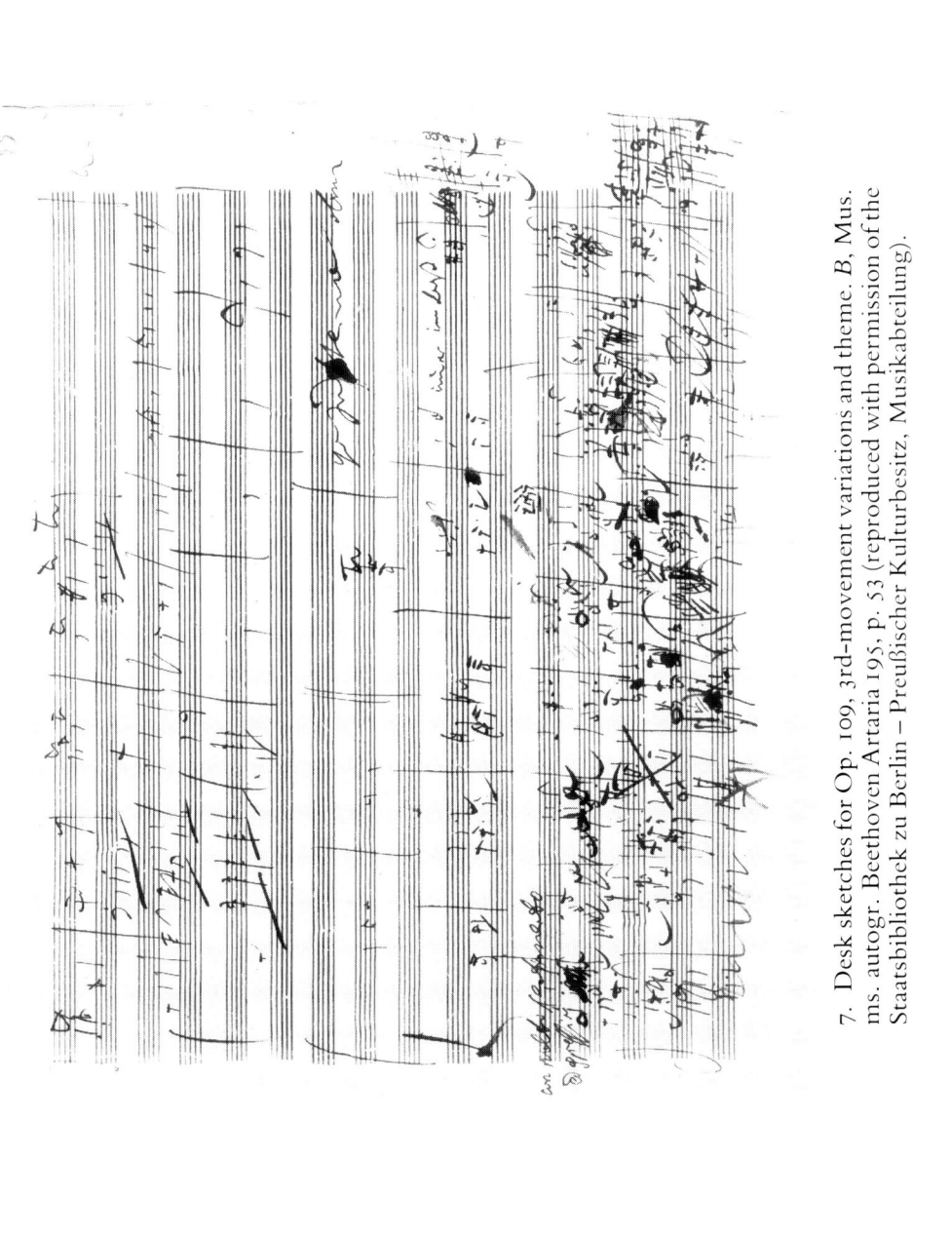

7. Desk sketches for Op. 109, 3rd-movement variations and theme. B, Mus. ms. autogr. Beethoven Artaria 195, p. 53 (reproduced with permission of the Staatsbibliothek zu Berlin – Preußischer Kulturbesitz, Musikabteilung).

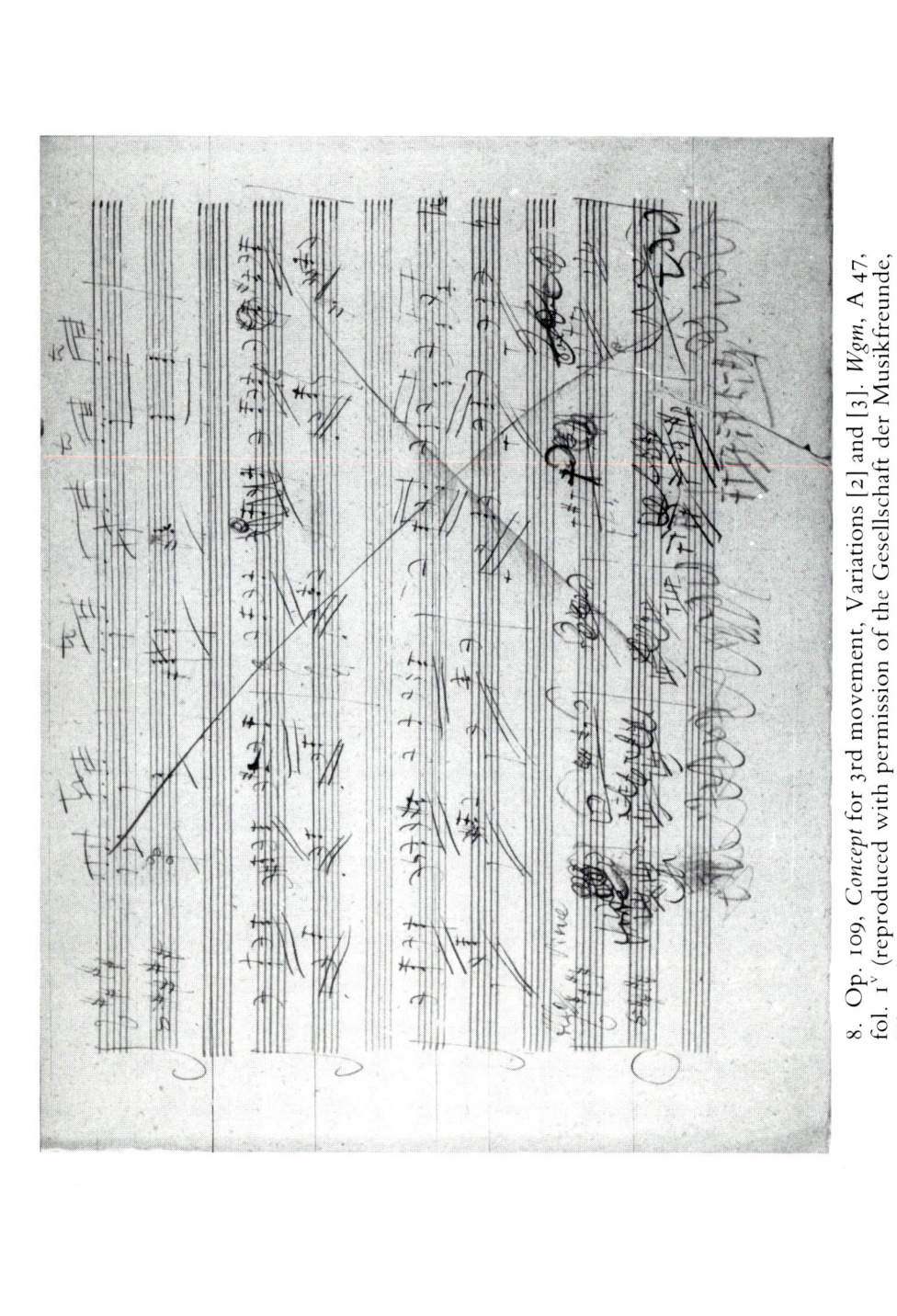

8. Op. 109, *Concept* for 3rd movement, Variations [2] and [3]. *Wgm*, A 47, fol. 1ᵛ (reproduced with permission of the Gesellschaft der Musikfreunde, Vienna).

Ex. 7.2. *a* Artaria 195, p. 57, st. 1/2

b Artaria 195, p. 57, st. 6/7

Diabelli Variations it is appropriate to give further consideration to the general question of relationships between variation sketches. This was touched upon in connection with Ex. 7.1 and has emerged as an important issue in the preceding paragraph. The extent to which the genesis of a Beethoven work may be (tentatively) reconstructed from its sketches depends largely upon the extent and scope of the relationships manifest between the sketches themselves on the one hand, and between the sketches and the final version on the other. Now it is the paucity of such relationships which makes the Op. 109 variation sketches so difficult to deal with. And yet there is a paradox here, for the very nature of variation form, coupled with Beethoven's procedure of creating a reservoir of variation possibilities, almost inevitably gives rise to numerous *apparent* musical relationships.

It has already been suggested that the relationships between the two pairs of sketches shown above in Ex. 7.1*a*–*b* may be fortuitous rather than consciously intended. A further example may help to clarify the point at issue. Ex. 7.2 shows two sketches which occur very close to one another on page 57 of Artaria 195. (The complete sketch is shown in part *a*; part *b* shows only the opening of a more extensive sketch.) The melodic similarity between the first bar of each is obvious. If these were sketches for the first subject of a sonata-form movement, for example, we might be justified in discussing their differences and similarities in some detail: at any rate, we would probably not hesitate to assume an intended relationship. But given that we are dealing with projected variations on a theme, can we be so sure that Beethoven 'composed' the relationships in Ex. 7.2? It seems inevitable that such melodic similarities will arise simply because of the musical constraints involved: the common thematic source, and (even for Beethoven in 1820) the stylistic limitations.[7]

Looking again at Ex. 7.2b we might note a number of similarities with Variation 4 in the final version. The triplet division of the crotchet beat creates an effective 9/8 metre; the imitative texture, expanding upwards in the right hand, and the appoggiatura figures (e^1–$d\sharp^1$, a^1–$g\sharp^1$) in the second and third bars all foreshadow quite specific features of that variation. But again: is this 'a sketch for Variation 4' in the same sense that Ex. 3.1a is 'a sketch for the first group in the first movement'? The distinction may seem excessively pedantic; but it appears that the nature of variation form, coupled with Beethoven's habit of jotting down potential variation openings seemingly at random, requires that the analyst of the compositional process be more than usually cautious when suggesting musical relationships here. In the case of the Op. 109 variations, where there are so few unambiguous relationships between sketches and final version, it is especially unfortunate that such apparent relationships serve only to complicate matters further.[8]

What of the sketches for the Diabelli Variations and the second movement of Op. 111? The composition of the gigantic former work straddles that of both Op. 109 and 111, and the sketches for it have been extensively surveyed by William Kinderman.[9] The main sources for the first (1819) phase of composition are the Wittgenstein sketchbook (including those leaves which originally belonged to it but are today located elsewhere) and a document which Kinderman calls the Paris–Landsberg–Montauban [PLM] Draft. This draft, most of which appears to have survived intact, consists of 'twenty-three variations in order, in addition to the copy of Diabelli's theme in

---

[7] It goes without saying that caution must always be exercised when positing relationships between sketches; the point to be stressed here is that variation sketches pose special problems in this respect.

[8] A particularly tricky case is that of a detailed draft of a complete variation, numbered 9, which begins on Artaria 195, p. 67, st. 1/2. Not only is this the final member of a projected variation cycle, its structure and details bring the definitive Variation 6 unmistakably to mind. On the other hand, it is sufficiently different from that variation to give pause for thought. I have elected not to consider it 'a sketch for Variation 6' in the strong sense discussed above.

[9] Kinderman, *Beethoven's Diabelli Variations*, esp. 3–60. In several cases Kinderman's identification of sketch material with variations in the final version seems far-fetched: the 'draft for Variation 20' transcribed on pp. 197–8 is a case in point. A more objective guide may be found in Sieghard Brandenburg's detailed catalogue of the sketches published as an *Anhang* to A. Münster, *Studien zu Beethovens Diabelli-Variationen* (Munich, 1982), 215–27. Brandenburg's account makes clear just how much of the sketch material was *not* taken up in the final version and also points out that a considerable quantity of sketches must have been lost.

Beethoven's hand'.[10] Its survival allows one to examine the relationship between it and the sketches in the Wittgenstein book, and to assess the role played by the sketchbook in the composition of this variation work.

Kinderman suggests that 'the bulk of Beethoven's creative labour took place in Wittgenstein. . . . The easily-legible [PLM] drafts represent work for the most part one step removed from creation itself, made after a store of ideas had been accumulated.'[11] This interpretation seems essentially correct, although the fact that some of the variations in the PLM Draft have no corresponding sketches in Wittgenstein implies that Beethoven must have worked outside that sketchbook as well. Conversely, the Wittgenstein sketches, like those for Op. 109 in Artaria 195, include ideas for several variations which were taken up neither in the PLM Draft nor in the final version of the Diabelli Variations; but they also differ significantly from the Op. 109 corpus in that a good deal of the sketch material did in fact find a place in the completed work. In particular, Wittgenstein contains a number of drafts for variations which Beethoven subsequently transferred to the PLM Draft, extending and revising them in the process. The Wittgenstein sketches betray clear signs of Beethoven's having looked through them on at least two occasions in an attempt to select those ideas which seemed suitable for development and inclusion in a possible final version: there are the beginnings of a numbering system in ink, and a more extended series of numbers in pencil. (The presence of a large pencilled *X* at the beginning of seven sketches, including three of the numbered ones, may represent part of a third selection process.) Table 7.1 shows the survival in the PLM Draft and the final version of the numbered sketches in Wittgenstein, and also the various renumberings adopted at each stage.[12] The purpose of the table is to emphasize the extent to which material present in Wittgenstein was taken over not only into the PLM Draft but even into the final version of the Diabelli Variations. There is considerable continuity between the sketchbook, the PLM Draft, and subsequent phases of composition; as we have seen, such continuity is almost wholly lacking between the Op. 109 variation sketches in Artaria 195, the two A 47 drafts, and the final version of the movement.

[10] Kinderman, *Beethoven's Diabelli Variations*, 13.
[11] Ibid. 26.
[12] Compare Kinderman's table 4, ibid. 39. Kinderman does not transcribe the pencilled numbers 9 and 10 and does not distinguish between ink and pencil in the Wittgenstein sequence. He observes, however, that the direction 'Hiernach Marsch' following the sketch numbered 15 allows us to assume the number 16 for the draft headed 'Ma[rsch]' on Wittgenstein, fo. 4^v, st. 1/2–5/6.

TABLE 7.1. *Variation numbering and sequence in the sketch and final versions of the Diabelli Variations*

Wittgenstein		PLM Draft	Op. 120
ink	pencil		
3	9	8	10
1	10	15	18
2	—	—	—
	11	9	11
	12	—	—
	13	16	19
	14	[6][a]	8
	15	[20?][b]	26/27

[a] Variations numbered 3–6 are missing from the PLM Draft; but since the variations numbered 1–2 and 7–12 became 3–4 and 9–14 in Op. 120 it may be assumed that the missing draft variations 3–6 corresponded to Op. 120, Variations 5–8 (see Kinderman, *Beethoven's Diabelli Variations*, 28–9, fig. 3).

[b] Only a fragment from the end of this variation appears in the PLM Draft, where it is succeeded by the beginning of a forerunner of Variation 30, numbered 21; hence the suggested PLM number 20 here.

Continuity between succeeding compositional stages is even more marked in the case of the second movement of the Piano Sonata in C, Op. 111, the sketches for which have been studied by William Drabkin.[13] The surviving sketches for the variation movement of this sonata far outnumber those for Op. 109—indeed, Drabkin was able to draw on fifty-four sketches for the Op. 111 theme alone—but there is no surviving document analogous to the PLM Draft for the Diabelli Variations. Perhaps it was the much greater length and scope of the Diabelli set, with its concomitant problems of variation ordering, which dictated the writing of the PLM Draft as a means of controlling the burgeoning work. Certainly, Beethoven seems to have been able to compose a good deal of the second movement of Op. 111 within the confines of the main sketchbook, Artaria 201, forty pages of which (pages 22–62) are devoted to variation sketches. In chapters 7 and 8 of his dissertation Drabkin separated the 'early' sketches from those which document the 'final genesis of the variations'. Some of Drabkin's descriptions of the 'early' sketches fit those for Op. 109 equally well. For instance, 'nearly half of the sketch material for the [Op. 111] variations consists of a series of outlines having little more than the 16-bar bipartite form, a basic triple meter and the key of C in common with the variations in their

[13] 'The Sketches for Beethoven's Piano Sonata in C minor, Opus 111', 2 vols., Ph.D. diss. (Princeton, NJ, 1976).

final form'. Or again: '[Beethoven] did not actually provide a complete 16-bar outline of any variation, but for the most part jotted down an incipit, an outline of bars 1–8, or the beginning of each half of a proposed variation.' On the other hand, the statement that 'the variations are essentially the result of work in the main sketchbook for the sonata' cannot be applied to the Op. 109 sketches with anything like the same justification.[14]

The sketches in Artaria 201 certainly bear out Drabkin's remark. Although a good many refinements remained to be made, the movement as we know it emerges clearly by the end of the sketching. Moreover, a number of significant features, such as the progressive rhythmic diminution from one variation to the next and the turn to E♭ major in the transition following Variation 4 (bars 106–36), appear to have been fixed at a relatively early stage. More importantly, the sketches convey an unmistakable impression of wholehearted engagement on Beethoven's part: not only are many sketches marked by heavy internal revision, Beethoven's interest and faith in much of the material was sufficient to lead him to rework it at other locations in the sketchbook. Thus, a projected series of three variations (clearly foreshadowing Variations 1, 2, and 4 in the final version) sketched on pages 37–44 was reworked and enlarged on pages 48–58. As we have seen, Brandenburg noted such reworking as characteristic of 'elaboratory' sketches.

It is precisely this sense of engagement with the material, the sense of a commitment to developing its potential, which seems lacking in the Op. 109 variation sketches in Artaria 195. Comparing these sketches to those for the second movement of Op. 111 and for the Diabelli Variations, one is struck by the much greater volatility of Beethoven's ideas for Op. 109: if he actually felt capable of developing this material at this stage, he was apparently uninterested in doing so. Admittedly, the Diabelli and Op. 111 variation sketches likewise include much material which was later abandoned. In both those cases, as in that of Op. 109, Beethoven began by jotting down ideas for variations more or less at random; the dual process of

---

[14] Ibid. 186–7, 190, 187. The last quotation from Drabkin seems somewhat at variance with his statement (p. 187) that 'the details of Variations 2, 3 and 4, the "reprise" variation (Variation 5) and the coda were mainly worked out at the autograph stage.' The surviving autograph of the second movement of Op. 111 (*Bds*, Artaria 198) is an *Urschrift* rather than a *Reinschrift* (the reverse is true of the first movement in Artaria 198), yet much of it is surprisingly clean; the evidence of major compositional activity here is not as extensive as Drabkin suggests. For a facsimile of Artaria 198 see *Ludwig van Beethoven: Piano Sonata No. 32 in C Minor, Op. 111*, with introd. by E. Simon (New York, 1968). Further discussion of the sources for Op. 111 can be found in H. Unverricht, *Die Eigenschriften und die Originalausgaben von Werken Beethovens in ihrer Bedeutung für die moderne Textkritik* (Kassel, 1960), and C. Timbrell, 'Notes on the Sources of Beethoven's Opus 111', *Music & Letters*, 58 (1977), 204–15.

selection and refinement of individual sketches followed later. But while the Wittgenstein sketchbook and Artaria 201 played a prominent part in that process for the Diabelli Variations and Op. 111, the Op. 109 variations appear to have been developed largely independently of Artaria 195. Ideas which were eventually taken up in the final version were liable to be left untouched in the sketchbook (witness the draft on page 59 for what would become Variation 3); very little of the material appears to have held Beethoven's attention for much longer than it took to be written down.

The nature and extent of the presumed missing sketch material for the Op. 109 variations must remain speculative. The sudden appearance, near the end of so much apparently aimless sketching in Artaria 195, of the melodic line of Variation 1 might suggest that Beethoven had been developing such details in another source while at the same time continuing to add to the reservoir of sketches in the sketchbook. Alternatively, the sketch for Variation 1 might represent the start of work on the individual variations—a process which must again have continued elsewhere, since the rest of Artaria 195 was devoted to other compositions (see Table 2.3).[15] Beethoven himself testified to the fact that he had made a preliminary *Urschrift* or *Concept* (his own term) of the sonata, and the amount of correction and revision in the two A 47 drafts testifies to the unfinished state of the variations at the *Concept* stage. Furthermore, the autograph manuscript is generally more heavily revised in the third movement than in either of the first two (some of these third-movement revisions are considered in Chapter 9). Even if we postulate no other missing sketch sources, then, it is clear merely from the A 47 *Concept* drafts and the autograph that the composition of the variations went considerably beyond the material in Artaria 195.

At this point it is necessary to enter an important clarification. Throughout the preceding discussion the main point at issue has been the slender extent to which the final version of the Op. 109 variations can be traced in the surviving sketches. Our intrepid musicologist, bent on reconstructing Beethoven's works in an imaginary world devoid of editions of any kind, would in theory be able to make a much better job of the Diabelli Variations or of the second movement of Op. 111 than of the final movement of Op. 109 (that any such reconstruction would fall hopelessly short of the authentic version is irrelevant). But to admit this much is not necessarily to concede that the Op. 109 variation sketches reveal nothing

---

[15] However, further sketches for the variations may have been made on some of the four leaves missing between the present pp. 80–1 of Artaria 195.

whatsoever of interest. The following study of their physical characteristics encourages some qualification of the earlier suggestion that they represent more or less randomly notated ideas whose importance to Beethoven barely outlived the time taken to commit them to paper. Ignoring the early pencil sketch (Ex. 4.2), apparently for a variation, made on page 36 of Artaria 195 before Beethoven had sketched even the second movement, we shall focus on the main series of sketches beginning at the bottom of page 50, directly after the last continuity draft (CD 4) for the second movement.

The sketches on pages 50–70 are written predominantly in ink, and with three exceptions (on pages 55, 57, and 70) they are all sketches for the third movement of Op. 109.[16] Pages 50–69 clearly represent a sustained phase of work on the variations. The majority of the staves are used, even if in some cases Beethoven merely prepared the page by drafting a series of blank bars, many of which remained empty (page 52 is a good example). At least four sketches were added to the top two or three staves of a page in advance of the main sketching—this is evident from the fact that Beethoven was forced to use the lower staves for the continuation of sketches begun on the preceding pages.[17] Moreover, it is clear that the bottom staves of several pages were initially left empty and were filled retrospectively, after later pages had been used.

Despite the predominance of ink sketching, pages 50–69 also contain pencil entries of various kinds. Some are straightforward revisions or deletions of ink sketches (a heavily corrected sketch on page 56 is a good example of the former, while a variation drafted in ink on page 61 was deleted by means of a large pencilled cross); a few others represent entirely new sketches, while in one case (on page 60) a sketch for the first half of a variation has bars 1–2 written in ink and bars 3–8 in pencil. It is clear from the nature and position of all these pencil entries that they form a secondary compositional layer.

Clear signs of a break in continuity begin to appear around page 70. Staves 6–16 of page 70 are blank, as are staves 8–16 of page 71. Moreover, material unrelated to Op. 109 appears at the top of page 70, and while staves 1–4 of page 71 are written in ink, staves 5–7 are in pencil.[18] Pages 72–3 are entirely in pencil and contain only

---

[16] The exceptions are: p. 55, st. 12/13 (the late pencil sketch for the recapitulation transition in the second movement); p. 57, st.16 (an unidentified texted fragment); and p. 70, st. 1/2, 3 (a miscellaneous keyboard jotting).

[17] The four 'advance' sketches are: p. 63, st. 1/2, 3; p. 64, st. 1/2; p. 65, st. 1/2; and p. 73, st. 1/2. See Ch. 8 n. 8, below, for the more ambiguous case of p. 69, st. 1/2.

[18] The presence of braces at the beginning of st. 6/7 and 8/9 on p. 70 suggests that Beethoven intended to continue there a sketch begun on st. 4/5. However, the actual continuation of that sketch appears to follow on p. 71, st. 1/2.

180 *Approaching the Variation Sketches*

TABLE 7.2. *Ink numbering of selected variation sketches in Artaria 195, pp. 50–69*

Artaria 195, page, stave	Heading and/or number
51, 9	2
57, 1	Var: 2
59, 1	all[egr]o 3
60, 5	4
61, 5	all[egr]o 5
62, 13	6
63, 13	adag[i]o 7
66, 4	all[egr]o 8
67, 1	9

material for the Op. 109 variations. Page 74 is in ink, but none of the material is for Op. 109; it consists entirely of desultory jottings. Similar jottings, again in ink, continue on page 75 but are interrupted by the sudden appearance, as if from nowhere, of the melodic line of Variation 1 from Op. 109. A sustained bout of pencil sketching sets in with page 76, the first of several pages containing sketches for numbers 7–11 of the Bagatelles, Op. 119. The final sketches for the variations appear in pencil on page 78.

It is reasonable, on the basis of the preceding facts, to suppose that page 69 marks the end of a discrete stage of work on the variations in Artaria 195. Having used this page Beethoven probably went back over the sketches at least twice: first to filter out material which he considered worthy of further development, and secondly to make the pencil revisions and additions already noted. The filtering process involved the addition of numbers, in ink rather than pencil, to selected sketches; the sketches so numbered are listed in Table 7.2.[19]

It is noteworthy that many of the sketches in Table 7.2 are relatively extensive; those numbered from 4 to 9 are all sketches for variations drafted at full length, even if all that is present is a skeletal bass line, or if the sketch includes a number of blank bars. The most elaborate is the sketch numbered 9, a detailed draft for a double variation bearing an obvious affinity to Variation 6 in the final version. There will be an opportunity to examine this sketch closely in the next chapter; for the present, we need only remark that it represents the end of a projected set of nine variations followed by a coda. The coda sketches, moreover, occur at the top of page 69,

---

[19] That the numbering process preceded the stage of pencil revisions seems assured by the sketch numbered 5 on p. 61. This bears some pencil revisions and is also entirely deleted by means of a large pencilled cross. It would be illogical to assume that Beethoven assigned it a number within a projected variation cycle after deleting it.

lending further support to the idea that a distinct phase of sketching comes to an end on that page.

One further piece of evidence argues for a break in sustained sketching at page 69: it is on this page that the only surviving 'overview' sketch for the movement concludes. Beethoven must have left the bottom two staves of several pages blank during the first stage of sketching, for the 'overview' begins on page 64, staves 15/16 and continues on those two staves until page 69, where it breaks off in mid-variation with the direction 'etc etc sofort bis 100'. This direction leads up to staves 1/2 on the same page, where the connective '100' is repeated (see Plate 6).[20]

Table 7.2 contains a clue which can help further to refine our understanding of Beethoven's work on these variation sketches. As can be seen, two sketches—one on page 51, the other on page 57—are numbered 2. This must be because they belong to different projected variation sets; and the boundary separating one set from the other is surely the final, detailed draft of the theme which Beethoven made at the bottom of page 53. A closer examination of the sketches immediately preceding that draft (see Chapter 8) reveals that they are, appropriately enough, attempts to forge an ending for the variation movement. The suggestion that pages 50–3 and 54–69 represent different phases of work is further supported by characteristics of the sketches themselves: those made after the final draft of the theme are a good deal more extended and detailed than those made before it. It may also be significant that, starting with page 54, Beethoven seems to have planned to begin each new variation draft on a clean page, although this resolve broke down after about page 60.[21]

After the break in work at page 69, Beethoven appears to have started again in earnest with page 72. The concentrated nature of the sketching on pages 72–3, which contain drafts for four variations, is reminiscent of the phase of activity which begins on page 54. By contrast, the few pencil sketches beneath the ink ones on page 71 are less straightforward; they may have been added only after the main phase of pencil sketching had begun on page 72. Pages 72–3 represent the last reasonably sustained work on the variations in Artaria 195; Beethoven's attention began to drift towards other projects thereafter.

---

[20] The music following the '100' connective on st. 1/2 was probably written independently both of the 'overview' sketch and of the sketch for a variation 9, to which it forms a coda or *Schluß*: see Ch. 8 n. 8, below.

[21] Kinderman notes (*Beethoven's Diabelli Variations*, 14) that the early variation drafts in the PLM Draft each occupy a single page; 'Var. 10, since it is the first "double" variation with both halves written out and which therefore cannot be contained on one side, continues from the last side of Paris 77A onto the first of Landsberg 10'.

Of the three remaining sketches, that on page 75 for the melodic line of Variation 1 is so unique in its close relationship to a part of the final version that it is tempting to assume that it was copied from some other source rather than generated by previous material in Artaria 195. Much the same applies to the sketch for the second half of Variation 6 on page 1 of Artaria 197.

Summing up this account of work on the variations in Artaria 195, we may distinguish at least the following phases of activity:

1. A preliminary series of sketches for a projected variation movement, made on pages 50–3 before the details of the theme had been finalized.

2. A more substantial series of variation sketches covering pages 54–69. These were subjected to critical review, during which some sketches were selected and numbered to form a set and were subsequently revised and added to in pencil.

3. The addition of the 'overview' sketch, again outlining a projected variation set, on the bottom staves of pages 64–9.

4. An interim period of less sustained activity covering pages 70–1.

5. A return to drafting variations, now in pencil, on pages 72–3, and the addition of some pencil sketches to page 71.

6. The final sketches, made on pages 75 and 78 after Beethoven had turned primarily to sketching Op. 119, numbers 7–11. The sketch for Variation 6 on Artaria 197, page 1 may also belong to this phase.

With this summary before us we can begin to make some sense of the bewildering array of variation sketches, most of them unrelated either to each other or to the final version, with which we are confronted in Artaria 195. What stands out particularly is the fact that during the most sustained period of activity, that represented by the sketching up to and including page 69, Beethoven was concerned less with writing variations than with establishing a coherent variation set; the character and details of individual members of the set seem to have been less important to him than the shape of the whole. Brandenburg's opinion that 'the originality of [Beethoven's] late variation works is rooted among other things in their cyclic organization' is thus consonant with the evidence of these otherwise refractory sketches.[22]

Beethoven's evident concentration on large-scale form suggests in turn a strategy for the analysis of these sketches. Rather than struggling to glimpse elements of individual variations in the making,

---

[22] 'Beethoven's "Erste Entwürfe"', 110: 'Die Originalität der späteren Variationswerke beruht u. a. auf ihrer zyklischen Gestaltung.'

Approaching the Variation Sketches 183

Chapter 8 will concentrate on the three variation sets projected in the sketches on pages 50–69, and on certain other relevant sketches. This is not to say that parallels with parts of the final version will not emerge; several striking ones will. But bearing in mind the aforementioned problematic status of relationships between variation sketches and final versions, it seems preferable to think relatively loosely, in terms of 'parallels' or 'forerunners', rather than to affix labels such as 'a sketch for Variation 2' and so on. The eight sketches which relate unequivocally to variations in the final version and which throw light on individual details will be discussed in Chapter 9, along with the A 47 drafts.

8. Plans for a Variation Set

Artaria 195, pages 50–3

As explained in the last chapter, the first outline for a variation set in Artaria 195 comes in a series of sketches on pages 50–3. In that they preceded the final, detailed draft of the theme made at the bottom of page 53, these may be regarded as preliminary sketches. (It may be recalled from Chapter 4 that some details of the theme which do not appear in the theme sketches prior to the final draft are nevertheless presupposed by some of these preliminary variation sketches; such thematic details may first have been worked out in sketches which are now lost.) Table 8.1 lists the locations of the sketches and shows how much of the theme they represent, while the transcriptions in Ex. 8.1 are intended only to give an idea of their musical content. Some are short enough to be transcribed complete; in other cases only an incipit is given. The three parts of sketch 8 are transcribed in full because they require more substantial discussion.

Table 8.1 indicates that sketches 1–4 are partly or totally superimposed upon one another. They are unique in this respect; the rest of the variation sketches are written successively, the only instances of superimposition being occasioned by revisions or additions (and these are infrequent enough). Indeed, the very fact that superimposed passages in Beethoven's sketches are so often the result of revisions suggests that sketches 1–4 may be reworkings of a single variation idea. This is clearly true of sketches 1 and 3, in both of which the rhythmic profile of the first half of the theme gives way to constant quaver motion broken only by syncopations. The melodic profile of the theme is closely adhered to in each case: sketch 1 simply fills in the falling and rising thirds with passing notes, while sketch 3 combines this procedure with arpeggiations which allow greater registral expansion. Sketch 2 holds even more closely to the theme. With the exception of an upward transfer leading to a cadence on b^2 in bars 4 and 8, it adheres strictly to the thematic register and melodic line almost throughout.[1] And like sketches 1 and 3, it employs a persistent rhythmic figure.

---

[1] A significant divergence from the theme occurs in bar 11, where the leap $g\sharp^1$–e^2 is not preserved; the melodic line in the variation moves within the third $g\sharp^1$–b^1. This detail may

TABLE 8.1. *Artaria 195, pp. 50–3: a projected set of variations*

Sketch number	Artaria 195: page, staves	Portion of theme represented (bars)
1	50, 13/14–51, 1/2	1–8
2	50, 13/14–51, 6/7	1–16; 13–15 blank
3	50, 15–51, 2	1–8
4	50, 16–51, 1/2/3	1–8
5 [labelled 2]	51, 9/10–52, 1/2	1–5 + 10 blank bars
6	52, 4/5–15/16	1 + 12 blank bars
7	53, 1/2	1–4 + 1 blank bar
8a	53, 4/5–7/8	1–8
8b	53, 7/8	1 [–16]; 'ganzes thema oben'
8c	53, 9/10	1–4, preceded by 1-bar link from sketch 8b; 4-bar coda added in version [2]

It is not possible to ascertain the order in which sketches 1–3 were written. All three are notated in ink; sketch 4, however, is in pencil, which suggests that it was the last of this superimposed group to be added, probably as part of the phase of revisions which Beethoven seems to have undertaken after sketching up to page 69. Unlike sketches 1–3, sketch 4 is based on a distinctive rhythmic-melodic motive, although this is once again derived from the filled-in thematic thirds $g\sharp^1$–e^1 and $d\sharp^1$–b. In bars 5–8 of the sketch (not shown in Ex. 8.1) the motive passes to the left hand; the wide spacing at the cadence in bars 7–8, and particularly the attempted part-writing in the latter bar, bring the corresponding part of Variation 1 to mind (Ex. 8.2).

Sketch 5 in Ex. 8.1 bears the number 2, which suggests that one of sketches 1–3 was intended as the first variation of the proposed set.[2] And the preceding discussion has suggested that this first variation was intended to adhere closely to the melodic and harmonic details of the theme: sketches 1–3 have this much in common even if they employ different means to the same end. Such strict adherence seems still to have been on Beethoven's mind when he came to write sketch 5, for he began by transferring the first bar of sketch 1 up an octave and adding a semiquaver accompaniment which artfully anticipates, in rhythmic diminution, the right-hand falling third

reflect the state of the theme at this stage; indeed, we have seen that one version of bars 9–12 tried out in the final draft of the theme on p. 53 also avoids e^2 and keeps the melody within the span $g\sharp^1$–b^1 (see Ex. 4.9, version [2], and Ex. 4.10a).

[2] This assumes that the numbering of sketch 5 preceded the stage of pencil working which brought sketch 4 into being.

186 *Plans for a Variation Set*

Ex. 8.1. Artaria 195, pp. 50–3: a projected set of variations

Ex. 8.1. contd.

$g\sharp^2$–$f\sharp^2$–e^2. This opening was then replaced by another notable mainly for its relative independence from the theme. The falling thirds $g\sharp^1$–e^1 and $d\sharp^1$–b, rigorously preserved hitherto, are replaced by embellished arpeggiations downward from the fifth, as opposed to the third, of the tonic and dominant triads: b^1–$g\sharp^1$–e^1 and $f\sharp^2$–$d\sharp^2$–b^1. The substitution of the triadic fifth for the third was ultimately to be used to great purpose and effect not in Variation 2 but in Variation 1, which departs immediately and radically from the theme by substituting b^2 for $g\sharp^1$. Sketch 5, by comparison, approaches b^2 more gradually; and despite the relative freedom with which the right hand is treated here, the bass line remains strongly tied to that of the theme.

Ex. 8.2.

a Artaria 195, p. 51, st. 1/2

b Op. 109, third movement, Variation 1, bar 8a

Sketches 6 and 7 require little comment: their relationship to the theme is utterly transparent. But sketch 8a is a different matter, for there is a greater distance between variation and theme here. Also, as in sketch 5, specific features of Variation 1 are called to mind: the contraction of the bass in bars 1–4 to a stepwise ascent through the fourth E–A, and the thick chordal accompaniment; or, in the right hand, the appoggiaturas e^2–$d\sharp^2$ and $g\sharp^2$–$f\sharp^2$ in bars 2 and 4. These details combine to give the sketch a rhapsodic character similar to that of Variation 1.

Sketch 8a covers the first half of a variation and closes with a double bar which is immediately followed by sketch 8b. This consists simply of a trilled B^1 and the instruction 'ganzes thema oben' (see Plate 7). Although the reference to the 'whole' theme suggests that a further complete variation is projected, it is a fact that throughout his sketching for the variations in Artaria 195 Beethoven almost never wrote more than one incipit per stave or system; it is possible, then, that sketches 8a–b together outline a single variation rather than two separate ones. If so, we must interpret Beethoven's instruction to mean that the entire second half of the theme was to be supported by the trilled dominant pedal.[3]

[3] It is also possible that the word 'Thema' here refers literally to a statement of the theme itself (or at least of its melodic line) rather than to a variation. If so, sketch 8b would appear to project a thematic reprise or a reprise-variation. But the likelihood of this interpretation is lessened by the fact that sketch 8c clearly has the function of a reprise, as the following discussion makes clear.

There is a firm musical continuity between sketches 8*b* and 8*c*: B^1 is repeated before a stepwise ascent leads to E. At this point the first four bars of the theme are restated, although the harmony is deflected strongly towards the submediant through the substitution of B♯ for B in bar 2. In version [1] the thematic restatement gives way to the characteristic abbreviation 'etc', but not before Beethoven has indicated that it should continue in the low register—'im̄er im Baß'— in which it began. In version [2] Beethoven obscured the 'etc' by adding a series of fifth-related chords whose strong cadential function (V/ii–V⁷/V–V–I) suggests that they mark the close of the projected movement.

The three parts of sketch 8 yield provocative information about Beethoven's plans for the final stages of the variation movement. With hindsight, one of the most significant indications is that of a prolonged dominant pedal which resolves to the tonic (sketches 8*b*–*c*). This was to remain a constant feature of the movement throughout the later stages of sketching. More importantly, it survived into the final version. The dominant is present as a pedal in some register throughout almost all of Variation 6, but in bars 9a–16a (17–24) it is represented by a trilled B^1 above which the variation—and with it the movement—reaches its climax. And just as sketch 8*b* is connected seamlessly to sketch 8*c*, which appears to function at least partly as a thematic reprise, so Variation 6 leads into the almost literal restatement of the theme which brings Op. 109 to its close.

In view of its uncertain function, sketch 8*c* deserves closer consideration. (Furthermore, it will become clear that this sketch was not entirely without influence on Beethoven's subsequent plans for the movement.) The temporary but important turn to the submediant prevents it from being equated straightforwardly with the more literal thematic reprise in the final version; nor was there necessarily any need for a thematic reprise if the remark 'ganzes thema oben' linked to sketch 8*b* was intended to indicate a reprise-variation of some kind. On the other hand, the close adherence of sketch 8*c* to the theme, and particularly to its rhythm, damages its credentials as a true variation sketch, especially in comparison to the preceding examples. But one feature of sketch 8*c* which should be entirely unproblematic is the choice of the submediant for the harmonic deflection. Beethoven's near-obsession with this scale degree since his earliest work on the first movement had already affected the theme itself (see Chapter 4); small wonder, then, that C♯ minor should surface elsewhere in the sketches for the third movement.

From a stylistic point of view, the introduction of a measure of tonal and formal expansion at the end of a variation movement was not unusual. In a number of his early piano variation sets (that on *La stessa, la stessissima*, WoO 73 is a good example) Beethoven had introduced sometimes lengthy sections which depart from the hitherto rigorously maintained thematic structure: wide-ranging tonal motion is common, as is developmental treatment of one or more motives drawn from the theme. Such sections usually culminate on a dominant pedal which is resolved at the beginning of a final variation or reprise-variation (there is an affinity here with the cadenza–final tutti arrangement in the classical concerto). A closer model for the plan suggested in sketch 8 is perhaps the slow movement of the 'Archduke' Trio, Op. 97. Here the fourth variation leads into what sounds at first like a straightforward reprise of the theme in the tonic, D major; but although the first eight-bar half (bars 141–8) is maintained in outline, it is tonally altered so that F major is touched upon in bars 142–5. The process is repeated from bar 149 onwards. A literal reprise of the second half of the theme begins in the piano; but reprise soon becomes development, and a climax is reached in bar 155 with the reappearance, in E rather than D major, of the last four-bar phrase. The dotted neighbour-note figure ♩♩ ♩. from the penultimate bar of the theme is then made the vehicle of a further passage leading back to the tonic in bar 174.[4]

That sketch 8c marks the beginning of a section like that in the 'Archduke' Trio rather than a more straightforward thematic reprise, albeit with some harmonic innovations, cannot be decided from the version [1] ending, with its imprecise 'etc' conclusion. But the series of chords in version [2] is clearly not part of the theme and argues that Beethoven was planning some kind of free coda for the movement. On reflection, his chosen material proves to be less than entirely original; like the turn to the submediant at the beginning of sketch 8c, these cadential chords appear to be a throwback to ideas familiar from the first-movement sketches. The upper voice traces the 'B-tonicizing' progression g♯–a♯–b; and the final chord is none other than the closed-position tonic triad on which the first movement (in its final version) ends. If, as argued in Chapter 4, the variation theme is a recomposition and completion of the structurally incomplete first movement of Op. 109, it seems that in these sketches

---

[4] Both the Diabelli Variations and the second movement of Op. 111 preserve the tradition of tonal expansion towards the end of a variation set; and in both these C-major works it is the key of E♭ which serves this purpose. In the Diabelli Variations a fugue in E♭ precedes the final reprise-variation, while the transition between Variations 4 and 5 (the latter again a reprise-variation) in Op. 111 introduces part of the theme in E♭ before touching upon other tonal regions.

Plans for a Variation Set 191

on pages 50–3 of Artaria 195 Beethoven was planning to undermine that completion by using the end of the first movement to 'close' the variation set.

Artaria 195, pages 54–69

This section is concerned with the sketches which Beethoven made after the final draft of the theme at the bottom of page 53. As explained in Chapter 7, he appears to have worked up to page 69 before looking back through the sketches and numbering those which he thought worth revising and combining to form a set. It was presumably after this that he added corrections and additions in pencil to the numbered sketches before going on to make further sketches in pencil on pages 71–3. What will not be considered here is the 'overview' sketch for a variation set which occupies the bottom staves of pages 64–9; that sketch is sufficiently important to be treated separately.

In numbering his selected sketches Beethoven again neglected to identify any sketch as variation 1: his numbering begins with 'Var: 2' at the top of page 57 and continues through to variation 9, which begins on page 67. But whereas three ideas preceded the sketch numbered 2 in the set outlined on pages 50–3, there are only two presumed candidates for variation 1 here. Both are included under the number [1] in Table 8.2, which lists the locations of the numbered sketches and gives a brief indication of their scope and content. Ex. 8.3 provides incipits for all the sketches, in order to give an idea of their character.

A comparison of these incipits with those in Ex. 8.1 shows clearly that there is little question here of any reworking of the earlier material: what appears in Ex. 8.3 is a series of essentially new ideas. Obvious exceptions to this are the two unnumbered sketches, which might plausibly be considered extended reworkings of Ex. 8.1, sketches 1 and 2 respectively (compare Ex. 7.1). On the other hand, it would be incautious to regard the repeated-chord accompaniment which Beethoven rejected at the beginning of variation 7 as related to that in Ex. 8.1, sketch 8a. The incipits in Ex. 8.3 also illustrate the remoteness of most of these sketches from the six variations in the final version. Exceptions here are variation 3, which clearly foreshadows its counterpart in Op. 109, and variation 9, whose content and double-variation form similarly foreshadow Variation 6. Yet these isolated visions of the final version should always be considered in context: variation 3 was pursued no further in Artaria 195, while the first of two incipits on these pages for what became

TABLE 8.2. *Artaria 195, pp. 54–67: a projected set of nine variations*

Artaria 195: page, staves	Heading, number, metre	Description (bars represented)
54, 1/2–55, 9/10	[1], 3/4	Complete double variation, 32 bars
56, 1/2–10/11	[1], 3/4	Complete single variation, 16 bars
57, 1/2	Var: 2, 3/4	2-bar incipit only
59, 1/2–10/11	all[egr]o, 3, 2/4	Intended double variation; 1a–8a, 1b–2b notated + 7 blank bars
60, 5/6–61, 1/2	4, 3/4	Single variation; 1–15 notated, bar 16 omitted
61, 5/6–14/15	all[egr]o, 5, 2/4	Intended double variation? 1a–8a, 1b–2b notated + 4 blank bars; 9[a]–16[a] notated. Entire sketch deleted in pencil
62, 13/14–63, 10/11	6, 3/4	Single variation, 16 bars; 3–6 blank
63, 13/14/15–66, 1/2	adag[i]o, 7, 3/4	Double variation, 32 bars; 2b–8b, 11b–16b blank
66, 4/5–13/14	all[egr]o, 8, 2/4	Single variation with repeats indicated; 1-bar extension to end of second half
67, 1/2–68, 10/11	9, 3/4	Complete double variation; 1-bar extension to end of second half, leading into (independently notated?) *Schluß* on 69, 1/2–3/4

Variation 5—the sketch in question is on page 62, immediately above variation 6—was deleted without even being graced with a number.

Viewing the projected set of nine variations as a whole we can see that numbers 3, 5, and 8 were to be 'allegro' variations in 2/4 time rather than the 3/4 of the theme. The specific marking 'adag[i]o' for variation 7 may have been intended to indicate a tempo slower than that of the theme itself.[5] In most cases it is possible to tell from the sketch whether Beethoven intended a single or double variation, although variations 2 and 5 are ambiguous in this respect. In the case of variation 4, whose last notated bar contains only a single B^1, it is

---

[5] The final draft of the theme (Artaria 195, p. 53) is marked 'con molto sentimento ed espressivo', but in the final version Beethoven was more explicit about the intended speed: 'Andante molto cantabile ed espressivo'. And Variation 4 is headed 'un poco meno andante ciò è un poco più adagio come il tema'.

Ex. 8.3. Artaria 195, pp. 54–67: a projected set of nine variations

194 *Plans for a Variation Set*

Ex. 8.3. contd.

not clear whether Beethoven simply did not bother to notate the final bar or whether he actually intended this variation to be open-ended, with the required tonic closure being provided by the opening of variation 5. In this connection it may be significant that variation 5 employs an anacrusis, unlike the theme and any other of the numbered sketches; the anacrusis may have been conceived to ensure a smoother connection with the unresolved dominant at the end of variation 4. (In the final version Beethoven retained the downbeat opening of the theme in all six variations, but Variations 3 and 5 are not tonally closed and run directly into Variations 4 and 6.)[6]

As Table 8.2 indicates, the sketches selected for this projected variation set are of varying lengths; the shortest is that for 'Var: 2'. It needs to be emphasized that the selected sketches were by no means invariably the most extended or detailed ones; ideas which were clearly of sufficient interest for Beethoven to record them at considerable length did not necessarily survive the test of time. However, it may not be entirely coincidental that the three longest and most detailed sketches listed in Table 8.2 occupy strategic places within the projected set: they are the two unnumbered sketches presumed to be for the first variation, and the final sketch, for variation 9. And a moment's further reflection on variation 9 reveals that, like the unnumbered sketches, it probably represents a reworking of earlier material. The trilled B^1 and accompanying direction 'ganzes thema oben' which make up sketch 8*b* in Ex. 8.1 are clearly preserved and developed in variation 9; the connection is simply obscured by the highly condensed and abstract nature of the earlier sketch. As the incipit shows, variation 9 brings a literal return to the melodic line of the theme, while the trilled dominant pedal is now present as a covering voice above this line. The theme is preserved very much in its original form throughout, and the dominant pedal is also maintained: b^1 is present throughout bars 1a–8a, 1b–8b, and 9a–16a, but gives way to a trilled B^1 in the last, slightly extended phrase (Ex. 8.4).[7]

Despite its relationship to the earlier sketch 8*b* in Ex. 8.1 and to Variation 6 in the final version, the draft for variation 9 implies that Beethoven's conception of the ending of the movement was quite

---

[6] Kinderman, *Beethoven's Diabelli Variations*, 32, draws attention to the PLM drafts of Variations 19 and 21, both of which are tonally open-ended like the sketch for variation 4 being considered here.

[7] On p. 64, st. 1/2 there is a two-bar incipit which again combines a literal restatement of the theme with a trilled dominant pedal: in this case the melodic line of the theme is presented in the upper voice while the pedal B forms an inner voice immediately above the bass. The incipit, which is deleted and was an 'advance' entry on the page, may represent an earlier formulation of the idea worked out at full length in variation 9.

196 *Plans for a Variation Set*

Ex. 8.4. Artaria 195, p. 68, st. 4/5–10/11 [variation 9: see Plate 5]

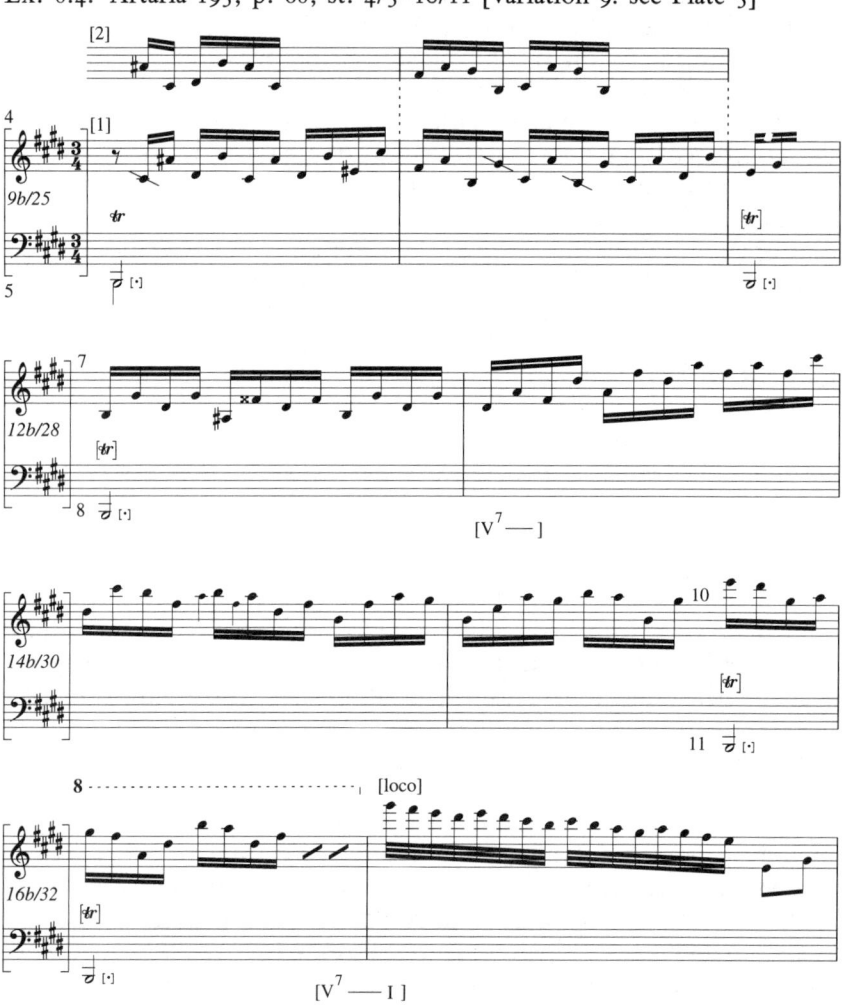

different at this stage. This matter requires extended discussion, and it may be useful to begin by examining the final version first. Variation 6 in Op. 109 works towards a climax at bar 9a (17). The climax is articulated in various ways: by the abrupt downward shift of the trilled dominant pedal to B^1 (prior to this the pedal has been confined to b^1 and B); by the arrival at a forte dynamic level; and by the dramatic change in the right-hand figuration, which receives its impetus from the diminished-seventh harmony anticipated at the end of the previous bar. Also significant is the dual process of rhythmic diminution leading up to this point. The dominant pedal is articulated in crotchets, quavers, triplet quavers, sextolets (the triplet quavers and sextolets appear as quavers and semiquavers within the temporary 9/8 metre), and demisemiquavers before being notated as a proper trill from the end of bar 4b (12) onwards. The rhythmic articulation of the melodic line of the theme undergoes a similar diminution, from crotchets to quavers and then triplet quavers; but the sextolet stage is omitted and the triplet quavers give way immediately to demisemiquavers at the climactic bar 9a (17).

The accumulated tension which breaks in this bar does not begin to subside until the very end of the variation. Prior to this, the left hand takes over the demisemiquaver motion in bar 9b (25) and shifts to a much higher register. In bar 15b (31) the descending line runs from b^1 back down to B^1 and then rises through a fourth to reach E on the downbeat of bar 16b (32), as previously in bar 16a (24). Bar 16b (32) is properly the final bar of the variation, corresponding to bar 16 of the theme. Now the first two beats of that bar carry a triple suspension over the bass E: a^1, $f\sharp^1$, and $d\sharp^1$ are suspended and resolve to $g\sharp^1$ and e^1 on the third beat (in figured-bass terms the voice leading, reading downwards from the top voice, is 4–3, 9–8, 7–8). In Variation 6 Beethoven extends this last bar of the theme in a surprising way. The triple suspension is held throughout bar 16b (32) and for a further three bars (33–5). Its resolution, displaced from the third beat of bar 16b (32), occurs with the first beat of the thematic reprise. And inasmuch as the theme departs from and returns to its initial root-position E-major triad with $g\sharp^1$ in the upper voice, the resolution of the suspensions in bar 16b (32) may be thought of as being 'composed out' across its sixteen-bar length. In other words, the final bar of Variation 6 is extended to a length of twenty bars: 4 + 16 (the thematic reprise). Only with the resolution provided by the reprise is the energy accumulated earlier felt to be wholly exhausted.

A similar scheme is hinted at, however vaguely, in Ex. 8.1, sketch 8b–c, where the resolution to E of the trilled dominant pedal B^1 calls forth some kind of varied thematic reprise. As in the final version, the tension built up in the last variation of this projected set requires a further event—the thematic reprise—for its complete resolution. Ex. 8.3, variation 9, on the other hand, works differently. As the incipit shows, the variation opens with the dominant pedal articulated in semiquavers and with the theme in its original note values. In bar 1b (9) the dominant pedal accelerates to a proper trill and the thematic voice moves in quavers. This arrangement persists throughout bars 1b–8b and 9a–16a, following which the trilled B^1 supports a thematic voice now moving in semiquavers (Ex. 8.4). The crucial point is that, unlike the situation at this stage in Variation 6, the climax of variation 9 has not yet been reached. Tension continues to build throughout bars 9b–16b as the semiquaver figuration rises inexorably, carrying a^1 up two octaves to a^3. The dominant harmony extends throughout bar 16b and the climax is finally reached in the ensuing 'extra' bar, where a significant reversal occurs: the previous rising semiquavers give way to downward rushing demisemiquavers as $g\sharp^3$ enters on the downbeat to resolve the preceding dominant seventh, a^3.

With this bar, variation 9 reaches its end. At the top of the next page (page 69) in Artaria 195 Beethoven outlined a plan for the ending of the movement as a whole.[8] This projected *Schluß*, as it is marked, is essentially an extended elaboration of the final bar of the theme, with its triple suspension over a tonic pedal (see the analytical stave underneath the transcription in Ex. 8.5a); more fundamentally, the purpose of the *Schluß* is to reiterate the A–G♯ resolution which had been the main business of the last section of variation 9. But it is clear that no thematic reprise was intended here. Whereas in the final version and in the set of variations projected on pages 50–3 the overall dynamic of the movement is conceived as a kind of arch, moving from the still, serene theme to the climactic frenzy of the second half of the final variation and back again, here Beethoven conceived a set of nine variations in terms of a long dynamic crescendo. There was to be no return to the point of origin; the brilliant, extrovert ending envisaged in Ex. 8.5a could hardly be more remote from the spirit of the theme. A similar kind of piano writing is to be found in one of the few sketches on pages 54–69 of Artaria 195 which are apparently not variation incipits (Ex. 8.5b); it is possible that this sketch too was intended as a bravura ending for the movement.

This radically reconceived ending compels us to consider again the preceding variations in this projected set of nine. And in order to do this it is necessary to take a harder look at the question of the first variation, which Beethoven did not specifically identify. For if his main purpose in these sketches was to establish a viable structure for the variation movement as a whole, it is reasonable to assume that the first variation would play a significant role in any such structure.

---

[8] There is a straightforward musical continuity from the end of Ex. 8.4 (Artaria 195, p. 68, st. 10/11) to the beginning of Ex. 8.5a (p. 69, st. 1/2). This is not matched by an unambiguous physical continuity, however (see Plates 5–6). Ex. 8.5a begins conspicuously far in from the left-hand margin at the top of p. 69, as if it were jotted down independently of the material on the preceding page. It is likely that at least the first four bars of this plan for a *Schluß* were actually notated some time before Beethoven finished the draft for variation 9.

Ex. 8.5. *a* Artaria 195, p. 69, st. 1/2–3/4 (see Plate 6)

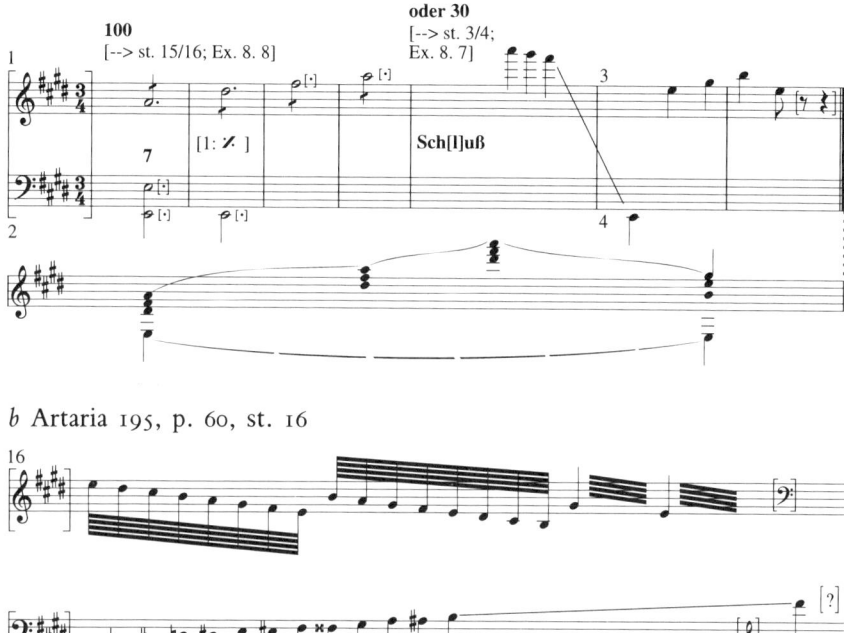

b Artaria 195, p. 60, st. 16

The obvious candidates for the first of the nine variations are the two unnumbered full-length drafts which precede the incipit for 'Var: 2' at the top of page 57 in Artaria 195. That the drafts are superficially quite dissimilar is apparent both from the incipits in Ex. 8.3 and from the descriptions in Table 8.2 (the first draft is for a 32-bar double variation while the second is for a 16-bar single one). Yet if our assumptions are correct—if Beethoven was sketching a structure in which the first variation was to play a significant role—there should be some point of contact between these two drafts. To put it another way, if Beethoven considered them equally suitable as the first variation of the set, then they should both relate to the eight succeeding variations in an essentially similar way.

The relationship hangs on Beethoven's treatment of register. The endings of the two unnumbered drafts are transcribed in Ex. 8.6*a*–*b*. In each case the melodic line is carried up to a^3 as part of a dominant seventh in E. This a^3, which corresponds to a^1 in bars 15–16 of the theme, represents the registral climax of the draft; and in each case it is reached by a relatively abrupt climb from a lower octave.

Ex. 8.6. *a* Artaria 195, p. 55, st. 9

b Artaria 195, p. 56, st. 10

c Artaria 195, p. 61, st. 14 [variation 5]

More important is the fact that a^3 is left unresolved in its own register: in the first draft there is a downward shift to $g\sharp^2$ during the final bar, while an even more dramatic plunge in the second leads to a resolution two octaves lower on $g\sharp^1$, the opening register of the draft and of the theme. The argument would be less convincing if the same registral strategy did not recur at prominent junctures later in the projected set of nine variations. Ex. 8.6*c* shows that the plunge from a climactic a^3 to $g\sharp^1$ occurs at the end of the central variation 5 also. Only in the climactic final bar of variation 9, then, was a^3 to be resolved in its own register, at the moment of reversal described above in connection with Ex. 8.4.

Thus a long-range structural plan for this projected variation set begins to emerge. The plan derives from a detail in the theme, namely the suspension and delayed resolution of a^1 to $g\sharp^1$ in bars 15–16. By establishing a^3 as the climactic point of a series of variations—and it is surely not coincidental that the chosen variations were numbers [1], 5, and 9, the first, middle, and last of the set—and leaving it registrally unresolved until the end of the final variation, Beethoven was able to create a sense of overarching continuity while at the same time providing satisfactory closure in a lower register for each individual variation. Either of the two unnumbered drafts could have served as the first variation of the set simply because of its treatment of a^3 prior to its close. As for the intended close, or *Schluß*, of the entire movement (Ex. 8.5*a*), it is notable that this rehearses for the last time the upward transfer a^1–a^2–a^3 before the cascading descent to the bass E four and a half octaves below.

Ex. 8.7. Artaria 195, p. 69, st. 3/4–9/10

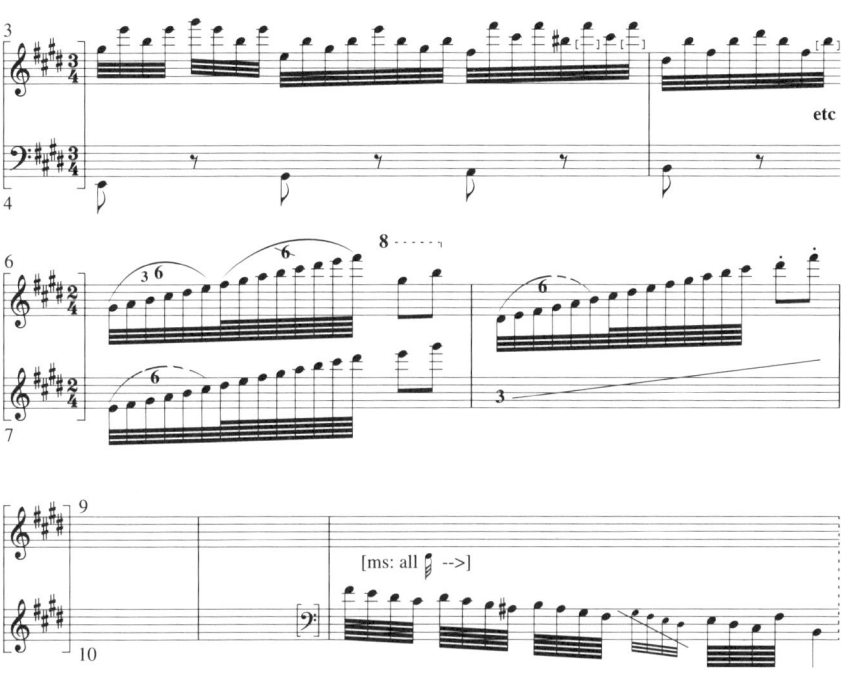

It might be argued that the a^3–$g\sharp^3$ resolution at the end of variation 9 is too fleeting to bear the weight of a structural resolution for the whole movement, and that it is undermined in any case by the return of a^3 in the bravura coda, which offers only a displaced resolution to $g\sharp^2$. If Beethoven was aware of these issues, he seems to have addressed them in a further pair of variations cued into Ex. 8.5a by means of the 'oder 30' connective. These added variations (Ex. 8.7) substitute a marked emphasis on $g\sharp^3$ for the former scalic descent from a^3; Beethoven's intention seems to have been to 'ground' the registral denouement introduced at the end of variation 9. Unfortunately, it is not possible to tell how he planned to conclude the movement following these additions.

The structural scheme envisaged in this series of sketches is of course intimately related to the incomplete structure of the first movement, in which (as the sketches show) Beethoven suppressed the harmonic–melodic resolution A–G♯ both at the point of recapitulation and at the close. Indeed, it is in its relationship to the first movement of Op. 109 that the difference between this set of (initially) nine variations and the shorter set outlined on pages 50–3 of Artaria 195 can most plainly be seen. The earlier set was apparently intended to reinforce the incomplete ending of the first movement by echoing its final chord, preceded by a slow unfolding of the 'B-tonicizing' progression g♯–a♯–b (Ex. 8.1, sketch 8c). The set sketched on pages 54–69, on the other hand, was designed to supply the structural resolution lacking in the first movement.

Artaria 195, pages 64–9, staves 15/16

Beethoven's final attempt in Artaria 195 to fix the structure of the third movement of Op. 109 came with the writing of the 'overview' sketch for a variation set which runs along staves 15/16 of pages 64–9 before feeding into the pre-existing plans for a *Schluß* on staves 1/2–3/4. That *Schluß* was transcribed in Ex. 8.5a; the 'overview' sketch appears in Ex. 8.8. It contrasts starkly with the material discussed in the preceding section. While the nine-variation set was culled from a much larger number of sketches, there is no evidence of selection here: everything notated is a part of the whole. Accordingly, there is no numbering; the six projected variations are easily distinguishable from one another, and there is no unused material from which they need to be separated. Compared to the extended, perhaps sometimes leisurely, bout of activity which produced the nine-variation set, everything about this 'overview' sketch suggests haste and a conscientious avoidance of any superfluity. By its very nature it focuses attention on the variations *as a set*. There is in any case little opportunity to discuss individual variations, for all that is provided in each case is an incipit: the sole, significant exception to this is variation [6], for which there are ten bars as compared to a previous maximum of four. This is also the only one of the six variations whose position ('le[t]zte') in the set is specified.

Further comparison with the earlier nine-variation set must be almost entirely negative; there is no significant connection between any of the 'overview' incipits and the nine numbered sketches listed in Table 8.2. Once again, a slight exception must be made for variation [6], which was clearly intended to be a double variation like variation 9. However, two crucial features of that variation—the trilled dominant pedal and the undisguised return of the theme—are much attenuated here. (It is variation [2] which most powerfully suggests a literal recall of the theme.) Nor is there any sign in the 'overview' of a registrally unresolved a^3 which might link up with that note in the recycled *Schluß* material. And although variation [5]

Plans for a Variation Set 203

Ex. 8.8. Artaria 195, pp. 64–9, st. 15/16: the 'overview' sketch for a variation set

Ex. 8.8. contd.

is (erroneously) given a 6/8 time signature, none of the variations uses 2/4, which had replaced 3/4 in the three 'all[egr]o' variations (3, 5, and 8) of the earlier set.[9]

A cursory glance at Ex. 8.8 might also suggest that there is no point in pressing comparisons with the final version: once again, the specific features of the final version projected in the nine-variation set seem to have been rejected at some point before Beethoven put the 'overview' sketch on paper. Nevertheless, the final version and the 'overview' do share a number of characteristics worth examining. To take a rather obvious example, the number of variations now envisaged is the same as that in Op. 109. But a more subtle feature is the implied grouping of the variations in the 'overview' sketch. A double-single barline separates variations [1] and [2], and [4] and [5]; elsewhere there is a single barline or (as between variations [3] and [4]) none at all. The point might seem trivial were it not for the fact that in no other case in Artaria 195 did Beethoven close a variation incipit with a double-single barline: only if he had

---

[9] The 6/8 signature at the beginning of Variation [5] is contradicted by the metrical groupings and notation, which clearly imply 3/4.

sketched a first half (bars 1–8) or a complete variation did he employ this sign. While the use of double-single barlines in the 'overview' sketch is thus unusual, it directly foreshadows their use in the autograph, where also a double-single separates Variations 1 (second-time bar) and 2, and 4 and 5, a standard single barline being used elsewhere (see Fig. 1.1). In the 'overview' sketch and the autograph, then, the variations are given the larger grouping 1; 2–4; 5–6.

Another suggestive comparison may be made between variations [1] and [2] and their counterparts in the final version. With its rather conventional arpeggiated left-hand part and series of equal quavers in the right, variation [1] still stands at a considerable distance from Variation 1. Similarly, the literal statement of the theme as an inner voice between two counterpointing voices moving in tenths in variation [2] gives little hint of the varying textures which characterize Variation 2. If, on the other hand, we interpret the two incipits more broadly as the expression of a radical departure from the theme in the first variation followed by an equally firm return to it in the second, then comparison with the final version becomes more telling. In Variation 1 several factors combine to create the impression of a conceptual 'gap' between it and the theme from which it proceeds. Despite its more florid melodic line, the essentially homophonic texture is simpler than that of the theme; the harmonic rhythm is generally slower, particularly at the opening; the melodic line operates in a higher register; and most importantly, the substitution in Variation 1 of b^2 for $g\sharp^1$ on the downbeats of bars 1 and 3 destroys one of the theme's most conspicuous melodic features.

The opening of Variation 2 restores all these features of the theme; although it eschews the literal restatement of the melodic line found in variation [2], its proximity to the theme is none the less unmistakable. It is almost as though the proper sequence of variations begins with Variation 2, while Variation 1 is an interpolation which properly belongs elsewhere, at a temporal distance more appropriate to its conceptual distance from the theme. (This interpretation is reinforced by the disposition of double-single barlines in the autograph whereby Variation 1 is uniquely isolated.) Not that 'distance' should be construed here as lying necessarily in the direction of greater complexity. On the contrary, Charles Rosen's statement that 'in many of the late variation sets (opp. 109, 111, 127, etc.) there is a progressive simplification as the variations proceed—not of the texture but of the conception of the underlying theme' does not apply particularly well to Op. 109, where it is above all Variation 1 which gives the impression of immediate and drastic simplification and seems to be 'not so much decorating the theme as discovering its essence'.[10]

As well as foreshadowing Variation 1 both in its contrast with the theme and variation [2] and in its concluding double-single barline, variation [1] also shows the replacement of G♯ by B mentioned above as the most important feature of Variation 1. The incipit makes the point with a vengeance, indeed, since the revised version of the right-hand part consists solely of B repeated in three different octaves. (The letter h [= B] written above the notes in the first two bars clarifies the intended pitch.) A similar insistence on B sets in with the last two notated bars (they correspond to bars 1b–2b of a double variation) in variation [6]. The resemblance to variation [1] is quite striking, with a repeated b now struck on every second semiquaver while an ascending left-hand arpeggio crosses over this inner pedal to reach b^2 at the end of each bar. The 'overview' sketch breaks off here, of course, and the instruction 'etc so fort bis 100' leads to the recycled *Schluß* material of Ex. 8.5a (see Plate 6).

By considering the 'overview' sketch in relation to the already-projected *Schluß* it is possible to understand why a registrally unresolved a^3 plays no apparent role here. That note, which unifies the nine-variation set by spanning variations 1, 5, and 9 before finally resolving to $g♯^3$, is replaced in the 'overview' by B, which features most prominently in the two outer variations of the set. In variation [1] the melodic line rises rapidly from b^1 through b^2 to b^3. This high register is reiterated in variation [5] when b^3 returns on the downbeat of bar 2. And although the notated portion of variation [6] ventures no higher than b^2, it seems reasonable to suppose that Beethoven would subsequently have extended the compass up to b^3 in order to establish a registral link back to b^3 in variation [1]. The b^3 spanning variations [1]–[6] would lead forward to the protracted A–G♯ (specifically, a^3–$g♯^2$) resolution in the *Schluß*.[11] The direction of Beethoven's thought seems clear: he was seeking a means to employ

---

[10] *The Classical Style: Haydn, Mozart, Beethoven*, rev. edn. (London, 1976), 436, 437. Certainly, the first variation in other Beethoven cycles more frequently displays the close relationship to the theme (and the simple figurational embellishment) exhibited in bars 1–8 of Variation 2 than the radical reinterpretation offered in Variation 1. Compare, for example, the first variation of the second movement of Op. 111, which begins the variation process with a very simple elaboration of the Arietta. As the variations proceed, so what I have termed their conceptual (as well as strictly temporal) distance from the theme increases. For a similar procedure to that adopted in Op. 109, compare the theme and Variations 1–2 from the Variations on 'Rule Britannia', WoO 79, quoted in Rosen, *Classical Style*, 435–6.

[11] Since 'overview' Variation [6] is specifically marked 'le[t]zte' it seems unlikely that Beethoven intended the recycling of material written at the top of page 69 to extend to the additional variations transcribed in Ex. 8.7, although their emphasis on $g♯^3$ would have been registrally appropriate in this context.

the complete 'E-tonicizing' progression B–A–G♯, rather than the partial form A–G♯, as a large-scale unifying element in the variation set. The way in which this idea is worked out in the final version of the movement will be discussed below, in the Conclusion. In the mean time a number of other sketches invite comment.

Artaria 195, pages 70–3

It is clear that the two variation sets just considered—the one of nine selected from pages 54–69 of Artaria 195 and the one of six outlined in the 'overview' sketch—were to consist entirely of variations in the tonic key. No tonal or formal expansion of the kind hinted at earlier in Ex. 8.1, sketch 8c is indicated in either case. Moreover, variation 9 in the larger set was evidently intended to serve partly as a thematic reprise, following which the movement was to close in a blaze of cascading scales. It is uncertain whether Beethoven intended a different conclusion to follow the additional variations transcribed in Ex. 8.7; but we can safely say that among the sketches related to the nine-variation set there is no hard evidence that he was planning a literal thematic reprise like that in the final version. And since the 'overview' sketch feeds into the already-projected *Schluß*, the same conclusion applies here also. However, sketches written on the pages immediately following page 69 show that Beethoven did reconsider the idea of tonal and formal expansion towards the end of the set and that the possibility of closure achieved through literal restatement of the theme was also in his thoughts. Not surprisingly, the only tonal expansion envisaged involves the submediant (compare Ex. 8.1, sketch 8c).

Tonal and formal expansion appears linked to thematic reprise in the most substantial sketch (Ex. 8.9). The last four bars, which reproduce the bass line of the theme more or less literally, and the ensuing direction 'etc Ende' strongly indicate a thematic reprise; but the preceding material is less straightforward. Viewed as a whole, the sketch is built over the strongly cadential progression VI–II–V–I. (It may not be coincidental that essentially the same progression governs the ending of Ex. 8.1, sketch 8c, version [2].) First come five bars in 4/4 time; following these, and leading directly into the presumed reprise, there is a return to 3/4 for a four-bar sequence based on bar 14 of the theme.[12]

---

[12] That Ex. 8.9 does indeed constitute a single sketch is based largely on the very plausible musical continuity between bars 4–5; but it is curious that Beethoven should have turned from p. 70 to p. 71 at this point, leaving st. 6–16 on the former page entirely blank except for braces at the beginning of st. 6/7 and 8/9.

208 *Plans for a Variation Set*

Ex. 8.9. Artaria 195, p. 70, st. 4/5–p. 71, st. 3/4

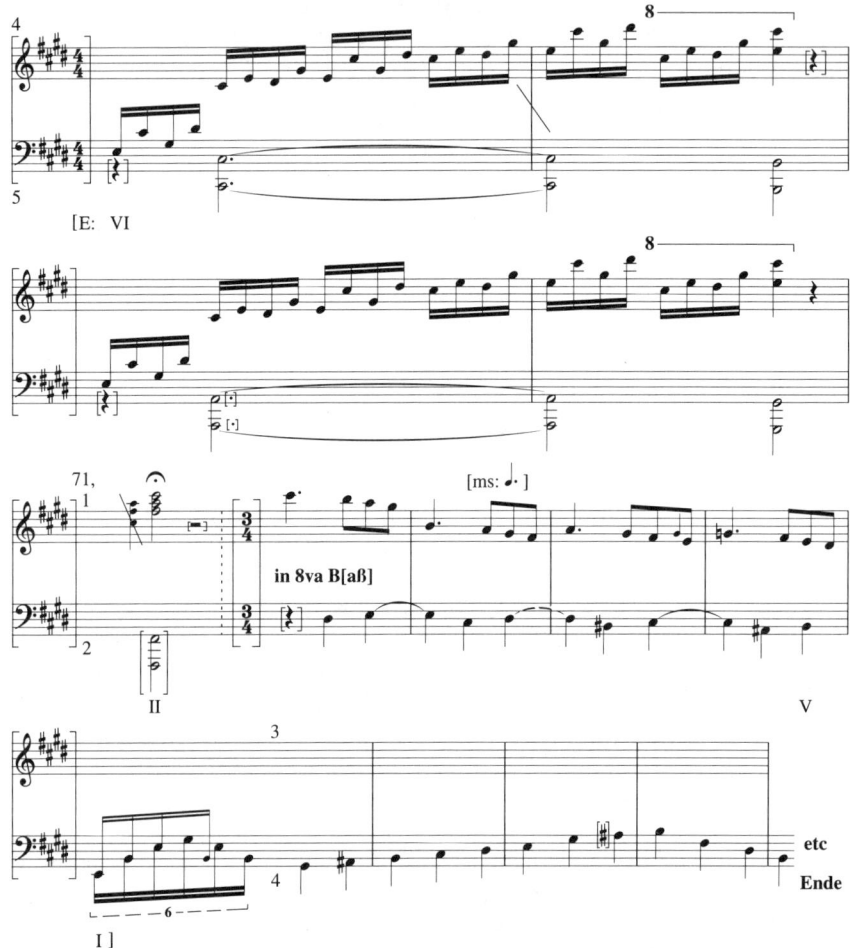

This material is obviously not just another idea for a variation; its most likely explanation is that Beethoven was planning a free coda of the kind discussed above. This interpretation is supported in several ways: by the change of time signature, by the free, 'developmental' use of a motive from the theme, and by the implied subsequent restoration of the theme itself in the concluding four bars. Ex. 8.9 captures an idea which bore fruit not in Op. 109 but in Op. 111, where a transition (bars 106–36) involving a modulation to E♭ separates Variations 4 and 5, the latter of which serves as a reprise-variation.

Ex. 8.10. *a* Artaria 195, p. 71, st. 5–7

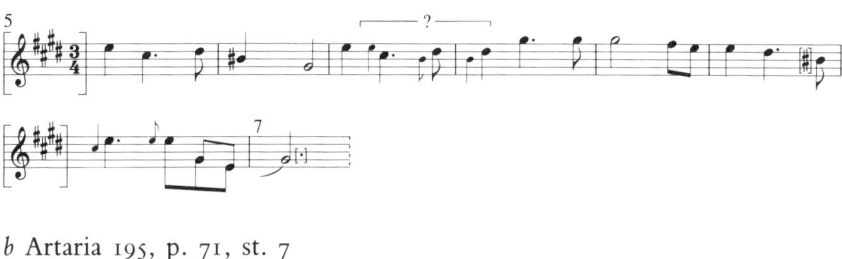

b Artaria 195, p. 71, st. 7

And Drabkin's sonata-form description of the second movement of Op. 111 as 'exposition (i.e. the Arietta itself), variations, transition, recapitulation' in which 'the transition is really a short development section, moving towards a new key (E♭ major) and fragmenting the melody of the Arietta into its motivic components' is relevant to the third movement of Op. 109 as Beethoven seems to have envisaged it here.[13] Rather than establishing a new local tonic Ex. 8.9 stresses a tonal area—the submediant—which is relatively underplayed in the theme and variations; but an actual tonicization of the submediant prior to the point at which the sketch begins cannot be ruled out.

Two further sketches in which the submediant is introduced are transcribed in Ex. 8.10; written in pencil on page 71, they immediately follow Ex. 8.9.[14] The first appears to be an idea for a minor-key variation, and the same may be true of the second although the difficulty of reading some of the pitches makes interpretation correspondingly less secure in this case. A notable feature of both sketches is the extent to which they replicate the rhythm of the theme, a characteristic they share with their precursor Ex. 8.1, sketch 8c.

It is appropriate that this discussion of plans for a variation set should close in the same way as the final version itself, with an unequivocal reprise of the theme. The series of pencil sketches on pages 72–3 of Artaria 195 may represent the beginnings of another projected variation set: four variations are clearly indicated, one of them even at full length (although a number of bars are blank). The second variation continues from page 72, staves 15/16 to page 73, staves 3/4; what prevented Beethoven from using staves 1/2 on the

---

[13] 'Sketches for Beethoven's Opus 111', 211.
[14] The possibility that these two sketches may have been added to p. 71 only after Beethoven had begun the longer series of pencil sketches on pp. 72–3 was raised in Ch. 7.

Ex. 8.11. Artaria 195, p. 73, st. 1/2

latter page was the presence there of the sketch shown in Ex. 8.11. Its similarity to the thematic reprise which brings Op. 109 to a close is obvious; even the downward octave transfer of the bass (bar 5) is in place.

Conclusion

To summarize: the first set of sketches, written on pages 50–3 of Artaria 195 prior to the final draft of the variation theme itself, indicates a set of possibly six variations—the exact number is uncertain since only one of the variations is explicitly numbered, and it is not clear whether Ex. 8.1, sketches 8*a* and 8*b* represent separate variations or not. Beethoven envisaged a measure of formal freedom and tonal expansion towards the submediant at the end of the set, possibly as part of a coda which would also make literal reference to the theme. The movement was apparently to conclude in a subdued manner, with a series of slow chords outlining the first-movement 'B-tonicizing' progression (g♯–a♯–b). The final chord, a tonic triad in closed position, would also strongly recall the end of the first movement.

While this projected variation set appears to reinforce the open-ended, incomplete structure of the first movement, the two sets which Beethoven planned after he had made the final draft of the theme were designed to echo the theme's special closural features. The set of nine variations selected from sketches on pages 54–69 uses the final cadence in bars 15–16 of the theme to give coherence and eventual closure to the movement as a whole. Specifically, a^3 (which corresponds to the suspended a^1 in the final cadence of the theme) is introduced in the first, fifth, and final variations; only in the last of these is it explicitly resolved in its own register, before being reasserted and resolved to $g\sharp^2$ above a tonic pedal in the projected *Schluß*. A sense that stronger 'grounding' of this important resolution was necessary may have led Beethoven to consider adding a number of supplementary variations in which g♯³ would be particularly emphasized (Ex. 8.7).

The final attempt to draft a variation set is recorded in the 'overview' sketch on the bottom staves of pages 64–9. Beethoven reduced the number of variations from nine to six, and used double-single barlines to indicate a larger grouping (1; 2–4; 5–6) which corresponds to that in the final version. Variations [1] and [6] show a marked emphasis on the note B in various registers, including b³. Since the concluding material of the nine-variation set was adopted for this set also, it seems that the large-scale unifying element was now to be not merely the final cadence of the theme but the 'E-tonicizing' progression B–A–G♯ which spans its second half. B would be 'suspended' across the entire variation set, and A–G♯ would again appear in the final bars.

Neither the set of nine variations nor that of six projected in the 'overview' sketch suggests that Beethoven was planning any kind of tonal or formal expansion, or that he envisaged closing the movement with a literal thematic reprise. But a number of apparently independent sketches show that at some point he reconsidered writing a developmental coda which emphasized the submediant and led into a reprise. Another idea may have been the inclusion of a variation in the submediant. These plans reach back to the very first variation sketches on pages 50–3, and particularly to the scheme adumbrated in Ex. 8.1, sketch 8c.

That Beethoven considered introducing such tonal and formal expansion helps to throw into relief the uncompromisingly strict form of the final version. All six variations are in the tonic key, and the harmonic structure and proportions of the theme are closely adhered to throughout. Variation 5 is slightly unusual in that the second half of the theme (bars 9–16) is represented not twice but three times. If the phrase structure of the theme be described as AABB, then that of Variation 5 corresponds to AA'BB'B': bars 9b–16b (25–32) are repeated in bars 33–40, a repetition not matched in the first half of the variation. Only in Variation 6 are the confines of the theme decisively shaken off: we have seen above that bar 16b (32) is extended to a total of twenty bars: four plus the sixteen-bar thematic reprise, which may be understood as a composing-out of the final chord of the theme. The reprise sets the seal on the strict character of the movement. Indeed, no other variation set by Beethoven returns so literally to its point of origin.[15] The reprise

---

[15] The reprise in the second movement of the 'Appassionata' Sonata, Op. 57, comes close to Op. 109 in this respect, but the registral shifts represent a degree of continuing variation. Nor does this reprise have the function of bringing the entire work to a close, as in Op. 109;

even simplifies the theme by omitting the repeats and the arpeggiated chords in bars 5 and 13 (the left-hand octave doubling in bars 4–7, on the other hand, represents a new feature).

The sketches suggest that in the variation set, as in the theme itself, Beethoven was again working out the issues left unresolved in the first movement. While the early sketches on pages 50–3 project a structure which returns ultimately to the incomplete ending of the first movement, the sketches for the two other sets indicate a reversal of this plan: like the theme—indeed, by drawing upon and expanding crucial features of the theme—these sets would supply the closure lacking in the first movement. The precision with which Beethoven planned this large-scale closure is most evident in the role assigned to the delayed resolution of a^3 in the nine-variation set, for it is precisely the failure of this pitch to link b^3 and $g\sharp^3$ which leaves the expected 'E-tonicizing' progression incomplete at the beginning of the recapitulation in the first movement (bars 47–8; Ex. 3.26).

The delayed resolution of a^3 plays an important part in the final version. The note is first introduced in Variation 1 when, after a brief return to the original register of the theme in bars 11–12, there is an unexpected two-octave leap up to a sforzato a^3, supported by supertonic harmony, on the downbeat of bar 13. This is the highest note heard in the movement so far, and is a seventh above b^2, the previous upper registral limit of Variation 1. The new, higher register is quitted immediately the a^3 has sounded and is regained only at the beginning of bar 15, where $g\sharp^3$ is introduced by an octave leap from $g\sharp^2$. Although $g\sharp^3$ provides some registral continuity for the preceding a^3, it is harmonized as V^6_4 and is therefore not harmonically stable. Variation 1, then, establishes the registral highpoints a^3 and $g\sharp^3$ but leaves them isolated and unstable. Ex. 8.12 illustrates two ways in which stability might be achieved: the harmony supporting a^3–$g\sharp^3$ might be extended to form the cadential progression II–V^{6-5}_{4-3}–I, combined with a melodic descent from a^3 to e^3. Alternatively, a^3–$g\sharp^3$ might be reharmonized as II–V^7–I in order to provide closure on $g\sharp^3$ rather than e^3.

The second of the two progressions shown in Ex. 8.12 does in fact occur fleetingly in bars 13a–14a (21–2) of Variation 2, but the extremely high register of the left hand robs this of any force it

---

the second movement of Op. 57 is not even tonally closed, but leads into the finale without a break. Beethoven's procedure in Op. 109 inevitably calls to mind the end of Bach's 'Goldberg' Variations, in which the goal of the entire, massive structure proves identical to its point of origin. For a more extensive treatment of the relationship between Op. 109 and the 'Goldberg' Variations, see Martin Zenck, *Die Bach-Rezeption des späten Beethoven* (Stuttgart, 1986), 219–31.

Ex. 8.12. Cf. Op. 109, third movement, Variation 1, bars 13–15

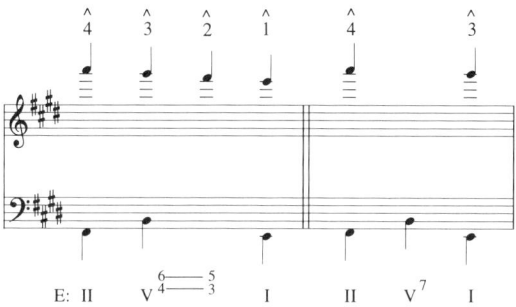

might have to resolve the unstable progression in Variation 1. In bars 15a and 15b (23 and 31) of Variation 2 g♯³ appears fleetingly within V⁶₄, but is again left registrally isolated (a continuation to f♯³ follows in bar 16a (24) but this note is then left hanging: e³ does not follow). And although g♯³ is again reached briefly in bar 7 of Variation 4 it is again given no local registral continuation.

The unprepared a³ in Variation 1 finds its first real continuation in Variations 5 and 6. In the former it appears in bar 15b (31) and its subsequent repetition (bar 39), functioning effectively as a dominant seventh in E. It is interesting that the second appearance occurs within the anomalous repeat of the B′ phrase (bars 25–32) referred to above; might this repetition have been inspired by an urge to reiterate the a³? As in Variation 1, a³ in Variation 5 is registrally isolated and is approached directly by a wide leap, in this case from e². Its harmonic setting as a dominant seventh is re-established in Variation 6, bars 14a–16a (22–4), where it is once again left unresolved in its own register (the resolution of the dominant pedal on the third beat of bar 16a (24) brings a²–g♯² rather than a³–g♯³ in the upper voice). In bars 9b–16b (25–32) of Variation 6 the melodic line of the second half of the theme is present in the upper voice, beginning on b³. Since it follows the theme closely, although not literally, it may be expected that bars 15b–16b (31–2) will at last bring the resolution of a³ to g♯³ above the cadential V⁷–I. The a³ duly arrives on the last quaver of bar 15b, but during the ensuing extension it is transferred down two octaves to a¹, which then resolves to g♯¹ at the beginning of the thematic reprise.[16] Ex. 8.13 shows how the second of the two progressions illustrated in Ex. 8.12 is composed out over

---

[16] The downward transfer of a³ here may be compared to the upward transfer a¹–a²–a³ in the *Schluß* transcribed in Ex. 8.5a.

Ex. 8.13. Composing out of I–II–V^7–I/$\hat{3}$–$\hat{4}$–$\hat{3}$ in Op. 109, third movement (cf. Ex. 8.12)

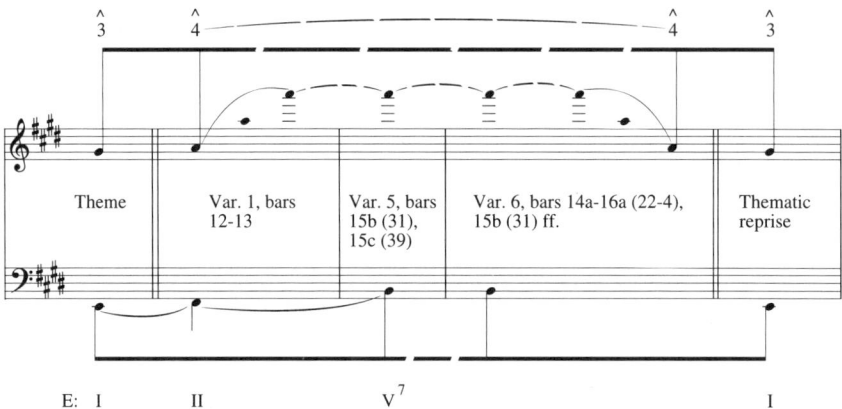

the course of the entire movement in connection with the eventual resolution to g♯^{1} of the problematic a^3 introduced in Variation 1.

Since a^3 does not resolve ultimately to g♯^{3} in the final version it might be argued that the compositional strategy outlined here, and embracing not just the third movement but also the first movement of Op. 109, fails to be properly concluded. But a^3 in the variations is essentially a projection upward of a^1 in the theme; in this sense, the downward transfer of a^3 through a^2 to a^1 and its resolution to g♯^{1} at the beginning of the thematic reprise stands as a reversal of the upward transfer by which a^3 is first reached from a^1 in Variation 1, bars 12–13. And the downward transfer at the end of the variations needs to be understood more generally as a response to the larger registral disjunction within the first movement. This is signalled most clearly by the fact that the recapitulation begins two octaves higher than the exposition, and by the juxtaposition of high and middle registers at the end of the movement. In its shift from the g♯^{1} to the g♯^{3} register and its eventual return to g♯^{1}, the third movement of Op. 109 retraces and closes the registral trajectory of the first: the sonata ends quite literally where it began, with an upper-voice g♯^{1}.

The strong assertion of B found in variations [1] and [6] of the 'overview' sketch also finds a place in the final version. The priority over g♯^{1} given to b^2 during Variation 1 has already been mentioned and needs no further comment. But we have also observed that a dominant pedal is present in almost every bar of Variation 6: this was of course one of Beethoven's earliest and most fixed ideas for the variation movement. In the first half of Variation 6 the pedal is

Ex. 8.14. The relationship between theme and variation set in Op. 109, third movement

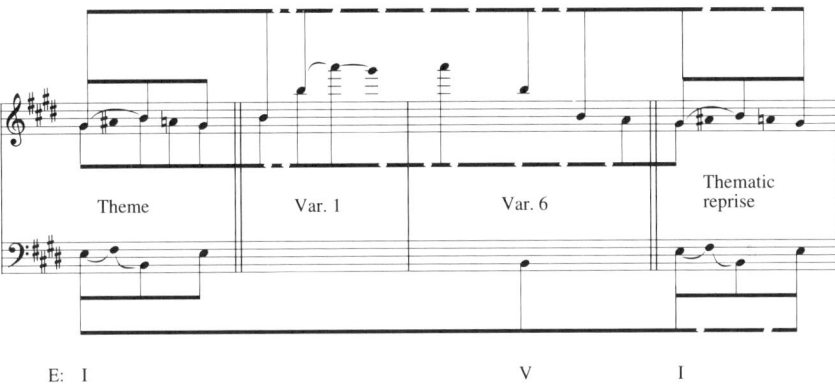

sustained on b^1 and B; it continues on B^1 from bar 8b to 16a (16–24) and then shifts into its highest register, b^2, for bars 9b–16b (25–32) and the first bar of the extension (bar 33) before returning to b^1 for the two bars preceding the thematic reprise. This arrangement closely matches what happens at the beginning of the movement: following the statement of the theme, Variation 1 begins with an octave leap up from b^1 to b^2. The strong assertion of b^2 in Variation 1 thus re-surfaces in this last section of Variation 6, where the suspended a^3 from Variation 1 is finally to be dealt with.

The final version thus combines elements of the two structural plans which Beethoven had tried out in Artaria 195. The combination gives to the movement as a whole a structure which reflects and magnifies that of the theme. Conversely, the theme summarizes the melodic-harmonic structure left incomplete in the first movement and thus acts as an exposition of the larger structure of the variation set, which is to provide the long-awaited closure of that earlier movement. As shown in Chapter 4, the melodic structure of the theme consists essentially of a stepwise progression from $g\sharp^1$ to b^1 and from b^1 back to $g\sharp^1$; at the most abstract level it may be represented simply by $g\sharp^1$. As we have seen, $g\sharp^1$ is supplanted by b^2 at the beginning of Variation 1, while at the other end of the movement b^2 yields again to $g\sharp^1$ for the thematic reprise. At the same time, the 'E-tonicizing' progression b^1–a^1–$g\sharp^1$ governing the second half of the theme is played out across the six variations in a more varied registral context and with B and A simultaneously suspended across the whole. Ex. 8.14 attempts to illustrate this large-scale reflection of the thematic structure in the total variation movement;

as well as showing the melodic features just discussed, it suggests that the dominant pedal in the second half of Variation 6 is structural at the level of the entire movement and creates a large-scale I–V–I progression which mirrors the harmonic structure of the theme. The symmetrical arrangement illustrated in the example is such that the almost literal repetition of the theme at the end of the movement, unique as it is in Beethoven's variation *œuvre*, comes to seem almost inevitable.[17]

While the structural relationship between the outer movements of Op. 109 operates at a very deep level, there are two points in the third movement where a connection with the first becomes almost audible. To begin with, the stark contrast between the two exposition subject groups in the first movement seems to be recalled in the contrast between the theme and Variation 1. The special characteristics of this variation have been discussed above, as has the fact that it is uniquely isolated in the larger grouping of the variations; to repeat, it is as if Variation 1 is an interpolation between the theme and Variation 2. The exposition second group in the first movement may also be experienced as an interpolation—indeed, a more shocking one than Variation 1, with which it shares its 3/4 metre.[18] And the clear metrical, textural, and registral continuity between the end of the first group in bar 8 and the beginning of the development at the end of bar 15 ('tempo 1', 2/4) is reflected in the precise match between the end of the theme and the beginning of Variation 2.

Along with the issue of contrast, there are more specific connections to be made between Variation 1 and the exposition second group in the first movement. Both employ a similarly dramatic rhetoric (the variation is marked 'molto espressivo', the first-movement passage 'adagio espressivo'). And the extraordinary leap up to a^3 in bar 13 of Variation 1 is more than a structural element with long-range implications for the rest of the movement: it very accurately recalls the introduction of the same pitch in bar 12 of the first movement. In both instances a^3 is prepared by a crescendo and is dynamically emphasized by a forte or sforzato marking; it is approached directly from a^2; and its supporting harmony (note the identical bass F♯) is anticipated on the last quaver of the preceding bar.

The second point in the variation set at which the first movement is almost audibly recalled comes in bars 9a–16a (17–24) of Variation 6; and this time it is the recapitulation, rather than the exposition, of

---

[17] Symmetry is also a feature of the treatment of register illustrated in Ex. 8.13.
[18] This interpretation of the first-movement second group is well known: see, *inter alia*, Kinderman, 'Thematic Contrast and Parenthetical Enclosure', and Jonas, *Introduction to the Theory of Heinrich Schenker*, 142.

the second group which we hear. The connection was pointed out by Allen Forte in his own analysis of the sketches for Op. 109, but it becomes more telling in combination with the one just discussed.[19] As well as sharing harmonic and voice-leading characteristics with its counterpart in the first movement (bars 58 ff.), the passage in Variation 6 is gesturally similar also. Like Variation 1 it is dramatic, almost improvisatory; it represents the dynamic climax of the movement, and the utter contrast it forms with the ensuing thematic reprise recalls and outstrips that between the initial statement of the theme and Variation 1. Thus the contrasting subject groups in the exposition and recapitulation of the first movement are very accurately recalled in the third movement: the theme and Variation 1 correspond to the exposition statements while Variation 6 and the thematic reprise correspond to a reversal of the recapitulation statements. The symmetry of this arrangement (theme–first variation; final variation–thematic reprise) enhances the structural symmetry already illustrated in Ex. 8.14.

At this stage it becomes possible to revise the pessimistic view of the variation sketches taken in Chapter 7. True, they throw almost no light on the genesis of the individual variations in the final version. But this chapter has tried to show that they illuminate much about the genesis of the variation set as a whole. To put it simply, it is as though Beethoven was intent on sketching not variations but a variation structure; it may not be over-exaggeration to suggest that he was to some extent indifferent to the detail of the variations in which that structure would be expressed, provided that they expressed it satisfactorily. It was almost certainly only after the structure of the whole had been more or less fixed that Beethoven began serious work on the variations themselves. That was a phase of work which took place largely outside Artaria 195, and for which little evidence survives. What evidence there is will be the subject of the next chapter, after which this interpretation of the sketches for Op. 109 will be complete.

[19] Forte, *Compositional Matrix*, 24–5, 78–9.

9. Sketches for the Variations in the Final Version

The paucity of sketches which may confidently be related to the six variations in the third movement of Op. 109 has already been stressed. Table 9.1 lists the ten sketches which may be so related; all are discussed in this chapter. The term 'sketch' does not properly apply to the two A 47 drafts, for these derive from Beethoven's detailed draft or *Concept* of the sonata rather than from a sketchbook or sketchleaves. The A 47 drafts are accordingly far more detailed and extensive than any of the other eight sketches listed; and even these eight vary considerably in length and content. Table 9.1 also shows that Variation 4 is the only one for which no material survives in any source. The only sketch which might possibly be connected with Variation 4 is one in Artaria 195, page 57, staves 6/7–12/13 (see Ex. 7.2b); but the relationship between this sketch and the final version of Variation 4 is not comparable to those listed in Table 9.1. Also excluded from the table is the important draft for variation 9 discussed in Chapter 8 (see Ex. 8.3). Although very similar to Variation 6 both in content and structure, it is nevertheless not 'a sketch for Variation 6' in the sense in which the first sketch in Table 9.1 may be labelled 'a sketch for Variation 1'.

The following discussion deals first with the eight sketches in Artaria 195 and 197 and then with the A 47 drafts. In distinction to previous chapters, the sketches are discussed here not in their presumed chronological sequence but according to the sequence of variations in the final version.

Variation 1

The sole surviving sketch for Variation 1 is transcribed complete in Ex. 9.1. It seems likely that Beethoven first conceived it as a sixteen-bar variation without repeats; the main evidence for this is the fact that the first-time version (version [1b]) of bars 15–16 appears only after the second-time one at the end of the sketch, and also the fact that there appears to be no first-time version of

TABLE 9.1. *Sketches for the definitive set of variations in Op. 109*

Variation	Location (MS., page or folio, staves)	Description (bars represented)
1	Art. 195, 75, 7–9	Complete single variation, 16 bars
2	A 47, 1^r, 1/2–1^v, 7/8	Complete single variation, 16 bars
3	Art. 195, 59, 1/2–10/11	Intended double variation; 1a–8a, 1b–2b notated + 7 blank bars
	A 47, 1^v, 10/11–2^v, 7/8	Complete double variation, 32 bars
4	—	—
5	Art. 195, 62, 7/8–10/11	1[a]–8[a]
	Art. 195, 64, 16	1[a]–4[a]
	Art. 195, 78, 5/6	1[a]–3[a]
	Art. 195, 78, 8/9–10/11	1a–8a, 1b–2b
6	Art. 195, 65, 1/2	2 bars; cf. 9a–10a (17–18)
	Art. 197, 1, 6–10	9a–16a (17–24)

Ex. 9.1. Artaria 195, p. 75, st. 7–9

bar 8.[1] As for version [2] of bars 15–16, this is written directly below version [1a] and the two are linked by corresponding crosses. The two versions are almost identical apart from the higher register indicated in version [2]. Beethoven would presumably have revised the preceding bars in connection with version [2] in order to avoid an inelegant leap from a^1–$d\sharp^1$ to $g\sharp^2$ in bars 14–15.

On the whole, the similarities between Ex. 9.1 and Variation 1 are obvious and need not be laboured; it is the differences which require attention. Perhaps the most pervasive difference is the way in which the sketch, in contrast to Variation 1, adheres closely to the melody of the theme in terms both of absolute pitch and specific register. This can be clearly seen in bars 1–4, where despite the placement of b^2 on the downbeat of bars 1 and 3 the thematic interval G♯–E is retained, in a melodic formula which was to appear only in bar 5 of the final version.[2] The immediate substitution of b^2 for $g\sharp^1$ in Variation 1 is all the more effective for the complete absence of G♯ in the remainder of the first bar: the thematic interval $g\sharp^1$–e^1 becomes b^2–e^2, and $g\sharp^2$ is only gradually introduced, first as an anticipation at the end of bar 3 and then as part of the descending triadic figure b^2–$g\sharp^2$–e^2 in bar 5.

The second half of Ex. 9.1 well illustrates Beethoven's adherence to the melodic line and register of the theme. The descending line b^2–a^2–$g\sharp^2$ in bars 9–11 of Variation 1 is not yet present: Beethoven would eventually create this by inverting the descending thirds $c\sharp^2$–a^1 and b^1–$g\sharp^1$ in bars 10 and 11, a move which would also maintain the prominence of the higher register in which the first half of the sketch unfolds. More importantly, there is as yet no sign of the vital pitches a^3 and $g\sharp^3$ in bars 13 and 15—surely the most striking difference in the deployment of register in the sketch as compared to Variation 1. As for the three versions of bars 15–16, versions [1a] and [2] simply fill out the corresponding part of the theme with chromatic passing and neighbour notes. It was from version [1b], the appended first-time ending, that bars 15–16 of Variation 1 were eventually derived.

Beethoven's use of register in Ex. 9.1 has implications which lead beyond the confines of the sketch itself. We have seen how the unstable progression a^3–$g\sharp^3$ in bars 13–15 of Variation 1 leaves the variation open-ended and points towards the end of Variation 6, where a^3 is reintroduced and transferred down to a^1 in order to

---

[1] The three versions of bar 8 may represent attempts to differentiate between first- and second-time endings, although no version provides a satisfactory link back to bar 1.

[2] Another feature of the theme which is retained in the sketch but not in Variation 1 is the rising fourth $f\sharp^1$–b^1 from bar 4.

resolve to $g\sharp^1$ at the beginning of the thematic reprise. In the sketch, by comparison, it is b^2 and b^3 (bars 1, 3, 5, and 9) which are left hanging. If we take the low-register version [1a] ending, b^2 and b^3 are provided with no melodic continuation whatsoever. The picture changes considerably once the version [2] ending is substituted, for the higher register now picks up the earlier b^2 and provides a stepwise continuation through a^2 to $g\sharp^2$ at the final cadence. This imparts much firmer closure to the upper voice as a whole, despite the registral isolation of b^3 in bar 5.

If we now reconsider Variation 1, Beethoven's use of register there seems all the more powerful. Having set an upper registral limit of b^2 throughout the first three quarters of the variation, he oversteps it magnificently with the introduction of a^3 on the downbeat of bar 13 and its continuation to the unstable $g\sharp^3$ two bars later. This audibly incomplete melodic-harmonic progression acts as a much more effective 'signpost' to later events in the variation set than does the isolated but essentially static b^3 of the sketch.

Variation 3

The opening bars of this sketch appeared in Ex. 8.3; the entire notated portion (that is, omitting the concluding seven blank bars) is given here in Ex. 9.2. As it stands, the sketch begins at the top of page 59. However, the left-hand part of the first bar also appears at the bottom (staves 15/16) of the preceding page, immediately following a draft for a complete variation which occupies staves 1/2–13/14. The single bar pertaining to Variation 3 is clearly a rejected opening

Ex. 9.2. Artaria 195, p. 59, st. 1/2–4/5

Ex. 9.3. Cf. Op. 109, third movement, theme and Variation 3, bars 4 and 8

which was probably discontinued due to Beethoven's preference, in this part of the sketchbook at least, for beginning each new variation draft on a clean page. Within Ex. 9.2 itself there appears to be a superfluous blank bar following bar 4: the ascending right-hand figure surely continues directly from $d\sharp^3$ to e^3 at the beginning of staves 4/5. This initial eight-bar phrase is followed by the first two bars of a varied repetition in which the right-hand figure is shifted to the second half of each crotchet beat; the seven blank bars presumably represent the remainder of the phrase. (When mapping out a series of blank bars prior to filling them in Beethoven did not always draft precisely the required number.)

The right-hand figure rising through two and a half octaves from e^1 to b^3 makes of this first phrase a single gesture corresponding to bars 1–8 of the theme.[3] This provides an interesting comparison with Variation 3, in which bars 1–8 appear superficially to consist of a basic four-bar phrase which is repeated with the voices inverted. Only Beethoven's subtle differentiation of the cadences in bars 4 and 8 hints at the underlying eight-bar unit: Ex. 9.3 shows how the two-voice texture of Variation 3 faithfully reflects both the V–I cadence in bar 4 of the theme and the approach to the dominant through the augmented sixth in bars 7–8.[4]

---

[3] The upward sweep through b^1 and b^2 to b^3 is similar to that in the first incipit of the 'overview' sketch (Ex. 8.8), which must have been written after this sketch for Variation 3.

[4] Bars 1b–8b (9–16) of Variation 3 likewise appear at first to consist of a repeated four-bar phrase, but the cadences are again carefully differentiated. In fact the augmented-sixth chord is explicitly stated in bar 8b (16).

Ex. 9.4. Artaria 195, p. 59, st. 15/16

A corollary of the continuous eight-bar unit in the sketch is the fact that it does not make use of the invertible counterpoint found in Variation 3. One might expect that this inversion would therefore operate between rather than within eight-bar phrases, but the final two bars notated in the sketch appear to rule out this possibility: only the metric displacement of the right-hand figure distinguishes the second phrase from the first. The discussion of the A 47 draft will show that Beethoven invested considerable thought in the phrase structure and disposition of voices in Variation 3. But as a postscript to the present discussion, Ex. 9.4 shows a variation incipit which Beethoven wrote on staves 15/16 of page 59 in Artaria 195. The handwriting suggests that it was made some time after the sketch for Variation 3 (Ex. 9.2) above it. Like that sketch, this incipit is in 2/4 time; and although it uses quite different musical material, it corresponds to Variation 3 in precisely those ways in which Ex. 9.2 itself does not, for the basic four-bar phrase is given a surface structure of 2 + 2 bars thanks to the invertible contrapuntal texture.

Variation 5

The four sketches for Variation 5 are transcribed in Ex. 9.5; although fragmentary, they provide some compositional insights. A comparison of the first three sketches shows how Beethoven gradually strengthened the relationship of the basic two-bar motive in the variation to bars 1–2 of the theme, from which the motive is derived. In all three sketches the rhythm of the motive is identical to that in the final version of Variation 5; nor does there seem to have been any doubt about the content of the first bar, the falling third G♯–E with which the theme also opens. Ex. 9.5b captures not only the falling third d♯^{1}–b from bar 2 of the theme but also the upper neighbour f♯^{1} on the last quaver of bar 1 (this f♯^{1} is delayed until bar 2 in Ex. 9.5b, however); neither of these thematic details is present in Ex. 9.5a, in which the motive stresses the fifth f♯–B in

Ex. 9.5. *a* Artaria 195, p. 62, st. 7/8–10/11

b Artaria 195, p. 64, st. 16

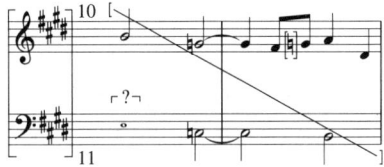

c Artaria 195, p. 78, st. 5/6

d Artaria 195, p. 78, st. 8/9–10/11

response to the initial third g♯–e. Only in Ex. 9.5c does the two-bar motive acquire its final form. All that was required was the substitution of C♯ for the e^1 forming the second of the pair of quavers in Ex. 9.5b. Even this C♯ originates in the theme, for it represents the inner-voice $c♯^1$ on the third beat of bar 1 there.

As well as recording the development of the basic motive, these sketches suggest that Beethoven experienced some difficulty in establishing the contrapuntal texture of Variation 5. In Ex. 9.5a he chose at first to work with overlapping entries of the motive: thus the second entry (b–f♯) begins in bar 2 while the first is being completed in the lower voice. This plan was rejected in favour of a series of four distinct entries; but by the time he wrote Ex. 9.5b Beethoven was again experimenting with overlapping entries, perhaps because the revised arrangement in Ex. 9.5a emphasized two-bar groupings at the expense of the larger eight-bar phrase.

A second feature of the contrapuntal organization in Ex. 9.5a is its indebtedness to fugal exposition procedure. The relationship between the first two entries is that of subject and answer, whereby the subject in the tonic is answered, here in intervallically modified form, at the dominant.[5] The third entry (that is, the second entry of the 'subject') is identical to the first except that it is two octaves higher; and the fourth preserves the basic shape of the motive while taking on the colouring of the flat submediant (augmented-sixth) harmony which occurs at the corresponding point (bars 7–8) in the theme.

The fugal model underlies Ex. 9.5b, where the overlapping entries create an alternation of tonic and dominant harmonies which reflects the harmonic structure of bars 1–4 of the theme. However, the initial falling third of the motive is lost after the first entry: the remaining three entries substitute a falling fourth. This intervallic modification may have been connected with the larger shape of the basic motive. The e^1 suspended between bars 1 and 2 resolves downward to $d♯^1$ on the third crotchet of bar 2. To correspond exactly with this arrangement, $f♯^1$ suspended between bars 2 and 3 would need to fall to e^1 on the third crotchet of bar 3. But if, in accordance with the basic motive, the upper voice were then to introduce $g♯^2$–e^2 in bar 3, then near-parallel octaves would arise (Ex. 9.6a). On the other hand, the combination of the hypothetical lower voice in bar 3 of Ex. 9.6a with Beethoven's notated upper voice e^2–b^1 is not entirely satisfactory either (Ex. 9.6b): the fifth b^1/e^1 is approached awkwardly by similar motion, and e^1–b in the lower voice follows the same interval in the

---

[5] Beethoven omitted the last two notes of the second entry in Ex. 9.5a; in accordance with the end of the first entry (see bar 2) they would presumably be g♯–e (possibly g♯–B), completing a V–I progression to balance the I–V underlying the first entry.

Ex. 9.6. Cf. Ex. 9.5b

Ex. 9.7. *a* Cf. Ex. 9.5c *b* Cf. Op. 109, third movement, Variation 5, bars 1–3

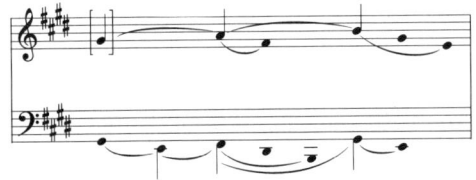 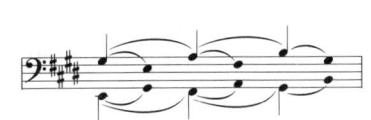

upper voice rather closely. Ex. 9.6c suggests a modification of the lower voice which would avoid these problems; the fact that Beethoven actually left the lower voice of Ex. 9.5b incomplete may signal his awareness of issues similar to those touched upon here.

In short, the fugal model used in Ex. 9.5a–b seems to have been incompatible with the falling-third motive; and that third, derived as it was from the opening of the theme, was clearly an important element which ought not to be lightly dispensed with. A more satisfactory arrangement appears in the three bars of Ex. 9.5c. Here the falling third is retained in all three entries of the motive. The second entry (a^1–$f\sharp^1$) begins essentially a semitone above the first; and although the third entry (in the lower voice) returns to G♯–E, the completion of the second above it brings in b^1 in such a way that an ascending series of parallel tenths ([$g\sharp^1$]/E–a^1/F♯–b^1/G♯) is created between the two voices (Ex. 9.7a). A similar two-voice framework supports the opening of Variation 5 (Ex. 9.7b).

The problem of the initial contrapuntal texture was not wholly solved with Ex. 9.5c, however. The autograph of Op. 109 reveals an interesting variant, not of bars 1–4 but of bars 5–8 in Variation 5. Ex. 9.8a shows what Beethoven first wrote for these bars, and Ex. 9.8b his subsequent revision of bars 5–6. The most important feature of the original version is the bass entry of the motive in bar 5, beginning with the falling third D♯–B^1. This extends the rising sequence of entries in the top voice of bars 1–4 and, in so doing, helps to bind bars 1–4 and 5–8 into a continuous unit.[6] In the final version this bass entry is modified so that D♯–B^1 appears in crotchets on the second beat of bar 5. But listening to the variation we are likely not to perceive the entry as such: instead, it is the inner-voice B–F♯ in bar 5 which most audibly marks a new entry of the basic motive. It is interesting to see that Beethoven himself at first 'heard' the variation in this way: in Ex. 9.8b he originally assigned the pair of quavers G♯–D♯ in bar 6 to the inner voice rather than to the bass, so that the inner-voice entry preserves the rhythmic shape of the motive intact.[7]

Since the bass and the inner voice merge on this second crotchet of bar 6, however, the question of stemming is to some extent trivial; ultimately there is little reason not to regard the inner voice in bar 5 as a true motivic entry. It preserves the rhythm of the motive and its metrical placement corresponds to that of all the previous entries. The claims of D♯–B^1 on the second beat of bar 5 seem weak by comparison, despite the fact that the thematic falling third is preserved here. And yet it is clear from Ex. 9.8a that the inner-voice falling fourth B–F♯ was at first a rising fifth, B–f♯. Beethoven could have retained this rising interval after he had modified the bass as shown in Ex. 9.8b.[8] But the abandonment of the bass entry D♯–B^1 on the downbeat of bar 5 seems to have been accompanied by the inversion of this rising fifth, with the result that a fifth entry of the basic motive is created by the falling fourth B–F♯.

The initial interval of the basic motive is freely modified throughout Variation 5: it is expanded to a sixth in bar 9a (17), for example, and to an octave in bar 13b (29). But the inner-voice entry in bar 5 is the only occasion on which it becomes a falling fourth; and this

[6] The rising sequence runs as follows: g♯–e (bar 1), a–f♯ (bar 2), b–g♯ (bar 3), c♯^{1}–a (bar 4), D♯–B^1 (bar 5). The D♯ resolves to E on the third crotchet beat of bar 6.
[7] Schenker (Ea, 49) forbore to reveal whether he heard B–F♯ or D♯–B^1 as the 'true' motivic entry in bar 5, observing only that 'in T. 5 erfolgt bei der l. H. der fünfte (letzte) Einsatz'.
[8] In fact he initially did precisely this: B–F♯ appears on the second beat of bar 5, creating a temporary fourth voice in the texture. Beethoven later delayed the entry of this voice until the second crotchet of bar 6, where the two left-hand voices merge. The fact that the beginning of the lower right-hand voice was deleted in pencil rather than ink suggests that it stood until a relatively late stage in the compositional process.

Ex. 9.8. *a* Op. 109, autograph manuscript, fol. 16ʳ, st. 3/4: Variation 5, bars 5–8

b Op. 109, autograph manuscript, fol. 16ʳ, st. 5/6: Variation 5, bars 5–6

[right-hand deletions in pencil]

entry is also the first one in which the interval is modified at all. In Ex. 9.5 we have seen Beethoven's attempts to 'answer' G♯–E in a quasi-fugal manner with B–F♯. The fugal character of those sketches is remote from the opening of Variation 5 in its final version, but the idea of the falling fourth answering the falling third remains. In the theme, g♯^{1}–e^1 in bar 1 is answered by b^1–e^1 in bar 5; in Variation 5, g♯–e in bar 1 is answered by B–F♯ in bar 5. The melodic differentiation of the two four-bar phrases (1–4 and 5–8) in the theme is subtly captured by Beethoven's manipulation of the basic motive in the variation, so that the variation itself 'answers' the theme.

Ex. 9.5*d*, finally, reveals nothing about the arrangement of contrapuntal voices; after setting down g♯–e in bar 1, Beethoven left the next three bars blank. But since this sketch directly follows Ex. 9.5*c* in Artaria 195, it is likely that Beethoven intended to retain the arrangement already fixed there, even if with some modifications. Two other features of Ex. 9.5*d* are worthy of attention. First, the last two bars clearly represent a return to the beginning of the theme: in other words, they correspond to bars 1b–2b of a planned double variation. Since Variation 5 is a double variation (albeit with an anomalous second repeat of bars 9b–16b) the sketch could imply that Beethoven's vision of this variation was now becoming more concrete. On the other hand, the free inversion of the basic motive in the sketch, whereby the opening third is replaced by a rising fourth,

Ex. 9.9. Cf. Op. 119 No. 11, bars 1–3

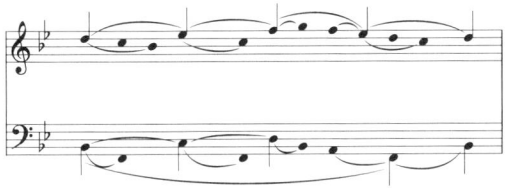

b–e¹, was not to find a place in the final version. The second noteworthy feature of Ex. 9.5d is the harmonic structure of the first eight-bar phrase, which closes not in the dominant but in the mediant, G♯ minor. This is the only instance either in the variation sketches or in the final version of a substitute harmony for the central dominant in the theme. And the reason in this particular case is not far to seek: the motion from E major to G♯ minor, while borrowing from the cadence in bar 12 of the theme, mirrors the falling third g♯–e of the basic motive.⁹

The influence of these sketches for Variation 5 appears to have extended beyond Op. 109. The last two (Ex. 9.5c–d) occur in the section of Artaria 195 which is otherwise devoted to sketches for numbers 7–11 of the Bagatelles, Op. 119. Indeed, after writing Ex. 9.5c–d on page 78 Beethoven turned to page 79 and began sketching Op. 119 No. 11. It seems hardly coincidental that the opening bars of the bagatelle, which appear already in their final form in the sketch, are structurally very similar to the first four bars of Variation 5: both pieces open with an ascending series of parallel tenths between the outer voices, and the notes of the upper-voice ascent are embellished by descending thirds. The voice-leading reduction of the opening of Op. 119 No. 11 given in Ex. 9.9 should be compared to that of Variation 5 (Ex. 9.7b).¹⁰

---

⁹ The rising third g♯¹–a♯¹–b¹ in bar 8 of Ex. 9.5d could imply an abrupt modulation to the dominant following the cadence in G♯ minor suggested by f𝑥¹–g♯¹, but this seems unlikely in the context.

¹⁰ Compare also P. T. Barford, 'Bagatelles or Variations? A Discussion of the Origin of Beethoven's Bagatelles, Op. 119 Nos. 7 and 8', *Musical Opinion*, 76 (1953), 277–9. Barford suggests that these two bagatelles may have been spin-offs from Beethoven's work on the Diabelli Variations. But Barford's belief that the bagatelles may have been written 'during the formative period of the Diabelli variations' is untenable. It is clear from the evidence presented in Ch. 2, above, that the sketches for Op. 119 in Artaria 195 belong to autumn or winter 1820; and Kinderman's research (*Beethoven's Diabelli Variations*, 3–8) has shown conclusively that the Diabelli Variations were composed in two separate phases, in the years 1819 and 1822–3. That there is a close chronological relationship between the sketches for Op. 119 Nos. 7–11 and those for the variation movement of Op. 109 is indisputable, however; and the connection illustrated by Exx. 9.9 and 9.7b suggests that Op. 119 No. 11 and Op. 109, Variation 5 may indeed be related in the sense discussed by Barford.

Variation 6

The two sketches for this variation occur in separate sources, one in Artaria 195 and the other on the first page of Artaria 197. The Artaria 195 sketch, which was undoubtedly written first, is transcribed in Ex. 9.10. To judge from its rhythmic and harmonic features, it represents an attempt to formulate what eventually became the climactic point of the variation and indeed of the entire third movement: the passage beginning with bar 9a (17).

Ex. 9.10. Artaria 195, p. 65, st. 1/2

One aspect of Ex. 9.10 calls for immediate comment. This sketch is unusual in being one of the very few which deal exclusively with an internal portion of a variation; the great majority present an incipit, a first half, or (less often) a complete variation. A possible explanation for this peculiarity is that Ex. 9.10 does not so much represent part of a variation on the third-movement theme as a variation of part of another movement of the sonata. Allen Forte's observation that the beginning of the second half of Variation 6, from bar 9a (17) onwards, bears a close affinity to the recapitulation statement of the second group in the first movement has been noted earlier.[11] Both passages begin with a diminished seventh supporting d^3 over B; and in both cases there is a stepwise descent from d^3. In the first movement the descent reaches $f\sharp^2$ in bar 60 before being interrupted; it is completed with the arrival of e^2 during bar 65.

The recall of this material in Variation 6 is in fact rather slight and does not extend much beyond bar 10a (18). Only the descent from d^3 to $c\sharp^3$ is presented in the correct register; c^2–b^1 follows at the end

---

[11] See Ch. 8 n. 19, above.

Ex. 9.11. *a* Cf. Ex. 9.10

b Cf. Op. 109, first movement, bars 58–65

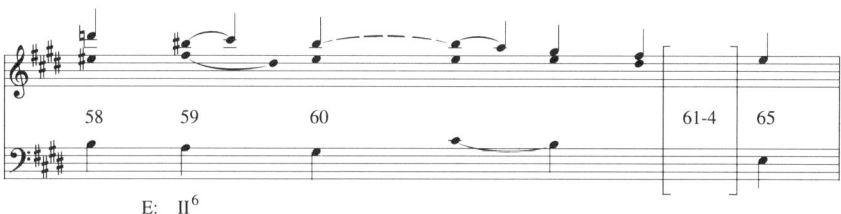

of bar 10a (18), and the continuation through a^1 to $g\sharp^1$ in the following two bars is obscured by the covering e^2 (this passage will be discussed in more detail below). Moreover, the harmonic context is altered by the dominant pedal supporting bars 9a–16a (17–24). But Ex. 9.10 comes considerably closer to its first-movement model. The voice-leading reduction in Ex. 9.11a shows that the outer voices in the sketch proceed in parallel tenths, from d^2/B to an implied $g\sharp^1/$E; and although the bass A supports root-position subdominant harmony rather than the supertonic found in the first movement (bar 59), the 4–3 suspensions in the sketch seem to recall in a general way the melodic embellishments of the descending line in the first movement: $b\sharp^2$ on the downbeat of bar 59 which delays the arrival of $c\sharp^3$, for instance, or the appoggiatura b^2 delaying a^2 in bar 60 (Ex. 9.11b).

The other sketch for Variation 6 is found on page 1 of Artaria 197 (Ex. 9.12). It presents a version of bars 9a–16a (17–24) which comes very close to the final one. There seems little danger in assuming that the unnotated left-hand part was to consist of the extended dominant pedal found in Op. 109.

Although the differences between the sketch and the final version might appear to be largely superficial, close comparison sheds interesting light on some of Beethoven's eventual choices. In Ex. 9.13 partial voice-leading reductions of the sketch and the final version, shown on the outer staves, are aligned rhythmically with bars 9–16 of the theme, which are reproduced on the middle stave. (Each

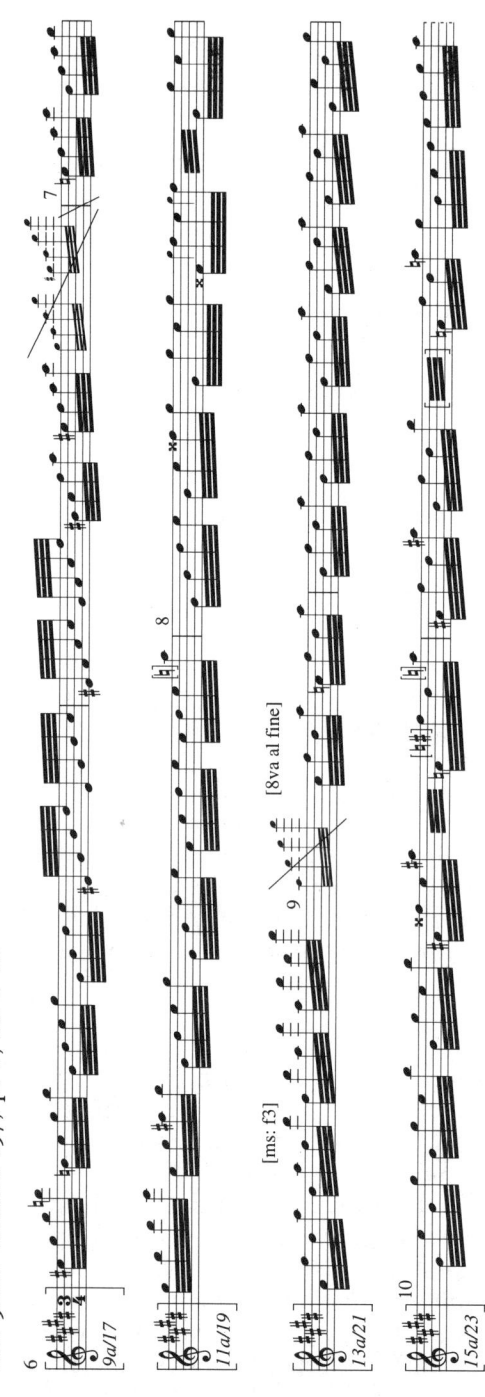

Ex. 9.12. Artaria 197, p. 1, st. 6–10

Ex. 9.13

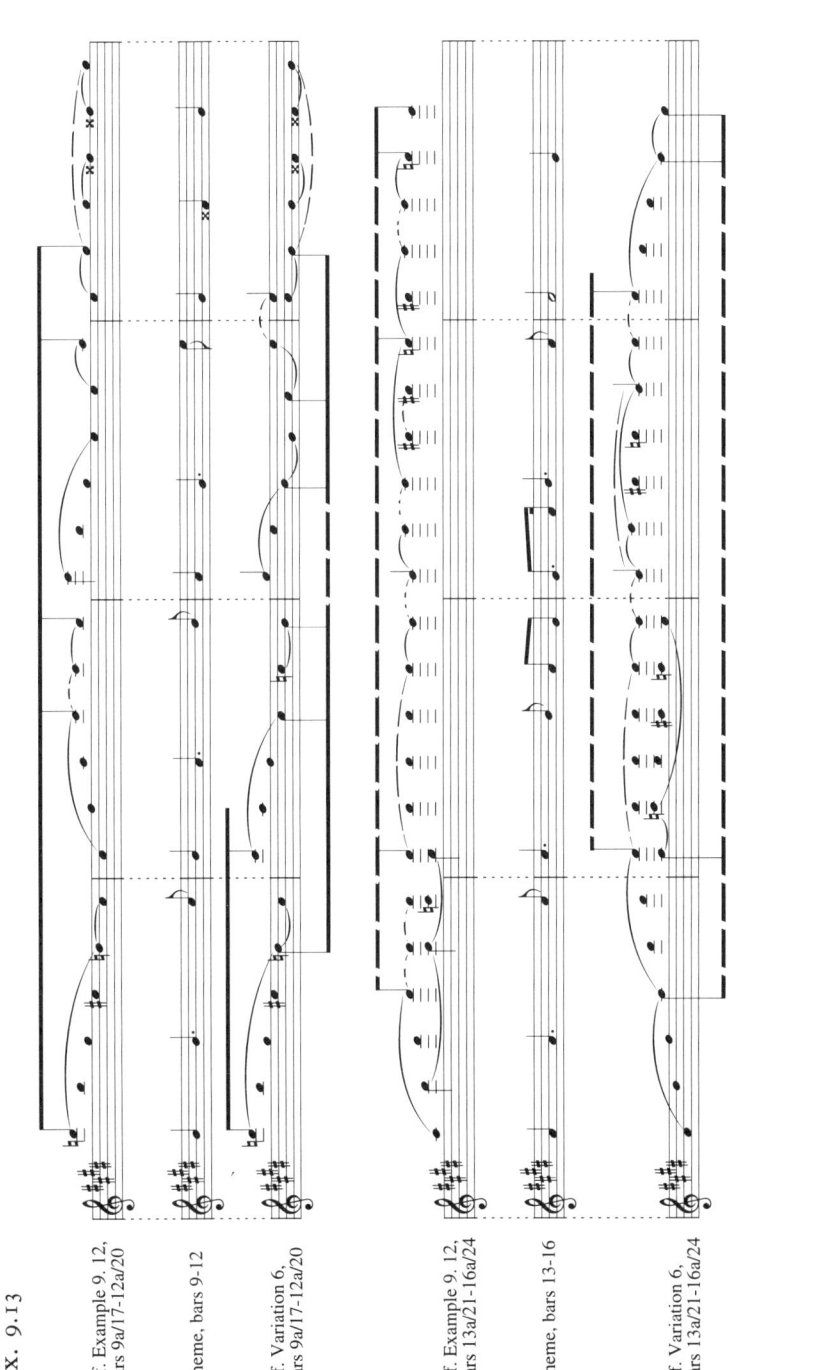

Cf. Example 9.12,
bars 9a/17–12a/20

Theme, bars 9–12

Cf. Variation 6,
bars 9a/17–12a/20

Cf. Example 9.12,
bars 13a/21–16a/24

Theme, bars 13–16

Cf. Variation 6,
bars 13a/21–16a/24

notehead on the outer staves represents one quaver pulse.) The first four-bar phrase in the sketch establishes a clear stepwise descent d^3–$g\sharp^2$: a vestige, perhaps, of the same descent tried out one octave lower in Ex. 9.10. In Variation 6 the descent from d^3 is severely curtailed and does not extend beyond $c\sharp^3$. But d^3 and $c\sharp^3$ are articulated more strongly than in the sketch: both fall directly on the downbeat of a bar, and $c\sharp^3$ is further emphasized by the octave leap up from $c\sharp^2$. Although the high-register descent is discontinued, a line from d^2 to $g\sharp^1$ is completed (compare again Ex. 9.10); and it is this lower register—significantly, the register of the theme itself—which governs melodic motion within the phrase as a whole.

The step d^3–$c\sharp^3$ stands isolated in Variation 6, then, with no immediate registral continuation. Beethoven's intention here may have been simply to concentrate the reference back to the recapitulation second group in the first movement by isolating the d^3 and $c\sharp^3$ from bars 58–9 there. Other changes made between the sketch and the final version also seem to have been prompted by the first-movement passage: the expansion of $c\sharp^3$–b^2 in the second bar of the sketch to become $c\sharp^2$–c^2–b^1 in the final version may derive from the presence of the identical progression in bars 58–9 of the first movement, where $c\sharp^2$–c^2–b^1 occurs as part of an inner-voice descent from d^2 (the descent appears split between the right- and left-hand parts in the score).

Comparing bar 11a (19) in the sketch with its counterpart in the final version we can see that in the former Beethoven introduced an emphatic e^3 within the downbeat, and thereby interrupted the descent from b^2 to a^2; a^2 is delayed until the last quaver. In the final version the descent from b^1 to a^1 is also delayed, but by $g\sharp^2$ rather than e^2. Like $c\sharp^3$ in the preceding bar, $g\sharp^2$ is emphasized by appearing directly on the downbeat and by its registral disjunction from the immediately preceding passage. While e^3 in the sketch appears unmotivated either by earlier events or by any relationship to the theme, $g\sharp^2$ in the final version does relate closely to the corresponding bar in the theme, in which the main note is $g\sharp^1$ supported by tonic harmony. And the remainder of bar 11a (19) in Variation 6 strengthens this thematic reference: the rising sixth $g\sharp^1$–e^2 in the theme is reflected in the variation by the descending arpeggiation $g\sharp^2$–$g\sharp^1$ followed by a^1–e^2 on the last two quaver beats.

The analysis of the theme given in Ex. 4.14 shows that the principal melodic event in the last four-bar phrase (bars 13–16) is the step a^1–$g\sharp^1$; this concludes the large-scale descent from b^1 which governs the second half and reverses the progression from $g\sharp^1$ to b^1 spanning bars 1–8. And in Chapter 8 we saw that the overall structure of the variation set depends largely on the appearance in Variations 1 and 6 of an unresolved a^3 which is eventually transferred down to a^1 before resolving to $g\sharp^1$ at the beginning of the thematic reprise. Looking now at bars 13a–16a (21–4) of Ex. 9.13, we can see that both the sketch and the final version adequately capture the descending step basic to the theme, and also that they both employ a^3. But subtle differences between the two versions also exist and these need to be more closely explored.

Consider first the way in which a^3 is introduced and maintained in each version. In the sketch the note is reached on the fourth quaver of bar 13a (21), following an ascending arpeggiation from a^2. The remainder of the sketch maintains this high register.[12] Relative to the sketch version, the appearance of a^3 in the final version is somewhat delayed. The upward arpeggiation begins on a^1 in bar 13a (21), but a^3 appears only within the downbeat of the following bar. Compared to the sketch, the final version makes the attainment of a^3 a more significant event; the preparation is longer, and the note itself is given a stronger metric placement. But looking ahead we can see that the high register is not maintained in the final version. Whereas the sketch closes (implicitly, at least) with a^3–$g\sharp^3$, a downward arpeggiation from a^3 in the final version leads to a^2 which resolves to $g\sharp^2$ together with the V–I cadence on the third beat of bar 16a (24). The a^3 is left unresolved in its own register: to bring in a^3–$g\sharp^3$ at this stage, as in the sketch, would be to short-circuit the structural plan for the variation set, which required a^3 to remain suspended until the beginning of the thematic reprise.

Returning to bar 13a (21) in the sketch, we can trace a subsidiary line $d\sharp^3$–$c\sharp^3$–c^3–b^2, closing on the downbeat of bar 14a (22). The metrical emphasis given to b^2 here is at odds with the corresponding point in the theme, where b^1 is merely a passing note within the third $c\sharp^2$–a^1. In the final version Beethoven avoided this undue emphasis: the downbeat of bar 14a (22) is in any case given over to the arrival of a^3, and the ensuing subsidiary chromatic progression, rising from a^2 to c^3 before falling to $g\sharp^2$, matches the upper voice of the theme much more closely. It was again probably his concern for fidelity to the theme which ultimately led Beethoven to revise the last two bars of the sketch. Bar 15a (23) accords well with the theme and follows its basic shape $g\sharp^1$–b^1–a^1 at a height of two octaves. But the direction of motion is reversed at the beginning of bar 16a (24):

---

[12] There is surely an *8va* indication missing before the third beat of bar 13a (21). It is clear from Artaria 197, p. 1 that there was no room for Beethoven to write the remainder of the sketch in the three-line octave because the space between staves had been taken up by the sharply sloping demisemiquaver beams of the preceding notation.

a♯³ leads back to b³ before the closing descent to g♯³. The final version removes the unwanted emphasis on b³ and follows the theme more closely: a³ is retained on the downbeat of bar 16a (24) and the downward arpeggiation to a² leads to the concluding g♯².

In short, the differences between Ex. 9.12 and the final version of bars 9a–16a (17–24) of Variation 6 seem largely motivated by a concern to relate the figuration in the variation more closely to the theme. But this concern cannot account for all of the changes made. Other refinements in the final version—the registrally isolated d³–c♯³ progression, the unresolved a³—may have been dictated not by the theme but by broader aims such as the reference back to the first movement or the large-scale unification of the variation set. Thus revisions and changes which appear to be of merely local significance prove to have wider implications; this thought may serve as a touchstone for the concluding study of the A 47 drafts for Variations 2 and 3.

The Concept *Draft for Variation [2]*

The headings for this and the following section err on the side of caution in referring to the A 47 drafts as drafts for Variations [2] and [3]; for although the variations were eventually given these numbers, neither draft is numbered and it is conceivable that even at this late stage the number and sequence of the variations was still not definitively fixed.[13] Indeed, the draft for Variation [2] (Ex. 9.14) shows just how different from the final version the third movement of Op. 109 may have been at this stage: it presents a single variation using only the material corresponding to bars 1b–8b (9–16) and 9b–16b (25–32) in the final version. The decision to make this a double variation had not yet been taken.

It will be clear from the transcription that the draft shows little internal revision; having realized that major formal expansion was pending, Beethoven simply deleted it by means of large crosses, one on each page (see Plate 8). It was presumably his decision to write a double rather than a single variation here which forced him to reject the A 47 bifolium from his *Concept* of the sonata: there would have been no space to accommodate the new subvariation in the manuscript as it stood. Before deleting the draft, however, he did make one major internal revision, a recasting of bars 1–4. The main difference between the two versions lies in the vertical spacing of the

---

[13] Recall the relatively irregular gathering structure, illustrated in Table 2.4, of the third movement in the autograph MS of Op. 109.

Ex. 9.14. A 47, fol. 1[r–v]: the *Concept* Draft for Variation [2] (The entire draft is deleted in the manuscript)

Ex. 9.14. contd.

entries of the two-bar motive. Version [2] may have been intended to enhance the quasi-polyphonic nature of the keyboard texture by giving a clearer impression of four independent voices (bass, alto, tenor, and soprano). But Beethoven eventually returned to his first thoughts in the final version, where the four entries are confined to the right hand; he also removed the appoggiatura at the beginning of each entry in the draft in order to clarify the thematically derived falling thirds $g\sharp^1$–e^1, a^1–$f\sharp^1$, and so on. (Ex. 9.14 shows that the appoggiature were in any case an afterthought.)

In considering the rest of the draft we may note certain revisions of detail which Beethoven made in the final version: for instance, in bar 7 of the draft the upper voice returns to $g\sharp^2$ rather than continuing the ascending line $g\sharp^2$–a^2 begun in bars 5–6; the substitution of b^2 for this $g\sharp^2$ in bar 7b (15) of Variation 2 strengthens the relationship of bars 5b–8b (13–16) to bars 1b–4b (9–12), creating almost a 'variation within a variation-within-a-variation'. And if we compare bars 13–16 of the draft with their counterparts, bars 13b–16b (29–32) in Variation 2, we can see that in the latter Beethoven adhered more closely to the melodic line of the theme: the draft version emphasizes b^2 in bar 14 at the expense of imitating the descent from b^1 to $g\sharp^1$ found in the theme.

Notwithstanding these details, the major significance of this A 47 draft lies precisely in what it does not include: the first subvariation, bars 1a–8a and 9a–16a (17–24), of Variation 2. Two questions arise. Why, at a late compositional stage, did Beethoven add what was effectively a new variation to the movement? And why did he add it as a subvariation of Variation 2? A plausible answer to both questions may be given, granted two reasonable assumptions: that the A 47 draft was indeed planned as the second variation of the set, and that what preceded it was to be essentially identical to the eventual Variation 1.

Reference was made in Chapter 8 to the special characteristics of Variations 1 and 2. Variation 1 departs radically from the theme in a number of respects, most significantly in its substitution of b^2 for the initial $g\sharp^1$ of the theme. By contrast, the first subvariation of Variation 2 relates to the theme very simply and directly: it immediately restores its melodic line, register, and harmonic rhythm, despite the upward register shifts which occur subsequently. This subvariation acts like a re-exposition of the theme following the disruptive events of Variation 1; it provides the opportunity for a new start.[14] The larger grouping of the variations suggested in the autograph by Beethoven's 'spelling' of their concluding barlines supports this reading, for Variation 1 stands isolated between the theme and Variation 2 while Variations 2–4 form a connected group (see Fig. 1.1). The late addition of the first subvariation in Variation 2 may therefore be thought of as a means of strengthening the connection between the theme and the variations, a way of bridging the 'gap' created by Variation 1. And by incorporating this re-exposition of the theme into a double variation, Beethoven created in Variation 2 a microcosm of the entire movement: the relationship between the two subvariations mirrors that between theme and variation.

This interpretation of Variations 1 and 2 has implications which go beyond Op. 109. William Kinderman has drawn attention to the 'parodistic' nature of a number of the Diabelli variations which were added to the work during the second (1822–3) phase of composition. He writes:

Most of Beethoven's other variations thoroughly transform the surface of Diabelli's theme. . . . In these late parody variations, however, the melodic outline and supporting context from the waltz are restored—recapitulated, in a sense. . . . Only in the added variations, furthermore, does the melodic outline of the waltz reappear in its original register, which strengthens the reference to the theme.[15]

The similarity between Kinderman's observations and our reading of Variations 1 and 2 in Op. 109 will be evident. Kinderman regards the added Diabelli variations, with their 'parodistic' qualities,

---

[14] A similar re-exposition is strikingly suggested by the second incipit in the 'overview' sketch in Artaria 195 (Ex. 8.8).
[15] *Beethoven's Diabelli Variations*, 71.

as Beethoven's solution to the problem of establishing 'a relationship between the theme and variations such that the waltz was not rendered superfluous, as a mere prologue to the whole'.[16] To be sure, there was a severe formal problem here: Beethoven's gigantic series of variations threatened to overwhelm Diabelli's rather trivial theme. There were far fewer variations in the Op. 109 set; moreover, the theme was Beethoven's and hardly trivial. But Beethoven may nevertheless have been concerned about the relationship of the theme to the variations; and the addition, late in the genesis of the movement, of a thematic re-exposition following the first, disruptive variation may well have been a conscious bid to shore up the coherence of the whole.

Indeed, we have observed on more than one occasion that Beethoven's revisions to individual variations for Op. 109 often seem designed to strengthen their relationship to the theme. If, as Kinderman suggests, the 'implicit contradiction' between Diabelli's theme and Beethoven's variations 'may have had something to do with Beethoven's uncharacteristic decision to lay this work [Op. 120] aside for several years', then it seems possible that it was not 'the apparent absurdity of building a monumental edifice upon such slight foundations [which] had, by 1823, supplied an unexpected stimulus to Beethoven's own imagination',[17] but rather the experience of composing Op. 109 in the meanwhile.

The Concept *Draft for Variation [3]*

While the A 47 draft for Variation [2] contains little internal revision, that for Variation [3] confronts the transcriber with a mass of deletions (see Plate 8). Not a single bar is left unchanged, and ink and pencil notations are freely intermixed. On closer inspection, it emerges that the A 47 bifolium contains not one but two drafts of Variation [3]. Each is written in ink; and since one version is deleted entirely and the other not at all there need be no doubt about which was written first. The separation of the two versions helps to clarify the role of the pencil notations, which are consistently closer in content to version [2] than to version [1]. The likely sequence of events is obvious. Beethoven wrote out the first ink draft and subsequently felt dissatisfied with it. He sketched his revisions in pencil before incorporating them into the second ink draft, each bar of which was superimposed on the corresponding bar of the first. Since each bar

[16] Ibid.
[17] Ibid.

Ex. 9.15. A 47, fols. 1ᵛ–2ᵛ: the *Concept* Draft for Variation [3]. Bars 1a–4a

of version [1] is deleted individually it seems that Beethoven proceeded bar by bar, first crossing out version [1] and then cramming version [2] into the remaining space between the barlines (Ex. 9.15).[18]

A swift reading of either version in Ex. 9.15 confirms that by this stage Variation 3 was essentially fixed; there was to be no large-scale recasting here, but rather changes within and between individual phrases. Two of the most notable differences between versions [1] and [2] can be seen in the final bar. First, it is clear that this variation was not originally intended to run directly into the next: both voices were to end on the third quaver, followed by a quaver rest (the upper-voice semiquaver motion originally continued throughout the bar, however). Even the pencil revisions originally preserved the

---

[18] The pencil sketches are shown on the indented staves supplied with small-print clefs and key signatures and sandwiched between the ink versions [1] and [2] in Ex. 9.15. It is not possible to determine the internal chronology of the pencil sketches with any consistency. A double deletion sign (\\) is used throughout the transcription to indicate a deletion in both ink and pencil in the original.

Ex. 9.15. contd.: bars 5a–8a

gap between this and what would presumably have been Variation 4. But the firm closure intended here was undercut by the arrangement of voices in version [1], which resulted in a final cadence on a first-inversion rather than a root-position tonic triad. Resolving this problem evidently led Beethoven to reconsider the sequence of contrapuntal inversions in the variation as a whole (see Fig. 9.1, p. 247; inversions are indicated by crossed diagonals).

Inversion occurs consistently *within* each eight-bar phrase in versions [1] and [2]. As for inversion *between* phrases, this occurs only once in version [1], at the midpoint of the entire variation. In version [2] an extra inversion takes place between the first and second

Ex. 9.15. contd.: bars 1b–8b (9–16)

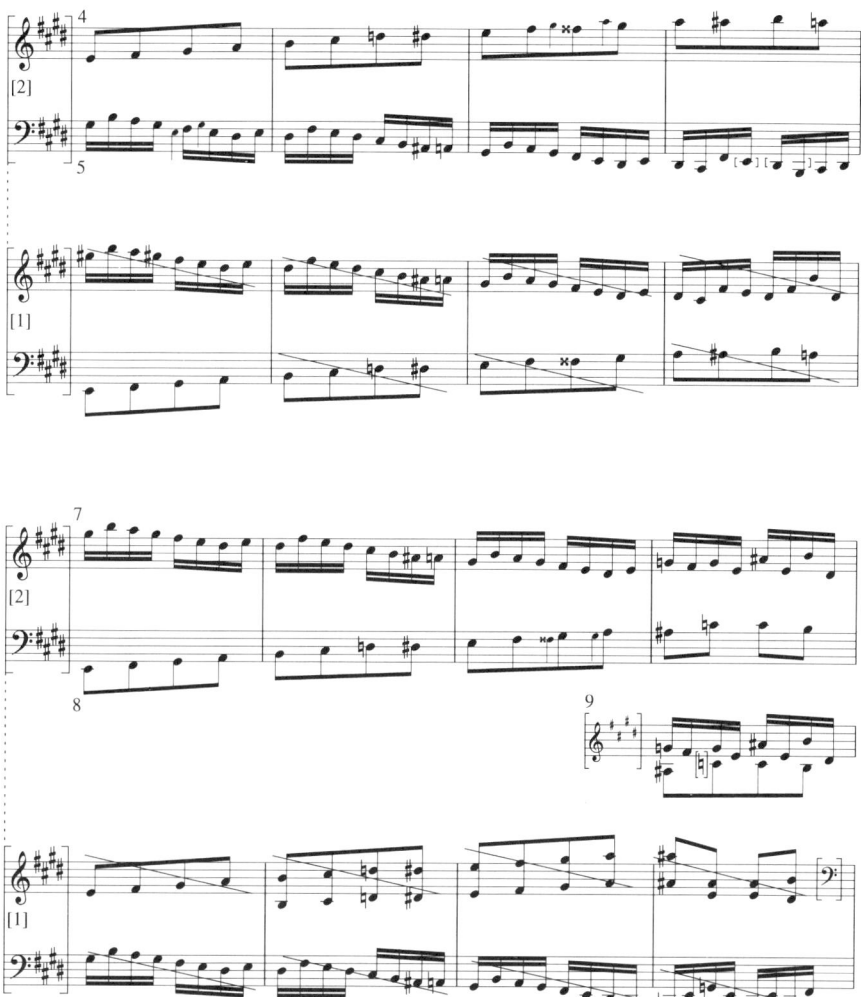

phrases (bars 8a–1b). The consequence of this is that all subsequent inversions run counter to those in version [1], with the result that the final intra-phrase inversion (bars 12b–13b) brings in the semi-quaver voice beneath the voice moving in quavers. Thus the lower voice is now free to create root-position support for the G♯ required in the upper voice, which carries the theme.

We might argue that Beethoven could have solved the problem of

Ex. 9.15. contd.: bars 9a–12a (17–20)

the version [1] ending simply by inverting the voices between bars 16a and 9b. But this would have disrupted the symmetry illustrated in Fig. 9.1a: the outer pair and inner pair of eight-bar phrases share the same inversion pattern, giving rise to an ABBA inversion scheme for the variation as a whole. At the same time, the second half of each subvariation inverts the pattern of the first. Bars 1b–8b and 9b–16b also invert the pattern of bars 1a–8a and 9a–16a, and thereby function as 'variations' of them. This variational aspect becomes more significant when we consider that, ignoring the voice inversion, bars 1b–8b in version [1] are an almost literal repeat of bars 1a–8a: it is precisely the inversion which distinguishes the two phrases as parts of separate subvariations.

The inversion pattern used in version [2] eschews any such sym-

Ex. 9.15. contd.: bars 13a–16a (21–4), 9b–12b (25–8)

metry: the overall scheme here is AAAB, and bars 1b–8b do not invert the arrangement of bars 1a–8a. Beethoven no longer needed that minimal variational element because he had altered the music of bars 1a–8a in order to distinguish the two subvariations more sharply. He reshaped the semiquaver voice so as to stress the thematic falling

Ex. 9.15. contd.: bars 13b–16b (29–32)

thirds g♯–e and d♯–B in bars 1–2. The removal of the passing notes from the upper voice gave similar prominence to the rising thirds e^1–$g\sharp^1$ and b^1–$d\sharp^2$. For bars 1b–8b he retained the corresponding material from version [1], inverting the voices and making other slight alterations. The result was a first eight-bar phrase which was more closely related to the theme than previously, while the second phrase was now more obviously a 'variation' of the first. This 'theme and variation' relationship between the two subvariations is retained in Variation 3: it parallels the definitive organization of Variation 2, which, as we have seen, was still planned as a single variation at this *Concept* stage.

The location of the pencil sketches in Ex. 9.15 is a useful indication of Beethoven's compositional concerns. The first pencil sketches for bars 1a–4a depart from versions [1], [2], and the final version in showing the semiquaver line commencing in the top voice. This arrangement makes the relationship between variation and theme even more obvious than in version [2], for it leaves the relative positions of the outer voices of the theme unchanged. Bars 1b–8b

FIG. 9.1a The *Concept* draft for Variation [3]: contrapuntal inversion in version [1]

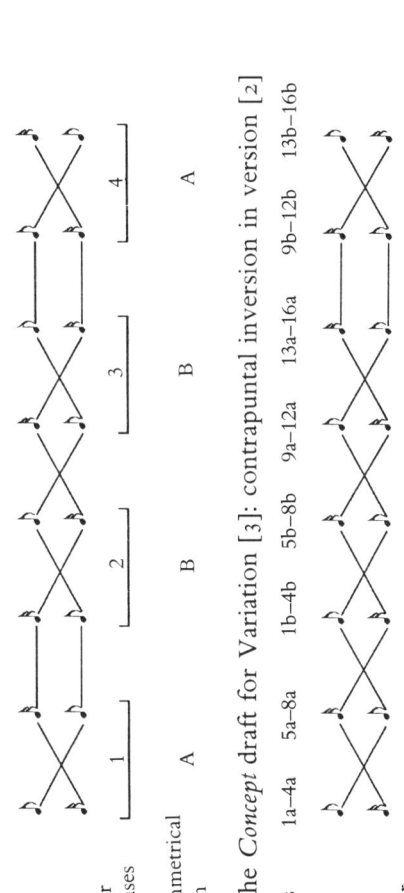

b The *Concept* draft for Variation [3]: contrapuntal inversion in version [2]

are almost entirely free of pencil sketches. This probably reflects the fact that Beethoven had no recomposition to do here; all that was necessary to produce version [2] was the wholesale inversion of the corresponding bars of version [1].[19] Apart from voice inversion, the main alteration required in bars 9a–16a and 9b–16b was the reshaping of the semiquaver line of version [1] in accordance with version [2] of bars 1a–8a: the new formulation again replaces a previously stepwise line by one emphasizing the important thematic interval of the third. Yet the pencil sketches for bars 9a–16a and 9b–16b are almost entirely devoted to the quaver voice, which underwent relatively little change between versions [1] and [2]. Such seemingly redundant sketching harks back to the problematic ending of version [1], where the quaver voice moving beneath the semiquaver one produced an unsatisfactory final cadence. Beethoven's careful mapping of the register and position of the quaver voice throughout the entire second half suggests his concern to resolve that problem.

Returning to bars 1b–8b, it is probably not accidental that the only bar in this phrase for which any pencil sketches appear is the last one. In versions [1] and [2] Beethoven distinguished carefully between the cadences on the dominant in bars 4b and 8b, so as to reflect the corresponding distinction made at those points in the theme. The arrangement of voices in bars 5b–8b of version [1] had allowed him full expression of the approach to the dominant through the augmented-sixth chord on C, but the inverted arrangement in version [2] made this less easy. The rising quaver line demanded a♯ on the downbeat of bar 8b, and the root (c^1) of the augmented sixth had to be shifted to the second quaver, producing a syncopation within the bar. In the final version of Variation 3 Beethoven avoided this syncopation by delaying c^1 until the second beat of bar 8b (16).[20]

Although version [2] in Ex. 9.15 comes very close to the final version, further changes were in store. The alteration to bar 8b was not the only one which affected the cadential bars. Whereas in versions [1] and [2] Beethoven had consistently distinguished the quaver line in bar 4a from that in bar 8a (in the former A♯ appears only on

---

[19] Alternatively, Beethoven's actual procedure may have been to transfer the material of bars 1a–8a in version [1] to bars 1b–8b (9–16) of version [2]. Although the distinction might seem overly pedantic, the fact that the final version of bars 1b–8b uses the dynamic scheme (piano . . . forte) associated with bars 1a–8a in version [1] should not be overlooked.

[20] Beethoven's special concern for the cadence points in this variation is again reflected in the pencil sketches for the second half of the draft, where the somewhat mechanical mapping of the quaver line is uniquely broken by a sudden switch to the semiquaver line in bar 12a (20). Not only must this bar observe the corresponding cadence in the theme, it is also the point following which the voices interchange. Beethoven had to devise a semiquaver line which would both express the cadence satisfactorily and allow for a smooth takeover of the quaver line from the upper voice.

Ex. 9.16. Cf. Op. 109, third movement, Variation 3, bars 9a–12a (17–20)

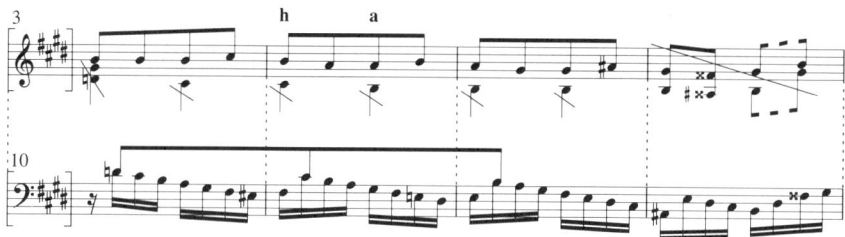

A 47, fol. 2r, st. 10 (upward stems and beam not in original)

the second quaver, while in the latter it appears on the downbeat), he eventually chose to make the two points identical, with A♯–A♯–B followed by a quaver rest in each. In the autograph, however, he first wrote the four-quaver group a♯–a♯–b–a in bar 8a: the passing a forms a smooth link to g♯ on the downbeat of the following bar. This was a formula which he had used in bar 4a of draft version [1] and bar 4b (12) of versions [1] and [2], where it served to enhance continuity across the midpoint of an eight-bar phrase; indeed, it serves the same purpose in bar 4b (12) of the final version. But in general Beethoven seems to have wanted to keep the eight-bar phrases 1a–8a and 1b–8b (9–16) more distinct from one another; therefore a♯–a♯–b–a in bar 8a of the autograph may simply have been a copying error which was quickly corrected.

The autograph version of Variation 3 holds other surprises. In bars 9a–12a (17–20) it shows that Beethoven considered expanding the texture from two to three voices by adding a right-hand inner voice descending in crotchets from d^1. This subsequently deleted voice is not entirely new, however; it derives from the semiquaver line in draft version [1] of these bars (Ex. 9.16). While this derivation is clear, Ex. 9.17 shows a passage from the autograph which is quite unprecedented in the A 47 drafts or anywhere else. In bars 13a–16a (21–24) Beethoven at first wrote a wholly new semiquaver line. When he deleted it he did so in pencil and went on to add the definitive version in pencil before inking it over.

Since there are clear traces of this new line in bar 13b (29) but not thereafter, it seems that Beethoven reverted to his A 47 plans fairly soon. But why experiment with this new material at such a late stage, when he was otherwise so satisfied with draft version [2] on the A 47 bifolium? It is impossible to be certain, of course; but one feature of this semiquaver line is especially striking. In bar 15a (23)

Ex. 9.17. Op. 109, autograph manuscript, fol. 14^r, st. 5/6–7/8 (original version only)

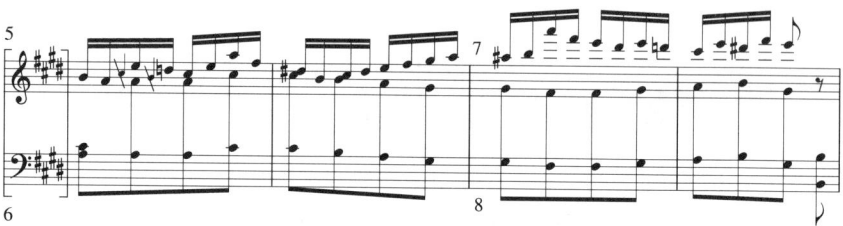

there is a sudden upward leap of a seventh from b² to a³. The leap is all the more conspicuous since b² has been the highest note in the variation up to this point. The a³ is left unresolved, an isolated highpoint within the phrase. We have seen in Chapter 8 that registral isolation of a³ was a major unifying tactic in the nine-variation set sketched in Artaria 195 and remains so in the final version. The material in Ex. 9.17 probably represents an attempt to introduce a registrally unresolved a³ in Variation 3, roughly midway through the variation set. It was an attempt which Beethoven soon abandoned. And while we can only guess at the reasons for his change of heart, the evidence of the attempt itself stands as a reminder that changes in surface detail, even at this late stage, might yet be but the means to a more large-scale end.

Conclusion

The stated aim of this chapter was to focus on the genesis of the individual variations in Op. 109; the intention was to turn aside from the large-scale structural considerations which have emerged repeatedly in preceding chapters, and to concentrate instead on matters of detail. That it has proved difficult, if not impossible, to do so should hardly come as a surprise; the separation of structure and detail in music of this kind is really no more than a convenient fiction.

The relationship between detail and structure—the dependence of structure on detail—in these variation sketches has emerged in various ways, not least in the many revisions which were apparently intended to strengthen the connection between variation and theme. Such strengthening took various forms. At one extreme there is the careful revision of the opening of the A 47 draft for Variation [3] which places heightened emphasis on thematically motivated rising and falling thirds; at the other extreme there is the addition of an entire subvariation within Variation 2, an addition which makes of this variation a 'theme and variation' and thereby a microcosm of the entire movement. But it is Ex. 9.17, the rejected passage for Variation 3 in the autograph manuscript, which remains the most telling, for it is precisely in an autograph that one might expect revisions to address local detail rather than large-scale structure. And while this rejected version of bars 13a–16a (21–24) highlights the inextricable relationship between the whole and its parts, it also points up the crude, expedient nature of the distinction made in this and the preceding chapter between sketches for the structure of the variation set and sketches for the detail of individual variations. There is an intimate connection between the deleted a^3 in Beethoven's autograph and the 'structure sketches' in Artaria 195, despite the ostensible evolutionary gap between these two manuscript sources.

10. Conclusion

I

The nature of Beethoven's original musical idea for Op. 109 remains concealed. However, the sketches and autograph revisions suggest that he had in mind a plan for the entire work, a plan which during the compositional process was amplified and refined until all elements had been coordinated to form a cogent totality.[1]

Allen Forte's conclusion to his study of the genesis of Op. 109 is no less pertinent here, although Forte's 'plan for the entire work', which emphasizes the 'developmental progression from one movement to the next' seen in the relationship between 'the bass lines of the thematic statements of each movement', is quite different to that which has emerged in the preceding pages.[2] Forte realizes the important role played in the first movement by melodic connections between G♯ and B, the constituent notes of the initial upper-voice interval. But he explicitly regards both notes as 'stable melodic points in the upper voice', whereas the analysis in Chapter 3, above, develops the idea that G♯ and B are mutually opposed.[3] In terms of the well-known characterization of sonata form as fundamentally the statement and resolution of a large-scale dissonance, B represents such a dissonance in relation to G♯ in the first movement of Op. 109. And lying at the heart of the 'plan for the entire work' proposed here is the idea that the 'resolution' of B to G♯ is massively delayed: it occurs not in the recapitulation of the first movement, where the primacy of B over G♯ is heavily underlined, but in the course of the third-movement theme and variations. The theme acts as a summary or re-exposition of the structural plan left incomplete in the first movement; the variation set and concluding thematic reprise reflect and magnify the structure of the theme, and thereby provide the definitive closure of the first movement and of the entire work.

The notion of the 'incompleteness' of the first movement developed in Chapter 3 is not touched upon by Forte, who also restricted his study of the third movement almost exclusively to the theme. Indeed, it is ironic that the strongest suggestion of structural incompleteness in Forte's analysis of Op. 109 comes in his reading of the

---

[1] *Compositional Matrix*, 85.   [2] Ibid., esp. ex. 38.   [3] Ibid. 19.

Ex. 10.1. Voice-leading connections between the movements of Op. 109

end of the theme, where 'in the final measure A is superimposed [over the melodic descent G♯–F♯–E in the tenor voice] and reintroduces G♯ in the upper voice, thus preventing a definitive melodic closure.'[4] Forte's demand for an orthodox $\hat{3}-\hat{2}-\hat{1}$ *Urlinie* descent at the close of the theme leads him to suggest structural incompleteness at the very point at which our analysis, accepting as it does an unorthodox $\hat{5}-\hat{4}-\hat{3}$ quasi-*Urlinie* descent, locates the definitive closure of the first movement and of the whole sonata.

By a neat reversal of readings, Forte argues for a structurally important $\hat{5}-\hat{4}-\hat{3}$ descent precisely where our analysis invokes the more conventional $\hat{3}-\hat{2}-\hat{1}$ *Urlinie*: in the second movement. 'The codetta', writes Forte, '... effects the definitive closure, resolving the triadic fifth to the third.'[5] By contrast, the analysis of the sketches and final version of the second movement in Chapters 5–6 above has stressed the sense in which this movement, like the first, is structurally incomplete. In this case, however, the incompleteness results from the careful manipulation of two melodic progressions, $\hat{3}-\hat{2}-\hat{1}$ and $\hat{3}-\hat{1}-\hat{2}$, and their related harmonic support (Ex. 5.20). The latter progression may be regarded as an elaboration of the more basic step $\hat{3}-\hat{2}$. It is this progression which governs the large-scale structure of the movement and prevents the completion of a $\hat{3}-\hat{2}-\hat{1}$ *Urlinie* (Ex. 6.21).

Ex. 10.1 provides a synoptic graph of the voice-leading structures underlying and linking all three movements of Op. 109 as analysed in this book. It suggests a 'plan for the entire work' whose development

---

[4] Ibid. 72.   [5] Ibid. 54.

has been traced with some clarity in the surviving sketches even though, as Forte rightly cautions, 'the nature of Beethoven's original musical idea for Op. 109 remains concealed.' The only aspect of Ex. 10.1 requiring further comment is the long-range connection G♯–G–G♯, whose audibility is ensured by the use of the tonic key in each movement (as in Beethoven's other multi-movement instrumental works in E: Op. 14 No. 1, Op. 59 No. 2, and Op. 90) and by the introduction of the triadic third, whether major or minor, as the initial upper-voice pitch in all three. This connection relates to a significant moment in the first movement: the varied repeat of the second group in the recapitulation (bars 61–4), where an unexpected and disruptive tonal shift from E to C major occurs. Our analysis of the few sketches for this passage has suggested that a more fundamental meaning may lie in the bass connection G♯–G–G♯ which ties this varied repeat into the surrounding music: G♯ is 'negated' by G and subsequently restored (Ex. 3.10). And to the extent that Op. 109 may be thought of in a highly abstract sense as a sonata 'about' the establishment, loss, and re-establishment of a single pitch, $g♯^1$, this long-range melodic connection between all three movements dramatizes that process.

II

This book began with an *apologia* for its limitations: limitations of scope and of analytical methodology, to name only two of the more obvious. Now that the 'full close', the *vollkommener Schluß*, is at hand, a measure of freedom will be introduced. In particular I wish to interpret the term 'sketch' in a more liberal sense than that employed hitherto, and to look more closely at an easily overlooked work whose relationship to Op. 109 is nevertheless striking for a number of reasons: the song 'Abendlied unterm gestirnten Himmel', WoO 150. In Chapter 2 it was established that Beethoven probably did very little compositional work in January and the first half of February 1820, a period when he was heavily preoccupied with the legal struggle for guardianship of his nephew Karl. The return to musical activity seems to be represented by the composition of 'Abendlied' and, shortly thereafter, the 'little new piece' which subsequently became the first movement of Op. 109. That both compositions share the key of E major is an obvious enough connection between them, although one which carries little weight on its own. But the links between the two works go much deeper than this; taken together, they permit us to regard 'Abendlied' almost as a further sketch for Op. 109.

Such an extended interpretation of the term 'sketch' has more frequently served to connect another, earlier song with Op. 109: 'Sehnsucht', WoO 146, written in 1815–16. This song is in E and in triple metre, and several writers have drawn on these features as well as upon the melodic shape of the opening bars to suggest a connection with the third-movement theme in Op. 109.[6] There is even a further connection in that 'Sehnsucht' is an example of a formal type labelled 'variirte Strophenlied' by Hans Boettcher and related to the prominence of variation form in Beethoven's late instrumental works.[7] But 'Abendlied' is itself a *variirte Strophenlied*; moreover, it employs a formal strategy which is foreign to 'Sehnsucht' but unmistakably similar to that found in its close chronological neighbour, the eventual first movement of Op. 109.

'Abendlied' begins with a short piano introduction in which G♯ is transferred downward through two octaves, from $g\sharp^3$ to $g\sharp^1$. Already, then, the song has opened up the two registers closely associated with the triadic third in the first movement of Op. 109. The lower register is maintained until bar 12 where the right hand, doubling the vocal line, leaps back up to e^3. A continuation upward from e^3 to $f\sharp^3$ follows in the next bar and events reach a momentary climax in bar 14, with $f\sharp^3$ retained above the dominant harmony; the second half of this bar brings an unmediated return to the $g\sharp^1$ register. The upward leap to e^3 and $f\sharp^3$ is repeated in each verse except the third, where in bars 49–50 e^2–$f\sharp^2$ is substituted. Far from being omitted, however, the leap is merely delayed: in bars 54–5 the accompaniment echoes the vocal cadence at the pitch-level e^3–$f\sharp^3$–e^3. The final appearance of these notes comes in the penultimate bar, in which the scoring of the chords emphasizes the connection with bars 12–14 and their repetitions. But while on all previous occasions $f\sharp^3$ had marked the registral highpoint, here it leads up to $g\sharp^3$ to complete the final cadence. The end of 'Abendlied' reverses its opening and at last completes a process which has been hinted at in each verse: the first melodic gesture in the song is the downward leap from $g\sharp^3$ to e^3, the last is the upward filling-in of that gap, e^3–$f\sharp^3$–$g\sharp^3$ (Ex. 10.2). The relationship of this strategy to that contemplated for, but eventually abandoned in, the first movement of Op. 109 needs no elaboration except for a reminder that in the sonata movement it

---

[6] See L. Orrey, 'The Songs', in D. Arnold and N. Fortune (eds.), *The Beethoven Companion* (London, 1971), 432; Lockwood, 'Beethoven's Sketches for *Sehnsucht*', 101; Cooper, *Beethoven and the Creative Process*, 62. Orrey is the only one of these three writers explicitly to suggest that 'one might almost imagine [the opening of 'Sehnsucht'] to be a first draft for that [Op. 109] theme.'

[7] H. Boettcher, *Beethoven als Liederkomponist* (Augsburg, 1928; repr. Walluf-Nendeln, 1974), 64.

256 *Conclusion*

Ex. 10.2. 'Abendlied unterm gestirnten Himmel', WoO 150

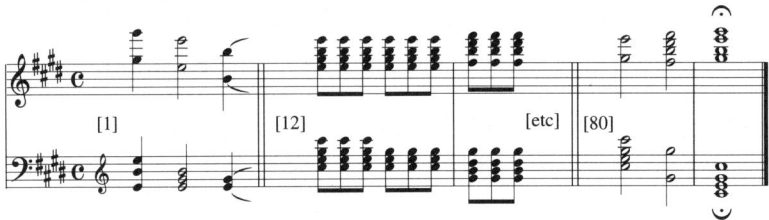

is the upper rather than the lower third of the tonic triad which is the locus of structural melodic progressions.

The structural similarity between the song and the sonata is reinforced by a number of more foreground features, such as the opening of the vocal line with $g\sharp^1$–b^1 followed by a descent to $f\sharp^1$, combined with the largely stepwise descent of the bass from $g\sharp$ to $G\sharp$. Another aurally striking connection between the two works emerges if bars 72–6 of 'Abendlied' are compared to bars 75–8 of the first movement of Op. 109: the turn to the submediant is handled similarly in each case. (The pocket sketch for the end of the sonata movement transcribed in Ex. 3.24*a* bears an even closer relationship to this passage from 'Abendlied'.)

III

In *Free Composition* Schenker reaffirmed, not without characteristic arrogance, his belief in the relationship between musical coherence and musical notation in a masterwork:

Since the musicians up to the present have been unable to perceive the musical coherence in the masterworks, they have been even less able to read the *autographs* of the great composers. These last present the additional difficulty of problems of notation which are highly individual, ever new, and never schematic, but which always correspond to the musical content. *Autograph-study*, a completely new and special field of knowledge, thus goes hand in hand with the theory of musical coherence. The extent to which I have surpassed my few predecessors in this subject—editors, analysts, and the like—is indicated by those works of mine which secure for me the honor of being the true founder of the discipline of autograph-study.[8]

---

[8] *Free Composition*, i. 7.

The Op. 109 *Erläuterungsausgabe* must be counted one of the most significant of 'those works' to which Schenker refers; thus it is all the more ironic that precisely in the case of Op. 109 Schenker failed to understand the structural significance of a notational detail in the autograph manuscript. The 'plan for the entire work' summarized in Ex. 10.1 is provocative in that it challenges the ostensible division of Op. 109 into three movements. However, that Beethoven himself conceived the work as a single, connected structure is attested by his striking orthography of concluding barlines throughout the autograph (see Plates 1–3). That orthography, which defeated Schenker, was studied briefly in Chapter 1 and summarized there in Fig. 1.1. To recapitulate the main points: only at the very end of the third movement did Beethoven write a true double barline of the kind conventionally used to close a movement or work. Elsewhere—at the end of the first two movements, and between Variations 1 and 2 and 4 and 5 within the third movement—he used the less final 'double-single' barline. His substitution of this form for the double barline which originally stood at the end of the first movement in the autograph leaves little doubt that he genuinely understood the two forms to signify different levels of musical closure. Thus, Beethoven's autograph supports an analysis of Op. 109 which locates definitive closure not at the end of individual movements but uniquely at the end of the entire work; this manuscript provides a classic instance of a 'highly individual' problem of notation which corresponds intimately to the 'musical content'.

Against this claim, however, we must consider the evidence of the first edition of Op. 109 published in 1821 by Adolf Martin Schlesinger. The arduous tasks undertaken by composer and publisher in the publication of this edition were touched upon in Chapter 2. Beethoven supplied the autograph manuscript as *Stichvorlage*, but its illegibility forced Schlesinger to have a new *Stichvorlage* prepared by a copyist in Berlin; the proofs which were sent to Beethoven were evidently made from (or checked against) the autograph rather than this copy, with the result that they were full of mistakes. On 6 July 1821 Beethoven returned the corrected proofs to Schlesinger and remarked that 'I have never had a more difficult and tiresome task to cope with' (Anderson 1053/Kastner–Kapp 997). In mid-November he was still sending corrections and requesting Schlesinger to have them entered by hand in the copies already engraved 'so that the work may appear as it should' (Anderson 1060). Now the first and second movements and Variations 1–5 in the third movement all end with a conventional double bar in Schlesinger's edition; Beethoven's carefully placed 'double-single' barlines have entirely disappeared.[9] Since it seems unlikely that even as poor a proof-reader as Beethoven would have overlooked something as conspicuous as a concluding double barline, perhaps we must conclude that he did not, after all, attach much significance to these signs.

Two pieces of evidence argue the contrary. First, there is the clear witness of the autograph itself: if Beethoven regarded double and 'double-single' barlines as interchangeable, why did he expressly substitute the latter for the former at the end of the first movement? Secondly, there is the witness of a textual source which has not yet been mentioned. The copy of Op. 109 which Schlesinger had prepared in Berlin to act as *Stichvorlage* appears not to have survived; but another manuscript copy, prepared for the Archduke Rudolph's music library and corrected by Beethoven, exists today and is housed under the shelf mark VII. 17379. Q. 11967 in the Gesellschaft der Musikfreunde, Vienna. A striking, indeed an apparently unique feature of this *überprüfte Abschrift* is the fact that it reproduces the concluding barlines of each movement and variation exactly as found in Beethoven's autograph.

On the face of it, the evidence is inconclusive. The Vienna *überprüfte Abschrift* supports the readings in the autograph; the first edition contradicts them; and Beethoven corrected both these post-autograph sources. Yet a case may be made for preferring the shared readings in the two manuscript copies to those in the first edition. Beethoven's dissatisfaction with the first edition of Op. 109 is obvious; the proof-reading and correction of errors clearly cost him an inordinate amount of time and effort. It is not difficult to imagine that, however much he wanted the sonata to 'appear as it should', there came a point at which he reluctantly decided to accept the text as it stood, knowing that it remained imperfect in certain respects.[10] If the arrangement of concluding double bars in the autograph carried the structural meaning suggested here, Beethoven may have come to regard this as a largely 'private' aspect of the score, one whose neglect would not mar performances of the sonata as obviously as would the presence of incorrect notes and accidentals. Future editors of Op. 109, however, would do well to 'exhume' this aspect of Beethoven's autograph; to do so would be to honour not only Beethoven's intentions but those of Schlesinger and Schenker also.

---

[9] Variation 6 closes with a single barline. The constituent thick and thin lines of the double bars closing Variations 3, 4, and 5 are in fact reversed; it is unclear whether this reversal is meaningful or merely the result of an engraver's error.

[10] Sieghard Brandenburg has argued for a similar attitude of surrender on Beethoven's part in the case of the repeats in the third movement of the Fifth Symphony: see his 'Once Again: On the Question of the Repeat of the Scherzo and Trio in Beethoven's Fifth Symphony', in Lockwood and Benjamin (eds.), *Beethoven Essays*, 146–98.

IV

'Even in my instrumental music I always have the whole in view' (Anderson 479/Kastner–Kapp 427). Beethoven's remark in a letter to Georg Friedrich Treitschke apropos the drudgery of revising *Fidelio* in 1814 is often quoted, and it is of the essence here. That Op. 109 forms a coherent whole is analytically demonstrable; that Beethoven himself planned such coherence—that there was indeed 'a plan for the entire work'—emerges from an examination of the compositional history of the sonata.

To be sure, the origins of Op. 109 suggest anything but a tight structure. We have seen that the first movement was conceived and written as an independent composition; but for Oliva's suggestion to Beethoven that he use the 'little new piece' in a sonata for Schlesinger, Op. 109 might have turned out to be wholly different from the work we know today. And notwithstanding Oliva's advice, Beethoven did a substantial amount of work on the Credo of the *Missa solemnis* before turning seriously to work on the sonata. When he did so, he composed the remaining parts in an unusual order: third-movement theme, second movement, third-movement variations. The remarkable relationship between the first movement and the third-movement theme, however, is highlighted by the fact that they were composed consecutively in this manner. Given that the theme effectively recomposes the first movement and concludes its 'unfinished business' while also foreshadowing the structure of the third movement, it was by completing the theme that Beethoven was first able to bring 'the whole' in view. Similarly, we have seen that in composing the third movement Beethoven was initially concerned with matters of large-scale structure. Only when the total structure was clear in his mind does he seem to have turned his attention to the detail of individual variations. That structural issues continued to hold sway throughout the compositional process is suggested by the autograph of Variation 3, with its striking original version of bars 13a–16a (21–24; see Ex. 9.17). Finally, Beethoven's sense of Op. 109 as a single unified 'whole' is rendered almost visible thanks to his careful spelling of concluding double barlines throughout the autograph.

And so at last to von Lenz, whose disparaging remarks on the first and third movements of Op. 109 stand counterpointed against Beethoven's famous remark to Treitschke at the beginning of this study. From our perspective, it is difficult to imagine any criticism less accurate. That Beethoven understood the meaning behind the 'whirlwind of notes' making up the third-movement variations is indeed beyond doubt; nor need that meaning continue to escape us. And even if it were chronologically accurate to describe Beethoven as being 'at the end of his days' in 1820, the claim that he no longer gave his full attention to sonata composition would be no less preposterous. If they do nothing else, the sketches for Op. 109 bear witness to the extraordinary attention which Beethoven brought to bear on the composition of this work. We are dealing, after all, with a master of musical structure; should we expect anything less from the record of musical genesis?

Bibliography

1. Primary Sources

Beethoven: Werke: Neue Ausgabe sämtlicher Werke, ed. Joseph Schmidt-Görg et al. (Munich and Duisburg, 1961–).
L. van Beethoven: Klaviersonaten: Nach den Autographen rekonstruiert von Heinrich Schenker, 4 vols. (Vienna and Leipzig, 1934); rev. Erwin Ratz (Vienna, 1946–7).
Ludwig van Beethoven: Piano Sonata Opus 109, with introd. by Oswald Jonas (New York, 1965).
Ludwig van Beethoven: Piano Sonata No. 32 in C Minor, Op. 111, with introd. by Eric Simon (New York, 1968).
Beethoven: Drei Skizzenbücher zur Missa Solemnis I: Ein Skizzenbuch aus den Jahren 1819/20 SV 81, ed. Joseph Schmidt-Görg, 2 vols. (Bonn, 1952 (trans.), 1968 (facs.)).
Beethoven: Drei Skizzenbücher zur Missa Solemnis II: Ein Skizzenbuch zum Credo SV 82, ed. Joseph Schmidt-Görg, 2 vols. (Bonn, 1968 (facs.), 1970 (trans.)).
Beethoven: Drei Skizzenbücher zur Missa Solemnis III: Ein Skizzenbuch zum Benedictus und zum Agnus Dei SV 83, ed. Joseph Schmidt-Görg, 2 vols. (Bonn, 1968 (facs.), 1970 (trans.)).
Beethoven: Ein Skizzenbuch zu den Diabelli-Variationen und zur Missa Solemnis SV 154, ed. Joseph Schmidt-Görg, 2 vols. (Bonn, 1968 (facs.), 1972 (trans.)).
Ludwig van Beethovens sämtliche Briefe, ed. Emerich Kastner, rev. and enlarged Julius Kapp (Leipzig, 1923; repr. Tutzing, 1975).
Beethoven: Entwurf einer Denkschrift an das Appellationsgericht in Wien von 18 Februar 1820, ed. Dagmar Weise (Bonn, 1953).
'Ungedruckte oder nur teilweise veröffentlichte Briefe Beethovens aus der Sammlung H. C. Bodmer—Zürich', transcr. and ed. Dagmar Weise, Beethoven-Jahrbuch, 1 (1954), 9–62.
The Letters of Beethoven, trans. and ed. Emily Anderson, 3 vols. (London, 1961).
Ludwig van Beethovens Konversationshefte, ed. Karl-Heinz Köhler et al., 10 vols. (Leipzig, 1968–).

2. Secondary Sources

ADELUNG, JOHANN CHRISTOPH, Grammatisch-kritisches Wörterbuch der Hochdeutschen Mundart, enlarged D. W. Soltau, rev. Franz Xaver Schönberger, 4 vols. (Vienna, 1811).

ARNOLD, DENIS, and FORTUNE, NIGEL (eds.), *The Beethoven Companion* (London, 1971).

BARFORD, PHILIP T., 'Bagatelles or Variations? A Discussion of the Origin of Beethoven's Bagatelles, Op. 119 Nos. 7 and 8', *Musical Opinion*, 76 (1953), 277–9.

BARTLITZ, EVELINE, *Die Beethoven-Sammlung in der Musikabteilung der Deutschen Staatsbibliothek: Verzeichnis* (Berlin, 1970).

BIRNBACH, HEINRICH, 'Über die verschiedene Form grösserer Instrumentaltonstücke aller Art und deren Bearbeitung', *Berliner allgemeine musikalische Zeitung*, 4 (1827), 285–7.

BOETTCHER, HANS, *Beethoven als Liederkomponist* (Augsburg, 1928; repr. Walluf-Nendeln, 1974).

BRANDENBURG, SIEGHARD, 'Beethovens "Erste Entwürfe" zu Variationenzyklen', in Carl Dahlhaus *et al.* (eds.), *Bericht über den Internationalen Musikwissenschaftlichen Kongress Bonn 1970* (Kassel, 1971), 108–11.

—— 'Die Skizzen zur Neunten Symphonie', in Harry Goldschmidt (ed.), *Zu Beethoven 2: Aufsätze und Dokumente* (Berlin, 1984), 88–129.

—— 'Once Again: On the Question of the Repeat of the Scherzo and Trio in Beethoven's Fifth Symphony', in Lewis Lockwood and Phyllis Benjamin (eds.), *Beethoven Essays: Studies in Honor of Elliot Forbes* (Cambridge, Mass., 1984), 146–98.

—— DRABKIN, WILLIAM, and JOHNSON, DOUGLAS, 'Viewpoint: On Beethoven Scholars and Beethoven's Sketches', *19th Century Music*, 2 (1978–9), 270–9.

CONE, EDWARD T., 'Analysis Today', in Paul Henry Lang (ed.), *Problems of Modern Music: The Princeton Seminar in Advanced Musical Studies* (New York, 1960), 34–50; repr. in Cone, *Music: A View from Delft*, ed. Robert P. Morgan (Chicago and London, 1989), 39–54.

—— 'Schubert's Unfinished Business', *19th Century Music*, 7 (1983–4), 222–32; repr. in id., *Music: A View from Delft*, ed. Robert P. Morgan (Chicago and London, 1989), 201–16.

COOPER, BARRY, *Beethoven and the Creative Process* (Oxford, 1990).

DRABKIN, WILLIAM, 'The New *Erläuterungsausgabe*', *Perspectives of New Music*, 12 (1973–4), 319–30.

—— 'The Sketches for Beethoven's Piano Sonata in C minor, Opus 111', 2 vols., Ph.D. diss. (Princeton, NJ, 1976).

—— 'Beethoven's Understanding of "Sonata Form": The Evidence of the Sketchbooks', in William Kinderman (ed.), *Beethoven's Compositional Process* (Lincoln and London, 1991), 14–19.

FEDERHOFER, HELMUT, *Heinrich Schenker: Nach Tagebüchern und Briefen in der Oswald Jonas Memorial Collection, University of California, Riverside* (Hildesheim, 1985).

FORTE, ALLEN, *The Compositional Matrix* (New York, 1961; repr. 1974).

—— and GILBERT, STEVEN E., *Introduction to Schenkerian Analysis* (New York and London, 1982).

GOSSETT, PHILIP, 'Beethoven's Sixth Symphony: Sketches for the First Movement', *JAMS* 27 (1974), 248–84.

HANSLICK, EDUARD, *Geschichte des Concertwesens in Wien*, 2 vols. (Vienna, 1869–70; repr. Farnborough, 1971).
HELMS, MARIANNE, and STAEHELIN, MARTIN, 'Bewegungen von Beethoven-Quellen 1973–1979', *Beethoven-Jahrbuch*, 10 (1983), 331–57.
JOHNSON, DOUGLAS, 'Beethoven Scholars and Beethoven's Sketches', *19th Century Music*, 2 (1978–9), 3–17.
—— TYSON, ALAN, and WINTER, ROBERT, *The Beethoven Sketchbooks: History, Reconstruction, Inventory*, ed. Douglas Johnson (Berkeley, Calif., Los Angeles, and Oxford, 1985).
JONAS, OSWALD, *Introduction to the Theory of Heinrich Schenker*, trans. and ed. John Rothgeb (New York and London, 1982).
KINDERMAN, WILLIAM, *Beethoven's Diabelli Variations* (Oxford, 1987).
—— 'Thematic Contrast and Parenthetical Enclosure in the Piano Sonatas, Opp. 109 and 111', in Harry Goldschmidt (ed.), *Zu Beethoven 3: Aufsätze und Dokumente* (Berlin, 1988), 43–59.
KINSKY, GEORG, *Das Werk Beethovens: Thematisch-bibliographisches Verzeichnis seiner sämtlichen vollendeten Kompositionen*, completed and ed. Hans Halm (Munich and Duisburg, 1955).
KLEIN, HANS-GÜNTER, *Ludwig van Beethoven: Autographe und Abschriften: Katalog* (Berlin, 1975).
KRAMER, RICHARD, '"Das Organische der Fuge": On the Autograph of Beethoven's String Quartet in F major, Opus 59 No. 1', in Christoph Wolff (ed.), *The String Quartets of Haydn, Mozart, and Beethoven: Studies of the Autograph Manuscripts* (Cambridge, Mass., 1980), 223–65.
—— review of *The Beethoven Sketchbooks: History, Reconstruction, Inventory* by Douglas Johnson, Alan Tyson, and Robert Winter, *JAMS* 40 (1987), 361–7.
—— 'The Sketch Itself', in William Kinderman (ed.), *Beethoven's Compositional Process* (Lincoln and London, 1991), 3–5.
KUNZE, STEFAN (ed.), *Ludwig van Beethoven: Die Werke im Spiegel seiner Zeit* (Laaber, 1987).
LENZ, WILHELM VON, *Beethoven et ses trois styles*, 2 vols. (St Petersburg, 1852–3).
LOCKWOOD, LEWIS, 'The Autograph of the First Movement of Beethoven's Sonata for Violoncello and Pianoforte, Opus 69', *The Music Forum*, 2 (1970), 1–109; repr. in id., *Beethoven: Studies in the Creative Process* (Cambridge, Mass. and London, 1992), 17–94.
—— 'Beethoven's Sketches for *Sehnsucht* (WoO 146)', in Alan Tyson (ed.), *Beethoven Studies*, i (New York, 1973; London, 1974), 97–122; repr. in Lockwood, *Beethoven: Studies in the Creative Process* (Cambridge, Mass. and London, 1992), 95–117.
—— '*The Beethoven Sketchbooks* and the General State of Sketch Research', in William Kinderman (ed.), *Beethoven's Compositional Process* (Lincoln and London, 1991), 6–13.
MARSTON, NICHOLAS, 'Schenker and Forte Reconsidered: Beethoven's Sketches for the Piano Sonata in E, Op. 109', *19th Century Music*, 10 (1986–7), 24–42.

MARSTON, NICHOLAS, review of *Beethoven's Diabelli Variations* by William Kinderman, *19th Century Music*, 12 (1988–9), 80–9.
—— 'Analysing Variations: The Finale of Beethoven's String Quartet Op. 74', *Music Analysis*, 8 (1989), 303–24.
—— 'Beethoven's Sketches and the Interpretative Process', *Beethoven Forum*, 1 (1992), 225–42.
MEREDITH, WILLIAM RHEA, 'The Sources for Beethoven's Piano Sonata in E Major, Opus 109', Ph.D. diss. (University of North Carolina, Chapel Hill, 1985).
—— 'The Origins of Beethoven's Op. 109', *Musical Times*, 126 (1985), 713–16.
MÜNSTER, ARNOLD, *Studien zu Beethovens Diabelli-Variationen* (Munich, 1982).
NOTTEBOHM, GUSTAV, *Zweite Beethoveniana: Nachgelassene Aufsätze und Mittheilungen*, ed. Eusebius Mandyczewski (Leipzig, 1887).
ORREY, LESLIE, 'The Songs', in Arnold and Fortune (eds.), *The Beethoven Companion*, 411–39.
POHL, C. F., and WARRACK, JOHN, 'Gebauer, Franz Xaver', in Stanley Sadie (ed.), *The New Grove Dictionary of Music and Musicians*, 20 vols. (London, 1980), vii. 210–11.
REYNOLDS, CHRISTOPHER, 'Beethoven's Sketches for the Variations in E♭ Op. 35', in Alan Tyson (ed.), *Beethoven Studies*, iii (Cambridge, 1982), 47–84.
—— 'Ends and Means in the Second Finale to Beethoven's Op. 30, No. 1', in Lewis Lockwood and Phyllis Benjamin (eds.), *Beethoven Essays: Studies in Honor of Elliot Forbes* (Cambridge, Mass., 1984), 127–45.
RITZEL, FRED, *Die Entwicklung der 'Sonatenform' im musiktheoretischen Schrifttum des 18. und 19. Jahrhunderts* (Wiesbaden, 1974).
ROSEN, CHARLES, *The Classical Style: Haydn, Mozart, Beethoven*, rev. edn. (London, 1976).
SCHENKER, HEINRICH, 'Vom organischen der Sonatenform', *Das Meisterwerk in der Musik*, ii (Munich, Vienna, and Berlin, 1926; repr. Hildesheim and New York, 1974), 43–54; trans. Orin Grossman, as 'Organic Structure in Sonata Form', *Journal of Music Theory*, 12 (1968), 164–83, repr. in *Readings in Schenker Analysis and Other Approaches*, ed. Maury Yeston (New Haven, Conn. and London, 1977), 38–53.
—— *Harmony*, ed. Oswald Jonas, trans. Elisabeth Mann Borgese (Chicago and London, 1954).
—— *Beethoven: Die letzten Sonaten: Sonate E dur Op. 109. Kritische Einführung und Erläuterung von Heinrich Schenker*, ed. Oswald Jonas (Vienna, 1971).
—— *Free Composition*, 2 vols., trans. and ed. Ernst Oster (New York, 1979).
SCHINDLER, ANTON, *Biographie von Ludwig van Beethoven*, 2 vols., 3rd edn. (Münster, 1860).
SCHMIDT, HANS, 'Verzeichnis der Skizzen Beethovens', *Beethoven-Jahrbuch*, 6 (1969), 7–128.
—— 'Die Beethovenhandschriften des Beethovenhauses in Bonn', *Beethoven-Jahrbuch*, 7 (1971), pp. vii–xxiv, 1–443.

SCHOFIELD, B., and WILSON, A. D., 'Some New Beethoven Letters', *Music & Letters*, 20 (1939), 235-41.
SOLOMON, MAYNARD, *Beethoven* (London, 1977).
THAYER, ALEXANDER WHEELOCK, *Thayer's Life of Beethoven*, rev. and ed. Elliot Forbes, rev. edn. (Princeton, NJ, 1967).
TILMOUTH, MICHAEL, 'Binary Form', in Stanley Sadie (ed.), *The New Grove Dictionary of Music and Musicians*, 20 vols. (London, 1980), ii. 707-9.
TIMBRELL, CHARLES, 'Notes on the Sources of Beethoven's Opus 111', *Music & Letters*, 58 (1977), 204-15.
TYSON, ALAN, 'New Beethoven Letters and Documents', in id. (ed.), *Beethoven Studies*, ii (London, 1977), 20-32.
UNVERRICHT, HUBERT, *Die Eigenschriften und die Originalausgaben von Werken Beethovens in ihrer Bedeutung für die moderne Textkritik* (Kassel, 1960).
WINTER, ROBERT, 'The Sketches for the "Ode to Joy"', in id. and Bruce Carr (eds.), *Beethoven, Performers, and Critics* (Detroit, 1980), 176-214.
—— *Compositional Origins of Beethoven's Opus 131* (Ann Arbor, Mich., 1982).
—— 'Reconstructing Riddles: The Sources for Beethoven's *Missa Solemnis*', in Lewis Lockwood and Phyllis Benjamin (eds.), *Beethoven Essays: Studies in Honor of Elliot Forbes* (Cambridge, Mass., 1984), 217-50.
ZENCK, MARTIN, *Die Bach-Rezeption des späten Beethoven* (Stuttgart, 1986).

Index

Augustinerkirche, Vienna 17, 18, 23–4, 25

Bach, Johann Sebastian:
  'Goldberg' Variations 212 n.
Beethoven, Karl van 19, 81, 254
Beethoven, Ludwig van:
  Piano Sonata in E, Op. 14 No. 1 33, 254
  Violin Sonata in A, Op. 30 No. 1 83 n.
  'Eroica' Variations for Piano, Op. 35 170
  'Appassionata' Sonata, Op. 57 211–12 n.
  'Razumovsky' String Quartet in E minor, Op. 59 No. 2 33, 112 n., 254
  Symphony No. 4, Op. 60 18
  Symphony No. 5, Op. 67 258 n.
  Symphony No. 6, Op. 68 18
  Cello Sonata in A, Op. 69 42
  'Ghost' Piano Trio in D, Op. 70 No. 1 112 n.
  Piano Trio in E♭, Op. 70 No. 2 108 n.
  Fidelio, Op. 72 259
  String Quartet in E♭, Op. 74 4 n.
  Mass in C, Op. 86 18
  Piano Sonata in E, Op. 90 33, 254
  'Archduke' Piano Trio, Op. 97 190
  An die ferne Geliebte, Op. 98 10 n.
  Ten Themes with Variations, Op. 107 30
  Twenty-five Scottish Songs, Op. 108 30, 34, 36, 37, 39, 40 n., 41
  'Hammerklavier' Sonata, Op. 106 123
  Piano Sonata in E, Op. 109: autograph manuscript 6, 9, 39–40, 41–4, 178, 227–8, 236 n., 249–50, 251, 259, double barlines in 9–11, 80, 205, 239, 257–8, 259; 'B-tonicizing' progression 52–3, 54, 58, 60, 70 n., 73 n., 79, 93–5, 122, 163, 190, 202, 210; 'E-tonicizing' progression 52–3, 58, 69–70, 73, 75, 76, 79, 93–5, 122, 163, 166, 207, 211, 212; first edition 257–8; lost manuscript copy (Stichvorlage) prepared for Schlesinger 39–40, 257–8; manuscript copy (überprüfte Abschrift) prepared for Archduke Rudolph 39 n., 258; structural incompleteness in 8–9, 10–11, 80, 94, 95, 163–6, 190–1, 201–2, 210, 215, 252–3
  Piano Sonata in A♭, Op. 110 29
  Piano Sonata in C, Op. 111 29, 34, 169, 172, 174, 176–7, 178, 190 n., 205, 206 n., 208–9
  Meeresstille und glückliche Fahrt, Op. 112 18
  Bagatelles, Op. 119 15, 35, 38, 180, 182, 229
  Diabelli Variations, Op. 120 169, 173, 174–6, 177, 178, 190 n., 229 n., 239–40
  Missa solemnis, Op. 123 15, 16, 23, 26, 27, 31, 35, 46, 81, 92, 95, 259
  Symphony No. 9, Op. 125 23, 33 n., 112 n.
  String Quartet in E♭, Op. 127 205
  Variations on La stessa, la stessissima, WoO 73 190
  Variations on 'Rule Britannia', WoO 79 206 n.
  'Gedenke mein,' WoO 130 23
  'Sehnsucht,' WoO 146 255
  'Abendlied unterm gestirnten Himmel', WoO 150 22, 25, 26 n., 29, 254–6
  'Hoffmann, sei ja kein Hofmann', WoO 180 16–17, 25
  'Schwenke dich, ohne Schwänke', WoO 187 16 n.
  'Sanct Petrus ist ein Fels', Hess 256 19, 26
  projected piano sonata in E 25, 31–4, 45
  piano composition in F minor 46
  'Sonate in E moll' 36–7
Boettcher, Hans 255
Brandenburg, Sieghard 169, 170, 171, 172, 174 n., 177, 182, 258 n.
Brentano, Franz 30, 45
Brentano, Maximiliane 15, 45

Caroline, Queen 23
Cone, Edward T. 96
Czerny, Joseph 16, 19

Drabkin, William 33 n., 176–7, 209

Forte, Allen 3, 4, 8, 11–12, 13, 63 n., 122 n., 217, 230, 252–3, 254
Frimmel, Theodor von 5 n.

Gebauer, Franz Xaver 17–18, 23–4, 25
George III, King of England 23

Handel, Georg Friedrich:
  Saul 23–4, 25
  The Ways of Zion do Mourn 23
Haydn, Franz Josef:
  String Quartet in E♭, Op. 64 No. 6 69
Hertzka, Emil 5 n., 6 n.
Hoffmann, E. T. A. 16, 108 n.

Jonas, Oswald 7 n.

Kanne, Friedrich August 17
Kinderman, William 174–5, 181 n., 239–40
Klein, Hans-Günter 38 n.
Kramer, Richard 13

Lenz, Wilhelm von 259
Lockwood, Lewis 167

Meredith, William Rhea 3, 4, 16
'Mittelsatz' 108, 151
Mozart, Wolfgang Amadeus:
  Violin Sonata in E minor, K. 304 33

Nottebohm, Gustav 167

Oliva, Franz 18, 30–1, 33, 36–7, 45, 259

Peters, Karl 19

Ratz, Erwin 5
Rosen, Charles 205
Rosenthal, Albi 34 n.
Rudolph, Archduke 24 n., 41

Scarlatti, Domenico:
  Sonata in C, K. 460 148 n.
Schenker, Heinrich:
  and autograph study 6 n.
  and cadence 7
  'Entwurf einer neuen Formenlehre'
    (unpublished) 10
  Erlaüterungsausgabe 4–5; Op. 109 5–6, 7,
    9, 63 n., 160 n., 227 n., 257
  Free Composition (Der freie Satz) 7 n.,
    52 n., 256
  Harmony (Harmonielehre) 5, 7, 57 n.
  Kontrapunkt 5
  Das Meisterwerk in der Musik 5; 'Vom
    organischen der Sonatenform' 6, 8 n., 68
  Der Tonwille 5

Schenkerian analysis 4, 12
Schickh, Johann 24
Schindler, Anton 37
Schlesinger, Adolf Martin 2, 15, 29–30, 31,
  34, 36–7, 38, 39–40, 41, 45, 92, 95,
  257–8, 259
Schmidt-Görg, Joseph 18 n., 19 n., 26 n.,
  35 n.
Simrock, Nikolaus 27, 30
sketch interpretation and analysis 2–4,
  12–14
sketch manuscripts (principal references to
  analyses of the sketches in each source
  are given in bold type):
  A47 Concept 41, 168, 172, 175, 178, 183,
    218, 219, 223, **236–50**
  Artaria 195 31, 34–5, 36–7, 38, 43–4,
    81–91, 96, **97–121**, **124–61**, 162, 170,
    171, 172, 173, 174 n., 175, 177, 178,
    179–83, **184–210**, 217, **218–31**, 250,
    251
  Artaria 197 38, 170, 171, 172, 182, 218,
    219, 230, **231–6**
  Artaria 198 177 n.
  Artaria 201 33 n., 176–7, 178
  BH 107 15–19, 24–5, 26, 27, 31, 35, 73,
    75–7
  BH 108 35–7
  BH 109 35 n.
  BSk 1/49 (Wittgenstein sketchbook) 20,
    21, 22, 24–5, 26, 27, 31, 33, 34 n., 35,
    81, 95, 174–6, 178
  BSk 27/75 16–17, 19, 24–5
  Grasnick 20b, fols. 1–6 15, 20–3, 25, 33,
    34 n., 36, **46–75**
  Landsberg 10 20, 21 n., 22, 23, 24 n., 25,
    181 n.
  Paris–Landsberg–Montauban [PLM]
    Draft 174–6, 181 n., 195 n.
  Paris, Ms. 77 21 n., 181 n.
Starke, Friedrich 15

Thayer, Alexander Wheelock 15, 25, 44–5
Treitschke, Georg Friedrich 259
Tyson, Alan 30 n., 34 n.

Universal Edition, Vienna 5, 6

Winter, Robert 16 n., 17 n., 18 n., 19 n.,
  26 n., 30 n., 35 n., 38 n., 146

Zmeskall von Domanovecz, Nikolaus 19